COLD CASE

Sudden Terror

THE TRUE STORY OF
CALIFORNIA'S MOST INFAMOUS SEXUAL PREDATOR

THE EAST AREA RAPIST

AKA

THE ORIGINAL NIGHT STALKER

BY

LARRY CROMPTON

authorHOUSE®

AuthorHouse™
1663 Liberty Drive
Bloomington, IN 47403
www.authorhouse.com
Phone: 1-800-839-8640

First published by AuthorHouse 7/23/2010

ISBN: 978-1-4520-5241-0 (sc)
ISBN: 978-1-4520-5242-7 (hc)
ISBN: 978-1-4520-5243-4 (e)

Library of Congress Control Number: 2010910823

Design and production by Cohographics.com
Salem, Oregon

Cover drawing by Tom Macris, San Jose P.D.

Printed in the United States of America

This book is printed on acid-free paper.

PROLOGUE

THIS BOOK IS BASED on the actual case of the East Area Rapist, later also known as the Original Night Stalker, a masked man who terrorized California communities for ten years; 1976 through 1986, and possibly to this day.

Because I was not involved in the initial rape investigations, they are written from hundreds of reports, notes, memos, newspaper clippings, conversations and interviews with those who were involved.

The crimes are factual. The crimes are real. While all characters and events have direct counterparts in the telling of the story, I have created some dialogue in the interest of readability. The cops in the initial rapes are not factual, their actions are. Their names and descriptions are completely fictitious. The names of the victims, witnesses and suspects are fictitious; the terror, the dialogue during the crimes, and the investigations are real.

The cops involved in the cases after I was involved are real, their names and dialogue is factual, the investigations are real.

The pain and terror may have diminished in the minds of the victims, I hope that the pain does not return. My intent is to tell the story without endangering the privacy or the dignity of the victims. They have suffered enough.

TABLE OF CONTENTS

Introduction

ON JUNE 18, 1976 at 4:00 a.m., an unmarried young woman alone in her Sacramento County, California home was sexually assaulted by a ski mask wearing rapist.

She was the first of thirty-eight women and children attacked by this serial rapist over a two year period.

Although millions of dollars were spent, law enforcement was not able to identify the man named by the news media as the East Area Rapist due to his first series of rapes occurring in the eastern area of Sacramento County.

His attacks occurred in several Sacramento County areas, and in the northern California cities of Sacramento, Davis, Modesto and Stockton.

Even though thousands of leads were followed up and thousands of suspects eliminated, law enforcement was no closer in identifying the rapist when in 1978 he began another string of attacks in the San Francisco Bay Area counties of Contra Costa and Santa Clara and the cities of Freemont and San Jose.

I became deeply involved in the investigation and saw the pain, the terror: the pain and terror that may have now diminished in the minds of the victims. The crimes are factual, the crimes are real, the cops are real. The names of the victims have been changed to protect them. My intent is to tell the story without endangering the privacy or the dignity of the victims. They have suffered enough.

I've thought a lot about the case since the rapes stopped. For years, as a member of an East Area Rapist Task Force investigating a serial rapist, it was my life twenty-four hours a day, seven days a week. Two in the morning, wide-awake, wondering, "Where is he? What am I missing? Who is he?" The years have slipped away, fewer sleepless nights, a little less intensity. We learn to live with life's unanswered questions. But I still wonder, not so much of who he is, but more of where he is. Does a serial rapist simply stop his hideous crimes?

Psychiatrists working with rapists tell us that many start out at an early age abusing, mutilating and killing animals. Soon they graduate to "Peeping Toms" and then, to rape. Seldom if ever are these sexual predators rehabilitated, their attitude towards women ingrained forever. Some return to mutilations and killings, the full circle. Unfortunately this circle ends with the rape and murder of women, and often to their families.

I wasn't part of the investigation when the rapes began but I thought through them all. I talked to many of those who were involved and read the many volumes of reports. Then I was involved, a part of it. There with the fear, the smells, the dark nights, the trembling victims, the stained sheets, the neat stacks of evidence, the sharp, echoing noises that come from nowhere.

More than sixty attacks by a rapist/murderer who terrorized California communities from Sacramento to Orange County. No one felt safe: not old, not young, not male, not female, not me. Hardened cops would check the locks on their doors and windows every night and would sleep with their guns within reach. Serial killers instill fear in certain segments of society, and readers of the newspaper account bristle with indignation and disbelief only to turn to Ann Landers, the want ads, or the comics. This serial rapist turned killer, entered and terrorized entire communities and left behind memories more terrifying than a childhood nightmare, memories that never really disappeared.

Ten years of terror, real to the victims and their families, real to the communities, and believe it, real to the cops. All of them felt the fear, the rage towards the man, and each of them knew that someone in their family might be next; a wife, a daughter, a girlfriend. No one was safe. The serial rapist/murderer doesn't need to be sensationalized, but the story needs to be told because people need to know that life is not a movie and these things actually happen and we must be prepared. And maybe finally somebody will come forward with the identity we need.

I never spoke to the man responsible for so much ruination, but I heard his voice on tape. Still, I don't know how his mind works. I have interviewed psychiatrists and psychologists, sex offenders and their counselors and learned their views. I have my own. I interviewed victims over and over. Some I watched under hypnosis, so I know what they experienced; stark fear. Those who didn't die believed that they would. I must assume that those who died spent the last hours of their lives knowing that they were about to die a painful, unfair death at the hands of a madman. Their last thoughts must have been only violent, terrible horror.

I'm a decent guy, maybe I was even a decent cop. Hardheaded, opinionated, yet dedicated to my job as most cops are, regardless of what you read in the papers or see on television. As a six-year veteran when I became involved in the search for the rapist, I had worked with the

Sheriff's Crime Lab, and prior to that, Patrol Division, Vice and Narcotics. I saw the ugly side of life as most cops have, and I learned to deal with it.

Most people think cops become hardened to crime. They don't. They just come to accept it. They cry when they see injustices of death and sometimes they cry when death doesn't come to someone who deserves to die. Cops are just a small part of a big cycle, just as you are. The only difference is, they are in the ugly part of the cycle. They see life, they deal with it, and they don't always like it.

I was stopped in traffic one day and wasted time reading bumper stickers on the cars creeping by. One bumper sticker stuck in my mind: "Old golfers never die, they just lose their balls." It made me think. What about rapists? What about serial murderers? What would their bumper stickers say? Do they keep on raping and murdering until they die? Do they suddenly find God and live a normal life? Someday, we may have the answers. For now, there is no answer; there is no end. Not yet, anyway. As a cop you learn fast that people are not always kind. Our job creates a moral loneliness that makes our lives so difficult. I knew this case would be like a cancer, destroying everyone it touched. The crimes went on for ten years and they may still be going on today. In my mind they are, especially when it creeps into my dreams, tugging at me, mocking me.

This case brought me into the lives of over sixty men and women violated by one sadistic criminal, to the edge of presidential politics, and to the fringes of San Francisco's gay community. It scared the living hell out of me to learn what humans can actually do to one another.

———————

What is it like to be raped? How does it feel to be violated? How does it feel to violate someone? A lot of time would need to be spent working on details to describe those feelings, and it really isn't necessary. This isn't a story about sex; it's a story about terror; the terror one feels when they know they are going to die and the feelings of helplessness when waiting to die. The rapes were horrible, make no mistake about it; but the victims all described the terror, the horror of the direct and constant threat that this man had over all of them. Every one of them, men and women, knew they were going to die. Rape was an acceptable alternative. For some it didn't end with rape.

The rapist tied them, blindfolded them, gagged them, and put guns to their heads; they listened while he cocked the weapon and they waited for that final pain that they knew would soon follow. He put knives to their throats, drawing blood from the passive, and he smashed his fists and clubs into the faces of those who resisted. He shot and clubbed to death those who kept resisting and then he clubbed to death those who didn't resist.

He broke into their homes while they slept, while their children slept. He kicked in doors, he slipped through open windows, he broke windows, and he prowled neighborhoods. He terrorized. Always he terrorized. If he had a pattern in choosing his victims, it was never understood. The victims certainly did not know why he chose their homes to invade.

One way or another, most of us believe we pretty much get what we deserve in our lives. We look back and see how things might have gone differently if we had acted differently. We accept responsibility for what we get. When we finally think it all through, we can understand why what happens to us happens. In this country we believe, or at least pretend to believe, that each of us is responsible for our own actions, and with that comes our acceptance of getting what we deserve: pay backs are hell, what goes around comes around, what you sow you shall reap, you make your bed and you lie in it.

But rape; personal, intimate terrorism goes against everything we are taught from birth. Retribution? For what? What could anyone do to deserve it? Stripped of all power, completely at his mercy, struggling to save life, self respect, freedom, sanity; most of all, sanity. A mother and her child, side by side, a husband and his wife, a woman alone, each were living with the terror of death. Could any of us remain sane? This is the worst crime in a horrible hierarchy of human abuse. Sexual violation is unspeakable. The breath against the victim's face, the smells, and flesh against flesh. A life will never be the same. How could it? And then to add to the terror, he made all of them know, deep within their hearts, straight to the marrow of their bones, that there was no question, he was going to kill them.

Marriages were destroyed because husbands could not live with the knowledge that they did not protect their wives. The love they had held could not overcome their feelings of inadequacy. Women left their homes screaming after being freed, unable to force themselves to return. A thirteen-year-old girl, not yet really understanding her virginity or the pleasure of losing her virginity to someone she loved, instead lost hers to a monster who had no human feelings. The pleasure of sex, the importance of it for a healthy life, was ripped away from these women.

Can she ever again be a partner in love without reliving those horrible moments? When she shuts her eyes, does she once again see the dark piercing eyes staring at her through the hideous mask? As her partner reaches climax does she only hear, "Bitch, fucking bitch. I'm going to kill you all!" Instead of the caressing fingers of her mate, does she only feel the sharp point of the rapist's knife? Will the sun ever shine again or will life be forever tarnished by the memories of the one thing that may be worse than death? Insane terror.

What type of person gravitates to such power? What blinders make it possible for that person to not see, or care, how they are damaging a human life?

Who is he? Where is he? What is he doing now?

There is no hero in this story, only victims. Yet if anyone deserves to be called the hero, it would be those victims who learned to live with the horrible memories. Those victims who were able to continue with their lives knowing that they did not cause the rapes and that they could do nothing to prevent them, short of death. A fact learned too late for those who resisted, and later for those who were simply unfortunate in their role – there for one purpose: to die.

Again law enforcement was stymied and in 1979 the serial rapist, after completing twelve more assaults, moved south to Santa Barbara County where he began another series of attacks, this time he turned to murder; ten violent killings over the next five years.

Over the years cops spent many hours talking, planning, and dreaming. It didn't matter who caught the rapist/murderer, they would all be part of it. They all had the same intensity. In 1997 Orange County Sheriff's Department formed their CLUE unit (County Wide Law Enforcement Unsolved Element). Their assignment was to look into unsolved murders in southern California. In 1998 DNA evidence linked six murders.

In July 2000, three northern California rapes were linked by DNA. Believing that the Santa Barbara double homicide and attempted rape were committed by the EAR, I requested the Contra Costa County Criminalist to contact the Santa Barbara Sheriff's Office.

In March 2001, I learned that the northern California rapist was linked to the southern California murders through DNA.

On April 25th I met with Detective Larry Pool and his CLUE investigators and provided them with reports and evidence from all northern California rapes, giving them an understanding of the serial murderer they were dedicated to finding, an insight they had been lacking.

INTRODUCTION

The victims, their need and their right to return to some sense of normalcy depended on the capture of their tormentor. The cops understand that. Their lives could not be the same either without a resolution to this case. A case that began as "EAR," short for the East Area Rapist, as the papers called him when they finally discovered the series of rapes, which began in the eastern part of Sacramento County, California. A case that was also investigated by the Orange County Sheriff's Department CLUE unit as The Original Night Stalker, the serial rapist/murderer, also without success.

In 2003, I was contacted by Pool. A Chicago based production company, Kurtis Productions Ltd. was interested in doing an episode on the rapist/murderer cases to be shown on their A&E Cold Case File program. They wanted to interview several investigators and others who had been a part of the investigation, and would I be willing to talk to them? After twenty-seven years of frustrations, a chance to open the case to a national audience. I agreed to the interview and met with the Production Company in Sacramento to tape the interview.

In September 2003, the A&E Network aired the production, "The Original Night Stalker" as their Cold Case File program. It aired several times over the years. Although the program dealt primarily with the southern California murders, each time it aired numerous calls came into the Clue unit. Again, over and over, they ended up a dead end in a growing heap of dead ends.

In April 2008, I was contacted by Todd Lindsey of E! Entertainment. His company was interested in doing a program on the rape/murder cases of the East Area Rapist/Original Night Stalker with an emphasis on the rapes. Again my hopes rose and I met with Todd and his producer Randy Ferrell in Concord, California on May 24, 2008

Interviews with other investigators from northern and southern California would take place with a proposed viewing date of May 6, 2008. Would this be the final chapter in the identification and capture of the most vicious predator in California history? Will someone watching this show finally come forward? Will there be closure? Time will tell.

Larry Crompton

ACKNOWLEDGMENTS

THE RESEARCH FOR THIS BOOK was extensive. Reports, books, articles, interviews, and too many people to list here.

One person I would like to acknowledge is retired Sergeant James Bevins. His expertise, his cooperation and his friendship will never be forgotten. Had there been more like Jim involved, I feel sure that the East Area Rapist would not have involved into the monster he became.

The investigations and the crimes in this story are real. The homicide victim's names are true. All other names have been changed. The names of the officers in the initial cases have been changed as I was not involved in the cases, and information was learned from reports, interviews and discussions and by using fictitious names and descriptions it made for easier reading. The sexual assault victim's names were changed to protect them from further scrutiny. They have endured more pain than anyone should ever have to endure. If I have caused embarrassment to any of the victims, their families or the officers involved in this investigation, it was not intentional and hopefully they will accept my apologies. The names of the officers involved after I was a part of the investigation are real so hopefully they will also accept my apologies.

The newspaper articles are factual although not all are complete. The names in the articles are the names as originally printed.

I dedicate this book to three friends who enriched my career and my life: Gary Ford, who achieved the rank of Captain before his untimely death due to cancer and John Patty, a Contra Costa County Sheriff's Department Criminalist who also succumbed to cancer at too early an age. The Contra Costa County Sheriff's Department and all those who came in contact with these two gentlemen benefitted from the association.

To Edward Besse, my best friend, my unpaid ranch foreman and the Captain of the Contra Costa County Search and Rescue unit, who passed away on July 4th, 2001, and whose friendship and help will never be forgotten.

To those who worked with me on the Task Force I thank you for your help and the opportunity to learn from some of the best.

ACKNOWLEDGMENTS

To my wife Barbara, thank you for standing by me all these years and for sacrificing the many hours, days, months and years it took me to complete this book.

To Larry Pool of the Orange County Sheriff's Department CLUE unit, thank you for your dedication and professionalism, and — good luck.

To Todd Lindsey, E! Networks, Los Angeles, thank you for your friendship, your help and your dedication to get my book in print.

To Michael Schott, retired Contra Costa County Sheriff's Sergeant/Private Investigator, thank you for your help and continuing dedication.

To Melanie Barbeau, Kay, and Robert Neville, webmaster of www.ear-ons.com, thank you so much for your help and dedication.

Larry Crompton

Sudden Terror

CHAPTER ONE

IN MAY OF 1975, twenty-three year old Carey Frank moved to Rancho Cordova to join her father who had retired from the Air Force while stationed at Mather Air Force Base. Her life had been uneventful since moving and except for her job as an insurance rater, her contact with the outside world was minimal.

Like most of the young women living in the twenty-year-old tract, she looked forward to the warm summer nights and blazing hot summer days familiar to the Sacramento area. She was looking forward to trips to South Lake Tahoe and the gambling casinos of Nevada. She loved the pine-tree-studded mountains and the cool waters of the lake. She also planned on several trips to San Francisco where she loved to walk along Fisherman's Wharf and Pier 39. San Francisco's restaurants, shopping, colorful Chinatown, the cool waters of the Pacific Ocean, and the foggy mornings would be a welcome relief from the sweltering heat.

Carey's thoughts weren't much different from the other young women she had seen in the neighborhood. Soon her thoughts would be exactly the same as theirs. When fear grips a community, all else is forgotten. Soon that fear would be experienced for hundreds of miles and would last for years.

Back in May, Carey thought she was being watched. On several occasions an older, dark, medium-sized American car drove through the neighborhood. Every time the car passed her the driver turned his face away. She told herself that it was just her imagination. Two weeks passed without her spotting the car and she began to relax as her suspicions disappeared. Then she received the hang-up phone calls.

The first one was nothing. Walking past the phone when it rang she casually picked it up. "Hello? Hello?" Only silence. The phone went dead as the caller hung up. Carey looked at the phone, shrugged, and placed the phone back on its cradle, a nothing event that has become increasingly common in our society.

CHAPTER ONE

Three days later, Carey was watching television when the phone rang. She picked up the phone expecting to hear her father's voice. He was in Boston on business and wouldn't be home until July.

"Hello? Hello?" Nothing. Just the sound of emptiness and again she heard the caller hang up. Rubbing a sudden chill from her arms, she quickly checked the doors; all locked.

⸻

A shadow emerged from the darkness and moved closer and closer. The moon bathed the figure in its subdued light. It took form, the form of a young man. As he moved closer the face remained featureless. Tennis shoes muffled the sound of his movements as he crept silently into the sleeping neighborhood.

The man disappeared over a backyard fence, a dog barked in the quiet neighborhood, and calmness returned.

Hours later the shadowy form returned and then disappeared back into the darkness.

June 17, 1976

June 17 was the same as any other workday for Carey Frank, except that when she got home, the house would be lonely without her father. She hated it when he was gone for so long: a month so far with two weeks to go. Even though it was nice to be alone, she missed his company in the evenings.

At five o'clock, Carey left her office and drove home anticipating a light dinner, a shower, and going to bed early. No other thoughts entered her mind until she pulled into the driveway of the comfortable, twenty-year-old ranch style home.

Later, she turned on the shower, allowing the water to run as she slipped out of her clothes. She was having menstrual cramps so when she slipped into her bed it felt good. She told herself that if she could get her mind off her stomach, she could sleep, so she tried to lose herself in a romance novel. After reading the same paragraph three times, she gave up.

Soon she fell asleep and the room darkened as the world outside slowly slipped under a dome of twinkling stars.

The moon watching over the quiet neighborhood slowly illuminated the railroad tracks, only two blocks away. The tracks were two ribbons of lights that eventually disappeared into a cave of darkness.

Out of that darkness and into the moon's glow emerged a solitary shadow, which slowly took the shape of a young man. No sound disturbed the stillness as he stepped from one railroad tie to the next, moving closer and closer to the quiet neighborhood and the sleeping woman.

He left the railroad tracks and weaved through the backyards of the neighborhood. Not pausing, he seemed to know the area, drawing closer and closer to Carey, pausing once, briefly, at the backyard fence. Quickly and quietly he entered the yard.

He unzipped the bag he carried with him, removed a cloth mask, and slipped it over his head. A knife, a pair of gloves, and two pieces of short rope were placed on the ground near the bag.

The masked man stood in the shadow of the fence and moved a plastic birdbath under the telephone line and climbed onto the bowl. The blade of his knife flashed in the moonlight as he tried to cut through the line. Unsuccessful, he jumped to the ground and moved toward the back door. Again, the knife flashed as he chipped away the wood from the door lock, then silently slipped into the house. He paused at the doorway, then crept toward the sleeping woman's room.

The hang-up phone calls over the past two weeks were not on Carey's mind. After tonight they would summon a fear that would remain with her the rest of her life, causing her flesh to crawl at the sound of a ringing phone.

The half-naked man silently moved through the house then stood in the doorway of Carey's room, staring at her sleeping figure through the eye holes of his mask.

A tapping sound from the doorway penetrated Carey's dreams and brought her out of a sound sleep. Her bedroom light flashed on, bringing her closer to reality.

She stirred, opened her eyes and looked toward the sound…tap, tap, tap.

Fear entered her dulled senses as she looked into the eyes of the masked intruder. She could see the knife in his gloved hand as he continued the rhythmic tapping against the doorjamb. His black T-shirt and erect penis drew her attention. She watched in horror as her eyes focused on his penis; she was unable to form thoughts as he leaped at her bed.

Instinctively she pulled the covers over her head to protect herself from an awful nightmare. But the nightmare didn't leave and she felt the weight of his body straddling her legs. The blankets were torn from her face and she stared into the eyes peering at her through the mask and realized this was not a child's dream; it was a living nightmare. The point of the knife pressed against her left temple and blood flowed from the wound and soaked her pillow.

Her ears were ringing as fear pulsated through her body.

"If you make one move or sound, I'll stick this knife in you," she heard him whisper through clenched teeth, "I want to fuck you."

He moved to the side of her bed and pointed his knife at her nightgown.

"Take it off."

His cold eyes were on her as she slid the nightgown over her head and automatically slipped her panties down and off. He paced the room, and then returned to the side of the bed. He pointed to the Tampax between her legs.

"Take it out," he whispered through his mask.

His eyes chilled her as he watched her remove the Tampax and drop it to the floor.

"Roll over!" She turned away from him and rolled onto her stomach. She felt his gloved hands grab her arms and pull them behind her. The rope bit into her wrists, hurting more as he pulled the rope tighter. She heard him move around and then her wrists were tied with something softer than the rope he had brought with him. Carey would learn later that it was a cloth belt from her closet.

"Roll over," he again whispered through clenched teeth.

Her eyes were closed tight to shut out the nightmare, but it remained. Years later the terror would still remain and she would never understand why it wouldn't go away. It wasn't the rape she would remember most vividly, it wasn't the rape that would make her want to scream and leave her trembling, drenched from perspiration, in the middle of the night. It was the terror he left her with. It was the fear that this night she was going to die. And tonight she knew she was going to die.

He touched her breasts with his gloved hands, only briefly, as he continued to push into her. She tried to shut out all thoughts. She just wanted it over. She felt him pull out, and wondered if he had climaxed, although she could not tell.

She fearfully opened her eyes. It was like watching a horrible movie. She wanted to close her eyes again, but still she watched him as he used the sheet to wipe off his penis and then let it slide to the floor.

"Do you have money?" he asked. When she tried to answer, he hissed, "Shut up!" His jaw didn't seem to move inside the tight fitting mask when he talked. His voice was a hoarse whisper, as though he had laryngitis.

He rummaged through the bedroom. She watched as he picked up her hair dryer and approached the bed. His eyes, outlined by the mask, watched, stared, until fear gripped her like a vice. She struggled to catch her breath as he grabbed her feet and tied her ankles together with the cord on her dryer. He tied her bra around her ankles, then left her bed and wandered around her bedroom. He picked up her slip from the floor and again approached the bed. He was still naked; the light colored cloth mask with the two eye holes, however, brought more terror than his naked body. Her eyes focused on the white slip as he twisted it in his hands. She could hear his heavy breathing as he wound the twisted slip around her head to cover her mouth and felt the pressure as he tied it in a knot.

Again he rummaged through the bedroom, and again he returned to the bed and placed the point of the knife near her right eye.

"Don't make a move while I'm here or I will kill you."

She waited, helpless, as he left the bedroom. She heard him rummaging through the drawers in the kitchen.

She heard voices, low whispered voices, believing it was two people talking.

Then, "I told you to shut up!" in a louder whisper. The whispering continued as she heard drawers being opened and closed.

Then she heard nothing. She waited, expecting the masked figure to return. And she waited. She began to struggle, but the bindings on her wrist only dug deeper. The feeling in her hands had left long ago. The slip fell down around her neck and she began to move her feet. The electrical cord and bra fell from her ankles and she swung her feet to the floor. Slowly she inched toward the kitchen, waiting for him to jump at her, expecting him to emerge at any moment. The door to the backyard stood open. She kicked it closed with her foot, only to have it bounce back as the dead bolt prevented it from closing.

She knocked the phone receiver from the wall and frantically tried to reach the dial. The panic grew as she realized she could not reach it. She ran back down the hall to her father's bedroom and knocked his phone off the bed stand. She managed to dial the operator.

Sobbing uncontrollably, she collapsed to the floor and begged for help.

CHAPTER ONE

As the sky lightened, a lone man jogged along the railroad tracks. The sound his tennis shoes made in the loose gravel fell silent as he lost shape and disappeared as though he had never been.

Deputies arrived at the front door of the Frank home to find it locked so they went to the backyard and entered the house through the open back door.

They found Carey lying on her father's bed, partially covered with the bedclothes. Her hands trembled as they cut the cords binding her wrists. Her hands were cold to the touch from her circulation being cut off and her wrists were raw and red from the bindings.

A quick search of the house and the backyard satisfied the deputies that the rapist had left. Carey was upset and frightened but there were questions the deputies had to ask, and she tried to answer. Remembering the night brought back the fear, stronger now than then. She trembled when she talked, her teeth chattered, as if she couldn't convince her body that she was now safe.

How long had he been in the house? They needed to know. Slowly regaining her strength, she was able to stammer, "Twenty minutes, I guess."

They asked her to describe her attacker.

She explained that when she first saw him she thought it was her dad returning home early, but he wore a mask and had no pants on. She had pulled the covers over her head to try to make him go away, but he didn't. She described him as about five-nine, and explained his mask fit tightly. She described the mask as dirty white or gray with two eye holes and a seam down the front. It didn't have nose or mouth holes, just eye holes and he wore a dark T-shirt. The rapist wasn't a large man; perhaps weighing a hundred and sixty pounds with possibly dark hair as the hair on his legs was dark. She was embarrassed when she told the deputies that the rapist had a very small penis. As the memories of the rape came back to her she started to sob, and trembled uncontrollably. "I thought he was going to kill me."

She was told that a deputy would take her to the hospital and that the nightclothes she had been wearing would need to be kept as evidence.

The deputies explained that investigators would be at the house for awhile, taking pictures and looking for evidence that would help catch the rapist. An investigator would meet her at the hospital to ask more questions.

They tried to show her the compassion she needed. They hated rapists, as most cops do, and tried to keep their personal feelings to themselves although they were sure it was a neighborhood kid.

"I don't know what to do. I'm sorry, I just can't think. He was going to kill me, that's all I could think of. I didn't want to die. I just wish my father were here. I'll have to call him," Carey sobbed.

They watched as she was led to the patrol car and then started taking notes, as Investigators would soon arrive.

Papers were strewn throughout and drawers were ransacked. Carey's purse was lying on the cement in the backyard and the contents were spilled on the lawn. A large block of wood and a plastic birdbath were under where the telephone wire entered the house. Cut marks on the wire indicated an unsuccessful attempt to disconnect the phone and a fresh crack on the base of the birdbath had probably stopped his efforts. Wood shavings on the ground from the doorjamb had been chipped away with a knife.

A Johnson's Baby Oil bottle and two towels balled up in the bathroom would lead investigators to believe the rapist had lubricated his penis prior to awakening Carey Frank. Two pieces of rope brought by the rapist would be an M.O. used to link the rapist to several more rapes over the next four years.

The bed sheets and towels were taken as evidence; however, it wasn't until March 26, 1977 that a request was made to examine the blood and semen stains to determine blood type. As the investigators knew no suspect, this was not an oversight that would have any great bearing on the cases to follow. On May 2, 1977 it would be learned that the rapist was a non-secretor.

In approximately 80 percent of the human population, antigens of the ABO blood typing system are found in other cells of the body, including semen, saliva, perspiration, vaginal secretions, gastric juices, hair, and bones. People in whom this phenomenon occurs are known as secretors and their blood type within the ABO system can be reliably determined from those body substances by means of absorption-elution techniques similar to those used in typing dried blood. All secretors display the presence of H antigens in their body fluids. In addition, people who have Type A blood secrete A antigens; people who have Type B blood secrete B antigens; and those who have Type AB blood secrete both. People with Type O blood secrete only the H antigen. If there is not positive reaction to anti-A, anti-B, and anti-H sera, the individual is not a secretor. People are secretors or non-secretors from birth and never change from one status to the other.

A year after the rapes began it was learned that the rapist was somewhere within twenty percent of the population. Not enough to give the investigators goose bumps, but it did narrow the field down to somewhere around two million potential suspects. This known fact about the rapist was used to eliminate hundreds of possible suspects. The lack of fingerprints left at the rape scenes would, however, baffle investigators for years.

Carey Frank's description of the rapist as a twenty to twenty-five year old white male, five foot nine inches tall, one hundred sixty-five to one hundred and seventy pounds, with muscular legs and an undersized penis would be repeated many times by other victims.

Chapter Two

Traveling westbound on Interstate Highway 80 from Sacramento takes the motorist through Yolo County and the university city of Davis, into Solano County and through Vacaville, site of the California Medical Facility where state prison inmates with medical and psychological problems, including sexual deviants, are housed. From Vacaville the motorist continues through Fairfield, site of the Travis Air Force Base, and on to Vallejo, Richmond, Berkeley, Oakland, and San Francisco.

Just west of Fairfield, Interstate Highway 680 will take the motorist south toward Contra Costa County and the city of Martinez where the Sheriff's Department is housed and then to Concord.

In the summer months this part of Northern California sports the golden hills of dead grass, one hundred-degree plus days and ninety-degree nights. In the years where there is no drought, lawns are a lush green from the daily watering. Other years the lawns match the golden hills.

August, 1978
Contra Costa County, California

Two years in Narcotics and three years in Patrol certainly hadn't made me a prize in anyone's book, but I had been selected to work as a crime scene investigator with the Contra Costa County Sheriff's Department Criminalistic's Laboratory.

Chief Duane Dillon, head of the Crime Lab, had a management style that demanded the best from his staff. Demanded might be harsh; instilled would be closer. I could see the dedication the criminalists displayed in their duties, and I was amazed by the unselfish enthusiasm each criminalist showed in teaching me the intricacies of the job.

Looking back, I realize that my transfer to the Lab led me into a part of my career that would be one of the most interesting, eye opening, yet frustrating times in my life. A time that still haunts my memory years later as I remember the victims of one of California's most savage serial rapists and of the victims of his violent murders when he finally reached his ultimate desire; the death of his victims.

This is a true story about a sadistic rapist/murderer. It's about life, real and horrible. It's about the victims of real life. It's about law enforcement and the lack of cooperation among agencies, cities, and counties.

It's about citizens who refuse or neglect to help their neighbors. It's about the terror that one man imposed on the citizens of California for ten years.

----•›‹•----

We all sat around the conference table in the back room of the Lab, waiting for the Chief to start our morning meeting. Books on evidence of all kinds, books on anatomies, fingerprints, photography, serology, books on things I couldn't even pronounce let alone understand lined the walls, each book dog-eared from continual use.

"Sacramento Sheriff's Office investigators will be at the Concord Police Department tomorrow to talk about a rapist who has been terrorizing their county for the last two years," Chief Dillon began, "They believe he is heading our way and the Sheriff wants us to be represented at the meeting. We don't know much at this time, but apparently their investigators have not been able to come up with anything of value on this rapist and they think we had better be ready.

"Sacramento formed a rapist task force and they are recommending that we do the same. If that occurs, we will be a vital part. John, I want you and Larry to attend. See what they have to say and we will discuss our role. Investigations and Patrol will also have representatives there," The Chief nodded at Criminalist John Patty.

"Why Concord P.D.?" someone asked. "Strange that a Sheriff's Department would go to the City instead of our Department."

"I don't know but I'm sure John and Larry will tell us after tomorrow. Maybe they think Concord is where he will hit," Dillon answered, "Now you know as much as I do, so let's get back to work. The meeting is at eight-thirty tomorrow morning at Concord P.D." Dillon pointed at John and me and left the room.

"Well Larry, looks like we are the chosen ones," Patty shrugged.

----•›‹•----

At 8:15 a.m. August 15, 1978 the room was already filling up. As with all cop meetings and church services, the back rows fill first. The front row is always reserved for the brass and they feel obligated to fill it, the padded seats were only a bonus. The rest of us filled in from the back forward, the hard metal chairs making more noise than needed on the green carpeted floor.

"I'm Lieutenant Ray Root and this is Sergeant Bevins", the man at the podium began. "We are with the Sacramento County Sheriff's

Department and have been working on a Task Force set up to catch who we call the East Area Rapist. I'll bring you up to date as to what an East Area Rapist is and why we are talking to you.

"In the last two years, since June eighteenth, nineteen seventy-six, we have had over thirty attacks that we have attributed to the same person. We think he is ready to move and we believe he is coming here. Don't really know why, we just feel it. Concord is a typical area for him to hit."

I looked around the room at the other cops, some were taking notes, some were listening, and then there were those who didn't care about Sacramento or their rapist.

Lieutenant Root told of their frustration, their lack of evidence, their inability to catch this rapist. He told of the ski masks, the gloves, and the shoelaces, usually white that he tied his victims with. Shoelaces that he sometimes brought with him into the residence. Sometimes, we were told, he entered the homes before the attack to set it up.

Late nights or early mornings were his attack times and all types of sex acts from sodomy, oral copulation on and from the victim, straight intercourse and terror, always terror the lieutenant emphasized were typical during the assaults. The threats to kill were consistent and the use of knives, guns, clubs and fists made the victims really believe that they were going to die.

"The psychological profiles that we have each says that he will kill and that he will kill a cop if he is cornered. We believe it and we suggest that you believe it also," Root admonished.

Well over a million dollars had been spent by the Sacramento Sheriff's Office and they were no closer to catching the rapist than they were in June 1976. No idea who he is, no idea where he works, no idea where he came from, but a pretty good idea where he was going to; the city of Concord, Contra Costa County, California.

"Our reports, our evidence, everything we have, is open to you. We have invented the wheel, but we can't seem to fit the spokes. He's hit in Davis, Stockton, Modesto, and all over Sacramento County including the City. I'll leave our business cards and when he hits, and he will, we would appreciate a call. Jim will respond at any time, day or night, and he knows more about this person than anyone does. He is heading up our Task Force and we want to be involved in any way we can to help you.

"All I can tell you is that unless you cooperate completely with each other, you're going to lose. I strongly suggest you form a multi-agency task force before he hits," Lieutenant Root finished his talk.

Looking around the room, representatives from all the central Contra Costa County agencies were represented: Concord, Walnut Creek, Pleasant Hill, Martinez, and of course, the Sheriff's Department. Antioch and Pittsburg were represented from the eastern part of the county. Richmond and El Cerrito from the west were apparently not suspected targets of the rapist.

Cooperation? Multi-agency task force? Get real. Some cops cooperate, even some agencies cooperate, but most cops don't, most agencies don't. Only when it's too late and the damage is done does any real sense of cooperation kick in and then only because outside pressure comes to bear. Egos, politics, budgets, laziness, incompetence, human nature, all play a part in the phenomenon known as "lack of cooperation".

Interesting meeting, but this is Contra Costa County and the citizens are selective in the types of crimes that occur. Serial rapists? Serial killers? Sacramento, Oakland, San Francisco, San Jose. Sure. Contra Costa County? Never. White collar criminals? Sure. Serial rapists? Never.

Contra Costa County, the gateway to the Delta, where fishing and boating abounds on the many waterways throughout the county. Nestled between the Sierra Mountains and it's ski resorts and gambling casinos of Lake Tahoe and Reno to the east and San Francisco and the blue Pacific to the west, Contra Costa County is the ideal area of northern California. Napa Valley and the wine country to the north and thousands of acres of cattle country, champion golf courses and the splendor of Mt. Diablo adds to the beauty of the county. The county is basically an affluent area with pockets of poverty, mainly to the east and west. The University of California, Berkeley and Davis are both within easy commute, as are the two community colleges in the county.

CHAPTER THREE

October 2, 1978

Minert Road, Concord, California

DUSK HAD NOT YET FULLY SET IN on the quiet neighborhood when Barbara Rivers was leaving her home to go to the store. She noticed a car parked across the street and the male slouched in the front seat appeared to be looking at houses. A chill went through River's shoulder blades and for some reason she couldn't shake the feeling of fright, a feeling she could not explain.

October 4,1978, 1:30 a.m.

Minert Road

"Dad," Seventeen-year-old Sydney Cannon ran to her father's bedroom and shook him from his sound sleep. "Someone's in the back yard."

"What?" Her father looked at the clock beside his bed. "What in the hell is anyone doing in our yard at one-thirty in the morning?"

They both heard what sounded like footsteps on the strips of aluminum that Hal Cannon had left in the back yard. He hurried to the bathroom window and looked into the back yard. Nothing, nobody.

"I guess whoever it was left," he told his daughter and both went back to bed.

Shortly after, he heard the noise again. Quickly he got out of bed, rushed to the closet and grabbed his shotgun leaning against the wall. Without turning on lights he again returned to the bathroom window where he saw the outline of a man just twenty feet from the house. He quickly unlocked the window, slid it up and pointed the loaded shotgun at the man standing just twenty feet from the house.

"What the fuck are you doing out there?" Cannon shouted.

"I'm looking for a friend," the male answered.

"Get out of my yard or I'll blow your fuckin' head off," Cannon yelled as the male ran from the yard toward the front of the house. Cannon ran to the front door, threw the dead bolt back and ran into the front yard. He didn't see anyone, he didn't see or hear a vehicle, he did see that his side gate was now open. He went back to bed.

CHAPTER THREE

The dark outline of a man slipped from one yard to the next as he made his way from Minert Road to the well-kept yard on Belamn Court. He stopped periodically until an occasional dog stopped barking and then silently moved on.

He approached the side door to the garage and peered through the window. No cars were parked in the darkened area and a gloved hand reached for the doorknob. Locked. He used a knife to silently cut away the wood near the lock, but it held, the deadbolt securely embedded.

Slowly he moved from one window to the next and eyes accustomed to the darkness peered into the empty house. At each window the knife flashed and scratches were left on the aluminum screens. He approached the living room window and pried the screen off, leaning it against the side of the house. Metal caught the reflection from a streetlight as a gloved hand placed the tip of a screwdriver against the glass near the lock. He hit the end of the handle, breaking a small hole in the glass, big enough to reach in and unlock the sliding glass window. He slid in through the open window, closing it behind him, making sure it remained unlocked.

Silently he moved throughout the house, then unlocked the deadbolt on the front door. He left then, closing the door behind him. Once again he entered the backyard and carefully replaced the screen to the living room window.

Bruce and Maureen McCandles drove into the yard of their Belamn Court home. As Bruce approached the garage he hit the automatic garage door opener, slowing until the door was fully opened then entered the orderly garage. Their baby didn't stir from her sleep as Maureen carefully lifted her carrier from the back seat and followed Bruce into the kitchen through the entry door from the garage.

Bruce turned on the lights as he moved through the house toward the baby's bedroom. As he passed he noticed that the door to his den was closed. *Strange*, he thought to himself as he always left the door open.

Before going to bed, Bruce checked all the doors as he normally did.

"Maureen," he called to his wife, "did you unlock the deadbolt on the front door after we got home?"

"No, I haven't been to the door. Why?" she responded.

"Strange. I could have sworn I locked it when we left," he muttered half to himself.

At 2:30 a.m., Bruce stirred from his sound sleep. He was still tired so it couldn't be daylight, yet the sun seemed to be playing across his closed eyelids. He tried to shut out the light but something hitting his foot penetrated his brain. He opened his eyes and looked directly into the eyes of the masked man standing at the foot of his bed. A flashlight was in the masked intruder's left hand and a revolver was pointed at the now fully awake McCandles.

"I just want food and money, that's all. I'll kill you if you don't do as I say," the man whispered.

Maureen was awake now, looking at the figure outlined in the darkness. Her fear was in her throat, her heart pounding so hard it hurt her ears.

"What?" she cried.

"Get on your stomachs," he ordered and pressed the gun muzzle against Bruce's head. "Put your hands behind your back," he hissed through clenched teeth.

Shoelaces landed on the bed in front of Maureen's face.

"Tie his hands," he ordered.

She began tying her husband's wrists. Her heart pounding so hard her head began aching.

"Tighter," he hissed. "That's not tight enough. Tighter. Get on your stomach," he ordered when she had finished and then he retied Bruce's wrists. Tight.

Maureen's arms were pulled behind her back and the shoelaces cut into her wrists. He was at her feet and she felt her ankles being tied, not tight like her wrists.

"If you look at me I'll have to kill you," he threatened. They heard him removing laces from Bruce's shoes and then he was back at the bed.

"Keep lying face down," he ordered. "If you look at me, I'll kill you. I'll blow your fucking head off," he hissed as he tied Bruce's ankles, tight like his wrists. They heard him rummaging through the dresser drawers and jewelry boxes.

"Where's your wallet?" he demanded of Bruce.

"On the bathroom counter," Bruce answered.

"Where's your purse?" he prodded Maureen when he returned to the bed.

"In the kitchen," she cried, and again he left them.

"Is that all the money you have?" he hissed when he returned to the bedroom.

"Yes," Maureen answered.

Again he was gone and they could hear him in other areas of the house and then he was back and they felt dishes being placed on their backs.

"If I hear these, I'll blow your fucking heads off," he hissed and was again rummaging. Maureen could feel the laces fall from her ankles and felt the dishes being removed from her back.

"Stand up," he ordered. "Don't look at me or I'll cut your fuckin' head off," He put the knife at Maureen's throat and pushed her from the room. "If you don't do everything I tell you, I'll kill you and everyone in the house. Lie down," he ordered when they were in the living room.

She heard him turn on the television and turn off the volume. She could see him put a blanket over the screen, the only light in the house, then he was gone again into the bedroom.

"If these dishes fall, I'll kill everyone in the house," he hissed at Bruce as he placed more dishes on his back. "My main man wants gold and silver," he whined as he left the room.

"If you don't give me a good fuck, I'll kill everyone, " he hissed as he cut Maureen's nightgown in several places, tearing it from her body. I'll cut off your baby's ear and bring it to you."

She could hear him lubricating himself with Vaseline and then he was over her.

"Maureen I've been seeing you for a long time," he whispered as he entered her. A short time later he went to a corner of the room and she heard him crying.

He was rummaging again. She heard him go into the garage several times and she heard him going into the backyard. Then there was silence.

————⟫●⟪————

At 4:42 a.m., Officer Wells, patrolling the Treat Boulevard, Oak Creek Grove area of Concord, received the call: burglary, rape, residential robbery. Wells arrived just minutes later to find Maureen and Bruce McCandles still tied. The rapist had left approximately twenty minutes before his arrival.

Approximately $4000.00 in jewelry, dishes, utensils, appliances, camera equipment, and miscellaneous items was missing. Apparently the rapist was setting up housekeeping. He was here to stay.

On October 8, a neighbor of the McCandles' found a security officer's badge in front of his house. The badge was a seven – point star with the California seal, made by the Hookfast Specialists Company in Rhode Island. The badge was turned over to the Concord Police. Could it belong to the rapist? Would it help identify him?

October 9, 2003
Contra Costa County Sheriff's Crime Lab
Martinez, California

At 8:30 a.m., Assistant Chief Mitosinka of the Lab informed us that a Concord family had been attacked by a masked rapist who had entered the residence, tied up the husband and wife and then raped the woman. Nothing else had been reported and no mutual aid had been requested. Was this the cooperation Lt. Root had so vigorously stated was needed to catch the rapist?

Concord Transcript, Monday, 10-9-78

Woman raped in her home

A 26-year-old Concord woman was reportedly raped in her bedroom early Saturday morning after a man carrying a flashlight and a gun threatened to kill the woman, her 29-year-old husband and their child.

The suspect apparently broke into the home of an Ygnacio Valley family at approximately 2:30 a.m. He proceeded to tie the hands of the woman and her husband and then warned them that if they tried to stop the attack, he would kill them and their sleeping child. The man allegedly stole some jewelry before he fled the house on foot. A canine search by the Concord police failed to locate the subject.

On October 10, a Concord police officer dropped off a rape kit at the Crime Lab. The evidence was tested and although no sperm was found on the vaginal slide smears, sperm was found in the saliva sample.

Major crime scenes in the unincorporated area of the county, are processed by members of the Criminalistics Lab. Although most of the larger city police agencies have their own technicians for processing, they are usually police officers transferred into the unit for a period of time. None of these agencies have the capabilities of examining the evidence and therefor evidence is sent to the Sheriff's Lab or to the State Crime Lab in Sacramento.

The Sheriff's Lab is also available at any time, to assist city police agencies on major cases when requested. After eight months of working in the Lab assisting on crime scenes, I had been part of the standby crime scene list with four of the criminalists. Each of us was on call for a week at a time. We would respond at any time of the day or night if we were requested. The week of October 9 was mine.

After the Concord rape, the chief informed us that it was believed that the East Area Rapist had committed the rape. It was also believed he would strike again. Concord had asked that the Crime Lab respond to any similar rape to assist in collecting any evidence. It was agreed that if I were called during my week, Criminalist Steve Ojena would accompany me.

On October 11, I contacted the lead investigator for Concord's rape. It would be beneficial to go through the victim's residence so we could prepare for any future rapes. It would help to know in advance what we could expect and what we should look for in processing the scene. Ojena and I were to meet the investigator at the residence at 3:30 p.m.

We met with Sergeant Johnson in front of the victim's home and he explained the sequence of events of the attack as we checked the exterior of the residence. When we checked the window screens we noticed scratch marks. They definitely were not pry marks, they were more like signature marks left there to taunt us. Another twist in the series of attacks.

The rapist was unsuccessful in entering through the garage door because of the two by four that McCandles had used as a brace across the interior of the door.

The security officer's badge found by the neighbor had not yielded any clues. Johnson had made several calls, however, and the manufacturer had told him that the badge could have been purchased directly from the company or one of its three thousand salesmen. The badge, a model B-617 with air-dried enamel, revealed some wear pattern on the face of the state seal, the back, and on each of the seven points indicating it had been carried in a wallet holder.

Several security companies throughout the Bay Area had been contacted, however, none could help determine the security firm that used this particular badge. Johnson had contacted Bevins and would send him a photograph of the badge.

The neighborhood canvass had discovered several unusual incidents, which separately meant little, however together they showed a pattern similar to Sacramento's attacks: open gates, suspicious males, barking dogs, hang-up phone calls.

A neighbor of McCandles', who lived on Hollis Circle, told investigators that Monday and Tuesday nights she heard noises in the backyard and a scratching noise at her screen door. She also heard the same noise the evening of the rape, however, did not check. Investigators had entered the yard of the twenty-nine year old female and found that the screen had been cut near the lock of the sliding glass door and a screen had also been removed from one of the windows. Scratch marks were found on several screens, similar to the marks found on McCandles' screens. Her gate was also left open.

The interior of the home had been cleaned, leaving no evidence associated with rape or terrorism, yet an aura remained that seemed to heighten at least one of my senses. I couldn't determine which one. Then, maybe it was my imagination.

We were invited to attend a meeting with Lieutenant Root and Sergeant Bevins as they were to give a thorough presentation on their investigation. Bruce McCandles had agreed to be hypnotized with the hopes of remembering some significant information that he had unconsciously buried in his memory.

On October 12, Root and Bevins were once again at Concord P.D. Prophets, maybe. Top notch investigators, obviously. Bevins displayed an intensity that only comes from being personally involved in the case and his need for closure paralleled that of the victims. Without it he would feel like a failure and past successes would not compensate for this one loss.

Bevins' dedication to this case would bring the two of us together to form a professional bond that would last for years, past our retirements, with one desire, one question: Who is he? A desire that would remain after all the task forces had been disbanded and most cops had forgotten and most victims would still be trying to forget.

Once again the brass settled into the cushioned chairs while the remainder of us settled into the metal ones. As I looked around I could tell that this time everyone would be listening. Cigarette smoke filled the room and empty Styrofoam cups served as ashtrays.

CHAPTER THREE

"Your rape," Bevins nodded at the Concord brass, "was committed by the East Area Rapist and he's going to hit again. He's going to hit you soon and he's going to hit you in the same general area.

"His M.O. hasn't changed since he first hit in June of seventy-eight except that he has become more sophisticated, more rehearsed, but basically it has worked and he has stuck with it."

As we heard before we learned again that fingerprints were never found, his face never seen and that he made sure his victims were secure enough to give him time to escape. Major thoroughfares and open fields were always close to his attacks.

"He likes to prowl the area and once he selects an area, come hell or high water, he's going to hit it. Sometimes he rides to the area on a stolen bicycle, sometimes he steals a bicycle to leave on. Many times he parks his vehicle several blocks from the scene and goes through neighbors' yards. Dogs don't stop him, neighbors don't stop him, and obviously we didn't stop him," Bevins told us.

"We think he uses different cars and different disguises when he checks out neighborhoods and it appears that many of those times are during the day as we have had neighbors tell us later that they had seen suspicious people and cars in the area.

"Lack of cooperation and the hesitancy or reluctance by citizens to call in suspicious activities has worked to his advantage for the past two years. Don't let it happen to you. I'm telling you, no one in the history of our department has caused more fear, cost more money to investigate, taken more man-hours, or caused more frustration, than this son-of- a bitch.

"One thing that is interesting is that he always disables the phones. We know he does that so the victims can't call us until he is long gone, but what that does for us is that we are sure that all the attacks are being reported. The victims have to get help to get free so several people get involved and anyway the rape is secondary when they call us. The terror and the thought that they were going to die are what they are reporting.

"He shot a teenager who chased him, so we know he is capable of murder and that includes the murder of a cop."

Everyone sat with their own thoughts and everyone knew "he" would be caught without outside help – everyone except Root and Bevins. They knew it would take teamwork, but cops are a strange breed, egotistical, secretive, defensive and possessive of their territory. We don't need help.

Looking around the room and seeing that although all the brass stood together talking, the rest of us broke off into little groups, groups made up of cops from each department.

On October 12, McCandles underwent hypnosis. Although nothing of importance was gleaned from the hour-long session, it did confirm that the attacker wore gloves and that he appeared to talk through clenched teeth. McCandles also confirmed that the weapon was a revolver and that he could see four or five bullets in the cylinder, further indication that the rapist was prepared to kill.

October 12th, San Simeon Drive, Concord

At approximately 10:00 p.m., a housewife heard a sound as if someone had bumped into a garbage can in her neighbor's yard. She looked out her window but saw nothing. Later during a canvass of the area it was learned that neighbors on Lyon Circle found that a board had been knocked free from the fence and that a side gate had been broken from its hinges.

Sacramento Bee, 10-13-78

East Area Rapist Now in Concord

Sacramento County sheriff's detectives traveled to Concord Thursday to talk with police there about the rape of a 26 year old woman in which methods similar to those used by the East Area Rapist were reported...

CHAPTER FOUR

A FORTY-TWO YEAR OLD HOUSEWIFE, mother of a nineteen-year-old son and a seventeen-year-old daughter, was leaving for work at 7:00 a.m. when she noticed that her side gate was open. In checking her backyard she discovered a bicycle missing. She returned to the house and called the Concord P.D. dispatcher. She was told that an officer would contact her later.

Ryan court is two blocks from the McCandles' home.

At 11:00 p.m. that evening, Paul West was watching television in his Ryan Court home. His girlfriend, Louise Simon, was sleeping on the couch, her head in his lap.

"Ready for bed, hon?" West asked as he nudged Simon awake.

"I'm ready," she murmured and turned the television off.

A cool breeze swept through the house from the open bedroom and living room windows. Both slept better when the house was cool and both fell sound asleep soon after turning out the light.

Louise Simon awoke with a start from the crash of the bedroom door being flung open. A beam from a flashlight illuminated the room and settled on Louise Simon's face and her now wide open eyes.

"Don't move or I'll blow your heads off," the masked man ordered in a muffled voice. Simon screamed. The masked intruder was more frightening than her worst nightmare.

"If you scream again, I'll kill you," the intruder warned.

Paul West sat upright in bed, looking at his screaming girlfriend. The flashlight beam drew his attention to the masked man and the gun pointed at his head.

"I don't want to hurt you. I just want food and money for my girl-friend and me," the masked man stated. "Roll over and put your face in the pillow. Put your hands behind your back. You, tie his hands. Tie them real tight or I'll kill you," White shoe laces landed on the bed near Louise Simon.

Simon did as she was told, still frightened but more in control of her fear. He only wanted food and money.

"Lie down on your stomach," he ordered her and tied her wrists and ankles. Her wrists real tight; her ankles, loose, then he retied West, tighter than Simon had.

The barrel of the gun pressed hard against West's head.

"If either of you move I'll blow your fuckin' heads off," he hissed.

Simon's eight-year-old daughter, Linda, ran into the room. She saw the ski masked intruder and screamed. Her hands went to her face, her body trembled and she continued to scream.

"Tell her to shut up or I'll kill you," he hissed.

"It's all right, honey. Stop crying and lie on top of me," Louise tried to calm her daughter who climbed onto the bed, still whimpering from the terror she just encountered.

The masked man grabbed the child and pulled her from the bed. "Get into the bathroom and be quiet," he ordered.

Once in the bathroom she reached for the light switch and turned on the light. A gloved hand quickly covered hers and switched the light off. He closed the bathroom door and slid the dresser in front of it, leaving the young girl in the darkened room.

He rummaged throughout the bedroom and then was back at the bed. The gun hit West on the side of the head, pain ripped through his body.

"All we want is food and money and then we'll get the hell out of here," he hissed and threw an afghan over West's head and placed dishes on his back. "If you move I'll drive this knife into your back."

Again he rummaged. This time they heard him throughout the house, cabinet doors slammed, dishes rattled, and then he was back. Simon was pulled from the bed, her ankles no longer bound. She was pushed from the room and down the hall.

"Get on the floor," he ordered, "on your stomach." She could hear him rummaging and going into the garage several times and then he was over her.

"Do you want to live?" he hissed.

"Yes," she stammered.

"Then this had better be the best fuck I've ever had or I'm going to kill you." She felt his thick leather gloves on her thighs, a fleeting moment, and then he was gone from her. She could hear him in the hall bathroom, drawers being flung open.

"Lift your head up," he demanded when he returned and tied a piece of towel around her eyes. "Play with it," he whispered as he knelt over her and placed his limp penis in her hands and moved back and forth.

She couldn't move her hands as they were numb from the ties around her wrists. Seconds later he grabbed her arm and rolled her on her back. "This had better be good or I'm going to kill you all," he threatened as he thrust his lubricated penis into her. Moments later, he was out of her, standing over her.

It didn't take long enough, she thought to herself, fear tightening her chest. *He's going to kill us because he wasn't satisfied.* Truman Capote's *In Cold Blood* ran through her mind. Knowing what had happened to the victims made her think of her young daughter imprisoned in the bathroom. Her greatest fear was that her rapist would kill her daughter.

She heard him in the garage again. Heard him opening a plastic garbage bag.

"Here, put this in the car," she heard him say. She heard no reply and no footsteps.

———

Around 4:00 a.m., fifty-seven year old Wallace Schuster was awakened by the sound of an intermittent beeping, similar to the sound of a car door being opened with the key still in the ignition. The sound shattered the predawn stillness near his Wilmore Road home less than half a block from where Louise Simon lay, all feelings gone from her tightly bound wrists and paralyzed with fear for her eight-year-old daughter who she could hear sobbing, locked in the bathroom. She pushed her face hard into the carpet wanting the pain to shut out the terror and the thought of her boyfriend, bound and helpless in the bedroom.

———

It was 5:45 a.m. when I was startled awake, fifteen minutes before the alarm was set to go off. As always, I jumped at the sound, sat up and looked around. It wasn't the alarm clock and it took me a few seconds to realize where the noise was coming from. I grabbed the phone. It was Dispatch.

"Sorry to wake you, but Concord just had a rape. Their watch commander called and requested the crime lab and we show that you're on call, so it's yours," the female voice advised.

"Okay. I'll call you from the Lab. Call Steve Ojena and have him meet me there," I hung up.

"What's the matter?" my wife rolled over and looked at me and immediately fell back asleep.

"Concord had a rape and they're asking for the Lab to help, so I've got to go." I mumbled to myself.

———⤞⬦⬦⤝———

We had been married for twenty years, less two and a half months and had moved across country three times since leaving Canada; California, Maine, New Hampshire and back to California. We had gone to school together in a small town in New Brunswick, Canada. Different grades, as I was a year older, but knew each other. She had taken an instant distrust of me, as I remember. But then, that didn't make her a minority. It would have been easier to count those who hadn't. Sometimes an embellished reputation isn't positive, even when you are the one doing the bull shitting. One time when I was in the eleventh grade I told her brother I was going to marry his sister. When he told her, she turned green. He was more descriptive when he told me what her reaction was.

I left home when I was seventeen, just after graduation, to join Canada's Navy. On one trip home on leave, we met again. For her it might have been my 1956 red and white Studebaker Hawk, or maybe the sailor uniform. On my part it was the five-foot tall blond bombshell with the green eyes. Whatever it was, we were married five months later, New Year's Eve, 1959.

After my five years were finished, I left the Navy and, like the Beverly Hillbillies, we loaded our station wagon and, with our sixteen-month-old daughter, moved to California.

A son, another daughter and a German Shepherd later we received our American citizenship. One day I saw an ad in the paper that the Contra Costa County Sheriff's Department was hiring. $580.00 a month. Hell, I was working two jobs and not making more than that so I applied. And now, six years later, I was on the sergeant's list, not near the top, but there never the less, enjoying my time in the Crime Lab.

———⤞⬦⬦⤝———

I met Ojena at the Lab and the two of us drove to the Ryan Road home where we met Sergeant Johnson who explained the assault. When we entered the house, the feeling was once again with me, that eerie feeling that seemed to close around me, to follow me as I walked through the house. A feeling that remained until I later left the area. I wondered how intense the feeling must be for the victims and how far away they would have to go before the feeling left them? Would it ever leave them?

Inside the attached garage, on the floor were two strips of a blue print towel, each approximately two to three inches wide. Another strip of the towel was lying on the victim's bed and a brown shoe with the laces missing was near the foot of the bed. Several white and brown shoelaces were on the floor and the bed. The rapist had brought the white ones with him.

In the living room, the television was unplugged and the cable missing. Some type of metal shavings were on the floor near the front door and when I stepped outside, I noticed fresh scratch marks on all aluminum window screens, including the window in the child's bedroom. All scratches appeared near the bottom left corner and did not seem to be pry marks. This was even more puzzling when I noted that all the screens were loose fitting and could have easily been removed.

The dust on the windowsill of the child's room was smudged, as was the dust on the living room windowsill, however no prints could be found.

I checked the backyard of the next door neighbor and saw that a screen had been removed from one window and placed against the side of the house. Another screen had scratch marks on the lower left-hand corner, identical to the marks on the screens of both the Concord rapes.

The neighbor's side gate was open, and trampled ice plants and striations in the wood of the fence indicated that the rapist had entered the victim's yard from this area. It also indicated that either house could have been the target.

"We had the Highway Patrol helicopter respond and check the area," Johnson advised. "but they didn't find anything. I also had dispatch call Sacramento S.O. and ask them to contact Bevins and he's on his way.

"We set up a hypnosis appointment for the eight-year-old daughter as she got a pretty good look at him, so maybe we'll get lucky. Bevins told us about victims getting phone calls after the rapes, so we put a phone trap on McCandles and we'll get one on this place today".

Linda Simon, the eight year old was hypnotized, although she had seen the attacker, nothing of importance could be drawn from her memory.

Sacramento Bee, 10-14-78

Two Concord Rapes In Week Ascribed to East Area Rapist

Sacramento County Sheriff's investigators Friday said two recent rapes in the Concord area were the work of the East Area Rapist.

Concord police reported that a man broke into an Ygnacio Valley home at 5:30 a.m. Friday, tied up a 29 year old woman and a 30 year old man, then rummaged through the house. He returned and sexually assaulted the woman.

On October 14, Concord investigators received an anonymous call that a California Highway Patrol officer should be checked as a possible EAR suspect. The officer had been working out of the Sacramento office during their attacks and had just been transferred to the Martinez office prior to the first Concord attack. It was also reported that the officer owned ski masks. The officer was eliminated as he had been working the night of Concord's first attack and had arrested a drunk driver at 2:30 a.m. and had an O positive blood type.

On October 19, Concord investigators received a call that a grocery manager who had worked in Sacramento from June 1971 until June 1977 had transferred to Stockton until May, 1978, and then to Contra Costa County, fit the description of the EAR. He had been in the military for one month in 1968 and had been medically discharged. A check of military records in St. Louis confirmed this fact and that he had a blood type O positive. Based on A positive blood found at a previous Sacramento rape, detectives eliminated the suspect as EAR without further contact.

That same day, an investigator received a call from an anonymous woman.

"I saw a sketch in the paper about the rapist," she began. "He looks like my old boyfriend. We were engaged, but broke up in April last year. He was real upset over our breakup and began to drink a lot so he was in the hospital for it and then moved back with his parents over in Solano County. I didn't hear about him again until December last year when I found out he was living with two friends who were going to college in Sacramento.

"I saw him again at a party in July, but he let on he didn't recognize me and then the next month I saw his father and he said his son had stopped in to see him and said he was working circulation for a major newspaper. The father thought it was strange because he hadn't seen him in years because they didn't get along too well. His father never had time for kids and his mother used to yell at him a lot, so he didn't get along with her, either.

"Last week he called me at work and said he broke up with his girlfriend and I should know how it felt. He sounded real strange on the phone and when I asked him if he was home he said, 'Let me look around. Yeah, I'm home.' He was real spacey."

The woman told the investigator that her ex-boyfriend had gone to Diablo Valley College for awhile, took Administration Of Justice classes, tested with Concord P.D. and the Sheriff's Department but failed the orals. He wanted to be a cop, and had worked security for K-Mart. The last time she had seen him he was dirty and was wearing run down, dirty tennis shoes and an old shirt. She described him as about a hundred and seventy pounds, brown hair and greenish blue eyes.

"I had to tell somebody just because of my intuitions," she told the investigator, "I'm not revengeful, I just think he is your rapist."

The detective took down the name and possible address and thanked the caller.

A records check showed contact with Sacramento Muni Police in 1977 for traffic and with Sacramento S.O. in 1978 for assault with a deadly weapon and possession of a silencer. His driver's license showed he was six feet two inches tall. Concord eliminated him because of his size without contacting him.

On October 18, Captain Warren Rupf, the S.O. Investigations Division Commander, sent an interoffice memo to Captain Harry Derum the Patrol Division commander, providing specific background information relating to the East Area Rapist. The memo relayed a psychological profile obtained from Sacramento S.O. and instructed that although the information was to remain confidential, the beat officers should be made aware of the potential danger. The memo was to be made available to the Patrol Division watch commander and asked for assistance in identifying potential county areas consistent with the area profile.

The nineteen page profile, partly a resume` of the meeting between the Sacramento S.O. Task Force and members of the California Youth Authority, cautioned that EAR's reaction to any field contacts with law enforcement personnel would be dependent upon interception being made before his entering the house or after leaving it. One part of the memo was of utmost importance to the patrol deputies and read:

"If the contact is made before he enters (during the preparation phase), the psychologists feel that his overall demeanor will be a cunning cooperativeness in the field interrogation. His mannerisms should be exceptionally calm, yet acutely alert since at the time he will be 'feeding' on the schizophrenic excitement made possible in this preparation/planning phase.

"If, on the other hand, he is intercepted while in the process of leaving the area, it is likely that a nearly explosive resistance will be immediately encountered. In the event that he exhausts such efforts as running, jumping fences, etc., to effect his escape, then he should 'resort to homicide and/or suicide' as the ultimate means of preventing his apprehension."

San Francisco Chronicle, 10-19-78

Concord Arming For Rapist

Gun sales were up and tempers were high yesterday as Concord residents tried to protect themselves against Sacramento's notorious "East Area Rapist."...

The East Bay City's Police Chief Chambers acknowledged yesterday that, unintentionally, he himself might have caused "frayed tempers" among "some would—be vigilantes" and "feminists."

The angry reaction followed a talk by the police chief when he warned against women wearing "Provocative clothing" and residents "arming themselves."

"All I said was that women were better off not wearing short shorts or bikinis when washing their cars in the front yard..."

Some women, including members of the Mt. Diablo Rape Crisis Center, were angered by what they called the chief's "sexist remarks" and his "blame of women" for supposedly inviting the attacks...

According to the chief, one drain on police efforts to cope with the attacks is the number of calls for information and help from the "considerable number" of residents who have just bought guns for the first time.

CHAPTER FOUR

"We've had a bunch of little old ladies who called to ask for an officer to come and show them how to load their guns. If some of these people don't shoot themselves in the foot, it will be a miracle."

———⟶⟩●⟨⟵———

Contra Costa Times, 10-19-78

Boggess Talk at Rape Meeting Hit

CONCORD – Organizers of a meeting on the East Area Rapist Wednesday charged Supervisor Warren Boggess was using the meeting to garner votes.

Boggess announced at the Tuesday night meeting the county will consider spending $200,000 in an effort to catch the rapist.

Boggess and his campaign co-chairman Gerald Rinell appeared at the meeting after being specifically asked not to by the organizers...

But during the meeting, Rinelle stood up from the crowd and asked Boggess what he knew about the situation.

The incumbent supervisor, facing a tight run off race for the seat November 7, strode to the front stage area and announced that he would ask the Board of Supervisors today to commit $200,000 to help capture the rapist.

He stayed on the stage through the rest of the meeting although two counselors from the Diablo Valley Rape Crisis Center were told there was not enough room for them, even though they had been invited.

"We didn't want this to be a political thing; I didn't want Boggess to speak," said Carmen Valine, president of the Parent Faculty Club of Woodside Elementary School which sponsored the meeting...

———⟶⟩●⟨⟵———

Contra Costa Times, 10-22-78, Letter to the Editor

Editor: I attended the police meeting at the Oakgrove School October 17 and left feeling that rapes will end when the east area rapist tires of Concord women. Unfortunately, judging by the large number of extremely attractive women attending the meeting, this may take some time... I would like to respond to the Rape Crisis Center's counselor's irate retort to the Chief's proposal that women refrain from wearing revealing clothing while washing the car or other public activities. She stated that places the responsibility for the rape on women.

The chief may or may not be a sexist, but the east area rapist certainly is sexist, sadistic, and violent. The responsibility for these attacks lies in a sick mind. While the woman feels it's fine to wear revealing clothing when a rapist is in our community, I doubt seriously she would pass through a high crime area flaunting $100 bills.

EDITOR'S NOTE: This woman requested that her name be withheld because the rapist is still at large.

CHAPTER FIVE

October 25, Montclaire Place, San Ramon

SAN RAMON is an upper middle class bedroom community of Contra Costa County bordering Alameda County. Most of the residents commute to work either north or south on Interstate 680 to Concord, Walnut Creek, San Francisco or Alameda County.

Ian and Sunny Walther were no exception. The young couple worked in Hayward, Alameda County, and were in the process of moving out of their rented home on Montclaire Place with their young son. As the Walthers and their friends made trips from the house to the rented moving van in their yard, Sunny Walther noticed a late model cream colored Toyota Celica drive into the court. She watched the car drive slowly around the court and as it approached her yard, it was going so slow that she thought it was going to stop. She didn't get a look at the driver as the car left the court.

October 26, Montclaire Place

The nights were getting longer, the days shorter. Indian summer in northern California: the days still warm, sometimes the temperature soars into the 100s; the nights cool enough to sleep comfortably and the rain still a month or two away. The leaves begin to turn color, from green to brown. No one ever says, "Let's go to California to see the leaves change color," but we do have the great weather.

Twelve-year-old Chris Jefferson was sitting on her front steps next door to the Walthers when she noticed a small cream colored car with black louvers over the rear window drive into the court. Although it wasn't quite dark, the vehicle had its high beams on illuminating the end of the court.

The young girl sat in the shadows of her porch and watched the car, stopped at the entrance of the court, for about two minutes. The car made a U-turn and left traveling east on Springdale Lane. Approximately ten minutes later it returned, again stopped at the entrance of the court for approximately two minutes, backed out and left west on Springdale. The car, which was in need of a washing, looked like a Toyota Celica and was driven by a white male with dark hair, styled into a pageboy with short bangs.

At 4:45 a.m. on the 28th, seventeen-year-old Morgan Feltch was returning home from an all night party. As he drove into the yard of his Pine Valley Road home he observed a man dressed in dark clothing climb the fence from the backyard of an Adams Place home and walk west on Pine Valley Road.

<hr />

At 5:00 a.m., a deputy working the San Ramon area received a call of a rape and robbery that had just occurred on Montclair Place.

Upon arrival, he met with Sunny and Ian Walther. Both appeared to be emotionally calm and cooperative, and with the help of covering officers, checked the area but found nothing. A ski-masked rapist who tied his victims with shoelaces and preferred greenbelt areas close to major thoroughfares: welcome to San Ramon.

The deputy contacted Dispatch, which relayed the information to the Watch Commander, and the rapist protocol was set in motion. Sergeant Carol Michener and her partner Sergeant Tom Coggan, the investigators assigned to handle an EAR attack in an unincorporated area, were notified as was John Patty, the on-call criminalist. Ojena and I were also called to assist in the processing of the scene. Ojena was requested to meet with Sunny Walther at John Muir Hospital, Walnut Creek, where she was to undergo a rape examination. Coggan and Michener also met with Walther and two Diablo Valley Rape Crisis Center counselors who sat in on the interview.

"Don't say anything or I'll kill you," was Walther's first recollection that someone was in their bedroom, she told investigators. A flashlight beam was shining directly into her eyes.

"He told me to 'Wake him up.' He was standing over me," Walthers began. "He tossed shoelaces near my head and said, 'Be quiet or I'll kill you, motherfucker. Tie his hands.' He leaned over Ian and said, 'Don't move, motherfucker, or I'll kill you.' It was like he was hissing the words.

"I tied Ian's hands and then the man tied mine after he ordered me to get on my stomach. He said, 'I want your money. All your money. I know you have some. I'll kill you if you don't tell me where it is.' I told him I had fifty dollars in my purse and he said he needed more than that. He left the room and when he came back I remembered that I had some silver dollars, so I told him. He got angry and said, 'Where is it? Where is it?'

"I heard him searching through the house and then he came back into the bedroom and told me he wanted me off the bed and away from Ian. He took me into the kitchen and told me to lie down on the floor. I always sleep naked and really felt vulnerable lying naked on my stomach on the cold floor. He tied my ankles and then left the room. When he came back he turned on the stove light and I could feel him walking around me. He threatened me several times telling me not to move or he would kill me. He also said he had seen me at the lake and I looked real good. He said every time he saw me he got hard and when I asked him what lake he said, 'Whisper. Whisper, motherfucker.'

"He blindfolded me with a piece of towel and I heard him searching the house again. I moved the blindfold a little and when he came back I could see he wasn't wearing any pants. He got down in front of me and said, 'suck on it and don't hurt me. You hurt me and I'll kill you.' I told him I needed a drink of water first. He got a glass of water and threw it on my face and neck and breasts and then he put his penis in my mouth. He moved back and forth for several minutes and climaxed on my face and then he left for a while. When he came back he raped me.

"He commented on my ring. He said it was unusual and I told him to take it. He tried to take it off and it wouldn't come off so I told him to pull on it and he finally got it. I told him that an airport limo was supposed to pick me up at five thirty and a short time later he was gone."

Walther also told detectives that the rapist was never fully erect, even when he climaxed.

When Coggan and Michener interviewed Ian Walther they learned that the attacker had shoved a gun against his head several times, threatening to kill him if he moved. The intruder had also placed dishes on his back and told him that if he heard them he would kill him. Ian Walther was certain that the attacker had not entered their young child's bedroom.

Both victims described their attacker as a white male with light olive skin, late twenties, five ten to six feet tall, one hundred and sixty-five pounds, dark hair, who talked through clenched teeth. They described the mask as similar to the upper part of a pair of nylon pantyhose, light beige or tan in color. Sunny Walther saw that her rapist had been wearing heavy, tan suede gloves similar to those worn by motorcycle riders, and dark blue cotton ribbed dress socks and royal blue tennis shoes.

John Patty and I met with a deputy at the Montclair Place address. He explained the scene and walked us through the residence.

When I entered, the same eerie feeling hit me like a blast of California fog on a cool, dark night. I knew it had to be my imagination, but cold beads of sweat on my partially bald head refused to disappear even though I wiped it dry several times as we moved from one area to the next. The rapist had turned the thermostat down to sixty-three.

We found that the attacker had entered the home through the unlocked garage door and left through the sliding glass patio door.

The home was photographed by Patty as were scrape marks on the board fence where the rapist had entered the yard. Several shoe impressions with a herringbone design were noted in the soft dirt in the backyard, casts were made and later determined to be a size nine and a half.

I noted how sparsely furnished the rooms were. We were told that the Walthers were in the process of moving and this was to be their last night in the house.

Two pieces of a torn yellow towel and a white shoelace were on the kitchen floor near where the assault on Sunny Walther had taken place. An empty Coors beer carton was on the kitchen counter near the refrigerator. In the master bedroom we located more shoelaces on the bed beside a cup and saucer. Dresser drawers were open, the few items of clothing that had been in the drawers were in disarray. The clothes closet door was open, revealing its emptiness. The phone, its cord cut, was lying on the floor near the bed.

Ojena and I processed the scene for fingerprints and several were collected and would later be compared against prints of anyone the Walthers could think of who had been in the house. Maybe this time the rapist had made a mistake and one of the prints would lead us to his identity. Maybe, but as Sgt. Bevins had warned us before, not likely.

Contra Costa Times, 10-31-78

May Not Be East Area Rapist

Doubts About SR Attack

MARTINEZ – Sheriff's investigators aren't sure the Saturday morning rape of a young San Ramon mother was the work of the East Area Rapist.

"There's no obvious way of eliminating [the East Area Rapist]," Sheriff's Captain Warren Rupf admitted Monday, "but on the other hand we're not satisfied it is him."...

Rupf warned Monday that authorities could be dealing with a "copycat," noting that many elements of the rapist's methods of operating had been publicized.

But, he warned, there's just as much danger with a copycat as with the East Area Rapist himself.

"We are concerned that there was a rape. We just can't say that it wasn't the East Area Rapist and let it go. We are working to solve it regardless, and if we catch the man responsible, it will be up to the other jurisdictions to prove he's the East Bay Rapist," Rupf said...

"It doesn't make a damn bit of difference if this rapist was from Sacramento or three blocks away — we're still going to solve the crime."...

Rupf, Sgt. Jim Layton, and Detective Rick Morgan told the group of concerned area residents they should take extra precautions in securing their homes to prevent an unwanted intruder.

Sgt. Layton told residents, "I'm not going to tell you not to go out and buy a gun, but unless you are skilled in firearms, a gun can get you in a lot of trouble."...

A woman asked whether it was a good idea to struggle with a rapist. Layton told her that was "a personal decision, I can tell you how to fight or how to submit, but not when to."

"We know how to submit," the woman retorted, "Tell us how to fight."

On October 1st, Sergeant Coggan and Detective Peggy Bowen drove Sunny Walther to Oakland where she underwent hypnosis. She described the vehicle she had seen drive through her court the day they were moving as a Toyota Celica, cream color with shiny hubcaps and two red stripes down the side. The rest of the hypnosis interview was consistent with the information previously obtained by the detectives. A composite was developed during the interview. Walther said it was of the person driving the Toyota.

The *Contra Costa Times* began a weekly series on "Rape: The Crime and Its Prevention." The first Article in the November 3rd, 1978 publication defined rape, according to California Penal Code, section 261.

It also explained how some victims could obtain compensation through the Victim of Violent Crime statute.

The *Tri-Valley Times* on the same day printed an article on residents coping with their fear of the serial rapist. Gun sales had doubled, people were sleeping with guns under their pillows, hardware stores could not keep up with the demand for security locks and pressure on the Contra Costa County Board of Supervisors caused them to once again re-energize streetlights. The lights had previously been turned off to save money in the aftermath of Proposition 13, the California tax initiative that rolled back property taxes to the 1972 level and that had overwhelmingly been voted in by the citizens.

October 4, San Jose, California

Forty miles south of San Ramon on Interstate 680 is the city of San Jose, the largest city in Santa Clara County. At approximately 3:45 a.m., thirty-four year old Phylis Akira, an Oriental housewife and mother of a year-old infant, was awakened by an intruder who told her not to make a sound or he would kill her and that he had a knife. When she screamed and cried, the intruder stated, "Don't you understand?" He told her he was hungry and just wanted to eat.

A knife was pressed against her face and she was pushed face down on her bed, her hands and ankles tied. She was then gagged and blindfolded with torn strips of towel and sexually assaulted by the intruder who lubricated himself with baby lotion before masturbating.

Because the victim could not describe the rapist, the investigator dispositioned the case as inactive. San Jose, as with many large cities, had so many crimes that without leads as to the responsible, the cases were not investigated. Rape was only one of the crimes handled this way. Robbery, burglary and lesser crimes without leads were also deemed inactive.

Sacramento Bee, 11-7-78

Assault in San Ramon Blamed on East Area Rapist

The rape of a 23 year old woman in her San Ramon home last month has officially been attributed to Sacramento's East Area Rapist.

Lt. Ray Root of the Sacramento Sheriff's Department said Monday a study of reports sent by the Contra Costa County Sheriff's Department last week "leaves no doubt" the sexual assault was committed by the man to whom 39 other rapes have been attributed...

San Ramon is approximately 18 miles south of Concord where the rapist is believed to have struck October 17 and October 13.

The rapist has not struck in suburban Sacramento since last January 28 nor in the city since April 14...

On November 7, the Contra Costa County Sheriff's Department underwent a major metamorphosis. Sheriff's Captain Richard K. Rainey had won an election to become the new Sheriff replacing retired Sheriff Harry Ramsey. Chief Duane Dillon, head of the Crime Lab, was appointed as the new Undersheriff. Both men brought a renewed spirit to the department. Youth with an eye to the future had emerged.

A man who worked for a major newspaper contacted a deputy who was checking a Danville pizza parlor. He told the deputy of a co-worker, just hired two months ago, who had previously lived in Sacramento. The person had been hired to deliver papers and was working in the Concord area during both of their rapes and he had been delivering papers in the San Ramon area during that rape. The subject, described as five foot ten, one hundred and eighty-five pounds, had bragged about stopping in San Ramon to help a person with car trouble. He said he had helped the person with burglary tools he had in his van. On all three nights of rapes, the person had taken off from work.

Investigators followed up on the information and found that the subject had been in the Marine Corps, was highly athletic and light footed. He had been diagnosed as having a split personality and felt women were subservient. Further investigation showed he was wanted on a felony wife-beating charge out of Los Angeles. A subsequent arrest eliminated the suspect because he was a blood Type A secretor.

On November 8th, members of the Walnut Creek and Concord Police Department along with Sheriff's Department personnel met with the California Highway Patrol to discuss the using of the C.H.P. helicopter in the event of another rape by the serial rapist. Walnut Creek requested the helicopter remain in the area for three days beginning November 9th as it was believed that the rapist was more active on the weekends. An extended use of the helicopter would be too expensive.

The helicopter would be housed at the Naval Weapons Station in Concord on November 9th and at the Sheraton Inn Airport on the 10th and 11th and would be available from 10:00 p.m. until 6:00 a.m. for three nights. The pilot and sheriff's deputy as the observer were to be housed at the Sheraton Inn each night. Nothing happened during those days.

CHAPTER SIX

IT WAS AFTER MIDNIGHT when the dark figure approached the yard of Clark and Heidi Tojo. The yard was in semi-darkness, illuminated by the moon, as the man moved toward the door leading into the garage, his tennis shoes leaving herringbone designs in the soft earth. A knife flashed in the man's gloved hand and splinters of wood broke from the door frame as the knife pried near the lock. He pushed on the door with his foot; the door held for an instant and then broke free, opening into the darkened interior. A flashlight beam searched the darkness and then disappeared as he backed away, moving toward the west side of the house and the window of the spare bedroom.

The knife appeared as the man hit the window near the lock with the handle, the sound of the breaking glass piercing the night silence. A small piece of glass fell to the carpeted floor and the gloved hand reached in and removed the lock. The window slid open six inches and then stopped. He pushed but the window held, stopped by the track lock in the upper portion of the frame.

He moved, this time toward the sliding glass door leading into the living room. The knife was used to break the glass of the window near the slider, the noise again reverberating through the stillness as he waited, listening for movement from the sleeping couple. The house remained silent and the gloved hand reached through the jagged hole in the window, this time to unlock and open the sliding glass door. Noiselessly he entered.

The masked man moved toward the bedroom and the sleeping Oriental couple. The beam from the flashlight searched the faces of the victims, their eyelids trying to shut out the invading light. Heidi Tojo woke and saw the ski masked intruder at the foot of their waterbed. She screamed, fear catching in her chest and again she screamed, louder. Her husband, startled awake, looked at his wife and then at the dark figure.

"Shut up or I'll kill," the intruder hissed. "Don't look at me."

Clark Tojo threw the blanket off his body and began to swing his legs from the bed, blind to the danger in front of him, his only concern was for his wife. The masked figure hit Clark's shin with the barrel of the gun; once, twice, hard. "Don't move, motherfucker, you try that again, motherfucker, and I'll shoot you," the voice snarled, "All I want is food and money and I'll leave in my van."

Heidi saw the gloved hand, the shoelaces dangling from the fingers, in front of her face.

"Tie his hands. Behind his back. Tight," he ordered as he threw the bindings at her. "On your stomach, motherfucker," Again he smacked Clark on the leg with the gun.

She tied his wrists, her hands trembling, her heart pounding.

"On your stomach," the masked man ordered and she felt her arms being pulled behind her and the laces bite into her wrists as they were drawn tighter and tighter. Her ankles were tied, not tight like her wrists and the circulation remained. The intruder retied Clark's wrists, and his hands burned as the blood flow ceased, then his ankles were pulled together as the laces once again stretched and bit into his skin.

"Don't move," he hissed through clenched teeth. "Shut up and don't move or I'll fuckin' shoot you both."

They heard him rummaging, ransacking throughout the house and then he was back.

"I only want money and food because I'm hungry," he stated.

"The food is in the refrigerator in the kitchen," Heidi mumbled, fear numbing her brain.

"Our money is in the hallway, under the linen closet. That's all we have," Clark answered, praying the man would take the money and leave.

The intruder left the room, they heard him in the hallway, and then he was back. The attacker used torn strips of a towel from the kitchen to blindfold the terrified couple. They were gagged with more strips of the towel.

Heidi felt the laces fall from her ankles and she was pulled from the bed.

"Don't you move, motherfucker," the intruder hissed at Clark as he pushed Heidi from the room, down the hall, and into the living room.

"On your stomach," he ordered as he pushed Heidi to the floor. She heard him in the kitchen, opening and closing cupboard doors, and then silence.

He was beside Clark again.

"If these fall, I'll hear them," he hissed as he placed dishes on Clark's back. "I'll kill you if I hear them fall."

He was back beside Heidi, masturbating.

"I've been watching you for a long time, Heidi. I've been wanting to fuck you for a long time," he whispered.

"Play with it," he ordered, as he knelt over her and put his penis in her numbed hands.

He was off her, pulling her to a sitting position and then he slapped her hard on the side of the head, knocking her to the floor.

"You better not hurt it," he hissed as he sat her up and moved his penis near her face. The point of the knife pressed against her neck, the pain more intense than the slap. "You better make it feel nice or I'll cut your throat."

Several seconds later she was pushed to the floor. Her nightgown was raised, her red underpants pulled down over her legs and a gun barrel was pressed against her head. The fear grew with the thought she was going to die..

"If you scream, I'll blow your brains out," he hissed.

He was in her, just for short seconds and then he was gone. She could hear him crying in the kitchen. Deep sobs.

"You motherfucker. You motherfucker," she heard him cry.

The silence engulfed her. Was he gone? She started to get up, to run to her husband.

"Lie still or I'll kill you," he hissed at her and she fell back to the floor.

Dishes crashed to the floor in her bedroom and she heard her attacker run down the hall toward her husband.

"Just try that again, motherfucker, and I'll shoot your wife first, then you," he hissed at Clark as he picked up the dishes and replaced them on Clark's back.

Again he was in the kitchen, sobbing. Heidi heard him crying for several minutes and then, once again, silence.

At 4:30 a.m., San Jose police officers received the call.

Seventy dollars, a six-pack of Coors beer, Clark's gold nugget wedding ring, and a General Electric digital clock radio were missing. The suspect had also eaten a box of Nabisco crackers.

As the victims could not identify their attacker, the case was classified as inactive.

CHAPTER SEVEN

THIRTY-TWO YEAR OLD TERESA MCCRAE turned on the small stereo in her living room. Soft, easy listening music followed her down the hall and into the bedroom as she turned off lights on her way to bed. As it was cold outside, cold enough for frost, an event that was not all that common in the Bay Area, she had earlier set the thermostat for a comfortable seventy-two. She had moved here from Chicago two years ago and should still be used to the cold; however, her blood had thinned, like all Californians, and now the cold chilled her to the bone.

She had been living alone in her boyfriend's house since he moved out a month ago and, although she enjoyed her freedom since her divorce three years ago, the loneliness did close in at times. The house she was living in was for sale and she would soon move into her own home. She loved Danville, the quiet bedroom community along Interstate 680, just a few miles north of San Ramon. It was a wealthy community, yet everyone seemed to be friendly and she was only a few miles from the BART train that took her to her job in San Francisco.

As she moved around her bedroom she stared at the several unopened boxes on the floor that contained the items she didn't need until after her next move. Her furniture had been in storage in Chicago for three years and she had finally had it shipped out after she had been burglarized in October, and although the thief had been caught, the burglary was still on her mind as she rechecked the locks on her doors and windows.

She turned on the bedside lamp, a globe-type with a three-way switch, sitting on the night stand. She automatically held onto the base of the lamp as she turned the switch. Ever since she had uncrated the light and set it on the night stand three weeks ago, she had meant to buy some type of rubber matting to keep it from sliding when she turned it on or off. Problem was, the only time she thought about it was when she turned it on or off.

At midnight, after reading several poems from Rod McKuen's "Celebration of the Heart", Teresa McCrae turned off the bedside lamp and dropped off to sleep, the music from her stereo drifting softly throughout the house. Aker Bilk's "Stranger on the Shore" soothed her mind as she snuggled beneath the blankets.

"Don't scream. Don't make any noise," the whispered voice brought her from her sound sleep. "I won't hurt you," She felt the intruder straddling her, her face pushed into the pillow. A sharp point pressed against her neck intensified her fear, bringing her fully awake.

"All I want is money and food for my van," the voice hissed. "Put your hands behind your back. If you make a sound, I'll kill you," Her wrists were tied, the laces biting into her flesh and then the covers were lifted from her legs.

"Cross your feet," the intruder demanded and her ankles were loosely tied together. "Where's the money? Where's the money?" he hissed. She heard the bedside lamp being turned on. She turned her head and saw the dark figure, his back toward her. She saw the ski mask covering his head down to his collar and the dark blue windbreaker. And then she buried her face deeper into the pillow.

I looked at the clock beside my bed before I reached for the ringing telephone. Five-thirty on a Saturday morning. "Who would be calling me at this hour of the morning on a weekend?" I mumbled as I fumbled with the phone.

"Hello?"

"This is Lieutenant Simmons," the Patrol Division watch commander began. "There's been a rape on Liberta Court in Danville and you've been requested. Patty's been notified and wants you to meet him there and said he'll have the equipment. Mitosinka is going to meet the victim at John Muir Hospital."

"Okay," I replied as I wrote down the address. "How long ago did it happen?"

"We got the call at five fifteen. Investigators have been notified as it appears to be the Sacramento rapist," Simmons replied and hung up.

My wife stirred beside me. "What's wrong?" she asked.

"Another rape. This time in Danville, our area again," I replied as I moved toward the shower, now fully awake.

"Same rapist?"

"They think so."

John Patty and I arrived at the Liberta Court address at approximately 7:30 a.m. and met with a sheriff's deputy who showed us the residence and explained the scene as he knew it. As we checked the exterior, the heavy frost still on the ground worked its way through the soles of my shoes. My feet and hands were freezing as the temperature had dropped to thirty-two during the night, cold for the Bay Area. I took a series of color photographs of the exterior, noting pry marks on the outside of the patio door leading to the kitchen area. When I entered the residence, I again felt EAR's presence. It was like a blanket of fog; cool, damp. Or, as I said before maybe it was just my imagination.

The inside of the house was as cold as outside; freezing. Maybe the chill that ran up and down my spine was just mother nature. Maybe.

I noticed the lack of furniture and the sealed and unsealed boxes and that the house didn't seem to be ransacked.

In the bedroom, a phone, the cord cut, was on the floor near the bed. Two strips of an orange towel, the ends knotted together, were on the edge of the bed. At the foot of the bed on the floor, were a comforter, a woman's coat, and a pair of white panties, stained with blood. Near these was a white shoelace, also knotted and cut. A globe-type lamp on the bedside stand still burned, basking the room in a soft glow; stark contrast to the violence and fear that the room displayed.

As I began to photograph the interior, Captain Rupf arrived and conferred with Patty. The Captain had requested a search and rescue team with tracking dogs and also advised that Sergeant Coggan and the victim would be en route from the John Muir Hospital back to the scene shortly.

Myron and Judy Robb with their bloodhound, Pita, arrived with the unit team leader, Phil Annis. The Bloodhound Unit was one segment of the Contra Costa County Sheriff's Department's Search and Rescue Team that was made up of volunteers who specialized in different areas of search and rescue. First aid, jeep, equestrian, divers, and communications were some of the units manned by these dedicated individuals. Self sufficient and professional, they responded at any time for any emergency. Especially adept at searching for lost children and the elderly, when they weren't volunteering their time, they divided the hours between their full time jobs and training. This enabled them to remain an elite group, respected not only by Contra Costa County law enforcement, but law enforcement throughout California and adjoining states.

One of the team leaders, Edward Besse, a retired Coast Guard Senior Chief Boson's Mate, would be one of eight people honored by KRON-TV at their first annual awards banquet, "4 Those Who Care," on October 4, 1983. After six months of searching by KRON, a list was compiled of eight people who met the criteria. Each recipient received a $1,000 check and $1,000 to their favorite charity. Ed was honored for donating more than four hundred hours of volunteer time to the search and rescue team. This was in addition to working at his full time job.

Each member of the team supplied their own equipment with no monetary help from the county. Dogs, horses, jeeps, radio equipment, first aid supplies, transportation costs, uniforms, and, in many instances, the loss of pay from their full time jobs, was borne completely by the individual team members themselves.

The Robbs took Pita into the residence and immediately upon entering the front door, the bloodhound picked up a scent. Spittle sprayed in all directions as the sleepy eyed dog shook its head, its ears flapping, its body shaking. Judy led the dog down the hallway and into the master bedroom. The dog went directly to the bathroom where she became extremely excited, to the dresser drawers, the walk-in closet, and to the side of the bed where the phone was lying on the floor.

Judy had the dog scent the phone and then trailed her down the hallway to the sliding glass door in the kitchen and into the backyard. I watched as the dog went to the corner of the fence where she stood on her hind legs, her huge body balanced precariously as she reached for the top of the fence with her front paws, wanting to get to the other side.

"I'll take her out front and around to the back of the fence," Judy remarked as she led the dog away with Phil Annis and me following behind. As the dog approached the other side of the fence, she immediately picked up a scent. Judy unleashed the dog and she took off at a high rate of speed toward the railroad tracks behind McCrae's residence.

Phil Annis, a tracker whose job was to stay with the dog, was one of the best on the team. He ran behind Pita as Judy and I brought up the rear. I was out of breath within the first ten steps as Annis and Pita, her nose to the ground, grew smaller in the distance. What made it even more demoralizing was that Phil Annis was a dwarf, his short legs taking about four strides to my one, yet he left me in his dust. Frustrated, I just looked at Judy and shook my head as my strides grew shorter and shorter.

"Don't let it bother you," Judy laughed. "I don't know how he does it, but he'll stay with the dog for as long as it takes and I just follow along behind. If you want to see something really funny, join us sometime when Phil's partner is with him. His partner, Tim Glazier, is six foot five and the two of them get us going. Tim will pick Phil up and put him on his shoulders and away they go. It's a scene because they're both clowns, great friends, and damned good workers."

"If I was him, I'd put a saddle on the dog and ride it," I puffed.

Pita lost the trail on Hansen Lane after indicating that EAR had been in several backyards in the area. Apparently his vehicle had been parked where the scent disappeared approximately a half-mile from the victim's residence.

Beverly Mestressat, another S.A.R. volunteer, arrived with her bloodhound, Eli and again the scenario was repeated, although Eli followed an air scent about a block off from the first dog due to the time frame and wind velocity that moved the scent.

The handlers discussed the search and realized that the dogs had each picked up on the scent immediately upon entering the residence. It had become more apparent in the bathroom where the dogs had become extremely excited, a different kind of excitement than a normal human scent. The dogs had previously acted this way on other searches when the person had a physical or drug problem. Judy explained that by physical, it meant any kind of disease that might change the chemical balance and enzymes of the person. It could not be the lotion used by the rapist, she told us, as the dogs live with that type of substance all the time.

Sergeant Coggan arrived and met with Rupf and Patty. Teresa McCrae was seated in Coggan's county vehicle, still trembling from the attack, unable to force herself to re-enter the residence. Coggan explained the importance of her presence in the residence and persuaded her to walk us through the scene. She was so terrified of the ordeal that after quickly walking us through the residence, she never re-entered the house again. Friends packed and removed her belongings.

She had been asleep, she told us, when she felt someone straddling her body on the bed and telling her not to scream or he would kill her. The rapist had tied her wrists and ankles and blindfolded her and said something about needing money and food for his van and that he wouldn't hurt her. She told him that her money was in her purse on the kitchen sink.

When she heard her attacker turn on the light near her bed she turned her head toward it before he had blindfolded her. She saw his back and could see he was wearing some kind of ski mask. It had scared her so much that she had buried her face in the pillow and never opened her eyes again while he was there.

She heard him masturbating beside her and could smell an odor similar to Johnson and Johnson Baby Magic lotion she had in the bathroom. He untied her ankles, pulled up her t-shirt, and pulled off her underpants.

"He asked me, 'Do you like to fuck, Teresa?' I told him no and then he asked me if I like to raise dicks. I told him no and then he said, 'Then why do you raise mine every time I see you?' Then he raped me and then he searched the house some more and then he raped me again," she cried.

She felt he got her name off her drivers license in her purse and didn't think it was anyone she knew.

"It's cold in here," Coggan remarked.

"Yes, it got real cold while he was here," McCrae stated. "He must have turned the heat off and he also turned my stereo off."

"Sounds like he didn't want any noise so he could hear if anyone showed up," Coggan remarked. Teresa told us she heard her attacker close all the drapes and she could tell he had a flashlight but didn't really see it. She said he must have been wearing soft-soled shoes, as she couldn't hear him walking around.

A friend arrived and took McCrae to her house to stay, and we started processing the scene in earnest. McCrae told us that her driver's license was missing from her purse as were two rings, an antique stickpin, and two pendants from a jewelry box. During our processing, one of the rings was found near the stereo that had been unplugged by the rapist. He had either dropped it by mistake or left it there on purpose.

We began to process for fingerprints and although we knew that EAR always wore gloves, we were determined to find that one clue we needed. When I lightly touched the globe lamp near the bed with fingerprint powder, fingerprints jumped out at me.

"Damn. John come here!" I yelled at Patty. "Look at this. McCrae said she heard him turn on this lamp and the surface is so slippery you have to hold the globe to turn it on. Maybe he had his gloves off because she said she heard him lubricate himself and these three fingerprints look fresh."

"Well, they're the only prints on it and if he wore gloves there should be some smudge marks at least. We'll have it checked against elimination prints of anyone she knows has had the opportunity to be in here. Maybe we will get lucky," Patty replied as he spread tape over the prints and transferred them to a fingerprint card.

At 5:00 p.m., we left the scene, locking the residence as we exited.

On December 9, real estate agents from a Dublin, California real estate agency were holding "open house" at several area houses for sale. At around noon a white male, approximately five foot ten, brown hair, brown eyes, medium to thin build, thirty, thirty-five years old, arrived at a San Ramon open house. The agent, Barbara Mays, met the person at the door.

"I'm Greg Pippin, I work for a San Jose property investment firm and I was just in the neighborhood and noticed the sign on the lawn. I've been looking for a house for a friend and would like to look around," the man greeted Mays.

"Come on in," she replied. "Do you have a business card?"

"I don't have any on me," the pockmarked visitor remarked as he pulled a small ringed notebook from his dark blue jacket pocket. She watched as the man walked through the house, checking window locks, door locks, and periodically writing in his book. After about thirty minutes, the man left stating he could offer $68,000 for the house listed at $90,000. For some reason, she shivered when the man left and after closing the door she watched out the window as he got into an orange BMW and drove off.

At approximately 3:00 p.m., Jean Hughs, an agent holding open house at a Dublin, California home, answered a knock on the door and greeted the pockmarked man standing on the front steps.

"Hi, I'm Greg Pippin, I work for a San Jose firm and just happened to be in the area and saw your sign. I'm looking for a house for my brother and sister-in-law who live in Concord and would just like to look around," the man said and stepped inside the house.

"What firm do you work for?" she asked.

"It's a property investment firm. Sun Shine Investments," he answered.

After approximately twenty minutes, the man entered the backyard and seemed to be checking the adjoining properties and the side gate's lock. He offered $63,000 for the $75,000 home and then drove off in an orange BMW. Hughs felt a sense of relief when he drove off.

At 5:30 p.m., a pockmarked man knocked on the door of a Silvergate Drive, Dublin, home that still had the "open house" sign in the yard.

"Are you a realtor?" the stranger asked the owner.

"No, the agent left. She left the sign up because she's coming back tomorrow," the owner answered.

"Your yard looks good," the stranger remarked as the owner and his attractive wife stood in the doorway. Without giving a name the man drove off in an orange BMW.

On December 10, Detective Peggy Bowen met with McCrae and Sunny Walther, the San Ramon victim, to compare their personal lives in an attempt to find a common thread. As with previous victims, there appeared to be none.

During a neighborhood canvass, McCrae's neighbor informed Coggan that the night of the attack one of her dinner guests had seen a dark colored van parked in McCrae's driveway around 11:30 p.m. McCrae knew of no one who owned such a vehicle.

Contra Costa Times, 12-10-78

A New Attack By East Area Rapist in Contra Costa?

DANVILLE – Authorities suspect the notorious East Area Rapist was responsible for the early Saturday morning rape of a 32 year old woman at her home on the south end of town.

This is the first attack attributed to the rapist since October, when police believe he struck as many as three times in Contra Costa County and created a flurry of concern by residents.

Some 20 sheriff's deputies were summoned at about 5:30 a.m. to a home in a neighborhood south of Valley Road...

On December 11, 1978, Sheriff Richard K. Rainey promoted four deputies to the rank of sergeant. I was one of the four who took the Oath of Office at a swearing-in ceremony at 8:30 a.m.

CHAPTER EIGHT

December 11, 1978

I WAS SEATED AT MY DESK in the Crime Lab nursing a cup of coffee and finishing my lunch and the report on the McCrae home when Jerry Mitosinka, the new chief of the Crime Lab sat down next to me.

"Well, Sergeant, how does it feel?"

"To be honest, I don't think it has really sunk in yet," I answered.

Well, the good news hasn't ended yet. At least not for you. Because of the East Area Rapist attacks, Sheriff Rainey has put together a Rapist Task Force. There will be members of our department as well as some of the city P.D.'s," Mitosinka began. "He's meeting with the chiefs today. Undersheriff Dillon just got off the phone with me and you're being transferred to the Task Force as of today."

The Unit would be made up of personnel transferred from various divisions. Captain Warren Rupf would be the Task Force Commander out of the Investigations Division. Lieutenant Russ Pitkin would be in charge of the Unit with Sergeants Gary Ford, Ron Voorhies, Rod Carpenter, and myself as the investigators. Criminalist John Murdock from the Crime Lab and Sergeant Mike Weymouth in charge of three deputies working as the trap unit would be the Sheriff's Department portion.

"You're all to meet in Investigations at 10:30," Mitosinka said.

"There's going to be some pissed off investigators," I remarked.

"That's life. You've done a good job here, but when we heard you were going to be promoted, we knew you would be transferred. Good luck with the Task Force," Mitosinka finished.

Contra Costa Times, 12-12-78

Strike Force To Stop Rapes

A strike force of law enforcement agencies is being put together by Contra Costa County's Sheriff Richard K. Rainey in hopes of preventing further attacks in the county by the notorious East Area Rapist.

Chapter Eight

Early Saturday a 32 year old woman who lives alone near Para-iso was the county's third reported victim.

Rainey Monday announced he is organizing a multi-jurisdic-tional operation, including police from Concord, Walnut Creak, and Pleasant Hill, along with the California Highway Patrol and the Alameda County Sheriff's Office.

"We are dealing with an area problem and all resources, public or private, should be utilized in an effort to protect the commu-nity," Rainey said in a statement released from his office...

The Task Force was set in motion on December twelfth using a multi-level approach involving Patrol, Crime Prevention, Investigation, Crime Analysis and Dissemination, and outside agencies.

Patrol Division was to supply ten deputies on overtime to work 9:00 p.m. until 7:00 a.m. Thursday and Friday nights for the next three weeks, supervised and coordinated by Sergeant Weymouth. In addition, ten reserve deputies would be used with the regular deputies to form two-man units. The teams would be both reactive and proactive. Reactive to apprehend and prosecute, or proactive to force EAR to leave the area.

Phone calls began coming in to the Task Force office due to the newspaper article. Although the unit, still loosely knit, had not had time to bring themselves up to date, the help provided by Sergeant Tom Coggan was invaluable. Coggan had been in contact with Sgt. Bevins, Sacramento Sheriff's Rapist Task Force, on numerous occasions, had been brought up to speed on previous cases, and had become a ma-jor part of the current investigations. His disappointment in not being part of the Task Force was apparent. His professionalism overcame his disappointment.

"Who was that you were talking to?" Voorhies asked me when I hung up the phone.

"Some nut who said she has psychic powers and knows who the rap-ist is. She gave me two names that came to her in a dream or séance or whatever nuts have," I responded.

"Her name Elsa something?" Voo asked.

"Yeah. Friend of yours?" I answered.

"I think she's certified nuts," Voo replied, ignoring my remark. "I've talked to her four damned times today. I almost believed her the first time she called."

An anonymous caller gave the name of a person who had been fired from the Sacramento S.O. while he was on probation. Bevins was contacted and confirmed the information. The individual, who had contacts with Stockton, Walnut Creek, and Sacramento, was eliminated due to height: six foot three.

Concord, Walnut Creek, and Pleasant Hill Police Departments agreed to participate and each provided an officer to the Task Force. Sergeant Frank Fonda from Concord, Officer Tom Cassani from Walnut Creek, and Officer Jack Harper from Pleasant Hill transferred in on December 14th, as did District Attorney Investigator Harold Franklin.

The initial procedure would be that Sergeant Gary Ford and I would be the investigators for Team #1 and Sergeants Voorhies and Carpenter Team #2 would respond to any EAR attacks in the unincorporated area. If an attack occurred within city jurisdiction, we would respond, if requested, to assist in the investigation.

Under Lieutenant Pitkin, a paper-trail fanatic, the first two weeks was spent going over previous EAR attacks and producing forms, forms, and more forms to be used in any investigation of an EAR attack, and reinventing the wheel, using spokes from Sacramento's experience and expertise with EAR.

Sergeant Ford, an experienced investigator, and the most glib of tongue among us, finally convinced Pitkin that we should be investigating the past Contra Costa cases, and that the producing of forms and background material should be left to the one person on the team who was adept at making charts, graphs, and reinventing the wheel: Sergeant Carpenter. Rod, left to himself, with help when he requested it, undertook the task and lived up to his reputation.

In the meantime, office space, phones, furniture, and supplies were appropriated by Pitkin.

The Task Force remained in constant contact with Bevins, who supplied us with copies of all previous attacks, including Stockton, Modesto, Davis, and Sacramento P.D. cases. Bevins was also placed on our call-out list, assuring that he would be called immediately if an EAR attack occurred.

A female Criminalist from the Crime Lab was placed on-call to respond to John Muir Hospital to meet with any female EAR victim. The

Crime Lab also provided each patrol trap unit with rape kits to be used on all EAR victims.

It was decided that areas along the Interstate 680 corridor would be the focus of the trap units with a concentration on greenbelt, railroad tracks, and golf courses.

Through the combined input from the Task Force, it was decided that EAR would probably not attack over Christmas. Although he had hit three times in December, once in 1976, once in 1977, and not to our knowledge, once in 1978, as at this time we did not know of the San Jose attacks, EAR had taken a month or more off after the December attacks.

Due to the trap units, burglaries did decrease; an unusual yet appreciated fact, especially due to the Christmas season and the usual jump in theft reports.

On Monday, December 18th, I received a call from Barbara Mays, the real estate agent that had been at an open house when a subject identifying himself as Greg Pippin had shown up.

"I wouldn't have called, but I was at a Christmas party over the weekend and the subject of the rapist came up and I mentioned about a man showing up that made my skin crawl," Mays began. "Another agent, Jean Hughs, said that the same person showed up at a Dublin open house and acted real strange. He told Jean that he worked for Sun Shine Investments in San Jose." I took down the information and thanked her, telling her that I would get back to her after I did some checking.

There was a Sun Shine Property Investment Company in San Jose; however, the owner assured me that only two salesmen worked for him and both were in their fifties and had worked for him for over ten years. The owner, himself sixty-two, stated that they had not done business recently in the San Ramon/Dublin area and that no one by the name of Greg Pippin had ever worked for him.

In the afternoon I contacted the State Realty Board in Sacramento to see if a Greg Pippin was licensed as a real estate agent. Four Pippins were located, each with a different first name. Also, six realty and property investment firms beginning with the name "Sun" were listed for the San Jose area.

After running a driver's license check on the four Pippins, each was eliminated by contact being made by other California law enforcement officers.

On December 18th at 6:30 p.m., thirty-six years old Barbara Korbell arrived at her Thunderbird Place home. An upper middle class area of San Ramon, the house bordered the San Ramon National Golf Course, a beautiful eighteen-hole championship course.

Korbell fit the profile of the new neighborhood: young, professional, married, with a son in college. She also felt the panic, the fear that other women along the I-680 corridor felt although hers was more deeply rooted. Blond, slender, and friends of an EAR victim's neighbor in Sacramento, she knew details of the attacks. She knew that the beauty of the golf course during the day could be the black realm of EAR at night. Because of that knowledge, Barbara and her husband, Ron, followed a ritual each evening upon arriving home and again before retiring at night.

Five minutes after she arrived home she heard the garage door open to allow her husband to drive into the garage and park his BMW for the night. Soon after Ron entered, the ritual began: Ron checked all the locks on the windows and doors to make sure they were locked and had not been tampered with. They knew that EAR sometimes entered a home while the people were away and set it up for a later attack. They knew that he left windows unlocked and secreted rope and shoelaces to tie up his victims.

As Ron checked the locks, Barbara checked under the bed, in the closets, under the chair cushions in the living room, under the sofa cushions. This time as she lifted the cushion from the sofa, her heart stopped, her hand went to her mouth, and she screamed. Coiled like a white snake ready to strike was a long, single strand of white nylon rope. Nothing else took focus as the room seemed to close around her. Ron was besides her, holding her, sweat beading on his forehead as he too stared at what he knew had not been there the previous evening.

At 7:00 p.m., Deputy Michael Barkhurst arrived at the residence. A thorough search by Barkhurst failed to reveal where the rope came from or how anyone had entered the residence to place it there. Barkhurst collected the rope and after learning that the Korbells would leave to stay with friends for the night, had radio call a member of the Task Force.

At approximately 8:15 p.m., Voorhies and Weymouth arrived at the scene and met with the Korbells. With prior approval they had parked their vehicle at a neighbor's a block away with the intention of remaining in the residence during the night. After the Korbells left, the two sergeants pulled the drapes, turned the inside lights off, and left the porch light on as the Korbells had been doing each night.

As nothing developed, the two left the residence at 4:30 a.m.

At 8:30 a.m., Voorhies and Weymouth were back to work briefing the unit on the past evening's incident.

"Voo, you and Larry get a hold of the Korbells and go over the home with a fine tooth comb," Pitkin told Voorhies. "See if you can find any evidence of forced entry and get back to me."

"They're scared to death, Russ," Voo remarked. "The rope isn't theirs and it wasn't there the night before. They know because they even move the damned furniture each night to look under it."

"You didn't hear anything at all last night?" Pitkin asked.

"Nothing. Not even a dog barking," Voo answered.

"Well, if it was him he probably got scared off by the patrol deputy or else he saw you two arrive," Pitkin remarked.

At noon, Voo and I met with the Korbells at their Thunderbird Place home. I checked the residence, interior and exterior, and could find nothing to indicate forced entry. All the screens were intact with no evidence of tampering or marking. When I went into the garage the Korbells' dog met me. Although the Korbells were not with me, the dog did not bark at any time. I patted it, then it completely ignored me.

The rear yard was unfinished and because of recent rains the ground was muddy. No shoe impressions were found.

"I can't find anything disturbed outside," I remarked, "You're positive you locked all the doors when you left for work?"

"Positive," Ron answered. "I double check every morning before I leave for work."

"Show me again exactly where you found the rope," I looked at Barbara who went to the living room couch, hesitated as if another rope might be under the cushion, and then lifted the corner of the cushion closest to the living room window.

"It was right here. I lifted the cushion and saw the end of the rope and then lifted it all the way and it was coiled right there near the arm," she explained. I could see her tremble as she relived the incident in her mind.

"You mentioned you have a son. Does he live at home?" I asked.

"He's away at college. He was home for a few days and left last week. I called him today and he said he never saw any rope in the house and knew nothing about it. Sergeant, the rope wasn't there the night before. I know because I took all the cushions off and Ron even lifted the couch up and I looked under it. Since we talked to our friend in Sacramento we have been extra cautious.

"Another thing. I wrote a letter Sunday evening. I used my writing paper here in this hutch drawer and today I opened the drawer and one of our wedding pictures was on top of the package of writing paper. The picture used to be in this envelope in the drawer."

"Are any pictures missing?" I asked.

"I don't know. I don't remember what all was in here. I just know that this picture was taken from the envelope by somebody and I know it wasn't us," she answered.

"I would like to take the envelope and pictures to see if we can get some prints off them. I'll make sure that the pictures aren't ruined," I gestured toward the drawer.

"That's fine," she shrugged.

At 1:30, Voo and I left the Korbells and returned to the Task Force office to meet with Pitkin.

"Somebody was in the house, Russ," I remarked. "These two people are so paranoid over EAR that there is no way they could have misplaced that rope or the pictures. I think EAR was in the house and I have no idea how he got in."

"Well, apparently we scared him off," Pitkin responded. "so there's no need for us to sit on the house any more."

"I think we should continue to stay with it, Russ. This is the first real break and if we miss it we're going to look real stupid," I argued.

"Yeah, well, maybe. Why don't you and Voo stay there tonight and take tomorrow off," Pitkin answered.

"Russ, I've got a meeting with McCrae tomorrow. I'll work the overtime. We've got a lot going on and we can't afford to let it slide."

"It'll be all right. We don't want to work overtime just for the sake of working overtime. Go ahead and take tomorrow off. McCrae can wait."

"Russ, the Board of Supervisors gave the Sheriff money to work the Task Force. If you're worried about the money, I won't put in for the overtime. I just think we need to worry about our citizens and not our pennies," I continued.

"It's not the money. Just take tomorrow off," Pitkin walked off and left me shaking my head.

"Get used to it," Ford remarked. "Russ thinks that if he doesn't spend money, he's doing a good job. I'll talk to Warren."

CHAPTER EIGHT

At 9:00 p.m., Voorhies and I arrived back at the Korbells. Again we parked in a neighbor's yard and walked the two blocks. At 11:00 p.m., the Korbells went to bed and we took up our positions in the house to enable us to hear any movement outside. I sat on the floor beneath the living room window near the couch where the rope had been found. Voo took up residence in the spare bedroom, the one used by the Korbells' son when he was home.

As my eyes became adjusted to the dark I could make out objects in the living room. My hearing also became more acute as I sat in the darkness. Around midnight I heard a dog bark in the distance. My heart beat faster as another dog entered the conversation. The second dog sounded closer than the first and I removed my two-inch Smith and Wesson from its holster and placed it on the floor beside me. A third dog joined in the chorus and I strained so as not to miss any noise outside the house. Before I passed out, I realized I wasn't breathing.

A noise from somewhere in the house startled me. It was almost a growl and I placed my hand on my gun, afraid to make a sudden move. Was he in the house, watching me? I heard it again, clearer this time. It was Voorhies. My partner, my mentor, my savior, was sound asleep, snoring loud enough to raise the dead. My thoughts were many, but I knew that if EAR broke in and subdued Voo, I wasn't going to do anything until EAR sodomized him. Then maybe I'd shoot him. Hell, maybe I'd even shoot EAR.

The night turned quiet, at least outside, as I silently cursed my partner who continued his undisturbed slumber.

At 5:00 a.m., I decided it was time to leave and was getting ready to wake Voo when Barbara Korbell came out of the bedroom.

"Good morning," I greeted her. "I was just getting ready to let you know we were going to leave. I don't think anything will happen now."

"We really appreciate your staying. We'll be all right now."

"Sergeant Voorhies is in the spare bedroom. I'll get him," I started for the bedroom.

"That's our son's room. Up until last week he had his pet boa constrictor in there. He took it with him when he went back to college," she smiled and gestured toward the sounds of snoring. It would have been justice if the snake had still been there and Voo had awakened with it stretched across his body.

At 5:30 a.m., Voorhies and I secured the scene, stopped for breakfast, and returned to the office as other members were arriving to work.

"Well, anything happen?" Pitkin asked.

"Dogs barking in the area until around 1:00 a.m., nothing after that," I replied.

"If it was him, he's been scared off. He obviously saw the deputies or you fellows. He won't be back so we can forget them," Pitkin remarked.

"I don't know, Russ," Ford interjected. "we've been real careful and I talked to the deputies that took the report. They didn't stay long because they knew we would want to take over and didn't want to blow it. I think we should stay with it at least one more night. Sacramento agrees. They stayed in houses for weeks at a time."

"No. Two nights is enough. We're not going to waste any more time on it," Pitkin dismissed the conversation.

"I agree, Gary. I think someone should be in the house," I remarked. "I could almost feel the bastard out there."

"So do I. Let's take a walk," Ford started for the door. Ten minutes later we were in the Investigations Division with Captain Rupf.

"How are things going?" Rupf asked.

"Voo and I sat in the Korbell house last night. Dogs barking in the area but no movement around the house," I answered.

"Russ says we must have scared him off. We kind of felt we should stick with it, but Russ overruled us. Said it's not worth spending the overtime on," Ford remarked as he looked at me.

"I want somebody in that house," Rupf stated.

"Not our call, Warren. Russ says no," Ford shrugged.

"Someone will be in that house tonight," Rupf stated as he reached for the phone.

"Don't burn us, Warren. Don't tell Russ you talked to us," Ford implored. "We have to work with him."

"So that's the way it works," I remarked to Ford as we left.

"You got to do what you got to do," Ford replied. "Russ can be a good boss, he just comes from the old school where if you're given money to run an operation, you're supposed to give a bunch back. Someday he'll learn that if you spend it you'll get more."

"Damn, Voo snored all night," I talked as we walked back to the office. "He scared the hell out of me when he started and if EAR was around, probably scared the hell out of him. I thought EAR was in the house and we were all going to get screwed. Literally."

"Weymouth said the same thing. Said he was afraid to blink all night and Voo slept like a baby," Ford laughed. "By the way, we're still on to meet with McCrae. I told Russ we couldn't put it off."

When we arrived at the office, Pitkin called to Ford. "Maybe you and Weymouth better sit in the San Ramon house one more night, Gary. No sense in taking a chance. Call them and set it up."

"I'm going to call Bevins and let him know what's going on," I winked at Gary. When I got Bevins on the phone I told him about the events and Voo snoring.

"I got a better one than that," Jim laughed. "I was sitting on a house one night and one of my detectives was in another. Around 4:30 in the morning he called me on the radio and asked me to meet him. I told him I couldn't leave yet and he said it was real important. Anyway, I told him he could leave and meet me. About fifteen minutes later he drove up and parked next to me. Said he had a problem and needed to talk to me in confidence. I asked him what it was and he said he needed a promise I wouldn't tell anyone.

"I told him to tell me what it was and he said that unless I promised I wouldn't tell anyone, he couldn't tell me. I told him I would be quiet. Said he was on the couch and got uncomfortable so he moved around and started to take his automatic out of his waistband and it went off. Creased his ass and ended up in the couch. The people didn't even wake up. I told him he had to get to the hospital and at first he refused, so I ordered him to go. As soon as he left I went to the patrol briefing and told everyone that he had shot himself in the ass. He still hasn't lived it down."

"Well, at least Voo didn't shoot himself, but I was tempted to," I laughed. "By the way, I'll send you copies of the fingerprints from the Korbell residence after we get all the elimination prints done. Oh, one other thing. Did you know that San Jose had been hit twice and they look like EAR rapes?"

"No. No one here has heard anything," Bevins answered.

"Well, I went to Berkeley P.D. and talked to one of their sergeants working the Stinky Task Force. Larry Lindinau said he would send me copies of the reports but said not to expect to get too much cooperation from San Jose. I'll get copies to you as soon as I get them. Apparently the victims were both Oriental. Lone woman in the first and a married couple in the second. The first one was November 4th and the second December 2nd. From what he told me the second is a classic EAR," I explained. "I wonder how many other departments aren't talking."

"We're our own worst enemies. If cops could work together maybe we could win a few," Bevins remarked.

"Well, we're an open book. The lieutenant told us you were to be called on every hit we get and to be honest, I'd prefer you to be here."

"Look, if you hear of an attack anywhere, give me a call. We'll go on it together. If I get a call, I'll call you. I've got your home phone number and you've got mine. That okay with you?" Bevins asked.

"You got a deal. Maybe we'll get lucky," I responded and hung up.

"Anybody read last Sunday's *Oakland Tribune*?" Carpenter looked around the room and saw no response.

"I've been collecting newspaper articles on EAR from all the newspapers from Sacramento through the Bay area. Some reporter from the *Trib* interviewed Sunny Walther. He didn't use her name but described her as the San Ramon victim. Called her Kathy. She told the reporter that the rapist wasn't really brutal and didn't whack her around. Said the only part of his body she could see was his little eyes, just staring at her. Said he raped her on the cold linoleum floor in the kitchen. It's a three-page article. Says she really hates the guy but feels sorry for any guy who has to stoop that low to get sex. Also says she deducts twenty-eight cents a month from her phone bill now. She dialed 9-1-1 that night only to discover it's not in service in San Ramon," Carpenter finished.

"I don't know. If I got raped I think a reporter would be the last person I would want to talk to," I replied.

"By the way, Voo, I understand you scared the hell out of Larry last night," Ford laughed.

"I dozed a couple of times. No big deal. I would have saved him if EAR had broken in. I'm a light sleeper. Rookies," Voo replied.

"The first time you snored I had to swallow three times just to get my heart back in my chest. You scared the living hell out of me. All I could think was that if EAR broke in and screwed me I would have to kill you to keep it a secret," I laughed.

"His snoring scared the crap out of me the night before," Weymouth remarked. "I thought a train had left the tracks and come into the house."

"My wife and I moved here from Canada in 1962," I started, "Well, sometime in '63 or '64 we went to Lake Tahoe to gamble. I think we had been there twice before and were still a little baffled as to why people flocked there to throw their money away on slot machines. Anyway, this time on the way back home we heard news that a casino girl in Reno had been killed that weekend, cut into pieces and stuffed in a trunk. They found her body and the news went on to say the person suspected of killing her was thought to be heading for San Francisco.

"At that time we still didn't know our way around too well and thought the only way to get from Reno to San Francisco was through Antioch where we were living. We didn't even know about I-80. We talked about the murder on the way home. This was big news to us. Hell, in Canada things like this didn't happen, at least then.

"Anyway, we went to bed talking about this murderer traveling through Antioch. Our headboard was up against the window and we had one of those spring-loaded blinds. We hadn't been asleep ten minutes before that blind let loose, rolled up, flapped around, and scared the holy hell out of us. I thought for sure the bastard had come through our window. I thought of that when I heard you snoring, Voo. I don't need any more heart attacks."

At 9:30 p.m., Ford and Weymouth arrived at the Korbell residence and took up their positions. Nothing developed during the night. Maybe Pitkin was right, maybe we did scare him away. Another mystery unsolved.

On December 22nd, a fingerprint examiner lifted fifteen prints from the wedding pictures and envelope taken from the Korbell home. Thirteen were of possible value.

Steve Ojena examined the rope. No adhering hairs or fibers were noted and the rope was sent to the Aerospace Corporation in an effort to detect occupational residue. A sample of the rope was examined using an AMR 1200 scanning electron microscope equipped with a Kevex 5100 x-ray spectrometer. Unfortunately, the vast majority of the particles examined were typical of environmental mineral or building dust, the type found on the skin of hands of most people in general. No particles were found that would be helpful in the investigation.

Listen up," Pitkin got our attention. "John Murdock and the Crime Lab has put together a packet to use when we check on suspects. I want each of you to carry a bunch of these. The outside of the envelope is stamped so we can control the chain of evidence. Inside there's a packet with gauze. If you can, get the suspect to chew on the gauze. Make sure he gets it good and wet with saliva, then place it in the packet and get it to the Lab. They'll check it for secretor status. Also, if we have an attack, Jerry Mitosinka has it set up with John Muir Hospital to do the rape examination. They have a bunch of rape kits and the Lab will make sure they maintain the supply."

"We picked John Muir," Murdock broke in, "because two of our female criminalists live in the area and they're taking turns on stand-by. If we have an attack, all you have to do is have radio call the one on duty and make sure the victim goes to John Muir."

"Rod is going to put out a memo to Patrol that all EAR victims are to be taken to John Muir, but hopefully they won't do anything until one of you gets there," Pitkin remarked. "Any questions?"

No attacks occurred over the Christmas holidays. The Task Force was fully operational by December 26th , and Assistant Sheriff Dillon issued the first Operational Order outlining the duties of the Task Force, Crime Prevention Unit, Patrol Division trap units, and Dispatch bureau.

Sheriff Rainey sent copies of the order to each city police chief with a letter explaining that the Task Force would be available to assist them should they experience a similar attack to evaluate as to whether it was an EAR attack and to assist their investigators if requested.

"Russ," I got Pitkin's attention, "When I dusted for fingerprints at the McCrae rape, I dusted a bedside lamp and got instant fingerprints on the globe. It was a three-way switch type and it was on a slippery surface. McCrae knows EAR turned the light on and according to her, the lamp had been in storage for three years. As far as I know, everyone who has had access to the bedroom has had elimination prints taken and it doesn't belong to any of them.

"Only one person hasn't been eliminated and that's her ex-boyfriend. She was real reluctant to give up his name and address, so he's probably married. I talked to her on the phone and told her I would keep everything confidential but I needed his prints. She gave me his business phone number in San Francisco and I called him. He's willing to do anything to help. He's free today if Gary and I can break free."

"Sounds good to me. Take Jack, he's been nose deep in reports since he got here. I'm sure he'll appreciate some San Francisco fog. What about McCrae's ex-husband? Did you get his prints?" Pitkin asked.

"She says he hadn't touched the lamp. Bought it after the separation," I answered.

"Okay. See you two later."

At approximately 11:00 a.m., December 27th, Harper and I met with McCrae's friend at his San Francisco business. Polite and helpful, he explained that he owned the house that McCrae was living in.

He had been letting her stay there rent-free until she bought her own house.

"Look, I'm real upset about this. Teresa's a super lady and didn't deserve any of this. She never hurt anyone in her life and sure as hell doesn't prance around naked or in skimpy clothing. You know, she moved out after the assault, so the house is empty," he began. "You can use it for as long as you like. Put a female officer in there undercover and entice this bastard and when he breaks in, kill the asshole."

"We appreciate it, but I'm afraid you would have to lend us a decoy also. We might have a couple male deputies that could entice him, but we're a little low on sexy females," I laughed. "Honestly, he's never hit the same house twice. He hits the same neighborhood sometimes. By the way, one thing I noticed when I was in the house is that Teresa didn't have any pictures of herself anywhere."

"No. She really didn't decorate or unpack all her stuff."

"Well, we appreciate your help. If anything comes up I'll give you a call and if you think of anything that might help, please call." Harper and I shook his hand and left.

At 3:00 p.m., McCrae's friends' prints were eliminated as matching the ones on the lamp. I was becoming more sure that EAR had made his fatal mistake.

December 28th, I met with a thirty-two year old housewife living on Paraiso Drive in Danville. Attractive, slender, strawberry blond hair, she met the profile of an EAR victim. She had called the Task Force when she saw the newspaper article asking for information.

The morning of the McCrae rape, around 2:30 a.m., her two-year-old daughter had entered her bedroom, slamming the door, screaming and extremely frightened. This was very unusual for the child and she had stayed up for about an hour with the lights on comforting her. She did not hear anything outside and couldn't explain the child's actions. I checked the exterior of the residence and found neither indication of attempted entry, nor any shoe impressions. The child's bedroom window overlooked McCrae's backyard and backs up to the railroad tracks.

That afternoon I met with two men who had helped the Walthers move prior to the San Ramon rape. Elimination prints were obtained and turned over to the Crime Lab to check against fingerprints found at the scene.

By the end of the year, the Task Force members had researched the past EAR attacks. Twelve Sacramento victims had sufficient semen stains that could be examined by the various crime labs. All twelve, and the three Contra Costa victims, Louise Simon, Sunny Walther, and Teresa McCrae, each confirmed that the attacker was a non-secretor. In addition, blood found at the scene of a Sacramento rape was tested as type A+. Neither victim had A+ blood. The non-secretor status would be a significant elimination factor, as was the size 9B-shoe impressions found at the scenes.

Eleven scenes had fingerprints that had not been identified and eliminated, including the ones from the McCrae lamp.

Other information gleaned from the reports was that most attacks occurred on Friday or Saturday mornings between 1:00 and 4:00 a.m., and that the suspect wore gloves. Also in several cases it was known that EAR prowled the area prior to attacking and that on occasion had entered the victim's homes, prowled, and then left, waiting for the victims to return before re-entering and assaulting.

CHAPTER NINE

THE BEGINNING

SERGEANT JIM BEVINS, as with most cops, enjoyed his job. Cops don't always like what they see, but they work hard at being professional in what they do. Jim worked hard at being a professional and took pride in his closure rate, as did all the detectives working out of the Sacramento County Sheriff's Department Investigation Division.

Working Robbery/Homicide puts one hell of a dent in an investigator's personal life as it takes many hours of on and off duty time to accomplish the goal of closure.

Robbery/Homicide. The big boys; the elite of every department; the "Dirty Harry's" of the real world, at least in the minds of those less fortunate who will never be selected to work the "felonies."

Only a handful make it and if they do their job, they stay. Many times they stay until they retire. Some leave when they are promoted, although most shun promotions; they have already surpassed their wildest ambitions.

The deputies and investigators who worked on the East Area Rapist cases from June 17, 1976 until EAR moved to Contra Costa County in October, 1978 did professional work although the rapist was not identified. Sergeant Jim Bevins remained involved for professional and personal reasons. Jim Bevins wanted closure, not just for himself, closure for the victims who were traumatized, brutalized and terrorized by California's most infamous sexual predator.

Jim gave copies of all the rapes, all the investigations, the witnesses, the suspects, the evidence, every piece of information he had to our Contra Costa County Sheriff's Rapist Task Force. Jim became an important part of our Task Force and at times my partner, my mentor, my friend.

Because I was not involved in the early rapes, the following chapters are written from reports, conversations and news paper articles. In the interest of readability, some dialogue has been added and I have taken the liberty to change the names of the officers involved, their descriptions and sometimes their actions. The crimes are factual, the conversations between the victims and EAR are factual, or as factual as the victims could remember, and the investigations and the cooperation and some times lack of cooperation between agencies is factual.

The pain and terror may have diminished in the minds of the victims. Because of that I have chosen to write a fictionalized version in the hope that the pain does not return. My intent is to tell the story without endangering the privacy or the dignity of the victims. They have suffered enough.

CHAPTER TEN

CAREY FRANKS' RAPE by a ski-masked attacker on June 18, 1976 had lacked any physical evidence that could lead to an arrest. Detectives, overburdened with other felonies and at a dead end with the rape had set Cary's case aside.

Felony cases are assigned to detectives on a rotational basis. The luck of the draw – much easier talking to someone who had a gun screwed in their ear and their money stolen than talking to a sex crime victim. Unless the woman knows her attacker, chance of an arrest is slim. It is much easier to stake out convenience stores and work informants than work rapes. Usually rapists are loners and don't talk to anyone about their crimes. Robbers? Most of them use the money to buy drugs and are always looking for partners or dealers. Robberies and murders are much more exciting cases than sex crimes.

Like all agencies that depend on taxes, the Sacramento County Sheriff's Office was in trouble. They were understaffed and overworked; too many cases and too few people to work them. The load, the horror and brutality to deal with, the overwhelming numbers that always make it seem like the good guys are losing, makes it exhausting and discouraging at times. Some cops quit, some just shrug their shoulders and put in their time while others only work harder, worrying about each case, believing that they are going to save the world. They die young.

Carey Frank's case disappeared. Like her rapist, it faded into shadows, and even though it nagged at investigators, they could find nothing. Her neighbors could add nothing that was helpful. No suspects of similar description turned up anywhere. Soon the weather grew hotter as the harsh, heavy days of July arrived. Sacramento had its share of homicides, burglaries, and rapes, so the case faded away along with all of the other unsolved cases.

Carey Frank would have floated away into a memory, only remembered because of the horror she felt, the deep, real conviction that he would find her and kill her. But it turns out she was remembered for much more as her case came back to life and she was spoken of as "The First". Her attacker would be the cause of an extensive manhunt by hundreds of law enforcement officers over the next nine years.

Chapter Eleven

Carmichael, California lies just across the American River from Rancho Cordova, where Carey Frank was terrorized. Fair Oaks Boulevard is a major thoroughfare through the community, paralleling the American River. Ten miles of bike trails lie along the scenic river and joggers and bike riders can be seen night and day.

Rio Americano Senior High School on American River Drive is just four blocks from the bike trail. Upper middle class residents send their kids to this neighborhood school.

And at night they sleep secure in their comfortable surroundings.

But at night one person doesn't sleep. He fades in and out of the darkness. He of the mask. And then he is gone.

July 17, 1976

Sergeant Jim Stone was awakened from a sound sleep by the incessant ringing of his bedside phone. He grabbed the phone, more to shut it up than to find out why it was ringing.

"Yeah," he mumbled into the phone. He looked at his watch and saw it was five o'clock. "Damn," he thought, "I've only been in bed two hours." He heard someone on the other end.

"Sergeant?"

"Yeah," Stone mumbled. "What?"

"Did I wake you?" the lieutenant on the other end asked, laughing.

"No, I had to get up to answer the damned phone," Stone answered, recognizing Lieutenant Bill Green's voice.

"Got a good one for you, Jim," the lieutenant continued. "Some creep in a ski mask just broke in on two young girls and raped one of them."

"I just got to bed two hours ago. Just got off that shooting in the Highlands. Okay, just a minute, let me get to the other phone," he dragged himself out of bed and plodded toward the kitchen.

"Yeah, Bill. Whatda ya got?"

"Got two young girls in the hospital," Green began. "Some asshole in a ski mask broke in on them. Punched them a bit, raped the fifteen year old. Ransacked the place, tied them up, threatened them with death."

"Okay, Bill," Stone was now wide awake. "What hospital?"

"Sacramento Medical Center."

Stone made notes on the pad near the phone, hung up, then called his partner, Greg Wayne, and told him to meet him at the hospital. Green had called the crime tech who was responding to the house to process for evidence, so he could meet them later.

Stone showered, got dressed, and left for the hospital. The life of a detective can be hectic.

He half listened to the music on the country western station tuned in on the radio. Rapes were never nice; young kids were even worse. He thought of some of the bad ones he had been on. None were nice.

Stone parked his county vehicle in the no parking zone.

He entered the emergency room and contacted the receptionist, a heavy set woman in her fifties who exuded the energy of a hung over beautician. He showed his badge and gave his name.

"You've got two young girls. One was raped. I need to talk to them."

The emergency room, even at this early hour, was filled with the poor people who crack their heads on the bathroom sink, drive their cars into telephone poles, get Barbie doll heads stuck up their ass, break into mysterious rashes. All of them staring into space.

"Depressing," he thought. The receptionist just pointed toward the door to the nurses' station.

"Your partner's waiting for you."

Stone entered the nurse's station door and saw his partner talking to one of the nurses.

"Morning. Didn't I just kiss you goodnight an hour or so ago?" he joked.

Wayne and Stone had been partners for the last year. Wayne's time revolved around finding a date. There is someone on this earth for everyone. In Greg Wayne's case, the good Lord made an exception. Everybody knew that, except Wayne. To say he was homely was being polite. White straw hair, eyes that looked like when he was a kid the mumps went up on him instead of down like most of us worried about. And ears! Damn, he had ears. They flopped when he walked. None of that stopped him from telling everyone in the detective bay about his animal magnetism. Like the day he came in and announced he had got the best head job he ever had the night before. "Oh, yeah. How did it taste?" Someone asked.

He was a good partner. His dedication to finding a date was only surpassed by his dedication to this job.

"What do we have, Greg?" Stone asked.

"A shitty case. Two kids, one cherry, raped by an asshole. One kid has a couple of bumps on her head, but she wasn't raped. Nurse says she is doing fine. She's sixteen. The fifteen-year old wasn't so lucky. It appears she was a virgin and the son of a bitch did a job on her. Slapped her around, I guess, and raped her. More than once, according to the doctor. He's finished with her and she's getting dressed now. They've got two rooms for us to use so you can take one and I'll take the other. Your choice, partner," Wayne shrugged.

"Got their names, Greg? I didn't get particulars from the lieutenant."

"Yeah. Fifteen year old is Sally Graham, sixteen year old is Sara Graham. Parents are out of town but their aunt is in the waiting room. Both girls are in the room down the hall."

"Okay, why don't you go tell the aunt we will be talking to the girls for awhile. I'll talk to the fifteen year old, you can talk to the sister. If you get through before me, join me," Stone said and walked towards the room with the girls.

Stone gave the nurses a forced smile and craved a cigarette. It was going to be another long day. He suddenly felt old and tired. He was glad he had no kids at a time like this. Other times he wondered. At thirty-nine, it was probably too late anyway, he mused.

He knocked on the door and could hear the two girls talking. One of them replied, "Yeah?"

"Sergeant Stone," he replied. "I need to talk to you ladies as soon as you're ready."

The door opened and Stone looked at the two girls. They were both fairly attractive and were dressed in similar jogging suits. One was tall, about five foot seven, he noticed, and about a hundred and twenty or thirty pounds. The other was shorter, about five four and a hundred and forty, he guessed.

"I'm Sergeant Stone. Jim," he introduced himself, "I'm with the Sheriff's Department."

"I'm Sara," the shorter one replied. "This is my sister, Sally." She looked at Sally with a sadness that couldn't be hidden.

"I'll talk to Sally for awhile in here and Detective Wayne is going to talk to you, Sara, in the next room. He's talking to your aunt right now. If you want your aunt with you, that's all right," Stone explained.

Chapter Eleven

Both girls shook their heads no and Sally said," I know I have to talk to you, but I couldn't talk in front of my aunt. Can Sara stay with me?"

"I'm sorry, Sally, but we need to talk to you separately first. It's best, really."

"Okay, I understand."

Stone asked Sara to go with him. She followed and he signaled for a nurse to meet him. The same nurse who had been talking to Wayne when he arrived came over to them and smiled at Stone and the girl. He asked her if she would take care of Sara until his partner returned.

"Of course," she replied and put her arm around Sara's shoulder and walked toward her station.

Stone returned to Sally's room, closed the door and sat down next to the young girl.

"I know this will be hard on you, Sally," he began, "but I need to go over everything that happened tonight. If something bothers you, we'll work it out, okay? You just let me know."

Sally nodded.

"Okay, let's start before you went to bed. Did anything unusual happen? Did you hear anything that might have sounded different?" he asked.

"No," Sally began, "Sara and I were watching TV and I think we got tired and went to bed about 10:30. Our parents are away, so we checked all the locks and went to bed. I turned off all the lights because Sara was ahead of me."

"Okay. You turned out the lights and went to bed. What happened next?"

"I fell asleep and then....," Sally hesitated.

Stone could see she was beginning to tremble as she pictured in her mind what she had gone through.

"Okay," he soothed, "it's all right. Just try and relax a little and we'll go slow."

"I'm all right," she replied, "I think it was about two o'clock or maybe three. I felt a hand over my mouth and I screamed. It scared me. I heard a voice tell me to shut up or he would kill me."

"Try to remember. What were the exact words he used?"

"I'll never forget. It scared me so much I couldn't breathe. He said, 'Shut up. I have a knife and if you don't shut up I can kill you.' It was like a nightmare. I thought I was dreaming and then I knew I wasn't. His voice scared me."

"What was so scary about his voice?"

"I don't know. He talked like he kept his teeth together and he whispered real angry."

"Then what happened?" Stone urged her on.

"I rolled off the bed and bumped his leg. Then I got up and ran out of my bedroom. I was calling for Sara, but he caught me and hit me on the back of my head three or four times real hard. I fell on the floor and started yelling for Sara. He hit me two more times and told me to shut up. He said he already tied my sister up."

"Did he use Sara's name or did he call her your sister?"

"He called her my sister. I pretended I was unconscious and he got real angry. He said 'Get your hands behind your back.' Then he grabbed my arms and tied my hands real tight with some string. Then he whispered real close to my ear. He said, 'You do everything I want and I'll fill my bag and leave'."

"Were those his exact words?"

"Yeah, that's what he said. Then he put a sock in my mouth...pushed it in, then tied something around my head to keep it in. I thought he was going to smother me," she continued. "Then he tied my feet and then picked me up and took me into the bedroom."

"He picked you up and carried you?" Stone asked, thinking that Sally would be a big load to carry.

"No," Sally said, "he took me around the waist and dragged me in and then he put me on the bed. He just kinda' swung me up and laid me on my belly."

"Then what?" Stone urged.

"He said, 'If you move or make the bed twinge, I'll kill you'," she said.

"Twinge?"

"Yeah," she replied.

"Have you ever heard anyone use that word before?" It was certainly nothing he had ever heard before.

"Nope, but I knew he wanted me to stay still."

"Sally, what were you wearing when you went to bed?"

"A t-shirt and my underwear."

"Did he remove your clothes or touch you at all during all this?"

"Not then."

"Then what happened?"

"He left my room. I heard him opening and closing drawers, slamming them shut real hard. He would come back into my room and then leave again. One time he tied a towel around my eyes. After about fifteen minutes, he came back in and turned on the light. I couldn't see him but I could tell it was lighter. Then I felt him get on the bed over me and I felt his thing. It was hard and he put it in my hands and said 'Play with it, play with it.' I smelled baby lotion and felt his thing all slippery. I couldn't move my hands much, but I did a little. Then he got real close to my ear and asked if I had ever done it before." Sally stopped and Stone could tell she was trying to shut things out of her mind. Although she was embarrassed, she knew it was important to be as exact as possible.

"All right, Sally. I know this is tough on you, but can you tell me exactly what he said. Don't be embarrassed."

"He said, 'Have you ever'...you know...'fucked before?'" She averted her eyes from Stone and looked at the floor.

"What did you say?"

"Nothing. I couldn't because of the sock in my mouth. I just shook my head no," she said with tears in her eyes. "Then he untied my feet and rolled me on my back. He pulled my panties off and moved my legs apart and bent my knees. Then he got over me and put it in me. He did it for a minute or two and then he got up and tied my feet again."

"Did he climax, Sally?" Stone had to ask.

"I don't know. I didn't feel anything if he did."

Stone looked at his hands. He hated this part of the job. How much easier it would be on these victims if defense attorneys weren't such assholes. But they were, so he continued, "Go on, Sally."

"Then he said, 'Where's the money?' and I nodded towards the dresser. I had about sixty dollars saved. I heard him looking around and moving things. He dumped stuff out of my drawers onto the floor and then threw the drawers down."

Sally said that her rapist then left her bedroom and she could hear him in Sara's room. She heard him talking and rummaging. Then he returned.

"He said he saw me at the junior prom," she continued. "I had a picture of my boyfriend and me at the prom. It was on my dresser. He said, 'I knew when I saw you at the junior prom I had to fuck you'."

Sally said she had written on the back of the picture that it was the junior prom and their names.

"I don't think he was at the prom. I would have known him."

"What next, Sally?"

"He got on the bed again, but he had his head near my feet. He put it in my hands again and told me to play with it. He said, 'I'm in love with it. I'm in love with your fucking body.' After awhile he got up and got on me again and did it to me again. I was on my stomach and he put it in for a few minutes. Then he got up and walked around the room, then put it in me again. After awhile he got up and left my room. I could hear him searching things. He was out there for a long time and then he came back in and did it to me again."

Tears were running down her cheeks now and Stone was afraid she would stop talking. He gave her his hankie to wipe her eyes and blow her nose...the only break he dared give her.

"Let's try and continue, Sally. Can you tell me what happened next?"

"He wiped between my legs with the sheet. I don't know why he did it. Then he said, 'Where's the doctor's drugs? I looked in the refrigerator and they're not there,' but I didn't know, so I just shook my head. My father's a doctor and he may have seen envelopes with his name," she explained. No other explanation as to how he knew a doctor lived in the house ever surfaced.

"When he left my room, he breathed real heavy through his mouth a couple of times as if he was real mad because I didn't know where Dad kept any of his medicines."

Sally didn't hear any more noises. She waited approximately thirty minutes and when he didn't return, she rubbed the blindfold off her eyes and looked at the clock beside her bed. It was 4:30 a.m.

She then got up and went to her sister's room. Sara was just untying her hands. Sara got a pair of scissors and cut the string from Sally's hands. Sara then went to her parents' room and called the operators for assistance.

"Sally, one last thing," Stone asked. "Describe him." He tried to keep his voice calm.

"I think he was eighteen, maybe twenty," she began. "When I first saw him, he was wearing a stocking cap that had several colors. He was wearing some type of mask over his face, but I don't know what kind. It just had eye holes. He had on cord pants, but I don't know what color. Oh, he was wearing waffle stomper shoes. You know, the kind you wear hiking. And a shirt. I think it was a print shirt, but I don't know what kind," she said.

Wayne knocked at the door, stuck his head in, and said, "Whenever you're ready, Jim, I'll be at the nurses' station."

"I'll bet you will," Stone thought, but replied, "Okay, Greg. We'll be finished up soon."

He then turned to Sally. "Anything else you can think of, Sally?"

"No, I don't think so."

"Okay, let's go find your sister and your aunt. You're going to get tired of seeing me, but I'm going to have to talk to you whenever I have a question. I'll need to talk to your mom and dad when they get home, too."

Stone put a reassuring hand on Sally's shoulder as they walked toward the nurses' station. Wayne was talking to another nurse, but seemed to be just as enthralled as before.

"Okay, Greg. Let's get to work." Stone headed for the waiting room and Sally's aunt.

"No problem," Wayne replied. "I'll see you later." He winked at the nurse.

"I'll be here," she replied.

The aunt said she would be taking care of the two girls until their parents returned. She said they were due that evening. Stone gave her one of his business cards and told her to have the parents call if they needed anything.

As Stone and Wayne headed toward their cars, Wayne related Sara's version of the attack. She had also been awakened by the masked man. She, too, had been tied. However, at no time had she been molested, although he had hit her on the head several times. She told Wayne she had been sleeping on her stomach when she felt someone sitting on her back. He had placed a knife against her neck and pushed it two or three times, telling her if she made a sound he would push it through her neck and kill her.

Sara had seen his mask and described it as light brown and that it covered his whole head. He was not wearing a stocking cap as Sally had described. He had tied her hands and feet with the same type of string he had used to tie Sally. He had threatened to kill her several times; however, he had not touched her again after tying her up. He told her he was going to steal some stuff and he would go in a half hour. He had pulled Sara's phone out of the wall while he had been sitting on her.

Stone and Wayne decided to stop and talk to the crime scene investigators on their way to the office. They didn't expect to find too much evidence, but...maybe.

Two hours later they were in the lieutenant's office.

Stone knew he had a case that the news media would run with. This one would hit again...soon. Something was familiar about this one. He remembered talking to other detectives about a masked rapist about a month ago. He would look into it just in case. In the meantime, he would work this one with an interest bordering on personal. He didn't know it now, but before this masked criminal was through, detectives would be personally involved in many such cases.

Involved and frustrated.

Stone had talked to the crime scene investigators and had more questions than answers. Sally had remembered the rapist wearing a multi-colored ski hat, yet Sara had seen him with just the mask. Sara had checked her room and found her ski hat and mittens in her dresser drawer. She said they had been in her closet. Why did the rapist move the hat? Why had he worn it when he confronted Sally? It made no sense. What made even less sense was that he had moved her mittens.

Neither Sally nor Sara had mentioned gloves. When asked, they could not remember if the rapist had worn any. The lack of fingerprints indicated he had. Tight fitting and smooth. Did the rapist know that Sally and Sara were home alone? Did he care or was he watching before they went to bed?

The crime lab found footprints outside Sara's window. If he was watching her, why didn't he rape her? Had he already decided to rape Sally before he entered?

Stone went over the crime lab report and the diagram of the residence interior. Entrance was made by prying the sliding glass door leading into the backyard. This meant that the rapist had to pass Sally's room to get to Sara's. The rapist obviously planned to secure Sara before contacting Sally. Why?

The string used to tie up the girls did not match anything in the house. Four equal lengths were located and he had used them to tie their hands and feet. He must have known the two of them would be home alone. How many nights had he prowled their yard? Their parents had been gone on a church trip for three days. Had the rapist known when they would return?

Stone learned on his second contact with Sally that the rapist raised her shirt one time and fondled her breasts very quickly, then lowered her shirt and made no further attempts. He also had used baby lotion on his penis. Both of these seem out of the ordinary for a rapist. Sally said the rapist never put his full weight on her. Any special reason? Was he trying to conceal his weight?

Stone wondered about the doctor's medication. How did the rapist know it was a doctor's home and why did he look in the refrigerator for medicine? Why didn't he notice the doctor's bag in the master bedroom if he were looking for drugs?

The crime scene investigator found two empty beer cans in the kitchen. The girls swear they were not there when they went to bed, yet neither girl smelled alcohol on the rapist. Did he drink them just before he left, or did he simply pour them out as a ruse? How smart was this bastard?

No footprints were found outside Sally's window. Did he know she was asleep? How could he know? Stone felt he had too many damned questions and was beginning to wonder if they were important. Did he have a sophisticated rapist or was this just a chance rape? Scuff marks on the back fence indicated he left through backyards instead of the street. Where did he go? Was he a neighbor? Sally and Sara both said he was wearing his pants, yet when he came into Sally's room to rape her she didn't hear him take them off. Where did he take them off?

"Greg," Stone said, "Let's get a beer. I've got a damned headache and it's getting worse."

Wayne was in his sports coat before Stone closed his notebook. "Quit dragging your feet, partner, they may run out of beer."

Both left for the day. It was two p.m., July 24, one week after the rape. The rapist had, once again, disappeared into thin air.

———

Jim Stone worked the cases that ended up on his desk each morning. He worked them, but his mind was on Sally Graham and her masked rapist. He had always prided himself in the fact he didn't get personally involved in his cases. He never worried about sentences imposed by judges on criminals he had arrested. He only worried about his part of the case being professionally done. If a suspect skated because of his sloppy work, he worried and learned from his mistakes. If a case was lost because of the deputy district attorney, Stone didn't mope over it. If a deputy sheriff screwed up, he let them know.

He found himself becoming emotionally and personally involved in the Sally Graham case. As the song went, he didn't believe virginity was as popular as it used to be, but a girl, especially as pretty as Sally, who saves herself for whatever reason, doesn't need to have it taken by some masked pervert.

Stone had read over the reports time and time again. He had followed up on the neighborhood canvass. He had sat along the bike trail on the American River. Sally had said she had ridden her bike on the path several times a week. Had the rapist first seen her there? He watched the people riding and walking by. What would cause a rapist to choose one of the hundreds he watched? How would he select a victim if he was a rapist? No answers came. And Stone fell deeper into the case.

He talked to other investigators about similar cases. The one in Rancho Cordova was very similar, yet nothing caught his eye as the key to the mystery. He knew the rapist would strike again...but when? And where? A month passed. Each night he half expected to be called and each morning he checked all the reports. Rapes were not uncommon in the sheriff's jurisdiction, but none were similar to the two he was looking at. And he waited.

Chapter Twelve

THE RINGING SOUND of the wind chimes awakened twelve year old Kathleen Scott. It was a pleasant sound. Kathy had hung the chimes, a present from her best friend, on her curtain rod. Seven little silver bells that moved easily in the evening breeze. She loved the sound and slowly awakened enough to look toward her window. The moon shining through her window shone off the shiny bells.

But something else was moving. Unlike the bells, the other movement was silent. The light from the backyard silhouetted a figure and Kathy sat up in bed to stare at the figure. A mask at her window. A gloved hand prying on her screen. The masked figure stared straight into her eyes as though it had seen into her twelve year old heart, then slowly, not taking his eyes off her, lowered out of sight. A sweet odor of aftershave lingered in the room, strong and pungent.

Kathy, swallowing screams, jumped from her bed and ran into her mother's room. Her father had left for work at 10:30 that evening, so her mother was alone.

"Mom, Mom," she whispered, shaking the deeply sleeping woman's shoulder. "There's a man at my window and he's got a mask on."

Rose Scott leapt out of sleep with a mother's adrenaline. She followed Kathy back to her room and looked out the window into her backyard. She could see no one.

"Are you sure, Kathy?" she asked. "Are you sure it wasn't a dream?"

"I saw him, Mom, I really did. He was trying to get my screen off. He was wearing a mask." Kathy cried.

Rose entered her living room to look through her sliding glass door into the backyard. "I don't see anything, Kathy. We better wake up your sister."

The two of them entered fifteen year old Brenda's room.

"Brenda?" the mother whispered, "Wake up. somebody is in the backyard."

Brenda rolled over and looked at her mother.

"Call the police, then," she replied and rolled over to re-enter her world of teenage slumber.

Rose and Kathy returned to Kathy's bedroom and froze in two generations of terror. The masked figure was there at the window. It turned and ran toward the back fences. Rose ran to her kitchen with Kathy following. She took the phone from the counter and both sat on the floor. Rose dialed the operator to call for help. They heard a noise from Kathy's room...the curtain rod and chimes had just fallen to the floor.

"Please," Rose pleaded into the phone. "Answer." She caught a movement and looked up.

The masked figure stood in the doorway, naked from the waist down, a club in his right hand, a gun in his left.

"Freeze or I'll kill you," the masked figure whispered. "Hang up the phone...now!" Rose did as he demanded.

"Who else is in the house?" he hissed.

"Only my sister," Kathy blurted out in fear.

The mask was a nylon-type with a slit for the eyes. Neither Rose nor Kathy could see his face, just the tight-fitting hooded mask. He stood there in a brown t-shirt and black gloves. His pubic hairs were dark, but his slightly tanned legs had no noticeable hairs. He was wearing ankle-high boots and a wide brown belt, similar to a lineman's, hung from his waist.

The masked figure moved closer to Rose. Closer than he should, at least to a mother who would risk her own life to save her family from pain. She grabbed his gun hand to turn it away. He was not a big man, she thought. A mother's instinct is to protect her children—protect them at all costs. She felt the club hitting her on the head again and again. As she tried to break free, she could hear Kathy screaming, and still the club landed over and over until she no longer struggled. She lay, subdued, on the kitchen floor. He ordered them into the living room and told them to sit on the couch. The masked fiend grabbed her arms and pulled them behind her. He was going to tie her wrists.

"I only want your money," he snarled. Again, Rose fought and this time she ran. She ran toward the front door. She felt the club begin its familiar battering, but she was now at the door. She had it open and she was still on her feet, running, screaming. Kathy was now beside her. The masked, half-naked figure was no longer following and Rose led Kathy to the next door neighbor's, screaming for help. The door was opening. They were safe. They were inside and the door had shut out the horrible outside world.

Rose's head was bleeding. Her face was covered in blood and her shoulder ached from repeated blows. Brenda also came into focus and only then did the mother allow herself to fall into unconsciousness.

Brenda had heard her mother pleading with the suspect, talking about God to try and make him leave. She heard her mother's and sister's screams and heard them running from the house. She had climbed out her bedroom window, climbed her fence, and entered the neighbor's house with her mother and sister.

The half-naked monster was no longer amongst them. His vicious attack was over.

At 0328 hours August 29, 1976, Deputies Moore and Timmons received a call of a burglary in progress. They were two blocks from the scene. At 0329 hours they contacted Rose Scott, who was lying on a couch bleeding through a towel on her head.

"Next door, it happened next door. I don't know if he's still there," she cried. "He's got a gun."

The deputies immediately searched the scene for the masked intruder, however met with negative results. They got a brief description of the suspect and radioed it to their approaching cover officers.

Much later a neighbor who lived across the street reported that she had seen four people running from the victims' house. One of them, a man with light shorts or white pants ran across the street and hid behind the neighbor's bushes. She watched him as he crouched, watching the other three go into the house. Then he walked away, naked from the waist down, she determined, a mask covering his face. And then he was gone. And then the police arrived.

"He didn't seem to be in a hurry," she later advised.

Rose Scott was lifted into the waiting Foothill ambulance and Deputy Timmons watched as they drove off toward Kaiser Hospital. The bleeding had stopped; however, the head wounds would require numerous stitches and the bruising around her face, arms, and shoulders would remain for many days as visible evidence to the vicious attack.

Rose would later tell investigators she could mentally handle the situation. She knew she had saved her family many hours of agony at the hands of the masked intruder. And she knew she had saved her fifteen year old daughter, Brenda, from a brutal rape. The Scotts lived two houses away from the first rape victim. They knew of the terror.

Deputy Moore spoke to the neighbor who had let Rose Scott and her two girls into the house. The neighbor, Frank Strock, said he had heard the screams coming from the Scott residence and had gone outside to check. He said it was approximately 3:05 a.m. when he awoke, as he had looked at his alarm clock. When he saw Rose Scott and the two girls, he immediately took them into the house. He said that although the front yard and street were well lit, he did not see the man who had beaten Rose.

"To be truthful, officer. I was more frightened than curious," Strock offered. "I just wanted to get them inside. We had Rose lie down on the couch and tried to stop the bleeding and then put the towel with ice on her head. Mrs. Strock then called Glen, Rose's husband, at work and told him what had happened. He should be here any moment. Then I called the operator and told her I needed the police. She connected me to your office."

"Did you hear anything unusual tonight, Mr. Strock, before the attack? Earlier in the evening?" Moore asked.

"Well, yes, I did, come to think of it. I heard somebody climb my backyard fence. It has happened quite a bit lately. Kids, I guess," Strock continued. "You don't suppose it was the fellow who hurt Rose, do you? I mean, it was earlier, around ten o'clock, I guess. He wouldn't have been out there that long, do you think? No, it couldn't have been him," Strock answered himself.

"It might have been," Moore replied. "We'll check and try to find out. You said it happened quite a bit...somebody climbing over your fence, I mean. Why don't you tell me about it."

"Well," Strock began, "for the last couple of months someone has been climbing our fence. I have had to nail some of the boards back up two or three times. Seems whoever it is just kicks them down. They were kicking my gate open too and leaving it open. I took care of that, though. Nailed the thing shut."

"Did you ever report this?" Moore asked.

"Nope, no, never thought of that. But you know...yes sir, I did. I did. When Carey was attacked around the corner here, a deputy asked me if I heard anything. I told him I hadn't, but kids had been climbing my fence lately. I think he wrote it down."

"You didn't call tonight when you heard?" Moore asked.

"No, I turned out my backyard light so they couldn't see. Hoped they would break a leg or something," Strock remarked.

"Oh, shit, no wonder we lose," Moore thought to himself. "What in hell do they think goes on in the real world."

Timmons returned from his neighborhood canvass.

"Several neighbors heard the screams, but damned few looked outside," Timmons remarked in disgust. "No one wants to get involved any more. Not even in a neighborhood like this," he remarked to no one in particular.

"The neighbor across the street saw the suspect, but couldn't describe him," Timmon continued. "She heard screams and looked out. She saw the Scotts enter the house and our man ducked down behind some bushes. She thought he was wearing white shorts or something, but later when he walked off she saw he was naked from the waist down. Said it shocked the hell out of her. She checked and saw her daughter was still in bed asleep. When she got back to the window, the suspect was gone and we were here. She said the suspect didn't seem to be in any hurry when he left. Just walked off into the darkness."

Moore and Timmons went back to the Scott residence.

"Well, Cal, it could be a lot worse," Timmons remarked. "At least no one was raped. The fifteen-year old had to be his target."

"Yeah, it looks that way, Dan," Moore answered. "Let's go through the house and get our information before the techs get here to process."

As the two deputies approached the house, they noticed that numerous trees and shrubs surrounding the house blocked it off from the neighbors' view. The front door was open, and as they entered they saw drops of blood on the entrance floor. A picture frame, the glass shattered, was lying on the floor and blood was smeared on the wall and the inside of the door.

They entered the kitchen and saw more blood on the floor. The phone, the cord ripped from the wall, was upended near the kitchen cabinets. Nothing else seemed to be disturbed in the room.

The family room was neatly furnished and everything seemed to be in its place. Everything except an off-white towel on the floor. The ends had been tied together to form a circle. Rose Scott later confirmed that the towel did not belong to them.

As they walked through the living room, they noted the couch against the north wall. They would later learn that this was where the masked intruder had ordered Rose and Kathy to sit and from which Rose had struggled free. A two-inch by twelve-inch piece of torn towel was lying on the cushion. A chair was near the couch. A black shoelace was on the chair arm. Another black lace was on the floor near the chair. Neither belonged to the Scott family.

Items of clothing were lying around both girls' bedrooms along with various personal items. The rooms looked ransacked. All items were in their normal location...typical teenagers in typical living conditions. Because of the actions of their mother, both of these teenagers would be able to continue to live as typical teenagers. The fear would subside.

The sliding window in Kathy's room was standing fully open, the screen missing, the curtain rod hanging from one wall, a set of silver belled window chimes still attached. The masked intruder that was only a silhouette to Kathy emerged as a half-naked, vicious, woman beater through this window.

Brenda's window was also open with the screen missing. As one window allowed the attacker to enter, this one enabled an innocent teenager a means of escape.

Timmons looked through Kathy's window and saw a small wooden patio chair directly underneath. Used to stand on, it had been placed there by the attacker.

The I.D. techs arrived as Moore and Timmons were finishing their walk-through.

"Investigations will want this report first thing Monday morning," Moore commented.

"I'll write it, Dan, you're down three reports."

"Thanks, buddy," was the reply.

As the morning light began to wash the violated neighborhood, the two deputies drove down the same road the half-naked figure had earlier traveled. They, too, soon disappeared in the distance.

Stone arrived at his office in the Investigations Division at 7:45 a.m., Monday, August 30, 1976. He scanned the reports in the in-basket. His eyes fell on the Rancho Cordova report as he noted the description of the suspect. Masked, no pants. His heart began to beat faster as he read the synopsis and noted the address.

"Damn, it's him. The son of a bitch has struck again," he mumbled to himself.

Afraid he might miss her, Stone quickly dialed Rose Scott's phone number.

"Hello," a female voice nervously answered.

"This is Sergeant Stone, Sheriff's Department," he began, "Is this Mrs. Scott? Rose Scott?"

"No, she's sleeping," came the reply. "Do you want me to wake her?"

"No, please don't. I need to talk to her, but I want to make it easy on her. I also need to talk to...," Stone scanned the report for further names. "...Kathy," Stone continued.

CHAPTER TWELVE

"I'm Kathy."

"Kathy, I need to talk to you and your mother about the attack Saturday morning. Will you be home this morning?"

"Yeah. So will Brenda."

"Okay, I'm going to give you my phone number. I'll be here in my office for a couple of hours. Could you have your mother call me? I need to set up a time to talk to you all today."

"Sure, let me get a pencil," she replied.

Stone gave his phone number to Kathy and hung up. He sat back in his chair and started reading. He read the report through once and then began over. As he read, he made notations in his notebook. Questions that needed to be answered...at least asked; maybe there were no answers.

At eleven a.m. Stone arrived at the Scott residence. He had also driven past the scene of the masked man's first rape. The houses, although on different streets, were only two yards apart. He decided he needed to go over the first report again and do some more follow-up on his own.

Stone rang the Scott's doorbell and was admitted by Glen Scott, Rose's husband.

"Morning, Sergeant," Glen remarked after Stone introduced himself. "How about a cup of coffee? Rose will be with us in just a minute. She's having a little trouble doing her hair with all the cuts and bruises. Brenda is helping her. Kathy, I want you to meet Sergeant Stone. He's going to be asking some questions as soon as Mother is ready. Black, Sergeant?" Glen asked, pointing to the coffee pot on the counter.

"Black's fine, thank you. Hi, Kathy. I heard you had a pretty exciting morning Saturday. The deputies said you were real brave and remembered things real well. I'm going to go over the whole thing again with you and your mom. Think you can talk about it one more time?"

"Yeah. It was real scary, though."

Rose and Brenda walked into the kitchen and introductions were taken care of.

Stone noticed the bruising on Rose's cheek and arms. He also saw the cut on her forehead that was closed with stitches. He would later see the two other places on the back of her head that had been sutured. Thirty-two stitches in all and another cut that probably would have been sutured. She also said she had a bad bruise on her sternum.

"Why don't we sit at the kitchen table. Will that be okay, Sergeant?" Glen asked.

When Stone indicated it would be fine, Glen turned to Rose. "Coffee, hon?"

"Please, Glen. Thanks."

Stone looked at Brenda and Kathy as he drank his coffee. In his mind he ruled out Rose as the victim. Although she was not unattractive, at forty-one he didn't think she would be the target. Kathy was too young, so he turned his attention to Brenda. She was not too different from Sally Graham, the girl raped in Carmichael last month, Stone mused to himself. He knew the rapist's intended victim was the pretty fifteen-year-old. Silently he thanked God she did not have to go through what Sally Graham did. Life can be a real bitch, he thought, but it could be worse.

"I've gone through the reports," began Stone. "And I have a few questions that I need to have clarified. Just so you know, I will be investigating the attack on you so if you ever need to talk or if you remember something that you think might be important, call me. I know this has been an ordeal, but we are dealing with more than a burglar. This person needs to be caught—soon."

Stone pulled out his notebook.

"One thing really bothers me," he began, "When you saw him in the backyard, did he have his pants on?"

Kathy shrugged her shoulders, indicating she didn't know. Rose closed her eyes as if to conjure up an image.

"I don't really know," she began. "At the time, I thought he must have. I mean, I didn't see that he didn't have his pants on, but it wasn't well lit and I wasn't expecting anything like this."

"Was he carrying any clothes with him?"

"No. He had a club and a gun, but nothing else," Rose replied.

"The techs looked and never found his pants. They checked your backyard and your neighbors' yards. Rose, when you ran out the door, he followed, right?"

Rose nodded her head yes.

"Kathy, you ran out behind him, right?"

Again he got a yes.

"Did you see him stop or go back into the house?"

"No," Kathy said. "I think he ran to the street. I followed Mom across the lawn and I think he kept on running."

"Brenda, did you see him at all, at any time?" Stone questioned.

"No. I heard Mom talking to him about God and everything to get him to leave and then I heard Mom screaming. I heard him yell at Mom and tell her to stop or he would kill her, but I never saw him. When I heard them run out the door, I pushed my screen off and jumped out my window. I thought he would come back for me so I ran. When I climbed over our fence, I saw Mom and Kathy running toward the Strocks', so I went with them and didn't see anybody else."

"I can't believe he came here without his pants, but where would they be, unless he jumped over the fence and got them?" Stone thought out loud. "The deputies were only one minute away, but they didn't see anyone. Could he be that brazen as to go back after his pants?" Stone shook his head as if resigned to the fact he had no answer.

"Rose, why don't you describe him again. Kathy, if you disagree or remember something else, I need you to tell me, okay?"

"He was wearing a mask," Rose began. "It was like a hood and had a slit for his eyes, but didn't have any mouth or nose holes cut in it. It covered his whole head and I think it was nylon, but not like nylon stocking. It wasn't that tight. He had on a brown t-shirt that went to his hips and he had a wide belt around his waist, like something a telephone man would wear. I think it was brown."

"Was it a shiny brown or a dull, unfinished brown?" he asked.

"Shiny," she replied, and Kathy nodded her head in agreement.

"How wide?"

"About this wide," Rose indicated by spreading her middle finger and thumb.

"Three, maybe four inches," Stone calculated, then raised his eyebrows as an indication for Rose to continue.

"He had a gun in his left hand and a club in his right hand," Rose went on.

"Describe the gun first."

"It was black and small," Rose continued.

Stone saw Kathy shake her head in disagreement.

"You don't agree, Kathy?"

"It was shiny silver. I saw the light shine on it," Kathy replied.

"Rose?" Stone inquired.

"I don't know, maybe, but I think it was black. I might be confused. I guess it could have been silver—I'm sorry, I'm not doing too good, am I?"

"You're doing fine. I know police officers who don't do near as well as you are. Don't worry about it. That part's not important. How big was the gun?" Stone pushed on.

"It was small and just a little stuck out past his hand. When I described it to Glen he said it was a two-inch revolver," she went on, "I saw the cylinder."

"Good," Stone replied. "What about the club?"

"He had it in his right hand and it was real small, maybe a foot long. About the length of a ruler. It wasn't too big around and was light brown. I think it might have had leather on it. He kept hitting me, but it didn't knock me out. It cut me, though."

"What about shoes?" Stone continued.

"Well, at first I didn't remember his shoes, but after talking to Kathy I remember they were dark brown with laces. They came above his ankles. I guess they would be leather walking boots, or hiking boots, whatever they call them."

"Describe his legs," Stone nodded to Rose.

"Well, they weren't big, but they were muscular looking. They seemed tanned, but not real dark. He didn't have much hair on his legs, but his pubic hairs were dark."

"Was he wearing gloves?"

"I told the officers he wasn't but I remembered he was. They were black leather," Rose stated and Kathy nodded in agreement.

"How tall?"

"Five ten maybe. Slim. He wasn't very strong and I think if he didn't have the gun and club I could have handled him," Rose shrugged her shoulders to indicate she wasn't trying to brag, just being honest.

"I think he might be eighteen, nineteen. Maybe twenty. Not much older, anyway."

"Can you describe his voice?"

"At first it was like he didn't open his mouth. You know, kept his teeth together. But after he hit me it got higher and seemed to be shaky as if he was nervous or scared. He didn't use any obscenities."

"Brenda, did you hear anything outside your window at all?" Stone inquired.

"No, nothing. And I had my window open."

"Were your curtains closed?"

"Yes, but I guess a breeze would blow them a little bit. I open my window after I turn out my light, though."

"Can anybody think of anything else?" Stone asked.

"Just a couple of things, Sergeant," Glen began. "We only have one car so anybody checking would know I was gone. I just started working nights two days ago, so this isn't my usual routine. Do you think he knew I wouldn't be home?"

"I don't know. I think he knew who was in the house, but I can only guess," Stone answered.

"One other thing. Rose told me that he reminded her of somebody in the military or maybe a policeman. You know, stood straight. Had that bearing about him," Glen added.

"He did seem that way, Sergeant. He just didn't seem to be a, you know, long-haired punk or anything," Rose explained.

"Okay, folks, that about takes care of my questions. Thank you girls. Mr. and Mrs. Scott, would you talk to me outside for a moment?" Stone asked.

Both followed him to the door and outside.

"I didn't want to ask this in front of the girls, but did your attacker have an erection when he confronted you?" Stone asked.

"I thought of that, Sergeant. He didn't, and he seemed kind of small. If he was going to rape one of us, would he, you know, have an erection?" she asked.

"I don't know. Maybe not, I just don't know," Stone finished. "I'll be in contact. Remember, if you have anything or you want to talk, just call me."

Stone walked back to his car, looking at the neighborhood. He could feel a presence...he couldn't describe it, but he could feel the masked figure's presence. This feeling would grow stronger in the coming months.

CHAPTER THIRTEEN

STONE HAD TALKED to his street informants, the ones who thought they owed him and those who did owe him. The burglars, the prostitutes, the dope fiends. Nothing. Could this son of a bitch be a real loner?

No one had any leads on a nasty white guy with a tiny dick, unless the black prostitute who insisted that all white guys had small dicks counted. She could name several. Contact after contact with patrol deputies also turned up no leads. Nothing. Stone felt like he would keep getting nothing, nothing but more victims. More young victims who would have to talk to strange cops about intimate details, details they would want to forget but never would.

Stone needed a break.

He was at his desk writing: *Who? Where? When?* over and over on a yellow legal pad, breaking the chain now and then by including *Pattern?*, when the phone rang, jarring him back into the mundane office.

"Robbery, Sergeant Stone," he spoke into the receiver.

"Sergeant, this is Glen Scott. I might have something for you."

"Jesus, I need it. Let's hear it," His heart was beating in his throat in a way he had not experienced in years.

"I was talking to Mrs. Strock, and she told me she was talking to another woman who was looking for her son the morning when all this bad stuff happened to Rose. The neighbor said she was walking around about four in the morning looking for him because he was late getting home from work."

"Walking around at four in the morning? That's weird," Stone replied.

"That's what I thought. She said she saw the patrol car and she was wondering what had happened. Mrs. Strock told Mrs. Hamilton, that's her name, about the trouble and she left."

"Hamilton left?"

"Right."

"Who's her son?"

"Walter Hamilton. He's nineteen and he lives with them, his mother and father."

"Could be the one," Stone said and immediately regretted it. Never set up false hopes.

"There's more. He's weird, this Walter. After I talked to Strock, I went over to the Hamilton's and a bunch of young kids were outside the place. I asked if one of them was Walter and one of them stepped forward and said he was. I told him we had some trouble in the neighborhood and he said he knew what had happened. He was real calm, and he told me he had worked overtime Saturday night and got home after 3:30. Said he was stopped by a sheriff's deputy and had to show his driver's license. I asked him if he had seen any suspicious people when he got home, but he said he hadn't. He did say, and this is where it gets interesting, that somebody had been messing with his car last week and he went out with his gun to chase them off."

"He has a gun?" Stone asked.

"Everybody has a gun, Sergeant. He went out with his and a flashlight and said he scared the person off."

"If it was somebody," Stone remarked.

"Right, that's what I thought. I told him that it could be the same guy that went into my house and he said that it was real easy to get into the houses around here. I didn't ask him how he knew, but it sure sounded weird."

"You got an address?"

"Yup," Scott was proud of himself and his importance to the case. Hell, if this worked out, Stone would be proud of him also.

Monday, August 30, 1976, Stone arrived at the Hamilton house. Walter was there. So was his mother, who immediately took charge.

Mrs. Hamilton told the same story that Mrs. Strock had told Glen, adding only that she and Walter walked up to the house where all the police action was going on. They walked back to their house when the sheriffs turned a spotlight on them.

"Walter, can I ask you a couple of questions?" Stone asked, wanting Walter's version, not his mother's.

"Sure."

"Tell me about last Saturday night," As he asked Walter, he kept an eye on the boy's mother to see if she was reacting in any way that would show she was supporting a lie.

Walter spoke quietly, calmly, and politely. He told Stone he had worked from two in the afternoon until midnight in El Dorado County about half an hour away.

"After work, me and another guy sat around and drank a couple of beers, just shooting the bull," Stone looked over at the mother and noticed she was watching Walter with just a hint of a smile.

"We were there until about three and then I drove home. I got stopped by a highway patrol cop just before I got home. Had to show him my driver's license and he let me go. When I got home, I saw the sheriff's mess and I told Mom. She was up because she always cooks me something to eat when I get home."

Christ, that sounds normal. Everybody's mother stays up until all fucking hours to cook their son a breakfast, Stone thought to himself..

"Like Mom said, we walked down, but the cops shined a spotlight on us so we went back home."

"What were you wearing?" Stone asked, making a clear shift in the conversation, bringing in an unspoken accusation.

"I don't remember."

"I do," His mother remarked. "I just washed his clothes," She stood and left the room, and Walter raised his hands as if to say, *What am I going to do. She treats me like a child.*

While she was gone, Stone and Walter sat in silence, the implications of the question about his clothes heavy in the air.

"You thinking of me for this?" Walter asked.

"Maybe. You fit. Five eight, hundred and sixty. In the neighborhood..."

"Here they are," the woman said as she re-entered the room carrying a pair of faded jeans and a print shirt. "I remember washing them the next day. Yesterday."

"You own a gun, Walter?" Stone asked, taking attention away from the clothes.

"Two. One is a Marine Corps forty-five auto and the other's a five-shot revolver. I left them at the Marine Corps armory because I don't want my little brother fooling with them. I was in the Marine Reserves. I left them there a long time ago, so I don't know if they're still there."

Stone made a mental note of the discrepancy with Glen's story. *Not looking good, Walter.*

"Walter, we have a lot of work to do on this and we need to eliminate you as a suspect. I know you're not the one, but you know how bosses are. If I don't follow up on everything my boss gets real mad. We need to be sure for your sake and ours. Will you take a polygraph for us?"

"A what?"

"A lie detector test."

"I'll take any kind of test you want. I've got nothing to hide."

"He's not in any trouble, is he?" his mother asked, holding her son's fresh clothes against her breast.

"I don't think so," Stone replied. "As long as he's cooperative, he'll be fine," The detective turned to the young man and extended his hand for a handshake, hoping to learn from the contact. He was disappointed that the flesh told nothing.

———⟫●⟪———

First things first. Stone met with Lieutenant Burns in the lieutenant's office.

"I think we might have a break in the rapes," Stone began.

"What've you got?"

"I talked to a good suspect this morning. He feels right. He fits the description and he's weird enough. And he lives in the neighborhood of two of the attacks."

"Got a record?"

"No sex. No violence. Chicken shit mostly. Nothing we can put our finger on. Real strange mother fucker. Might be worth following for a couple of days. What do you think?"

"Christ, Jim, I don't have anybody to give you right now. We're short and you know it. We need something more concrete before we spend manpower."

"Thought I'd ask. I need something so I can feel we're getting somewhere on this son of a bitch."

Stone told him about the guns, the strange hours, the knowledge of the homes in the neighborhood. The feeling that this was the guy.

"Well, at least you probably scared him, if it is him, into laying low for awhile."

"Yeah, or gave him a hard-on for more. Whoever he is, he's a violent son of a bitch, Mike. Somebody's going to get hurt more than just a rape if we don't stop him. Got a real bad feeling on this one."

"Stay on top of it and keep me informed," Burns ended the conversation.

"I'm trying."

"The press will have a field day with this if they catch on. I'll talk to the captain about some more men, but I need more from you."

"Okay, boss, you got it."

"Jim?"

"Yeah?"

"It's just a case, Jim. No matter how bad, it's just a case. Don't take these cases personal. If it's yours, work it. If it's someone else's, they'll work it. You let these cases get to you and you're dead meat, pal. Experience talking."

"I'm okay. Just got a feeling this one's going to come back to haunt us. I hear you, but sometimes these things get to you."

September 4, 1976

Debbie Patrick drove from her apartment in Sacramento to her parents' house in Carmichael. At twenty-nine, she hated to rely on her parents, but divorced and living alone did have its drawbacks. To top it all off, her washing machine broke down. Usually her father could fix things for her, but this time the washing machine was being inconsiderate. Her parents were out of town.

What a way to spend a Saturday night, she thought as she drove east on U.S. 80 as the late summer sky turned pink in the west. As she saw the sign for the Madison Avenue exit, she knew she would soon be home. Funny, no matter how old you get, your parents' house is always "home."

At six o'clock she pulled into her parents' driveway. Just six blocks from Del Campo High School, the neighborhood reflected the $90,000.00 median cost of the homes. The one-story single family homes were all well landscaped and most of the ten year old homes were still occupied by the original owners.

Entering through the garage, she dropped her basket of clothes beside the washer, one that worked, as opposed to hers, like her marriage, and her ex-husband, did not. She went into the house and immediately relaxed, as she always did. First, the refrigerator and a glass of milk, then back to the garage for the wash.

She put the first load into the washer and settled in front of the television. It was good to relax in comfort. So much better than her apartment, and the movie with Burt Lancaster was good.

When the first load finished, she went back out, deciding to dry everything back at her apartment. Thank God the dryer wasn't broken.

The movie ended at eleven and she returned to the garage and lifted the heavy, wet clothes into the basket and walked toward her car. Time to head home. Her home.

Indian summer was so nice in the Sacramento area. Nights were still warm enough to enjoy. The warm night air was slightly erotic, but she put that thought away. She had to worry about her wash. She opened her trunk as she balanced her clothes basket on one knee against the bumper. She placed them in the trunk and closed it. Lock up the house and a fifteen minute drive home. A great Saturday night! She circled her finger in the air for a whoopee sign.

A hand fell on her shoulder. Startled, she turned out of instinct. The light from the garage washed the driveway in a soft glow and fell on the masked face. Darkness and eyes. Unblinking eyes from behind the mask. Only eyes.

She sensed the movement coming from below and then her face exploded in red, bright pain, her nose broken from the vicious blow. The bright lights from the pain subsided into blackness before her limp body fell to the concrete. Her parents would never completely remove the stain of blood from the porous driveway.

———⟶✦⟵———

One more time. How many over the years? Stone reached over and shut off his alarm. The ringing continued and he hit it one more time as he opened one eye to look through the darkness at the il-luminated numbers. Shit. His heart pounded in his throat. The time was wrong, the feelings were wrong. It was not time for his alarm. He remembered he had not gone to bed drunk, yet his brain refused to cooperate.

Finally he got the clock into focus. Two thirty? What the hell? The ringing persisted.

"God damn it!" he muttered as he reached for the phone. "Yeah?"

"Sarge, this is Deputy Timmons. Sorry, but I'm at a rape scene. Someone with a mask just raped a girl here in Carmichael. Some white shoelaces were used to tie her up. Thought you should know."

Stone fell back on his pillow. "Shit. I knew it. How long ago?"

"He must have left about two o'clock. Half hour ago. I called you as soon as I could. It just looked similar to the last one. Her sister took her to Kaiser. Got a deputy meeting her there to get more info."

"Thanks, Dan. I'll be at Kaiser in forty-five. Appreciate the call. Tell Radio I'm on my way, will you? I'll call the lieutenant and make sure everything else is taken care of."

September 6, 1976

Another warm day. The detectives, all but Jim Stone, lounged around the investigations area, drinking coffee, waiting for the reports to hit their desks. Stone paced, waiting not for his report, that would soon come. He waited, pacing, for Lieutenant Burns.

He kept a monologue going about his latest fixation, Hamilton. Even though no one really listened, he kept at it: "I knew it. We should have been sitting on that motherfucker. It's got to be that cocksucker."

At eight-oh-five, Burns showed. At eight-oh-five and fifteen seconds, he had company.

Lt. Burns, who prided himself on his appearance, was turning towards his mirror to adjust his tie as Stone came through the door.

"Morning, Jim," Burns said to the reflection in the mirror.

Stone was short on formalities. "It had to be that asshole Hamilton. It had to be that little prick."

"Really? Look, sit down and tell me what you have. Run it down to me."

"Like I told you Sunday, Patrol called me and said it looked like our ski mask rapist. I think it was, too. A little different, but a lot of similarities. Too many to be a coincidence. He raped a twenty-nine year old in Carmichael at her parents' house. She was there doing her laundry while her parents were away. She was putting her clothes in the car, getting ready to leave, when he coldcocked her. Knocked her out and broke her damned nose," Stone ran his fingers through his thinning hair.

"He went the whole fucking gamut with her. Rape, sodomy, oral cop, whacking off, and he even went down on her. Came in her mouth twice and made her swallow. Said he would kill her if she didn't do it. He kept a knife at her throat. She said he lubricated himself before he had her play with him, just like the others. Kept threatening to kill her. He was in the house for two and a half hours. Raped her twice and the son of a bitch even jacked off on her leg. For some reason, this one must have turned him on real good. Told her he was going to Bakersfield and needed money and then stole her car when he left. They found it last night around 6:30 about a mile from the scene. A couple of times he told her he was in the army. She gave the same description as the others, small cock and all. As usual, the techs got nothing. She said he was wearing a gray flannel hood with eye holes."

"Sure sounds like the same guy, all right. What do you want to do with Hamilton? Tell me so I can argue with the boss."

"Got one problem, Mike. I don't think he was after her. She was there by chance and there was no way anyone knew she would be doing laundry there. He was either prowling the neighborhood and came across her, or he had someone else picked out to hit. No one could remember anything unusual lately, so maybe it was his first time in the neighborhood. All I know is, the son of a bitch disappeared again."

CHAPTER THIRTEEN

"Disappeared?"

"Like fucking San Francisco fog."

By the middle of the next week, Stone had no real information that shed any light, but he had started a list of things that might help:

Thursday: Hamilton's poly

Check with H's girlfriends: Sharon Gibson, Joan Rogers, Marilyn Warren (Engaged. She broke up with him)

Employer verifies he worked night of rape, but he left at 11:02. Plenty of time. Lied.

STILL NOT ELIMINATED!!!

September 16, 1976. 0930 hrs.

Walter Hamilton, affectionately known to all those around Stone as "that son of a bitch," appeared for his lie detector test. Stone was there to greet him.

"Walter, you won't mind if we search your car, will you?"

"What for?"

"Usual stuff. Guns, knives, dope, bombs, dead bodies. You know." *Maybe some white shoestrings*, he said to himself. "Mask. Anything."

"Go ahead. You won't find shit."

Stone had Hamilton sign some Consent to Search papers giving them permission.

The search turned up nothing except a *Penthouse* magazine under the seat, which caused one searcher to ask if the pages were stuck together.

"Nope, but at least we know he likes pussy," was the reply.

"Ain't it great to live in America?"

At the same time Hamilton was taking the poly, officers were at his house asking his parents' permission to search it. His mother asked the same question as her nineteen year old, one hundred and thirty pound, five foot eight son had asked: "What for?"

"Weapons."

The family was very cooperative and the investigations division detectives found nothing, which Stone fatally accepted, saying, "Could prove he's innocent. Could prove he's smarter than he looks. And acts."

September 17, 1976, Stone and the rest of the detectives decided to continue considering Hamilton as a suspect in spite of the poly. Detective Merton, a new addition to the detective bureau, whom Stone thought looked like a poster boy for the Church of Latter Day Saints, questioned Hamilton's girlfriend, Joan Rogers.

He reviewed his discussion with the girl with Stone who was, by now, so frustrated with the case that he listened to the detective in the hopes that something, anything, would bring them closer to solving the case.

"She dated him from '73 to '74, two years ago. He was doing a lot of drugs at the time."

"What kind?"

"Serious stuff. Coke and speed. Also did some dealing while he was at it. She said he was real weird, but he didn't do drugs in front of her because she didn't approve."

"Right."

"That's what the lady said."

"The lady say what she meant by 'weird'?"

"Weird. Basic weird, like talking to himself all the time, even when other people were around. Sometimes he would go from real calm to real violent... ."

"That ain't weird," Stone broke in, "I do that all the time."

"Yeah, but this asshole isn't a cop, so he doesn't have any excuses. Anyway, she said he could be real scary."

"Tell you the truth," Stone said seriously, "he's scaring me. Did she say if he had any weird sex shit?"

"No real weird stuff that she knew of, but listen to this. He had a narrow dick. She said it didn't grow much."

"What do you mean, narrow?"

"Fucked if I know. She just said he had a small narrow dick. I didn't ask her to draw the damn thing or describe it further. I thought she might want to compare it to mine and then tell me his wasn't so small after all."

"What else did the lady have to say?" Stone asked, smiling at the image of the comparison.

"Said he wanted to get away from his old lady, his mother. She was a pain in the ass, real domineering, and..."

"Don't tell me. Weird."

"You got it. Domineering and weird. And this time, she really means weird, like she liked to sleep with the youngest son on the couch while the old man was in bed upstairs. The old man, according to her, didn't mind. Probably appreciated it."

"How old is the kid?"

"Forgot to ask. Sorry."

CHAPTER THIRTEEN

Stone decided to talk to Sharon Gibson, Hamilton's fiancee, himself, hoping to get more information. The fiancee was, like everybody else, very cooperative, however, a little protective. She did not give any new information except that Hamilton had told her he had two guns at the Marine Armory and one at home.

"Have you ever seen him dressed in weird clothes?" Stone asked.

"What do you mean, weird?"

"You know, costumes, masks, anything like that."

"We never did nothing kinky, if that's what you mean," she replied.

"I don't mean that. I mean like Halloween."

"Sometimes he wore green army fatigues and those big lace-up boots."

"What color?"

"The boots?"

"The shoelaces."

"Black, of course."

"Of course."

On the way back from interviewing Gibson, Stone stopped at the Marine Armory. He showed his identification to a straight standing, crew cut young man who called him "sir" too much. Stone asked the excessively polite Marine, "Can reservists store their guns here?"

"That's why they call it an armory, sir."

"Good point. How can I find out if someone is storing some weapons here?"

"I could facilitate that, sir."

"I'd appreciate it. I need to know if a Walter Hamilton is storing any guns here."

"Let me check, sir."

The young marine went through a small, black, metal box just designed for three by five cards, quickly going through the H's.

"No sir, nothing listed for Walter Hamilton, sir. Could it be another name, sir?"

"Just Walter Hamilton. Could the information be somewhere else?"

"If it ain't here, it ain't anywhere, sir."

"No guns for Hamilton."

"No guns, sir."

"Could he have stored any here at anytime?"

"I doubt it, sir. The cards are maintained even after the weapons are removed."

Stone thought to himself: *Things are looking good for me by looking bad for you, Walter.* A further check with the California Highway Patrol determined that no officers had stopped anyone named Hamilton the night in question. If you lie about one thing, you'll lie about others. At least Stone had established that, if nothing else, Walter Hamilton was, in fact, a liar.

Tuesday, September 21, 1976, at nine-fifteen in the morning, Stone decided that it was time to put some pressure on Hamilton. As he put it to the two detectives, "Bring the little cocksucker in for questioning."

Merton and Wayne contacted Walter Hamilton at his parents' home. Hamilton was told he was being investigated as a possible suspect in the Rose Scott attack as some of his story did not check out. He was advised of his Miranda rights in front of his parents and agreed to talk to the detectives. He was transported to the investigations division for questioning.

Hamilton, true to type, sat slouched in front of the table at a sideways angle, a stupid grin on his face that was supposed to say, *Take your best shot. I've got nothing to hide,* but which, instead, proclaimed, *I'm a fucking duffus and it shouldn't be too hard to trip me up.*

Stone began: "Walter, we've met before. I'm Sergeant Stone."

Hamilton nodded a greeting that ran somewhere between arrogance and stupidity, slipping into the stupid more than he knew.

Stone turned to Wayne, who was standing against the wall. "Has he been read his rights?"

"At his house."

"You understand your rights, Walter?"

"Yup."

"Good. I want to go over the events of the night of the attack on Rose Scott."

Hamilton shrugged to give the detective the go-ahead.

"Tell me what you did that night."

"Told you already."

"Tell me again, why don't you? Humor me a little."

"I got off work at midnight and my boss and me sat in my car and drank beer. I had two six packs and he had one."

"Are you sure it was midnight when you got off?"

"Yeh, I heard the whistle," His left eyeball quivered and darted toward the wall. "We drank our beer and talked. I shouldna' drank so much, I know, but I drove home and was stopped by the highway patrol near my house. He asked me for my driver's license and I gave it to him. Guess he thought I was all right, because he let me go."

"Did he say anything about your drinking?"

"Nope. I can handle myself pretty well."

"You don't drink and drive often, do you?"

"Nope. Just once in awhile."

"Okay. Tell me what you did next."

"Well, when I got home, my mother and me saw all the crap down at Rose's house, so we walked down to see what was happening. Somebody shined a light on us so we went back home."

"Tell us about your guns, Walter."

"Already told you about them. Locked them up at the Armory."

"Walter, my friend, let me ask you a question."

"Sure."

"Do you think we're a bunch of idiots? Do we look like a bunch of idiots?"

"What do you mean?"

"Walter, you have a real problem here. Your story is bullshit. We checked with the Marine Armory. You don't have any more guns there than I do. You never have had guns there."

"I..."

"You got off work at eleven, not midnight, and you weren't stopped near your home by highway patrol or deputies. You're digging a deep hole, my friend. We can't help you if you lie to us. If your convicted of this, you could go straight to prison. You might as well tell us the truth and maybe we can help you. You're being looked at for the attack on Scott and two other rapes."

Walter's face collapsed in surprise. For a moment it looked like he was going to cry, then he got himself back under control and said, "What in fuck are you talking about? Look, I thought this was a game. I was fuckin' with you. Rape! That's serious shit, man. I was just kiddin', just foolin' around. Look, I'll tell you the truth. I lie sometimes and I just can't help it. I don't know why I make up stories, I just do. Fuck, no one said anything about rape. Shit, I ain't never raped no one. I'm fuckin' engaged. This is bullshit, man," Hamilton started to stand, but Wayne's hand on his shoulder sat him back in his chair.

"Don't get excited, Walter. We're just doing our job and only want to get to the truth. Why don't you start over and tell us what really happened?" Stone urged.

"Okay. I understand what's going on now. I know this is serious. This is what really happened. I don't know why I lie, I just do," His eyes darted around the room. "Okay, look, here's the way it was. I got off work at eleven, not midnight. We did drink beer until three-thirty and then I drove home. I didn't get stopped, but I did see all the cop cars, so I went and got my mom and we walked up the street. When the deputy shined his light on us, we went home. Shit, I thought this was a fuckin' game. I didn't think you guys were serious."

"You better believe we're serious."

"I believe, man."

"What about guns?"

"Guns? What about them?"

"Tell us about your guns, Walter," Stone said, feeling a lightness in his stomach that always came with big events.

"I never put them in the Armory. I don't know why I told people that. I only have one gun and that's the one in my room. Hell, I've never been a Marine. I just tell people that to impress them."

"Tell us about your dope habit, Walter."

"I'm quitting. That shit's bad for you. I finally know that. I'm going to get married so I don't have time for dope. I outgrew it."

"Outgrow it enough so you didn't use it before your polygraph?"

"Huh?"

"Did you get loaded before you took the test?" Stone asked, taking a long shot.

"No dope. No serious shit, if that's what you mean."

"Walter, stop jerking us around. Did you get high before the test?"

"A joint, but I didn't do no dope."

Stone looked at Wayne with raised eyebrows. "You used dope before you took the god damned test?" Stone stated with disgust in his voice.

"No, I told you. No dope. I just smoked some grass."

Criminals are such stupid shits, Stone thought. Or maybe we are.

"When?"

"When what?"

"When did you smoke the damned dope?"

Christ, thought Stone. What do we do now? He decided to try a new tack. "Walter, tell us about your mother. How do you feel about her?"

"What do you want to talk about my mother for?"

"Just tell us about your mother, Walter."

"What about her?"

"How do you get along with her?"

"Man, I got to get away from her. She is on me all the time. Tries to run my fuckin' life, always checking on me."

"Afraid of her, Walt? Most people aren't afraid of their mothers."

"Yeah, I'm afraid of her. If I don't do what she says, she gets madder'n hell at me."

In one of those coincidences that run through all police work, a detective softly knocked on the door to let Stone and others know that someone was entering, and stuck his head in the room. "Stone, phone. Walter's father is what you might call upset."

Stone pushed away from the table he was leaning against and said, "What is he upset about, Walter?"

"I don't know."

"Well, let's hope it's not bad news," the detective said with a light smile. He left the room without looking back at Walter, who was staring at the floor between his feet.

In the open office that he shared with all other detectives, Stone scanned a form about donating to the United Way, picked up the phone, and punched the blinking button, and said "Sergeant Stone."

"Stone, this is Walter's father. What are you doing to my son? My wife is getting very upset."

"We'll be another thirty or forty minutes."

Stone heard a scream in the background. "What the hell is going on?"

"I have to leave," the father whined and the phone went dead.

Stone went back to the small room in which Walter was being questioned. Nothing had changed. Wayne still leaned against a wall looking at Walter, who was looking at the floor. High drama.

"You having fun yet?" Stone smiled.

"Not yet," Wayne replied.

As Stone was telling Walter that he would be best served by telling the truth about all of this, the same soft knock with the same message was repeated, only this time it was from Walter's fiancee, Sharon Gibson.

Stone went back to his desk. "This is Sergeant Stone. Can I help you?" He spoke into the phone.

"This is Sharon Gibson, Walter's girlfriend. I mean fiancee. I'm at Walter's house."

"And how is everything at the Hamilton residence?" Stone asked with a little sarcasm in his voice.

"Not good. Walter's father went to work and I'm here alone with Walter's mother. She's threatening to commit suicide because Walter isn't here."

"Oh, shit," Stone thought. "The ruined poly and now this," he heard screaming over the phone.

"Sharon," Stone yelled into the phone. "What is going on?" Stone looked around for a detective and motioned to him. "Tell dispatch to get a unit over to the Hamiltons'. The mother is screaming and saying she's going to commit suicide."

"Sergeant Stone?" A woman's voice spoke over the phone.

"Yes?"

Her voice had a ragged, weeping quality to it. "This is Walter's mother," she screamed. "I know all about concentration camps. I've been there."

Stone tried to interrupt. "Mrs. Hamilton! Mrs. Hamilton! You are very upset. Put Sharon back on the phone!"

"If Walter isn't home in five minutes," she screamed, "I'm taking some pills and a glass of wine. Do you hear me?" The phone went dead.

Having faith in the patrol car that was on its way to the Hamilton residence, Stone shrugged his shoulders and went back to question Walter.

"Anything wrong with my mother?" Walter asked, starting the questioning for Stone.

"Nothing to worry about. She's fine, just worried about her son."

"I should talk to her and let her know I'm all right. She'll be pissed at me."

"I told her you were fine," Stone assured him. "Tell me, Walter, why do you talk to yourself?"

"I like to. When I get upset, I talk to myself. It helps me."

"Are you upset a lot?"

"What do you think? You've met my mother."

"Good point, Walter. I'm going to let you talk to yourself for awhile."

"What?"

"I'm serious, Walter. I think you can sort some of this story out. You know, talk it out with yourself and see where this thing went wrong. Think you can do that?"

"Sure, whatever," Hamilton shrugged.

Stone motioned for Wayne to follow him out of the room, leaving Hamilton alone behind closed doors, assuring him, "We'll be right out here. If you have any questions, just knock on the door. We'll be back in ten minutes."

"Sure," Hamilton seemed to be in a slow daze and he nodded to the departing men, leaned forward, elbows on his knees, eyes intent on the wall. No sooner had the door closed than Hamilton began talking to himself. "Fuckin' A, these guys are serious. They want to stick my ass in jail. I don't like this at all. I didn't come down with no fuckin' rape. No fuckin' way. They think I did. I shouldn't have lied to them. This is some serious shit. I'm in it now, but I didn't do no fuckin' rape. Check it out. I'll prove it to them. I'll go under hypnosis to prove I didn't do no rape and I didn't do nothin' to Rose," He went on for about ten minutes, all of it recorded.

When Stone re-entered the room to talk to Hamilton, the young man blurted, "Hypnotize me, man. That's the only way to solve this!"

"I'm no hypnotist."

"Then get one. Let's end this shit. Get me a fuckin' hypnotist and we'll settle this."

"Walter, if it becomes necessary, you'll be hypnotized, but right now we're going to get you back home. We've asked enough questions for today."

"You got that right."

At 1300 hours, Stone and Wayne arrived with Hamilton at his house. When they pulled up, a patrol car was parked at the curb. Walter was asked to wait in Stone's car. He seemed relieved that he didn't have to face his mother first.

Inside, Mrs. Hamilton was walking around as if she were drunk. "She's taken some pills and is real uncooperative," the deputy advised Stone.

"I want to talk to you, Sergeant Stone. Where's Walter?"

"Mrs. Hamilton, no one is going to talk to you until you give us your pills. Do you have any more?"

The swaying woman reached into her dress and fished around in her ample bosom until she located a napkin that contained a handful of pills. "I took seven thorazine tablets," she mumbled as she handed the napkin to Stone.

Stone asked Sharon who the family doctor was and she went to the family phone book and flipped through the pages. She found the number she was looking for and handed the tattered notebook to the detective.

"Here it is," She pointed to the number that was written with a broad, primitive point in a child-like, crooked hand.

Stone dialed, keeping an eye on the dazed woman. When the phone was answered, Stone quickly introduced himself to the nurse and explained the situation. She quickly put the call to the doctor. When Stone repeated the problem, the doctor stated, as Stone expected, "I cannot give medical information about a patient over the phone. You understand there are laws, Sergeant."

"I understand. Now this is an emergency and I need some answers. I'm Sergeant Stone with the Sacramento County Sheriff's Department and Mrs. Hamilton has taken seven thorazine tablets. What are we dealing with, doctor?"

Stone listened to the doctor as he explained: "It's a very sad situation, Sergeant." Tell that to the girls who have been raped, Stone thought. "She's an alcoholic and I've been trying to get her to seek psychiatric help, but she will not. To tell the truth, the whole family could use some help. The amount of thorazine she took is not enough to substantiate an overdose; however, she will get rather drowsy," No shit, thought Stone as he watched Wayne direct the woman to the couch for the fourth time since Stone began to talk to the doctor.

"Thanks, doctor. At least we won't have to worry about her dying."

"That's right."

Stone thanked the doctor and turned his attention to the dazed woman. "Can you understand what I am saying?" he asked, getting the feeling he was talking to a shit-faced old bag as his politeness drained away.

"I understand everything," she replied with a goofy nod.

"Walter has told us some lies, Mrs. Hamilton. He will explain it all to you after we leave. He's all right, he's just outside."

"Okay, just as long as you didn't hurt him. I know all about your ways of getting people to say what you want to hear."

"Come on," he directed the other officers, "let's get out of here."

Stone opened the car door and let Walter step out. "Walter, we will be in touch. Understand?"

"Yes, sir," He walked toward the house with his head down, obviously dreading his next encounter with his mother.

Stone and the other deputies leaned against the patrol car. "What do you think?" one asked Stone.

"Well, he sure as hell ain't eliminated."

"Well, if I had a mother like that, I'd be fuckin' nuts," the deputy replied. "He's crazy enough to be a rapist."

"Yeah. Too bad abortions aren't retroactive. Nobody would vote against that bill after talking to this fucked up family," Wayne replied.

CHAPTER FOURTEEN

SEPTEMBER 20, 1976, Deputy Phil Abbott was detailed to the scene of a possible burglary in the Citrus Heights area east of Sacramento. He was met at the door by Francis Woods, a twenty-nine year old house-wife. In tow was her three year old son who hid behind his mother when he first saw Abbott.

"Come down here," she said, walking down the hallway to her son's bedroom. The attractive woman explained, "We didn't notice anything until I vacuumed this morning. I was vacuuming Billie's bedroom and noticed mud on the carpet under his window." She pointed to the window that looked out into the backyard. "We have automatic sprinklers back there so the ground is wet. I guess someone stepped in the flower bed and then came in through the window."

As Abbott examined the mud and window, he asked, "Are you missing anything, ma'am?"

"That's the first thing I checked when I saw the mud. I probably wouldn't have ever noticed if I hadn't seen the mud. I'm missing some earrings and a bracelet I never wear. I'm not sure if I even lost it or not, it's been so long since I wore it. None of the things are expensive, but that's all that's missing. They were in my jewelry box in our bedroom. My expensive jewelry wasn't even touched. I think my dresser drawers were gone through, though. It's creepy."

"I know," Abbott replied. "Let's check the backyard."

She confidently led him to the backyard, surprising him with her calmness and composure as he thought to himself that he would be all over the place if some creep came into his house and rummaged where ever he wanted to. The first thing he noticed was that someone had stepped into wet mud under the window. No shoe impression was vis-ible; however, on closer inspection, he saw pry marks near the window lock. A man's dark blue sock was lying on the lawn several feet away.

As Abbott picked it up, Woods stated, "That's my husband's sock. How did it get out here?"

"Looks like whoever was in your house used it as a glove so he wouldn't leave fingerprints inside. It's an old trick kids use a lot."

"Kids? Do you think kids would do something like this?"

"Sure, they do things like this all the time. Someone was here, all right. Have you noticed anything suspicious lately?"

"No, nothing in the neighborhood, but we have been getting a lot of phone calls for the last two weeks where the caller just hangs up. My husband and I have both gotten them, but whoever it is doesn't say anything. They stay on the line for a few seconds, and then hang up."

"Has this happened before?"

"No, not really."

"Well, it's probably a neighbor kid. I don't know if the calls are connected to the burglary or not. I'd hate to say for sure. If it was a professional burglar, I'm sure he would have taken the expensive jewelry rather than the cheap...I mean, inexpensive. I'd suggest your husband put better locks on your windows and doors. No need to make it easy for burglars. Most of them are lazy and if you make it difficult, they will go somewhere else where it is easy. They didn't become burglars because they are overly ambitious."

Abbott got some more information for his report, thanked her, and left.

For two weeks, the phone calls continued. The phone would ring. Silence. Hang up. Abbott never knew it, but after the third one, Francis Woods started to cry.

After dropping her son off with her mother, Francis Woods drove west on Highway 80. Travis Air Base is located in Fairfield, a Solano County city halfway between Sacramento and San Francisco. The route was familiar to her because one weekend a month she traveled it to attend her Reserve training. On Saturday, she was on flight duty and would work with the pilots. Her next training would be October 2nd and 3rd. She enjoyed the Reserve duty, and it was good to be able to talk to her husband about the military. She was proud of his captain rank and the way the others respected him and she took great pleasure in the fact that he admired her work in the military, also.

Good music came from the radio and she felt like she could just drive forever, keep going through San Francisco, across the Golden Gate Bridge, and right on to Oregon and Washington, not because she had anything to run from. It was just the opposite, because she had everything to be happy about. Her five year marriage was going well and her life married to a military man was comfortable and secure. She was improving herself with her nursing courses at Sacramento State and Sacramento was a welcome town with the right smallness. Even the burglary was behind her. The creepy feeling was fading, the feeling that had made her shiver when she walked through her house knowing that someone else had invaded her privacy. She had a good solid circle of female friends, and she and her husband shared everything so he was as much a friend as husband. Her mother and father were close. Almost perfect.

She drove onto the base, showing her ID card to the Marine at the gate, pleased with his deference. She stayed in her car in the parking lot to hear the end of "Afternoon Delight," a song she and her husband enjoyed because of its endorsement of making love all afternoon when you are supposed to be working. Something they had not been doing enough of since the baby arrived, she thought as she stepped from the car. She went into the club, the interior cool and slightly damp from the air conditioning. She stopped at the doorway to the restaurant and watched her friends who were there waiting for her.

She decided to use the bathroom just to make sure she looked her best. The hallway to the bathroom was darker than the restaurant, and as she entered it, a short, thin man fell in step with her. She did not turn when he spoke to her.

"Excuse me. I haven't seen you here before. Do you mind if I ask your name?" The voice was dry and cold and the words were spoken through lips that barely moved.

Shocked, a chill going down her spine, the image of her husband's sock lying on the grass in its floppy L-shape flashed through her mind. The man's voice had the same quality as the dried mud on the carpet below her son's window.

She could not turn and look at him. Her fear tightened her muscles, but quickened her brain.

"I'm with friends," she said, "and my husband is a captain here."

"Sorry, I didn't mean anything," he mumbled as he turned and entered the men's bathroom. She turned enough to get a glimpse of his camouflage pants and white t-shirt disappear behind the closing door. In the bathroom, her hands trembled. She couldn't figure out why she flashed on the break-in to her house when she heard his voice. She knew there was no connection, no reason to be. And she was being paranoid for no reason. She left the bathroom and joined her friends.

That night she jokingly told her husband about the incident and the way she had reacted. She tried to laugh it off, but the talk soon turned to the break-in and the need for more secure locks.

"I'll do something this week," he assured her. "Don't worry about it. Nothing will happen."

But Francis Woods did worry about it. She worried about it enough to forget any thoughts of "Afternoon Delights."

As Francis pulled into her driveway returning home from her morning class at Sacramento State, Rosalie, her next door neighbor, was taking groceries from her car's trunk. Francis went over to help, picking up a bag in each arm, following the woman into the house. As Rosalie put away the groceries, Francis sat at the counter that separated the kitchen from the dining area. She had only one thought on her mind to talk about.

"This has really been bothering me, the thing about the break-in."

"Me, too," her neighbor replied. "It's real creepy to have someone break into your home."

"What gets me," Francis continued, "is what if Billie and me were home alone and someone broke in."

"Especially with some asshole going around rapeing."

"It scares me. Bill says that I shouldn't worry but I can't get it out of my mind. He says its just kids and they won't be back."

"That's what Jimmy says, too. But I'm not sure. Did I tell you I...we... have a diamond ring missing?"

"Really? You're sure?"

"Yeah. We're going to get an alarm system put in."

"That's a good idea. At least it's something. Maybe I can convince Bill to get one. Or maybe Jimmy can convince him, because so far I'm not doing so good."

"I'll have Jimmy talk to him, maybe we can get a deal with the alarm company if we both do it."

The next day, Francis was at the kitchen table working on a paper for her class when the phone rang. Calls at this time of day were unusual. Sometimes Bill called, but he had been in the field so much at work that he hadn't been able to call and her mother very seldom called because she knew this was the time Billie took his nap and she didn't want to wake him.

As it always did since the break-in, a shiver ran through her as the phone rang. The thought of someone she did not know having this power frightened and angered her. She hoped it was Bill calling from Travis, but she knew it wasn't. She slowly moved to the phone, dreading picking it up. A silence, a fuzzy, electric emptiness was all she heard.

"Who is this?" She hoped her pounding heart could not be heard in her voice. "Stop calling like this. The police know all about it. They know who you are," she lied.

"I'm going to kill your husband," The voice was a whisper, a man's voice, soft and deliberate. No childish laughter. This was not a kid.

Her heart stopped and her body turned cold. She slammed the receiver down and leaned against the wall, shaking. She then ran from room to room locking the doors and windows. She tried to call her husband at the base. Three times she misdialed, finally getting the number right. Her husband could not be located, but they would let him know she called as soon as he returned to his office.

She called the sheriff's office. A deputy arrived twenty minutes later but did little other than tell her it was probably kids playing games. As soon as the deputy left, she dressed Billie and went to Rosalie's until Bill arrived home.

"It's just kids," he tried to convince her, "who like to play games when their parents aren't home. It's nothing to worry about. Believe me, no one wants to kill me. If they call again, we'll get the phone number changed."

<hr />

Mondays were always awful. Feeling slow and logy because he did not catch up on sleep as he had hoped he would, and because he had a nagging depression because the '49ers lost, Jim Stone went through the Monday morning reports without the usual excitement.

Sacramento could keep an army of detectives busy. Every city, every county across the nation could do the same. That's the trouble with criminals, they commit crimes, no vacations, no holidays, just crime after fucking crime. There are just too few of us and too many of them, Stone often thought. As he read over each report, he knew they would not get the attention they deserved. You prioritized and you shoveled shit against the wind, and you ducked. Sometimes you were lucky. You solved a case. Other times, it just blew back and hit you in the face. And this was just one more shitty Monday morning.

"I've got to do something to get myself going," Stone thought to himself, and then called for one of the detectives.

"Fred, we've got fourteen in-custodies to take care of and then I need you to work on some sex offenders."

"Sure, you want I should kill some for you?"

"I wish. I've got a list of fifty for you to start on. We've got to do something about this rapist."

"I should be able to start this afternoon. You think it's somebody we've worked before?"

"Shit, Fred, I don't have a clue. I'm really screwed on this one. Just give it your best shot and see what you can do to eliminate some of them and keep me informed."

"You got it. Still think it might be Hamilton?"

"I don't know. He looks good in certain ways, terrible in others. I know it's getting me down and on top of that, it's Monday."

"Tell me about it. I'll do my best, Jim."

Bill Woods was not too fond of Mondays, either. Francis had six months of her Monday night classes to get her degree. And this was one more night to take care of Billie, whom he had just put to sleep. Now he could sit and watch dumb television shows and worry about Francis getting home safely. She would be home by ten. Tomorrow for sure he would get new locks for the windows.

When the lights of her car briefly filled the front room window with their glance yellowing, he breathed a sigh of relief.

Tuesday, October 5, 1976. The alarm woke Francis Woods and she turned to see her husband groping for the alarm.

"Ooh," she said with a yawn, "Five already?"

"Five already," He rolled toward her, kissed her on the bare shoulder, then rolled back to the edge of the bed and sat up. She reached sleepily in his direction and touched his back.

"Go back to sleep," he said.

"I was going to jog today," she said in a lazy voice.

"Yeah, right."

"Why don't you come back to bed?"

"What for?"

"You know."

"I've got to get ready for work."

"Good. I'll sleep instead."

"How come I knew that."

She pulled the covers up around her neck and was sound asleep as he stepped into the shower.

At six thirty, little Billie woke her by climbing into bed. That meant she should get up and take care of the last minute things that Bill needed to get off to work, but she stayed in bed and played with Billie. She enjoyed this time of the morning. They would play for awhile and then they would get up, she thought to herself as she heard Bill close the door on his way out.

She heard a series of clicks that sounded like the light was being turned on and off.

"Daddy must have forgotten something." she said to her son. "Funny, I didn't see any light go on."

She listened more intently, and heard footsteps running down the hallway. Then he was there, eyes glowing in the dark mask, burning into her from the doorway. She screamed and pulled her son to her as the man in the mask walked to her, knife raised above his head. As stark, raving fear took over her body, she tried to scream. She was only able to whimper as she hugged her son even closer to her shaking body.

At eight thirty that same morning, Jim Stone leaned back in his battered office chair, sipping his fourth cup of coffee. The three cups that preceded it sloshed in his gut, creating some minor electric storm in his innards, intent on making his life miserable until he opened the flood gates, making room for coffee yet to come.

Behind him a detective yelled, "Phone, Jim. It's Radio."

Stone catapulted himself forward in his spring-loaded chair, spilling coffee on the report spread out on his desk. He punched the blinking red button with his finger, spilling more coffee and swearing to himself.

"Yeah, Stone here. What is it?"

A woman's voice. "Dispatch, Sarge. We just got a call about a rape in the Heights. Sounds like it could be your man. The caller was pretty upset and excited. Talked about a ski mask and shoelaces. Said her neighbor was attacked. Apparently her young son was with her. Patrol said to call you."

"Damn," Stone again felt the excitement of the chase. "Okay. I have some things I need you to do. Make some calls for me, real quick. Get a hold of the on-call dog. I want a tracker over there ten minutes ago. Then get the scene tech on it. Go ahead and give me the address and I'll get a team over there from here," As he took down the information, the constant background hum of the office stopped. He looked up as he hung up the phone and saw everyone looking his way.

"It's son of a bitch him," he yelled. "He fuckin' hit this morning. Peg, you and Frank head out to the scene," he spoke to two of his detectives. "Let's try and get something this time. Peg, interview the woman on the way to the hospital. Frank, stay with the techs. Make sure they don't miss anything. I'm going to meet up with the dog team. With luck we may be able to track the cocksucker."

Stone had some misgivings about giving Peg the responsibility of interviewing the victim. Not that he was against her, it was that he was against the decision the captain made to have her do it just because she was a woman. Stone felt that any good detective could question anybody under any circumstance. The problem was not the gender of the questioner, it was the skill. But the captain wanted a woman interviewing women. Next, Italians interviewing Italians, Chinese interviewing Chinese, gays interviewing gays and on and on. We'll never get anything done, and it's only going to get worse, he told himself with real regret. We are smart enough to solve one problem, but we cannot even anticipate the problems we create by trying to repair what isn't even broken.

As he hurried to get to the scene, he stopped at the door of his boss.

"Mike, I'll fill you in later from the scene. Looks like our man just did another rape in the Heights. I've got Peg and Frank on it and I'm going with the dog handler. You can let the boss know before he reads about it in the newspaper."

Stone arrived at the scene five minutes after Vickers and Lawson. Vickers was talking to Francis Woods at a neighbor's house while Lawson was doing the exterior investigation. As the dog team had not yet arrived, Stone talked to the deputies who had received the first call. No leads. They had not interviewed the victim.

Stone entered the house. He could feel the presence of the masked son of a bitch. Without talking to the victim, without searching the house, he knew he was dealing with the same man who had attacked four times already. It was in the air, not a scent, not that he could detect anyway, but presence, a feeling in the air. A cold chill swept over him, a chill that would return many times over the next few years, and he involuntarily put his hands under his arms for a brief moment as a shiver worked its way throughout his body.

"This is weird," he thought to himself as he started to work.

The first things he saw as he walked through the house were pieces of white shoelaces and the strips of torn towels that had been used to tie up the victim. The shiver went through him again as he thought what she went through with her kid.

He was staring at a shoelace that seemed for a moment to move on its own, like some exotic snake from a seldom visited glass cage in a zoo, when he heard the front door open as a deputy with a dog entered the house.

"Anybody home?" the deputy yelled from the front room.

"Back here," Stone replied.

Chapter Fourteen

The dog entered first. A heavy, thick bloodhound with a bright light of intelligence in his dark eyes. He was ready to work and ready to please. Stone liked the way the dog and his handler worked in sync.

"His name is Omar," the deputy said, rubbing the dog's neck affectionately. Omar looked at Stone and slobbered.

That would be a good way to work, thought Stone. As a team, and for some reason his thoughts turned to his ex-wife.

"Christ, I hope I'm not getting lonely," he thought to himself as he worried for a brief moment. "How would she protect herself from a maniac like this. What would I do to help her if such a terrible thing ever happened. Hell, would she even call me?

He felt completely powerless as though hit in the stomach by the blow of realization what a horrible thing it would be to be raped, to have intimacy forced on your body, into the most secret parts of your person.

The dog strained at his leash, anxious to get on with its job, interrupting Stone's morbid thoughts.

"Let's start out in the backyard," Stone said.

"You got it. Let's give him a scent of something we know the rapist touched," The deputy looked around.

"How about this piece of towel? Is it big enough?"

"You bet. He doesn't need much, and he won't forget, either," the handler replied as he led the dog to the piece of towel. Stone watched as the dog stuck his nose into the towel, seeming to relish the odor as a pipe smoker relished the aroma of his tobacco.

"Let's go," the handler remarked as he led the dog toward the kitchen. The dog's toenails clicked on the linoleum on the way to the glass doors leading to the backyard. In the yard the dog went in crazy patterns around the lawn, working in mysterious ways to Stone's way of thinking. He stopped under the window, the same one the burglary suspect had entered through a month ago. A coincidence? Maybe, but probably not. The dog, slobber flying from both sides of his mouth, went in a straight shot from the window to the rear fence. The same place where the blue sock was located after the burglary. Had the rapist been here before? Had he been in the house, prowling, searching, setting up his plans to enter, rape, and terrorize?

The dog whined at the fence, wanting to be on the other side, knowing the fence was too high.

"Now what?" Stone asked.

"Can we go around?" The handler asked.

"Christ, what with dead ends, cul de sacs, and traffic lights, it would take a month. Not only that, I don't think you can get there from here."

"That's the trouble with the suburbs, blocks of fences. California ain't the place to be."

"Tell me," Stone replied. "Now what?"

The handler got down on his haunches near the dog, which was staring at a spot on the fence and trembling.

"Help me lift him over the fence."

"Are you kidding?" Stone asked, hesitant to touch the dog, let alone lift it over the fence.

"No problem. I do it all the time. He likes it. Just get him to the top of the fence and he'll do the rest," The handler rubbed the dog's ears and then stood at the fence and snapped his fingers. The dog raised himself onto his back legs and leaned his front paws against the fence.

"You balance his shoulders and head and I'll push his butt up."

"You sure about this?"

"Come on, Sarge. I do this all the time. It's my job," The dog wagged its tail and slobbered, urging them to quit talking and get on with the job at hand. Dogs don't have unions. They don't know that there are such things as breaks and overtime. Some animal rights activist will eventually rectify this major oversight.

"I've done a lot of stupid things in my life, but I have never helped a dog jump over a fence," Stone shook his head.

"That's sad, Sarge."

"What do you mean, sad?"

"Just think, you'll never be able to say that again," the handler laughed. "Anyway, what's life without a little learning?" The handler replied as he squatted, putting his basketed arms under the dog's flopping tail.

"Hold him steady."

Stone tried to find a place to hold onto to steady the dog, but every place seemed to be nothing but loose skin. As the handler pushed, the dog bent. It was like trying to push a used mattress up three flights of stairs.

"One, two, three, up," The handler pushed. Omar strained and scratched at the fence, and Stone pushed and tried to keep the dog from folding in two. As the two men grunted, Omar got one paw on the top of the fence, its back legs kicking like crazy, the way some dogs do when you hold them over water and they swim in the air. As the handler began to straighten his legs to get altitude on the dog, the other paw finally found the top of the fence. With the handler finally getting both hands under the dog's ass and pushing upwards, and the dog grunting and groaning, trying to do a canine chin-up, pulling itself higher, the ultimate balancing act occurred, with Stone stepping back out of the way in fear that the animal would choose to fall on him rather than the hard ground on the other side.

The dog, looking like some furry gymnast, hugged the top of the fence.

"Jump, Omar," the handler ordered. The dog looked back at him as if to say, "You're fucking crazy," He swayed and whined and then fell forward awkwardly. Stone was glad there were no little kids to see the dog's plight. Animal rights activists think rodeos are rough on animals. Give this bloodhound a choice and he'll take a cowboy and spurs any day.

Stone heard the animal hit the ground with a woof.

"Let's go!" the handler yelled at Stone.

"What do you mean, let's go?"

"He's not going to run around out there by himself and come back and write a report for you."

After a lot of swearing and straining, Stone finally made it over the fence. This fence was a long ways from the police academy and the days of being in shape. It was also a long ways from the dog and his handler who were now about a football field length away. Stone followed as best he could, watching the dog follow the scent across the field, past a house trailer, through an orchard that was being bulldozed for progress, and then onto a familiar street of a new tract of homes. Omar sniffed at an oil spot on the street and then looked up at the handler as if to say, "That's all, boss. This is as far as we go."

"He drove away from here," Stone remarked. "This is where he parked."

The three of them walked the wandering streets back to the Woods' home, Omar's tail wagging all the time, Stone's thoughts growing darker and darker.

Detectives had the job of canvassing the neighborhood, and they got good results. A strange vehicle, dark in color, was seen at 0700 hours by a man leaving for work. It had been parked where the dog had lost the scent. The car was not there when the woman of the house left for work an hour and a half later.

More news. Another neighbor said that four or five days before, she had gone out onto her porch at 6:15 in the morning and found a strange man standing in her driveway. They stared at each other for about a minute, and then he arrogantly walked across the street and got into a green car that looked like a Chevy Vega. She described the man as about five ten, medium build, dark hair, thirty to forty years old. His car was parked where Omar had lost the scent.

At 12:35 that afternoon, Peggy Vickers finished her interview with Francis Woods and then took her to the Sacramento Medical Center for a rape examination. A humiliating, yet necessary, probe of the victim's body, a clinical insult added to grievous injury. The medical team would take swabbings of each and every orifice penetrated by the rapist. Swabbings for the presence of sperm, internal examinations for bruises or abrasions to confirm that force was used. Pubic hair combings to detect foreign hairs: head, pubic, beard, mustache. The foreign hair could be used later to match against that of suspects. Francis Woods' body was treated like a thing, like a place, like a crime scene. It was examined carefully, swabbed, probed and photographed. People she did not know stood over her exposed parts and talked about her as if she was dead. At times she wished she were.

By about 2:00 that afternoon, the examination was complete and a rape crisis counselor talked to her.

Sometimes a rape victim is like a battered wife who is convinced she caused the violence. The counselor has to dissuade them of that notion. The counselor has to prepare her for the recurring flash floods of guilt and self loathing, the vast plains of depression. The endless cycles of nightmares and daydreams that are as original as the rapes. The horrible knowledge that one person took a huge portion of her life for a small moment's perverted pleasure. It helps a little to know about it all in advance, but then, it doesn't help all that much.

Later in the day, around dinnertime, Vickers was back at the Woods' home. She rang the bell, and when Bill Woods answered, she asked if she could talk to his wife. He asked her to come in, and Vickers did so, noticing the semblance of normalcy as Billie watched late afternoon cartoons and the smell of a dinner and sounds of its preparation came from the kitchen. Woods made a gesture to the pleasant odors and domestic noises.

"She's in there," he said, adding in a louder voice. "It's the detective from the Sheriff's Office."

Francis Woods stood at the kitchen stove, adding pasta to boiling water. Bill Woods stood slightly behind Vickers. Francis Woods looked at both of them, first at Vickers, and then at her husband.

"I'm all right," she said to her husband, who returned to the living room.

"I'll be with Billie," he replied.

"How are you doing?" Vickers asked.

"Life goes on."

"I've got some bad news."

"Let's hear it. Everything has been shit so far. Pretty hard to ruin a day like this," Francis tried valiantly to follow with a smile. It really didn't work.

"They found sperm."

She kept stirring as the long strands slowly collapsed into the boiling water.

"I got worse news," she finally said. "I checked when I got home. I'm in the ovulation part of my cycle. He couldn't have known that, could he?"

"I doubt it, but anything is possible with this guy."

Drops of water popped out of the pot and sizzled on the stove, but not even those were as hot as the tears that Francis could not stop from streaming down her cheeks.

The following morning, Stone, Vickers, and Lawson met with the investigation division staff. The Captain knocked on the table with his ballpoint pen. Stone, staring at the table, noticed that the point was retracted.

"Okay, let's get started," the Captain began. "I need good information here. The Sheriff is going to meet with the *Sacramento Bee* reporter in an hour, and he has to have this right. He wants to keep this out of the limelight for a while longer, but the *Bee* wants to sell newspapers. It's a bitch, so let's begin," All business, he nodded to Stone, giving the detective control of the meeting.

Stone leaned forward, his elbows on the table.

"Peg, we'll start with you and your interview of Francis Woods."

"Well, basically," she began, "we have the same pattern as before. This one was just as violent. Only difference was that this one was a little later in the morning."

The Captain did not like hearing this. He broke in.

"You sound like you have already determined that we have a serial out there. You know what the press will do to us and how the community will react. What do you have that's concrete, Jim?"

"Captain, first, I'm sure it's a serial. Same M.O., same type of violence. Always wears a mask and likes knives. He ties the victim's hands and feet and scares the living shit out of them. He talks through clenched teeth and continually tells them to shut up. Neighborhoods are all the same type, and he does a lot of prowling before he hits. I don't doubt it for a minute. You won't either after you hear what Peg has to say. Peg?" Stone nodded at her to indicate that she was to continue.

"I interviewed Woods right after it happened," Vickers began, checking back as she talked, to a stenographer's notebook in which she kept the notes of the interview. "She's an Air Force Reserve captain and her husband left for work about 6:30. He's a captain in the regulars. She was still in bed and her three year old son climbed in with her. She heard a noise and thought her husband had come back for something he had forgotten. Then she saw the rapist in her bedroom doorway. All she can remember is he was wearing a ski mask. Khaki color as near as she can describe it. She knows it had eye holes, but she doesn't think there was a hole for his mouth. She knows he was wearing a jacket, had a knife in his hand, but she either shut the rest from her mind or she really didn't see anything else. She said she grabbed her baby and kept saying, 'please don't hurt us. I'll tell you where my money is, just please take it and leave us.' Like Jim said, he told her to shut up and he talked with his teeth clenched. He blindfolded her and then tied her hands behind her back. Pulled the sheets up from the bottom of the bed and tied her feet. Kept saying all he wanted was money. And here's the creepy part, as if the other stuff isn't. He tied her kid up, hands and feet, and put him on the floor. The kid was good all through it, bless his heart. Come to find out, he thought the rapist was a doctor."

"Gynecologist?" one of the detectives quipped.

"That's not funny," Vickers snapped back.

"Life's not funny. Lighten up."

Vickers went on as if the remark was not made.

"He thought she was being bandaged. Anyway, he jabbed her several times with the knife and put it to her neck. Told her if she didn't do what he wanted he would kill her and her son. She heard him tearing cloth, same as before in the other rapes. He tore towels into strips to use for the ties and gags, and roamed around the house. He kept returning to the bedroom and one time told her he had the money and was going to leave soon. She felt relieved but then heard him tearing cloth again and she knew he was near the bed. He put his penis in her hand and told her to play with it and when she tried to tell him her hands were tied too tight, he just told her to shut up. He untied her feet, spread her legs and got on her."

Vickers went on, talking in a calm, professional voice as if she were describing a traffic incident, not a brutal rape.

"He told her she had a beautiful, big pussy and told her she looked good at the club. He also asked her if his dick was like the captain's. She didn't know if he climaxed, but apparently he did. The doctor found sperm. After awhile, she said he pulled out and told her to play with it some more. She said he had a small penis. He told her he was going to fix something to eat and she heard him in the kitchen with a frying pan. Oh, one other thing, before he raped her she said she heard him moving a chair near the front door. Apparently he put it there so if anyone opened the door, it would hit the chair and alert him. He covers his bases. After he didn't return to the bedroom, she struggled up and hopped to the backyard and called for her neighbor's kid to get help. As far as description, not a hell of a lot. Figures he's about five nine or ten from where she first saw him in the doorway. She also feels that he knows her from the Travis Air Force Club. That's about it from my side," Vickers concluded, closing her notebook.

"Thanks, Peg," Stone said, and then turned to his other detective. "Frank?"

"Can't really add too much. He did a lot of ransacking. Took money, about a hundred and sixty. Entered through the kid's bedroom window and left through the patio door. Jim worked with the dog, so he can fill you in on that. We got a lot of pictures and some prints, although he probably wore gloves. We have names for elimination so I don't hold much faith in getting anything out of prints. The shoelaces don't belong to the Woods', so he must have brought them with him. We are not sure about the torn towels yet, but it looks like they probably belong to the house. The tech found two hairs on one of the laces and the lab will be looking at them. We did a canvass last night and found a couple of witnesses. One may have seen his car at 7:00 a.m. It was gone by 8:30. Only described it as a dark colored car. Another neighbor saw a fellow around 6:15 one morning, four or five days ago. He just stared at her and then got in a dark green Vega type vehicle and drove off. The car was parked in the same place as the one yesterday. Looks like he may have been prowling the neighborhood for a week or so, maybe up to a month. There have been reports of burglaries in the area, so maybe Burglary can help us out. Anyway, we're checking on it," Frank shrugged his shoulders as if to say, "That's it."

Stone watched the captain who moved forward in his chair, taking in a lungful of air and slowly blowing it out through closed lips.

"I have to fill in the Sheriff and bring him up to date before he talks to the press. I'll press to get some extra help on this. In the meantime, put all you can into it. Keep me advised. Jesus, we don't need a serial rapist running around here. Push him into the damned city."

Friday, October 8, 1976

A lone figure sat on a wooden chair in the darkness of his bedroom. He stared out his bedroom window into the window of the house next door. As always, he could feel the blood pumping through the veins in his neck. He breathed shallowly. The window into which he stared was partially blocked by a hanging plant, the leaves and light branches of which swayed in the cool, fall breeze.

That same breeze gently brushed across the pretty nineteen year old girl who had just turned on the bedroom light and began undressing.

He had been watching her for the past five months, catching glimpses of her naked body ever since she moved back into her parents' home. Loneliness engulfed the lone figure as darkness suddenly covered the naked body of the young girl. In the darkness he rolled onto the bed, looking at the ceiling, his arms up, his hands under his head.

Heather Williams, naked, slipped into bed. She went quickly to sleep, no thoughts of the man next door. At midnight, the grandfather clock rhythmically struck the hour. The girl faintly heard the soft sounds, taking comfort in their familiarity, fading deeper into the sleep, no thought of being alone in the house.

At 3:30 a dog barked in the night's distance. A masked figure looked directly into the sleeping girl's darkened room. It moved away from the window and moved to the next, that of the dining room. Silently, the figure removed the screen and reached into the room to remove a silver candy dish from the grand piano near the window, and placed it on the ground at his feet. He slipped through and onto the piano and dropped lightly to the hardwood floor. The beam of his small flashlight flashed across the room and as suddenly, extinguished itself into darkness. He went directly to the phone, felt for the cord, and cut it with the knife he removed from the bag hanging from his shoulder. Using the flashlight in short bursts, he went down the hall into the bathroom. He took a length of rope from his bag and tied one end to the bathtub faucet. Quietly he played the rope out as he left the bathroom and crossed the hall to a closed bedroom door. Without checking the room, he tied the rope to the doorknob and pulled it tight so the door could not swing in. He tied the rope the same way to the knobs of bedrooms two and three. He knew where she slept as he moved closer to her room.

The plant in her window continued to sway in the night breeze.

He stood in her doorway, looking down at the sleeping girl. In the faint, shifting light that came through the window he saw her purse on the bureau. He opened it and found her driver's license. The beam from his flashlight quickly sprayed across the picture, revealing her name. He moved back toward the bed. Looking down on the sleeping teenager, he began to whisper, "Heather...Heather...Heather."

She heard her name as part of a dream.

He leaned over her. His presence woke her, and as her eyes slowly opened, she saw the masked face. She tried to scream, but could not get air into her throat. Before her body could overcome its paralysis, his gloved hand was clamped over her mouth. Only her eyes could scream out the fear that she felt as she stared at the mask, and only her brain could hear the screams that tore through her body. Though her ears were pounding with the panic she felt, she heard him hiss, "Don't scream or I will kill you." He put the knife against her where her bare shoulder met her neck. She knew she would not scream. She knew she might never scream again.

Saturday, 0900, October 9, 1976

"Any available unit in the Rancho Cordova area, 10-63, possible 261," the dispatcher's voice broke the silence. In his patrol car, Deputy Paul Burton checked his watch as the call came over his radio. The 10-63 was the code meaning a message was to follow. The 261 was the California penal code for rape.

"Shit. God damn it, I haven't even had coffee yet," Burton yelled at his steering wheel. Then, as all cops do, he grabbed his radio mike. "31A1, go ahead."

"Priority detail," the dispatcher began, "Meet the victim at LaLoma Drive. We're calling Investigations out also."

"10-4, three minutes away."

Stone stepped out of the shower to the sound of the phone ringing. Leaving wet foot prints, he sat on the edge of his bed, shivering from the beads of water on his skin.

"Stone here," he spoke into the phone as he pulled the covers over his naked body.

"Bad news, Sarge," the female voice began.

"Another rape?"

"You got it. Your man hit again. It looks like another of your weekends shot. We have you as the on-call detective, so congratulations."

Stone trembled and wiped himself partially dry with the sheet.

"Son of a bitch," he mumbled into the phone. "Okay, look, try and get Detective Vickers. Have her meet with the victim at the hospital. If you can't get her, try Greg Wayne. I'll go to the scene."

"Okay, Sarge. Sorry to ruin your day."

Forty minutes later, Stone met Deputy Burton at Heather Williams' parents' house. The crime scene techs were not there yet.

"Hell of a way to start a morning, Sarge," Burton greeted Stone. "No one's been inside yet. I've got a reserve in the backyard and a couple of units have checked the area. Nothing unusual. They're doing a neighborhood canvass now. The side gate was open when we got here and the back patio slider was open."

"Thanks. I haven't talked to the victim yet. I want to look around inside before I do."

"Okay, Sarge. Be careful when you go into the backyard. The reserve might be a little jumpy. He's pretty new."

Stone held his badge in front of himself as he entered the backyard. You can never be too careful.

"Sergeant Stone. Going to take a look around. Anything been touched?"

"Not by me, Sarge, and no one else has been back here since we arrived," Stone knew he was correct putting his badge out front. This reserve was nervous, but then who wouldn't be. He was a young kid who looked like he should be bagging groceries. He looked like he had rented the uniform for a costume party.

The reserve stood in the well maintained yard, on the neat, deep green grass. Roses of various kinds and colors were in the fresh dirt border along the fence. An overhead covered a cement patio containing wrought iron furniture and a brick barbecue pit with a chimney going up through the overhead.

Stone saw a piece of carpet near the corner post of the overhead, a rope tied to the post, and a knotted strip of towel on the cement. His stomach sank with an over-the-edge feeling. A shivery brief coagulation of fear was in his stomach as he thought, "This is enough. This is going too far, way too far."

He checked the outside of the house and saw the candy dish on the ground and the window screen leaning against a bush. He entered the house through the patio door and saw the opened drawers in the kitchen, the ransacking, and he felt the presence of the masked rapist. As he started toward the bedrooms he saw the cat's cradle of ropes stretched across the hall, holding the doors shut. To stop someone from getting out, or to stop someone from getting down the hall if they came in unexpectedly? He ducked under the crisscrossed ropes and entered the bedroom of the young victim. Quickly he took in the open window, the parted curtain, the plant hanging from the curtain rod. The room had been ransacked and her things had been thrown on the floor. On the bed were the torn strips of towel and the white shoelaces. Mesmerized, he stood staring.

"You son of a bitch. You miserable son of a bitch," he whispered.

Stone was checking the phone cord in the kitchen when the techs arrived. They came into the house with the objective and unattached air that Stone always envied. They seemed to enter and exit with so little connection to the chaos and grief that Stone and others had to deal with time after time. He could come in and check the air conditioning system with as much emotion. They looked around the room nonchalantly.

"Looks like we're going to be busy," one of the techs commented.

"I haven't talked to the victim yet. They took her to the hospital before I arrived. I'm going there as soon as I leave here. I'll try to get her to come back so we can walk through this," Stone remarked.

"Good. We've got enough to keep us busy outside until you get back."

Stone was walking down the hall, ducking under the ropes that went in odd x's down its length when the doorbell rang. Stone figured that the techs had gone around to the front of the house and needed to get back in. He was surprised to see a young man in his mid-twenties holding a plastic bag of jewelry.

Jesus, who is this guy? Stone thought. "Can I help you?"

The kid looked like he was going door to door harmlessly selling subscriptions to a family magazine. He did not give any hint that he was talking to a strange man at the door of his neighbors nor did he give any indication that he was aware of the fleet of diamond E plated county cars in front of the place. He simply introduced himself.

"Hi, I'm Tracy Earle."

"I'm Detective Stone. Is there something you need here?" Stone asked. He could hear his own official version of himself in his voice. As Stone was introducing himself, the young man walked through the front door, past Stone, through the front room to the patio doors. He pointed through them.

"That's my house there. That's my bedroom window up there. Is Heather all right?" As the young man talked Stone noted that he was intent on looking at as much as possible in the house, the way an anxious employee tried to read upside down all the papers on his boss's desk.

"Excuse me, but you're going to have to go outside. We're processing a burglary in here," Stone took Earle's arm, leading him to the door.

"Oh, yeah. Look, I found this bag of jewelry in my mother's room. My parents are out of town, but I don't think it's theirs. I don't know how it got there, but I'll check with her when she gets home. I saw the cops here so I thought I better show you in case you're looking for it."

What in the fuck is going on here? Stone thought to himself. *This kid is a fruitcake.* Out of pure frustration, Stone remarked, "Before I look at that, let me ask you a few questions. Did you see anything last night?"

"Nope. I'm a pretty heavy sleeper, though. I don't usually hear anything."

"Okay, give me your phone number and I'll get in touch with you later about that bag of jewels," Stone could see that they were cheap pieces of jewelry. "You better go home now."

"Okay, but I'll check with my mother about this," he held up the bag and turned to leave.

"What in the hell was that all about?" the tech who was checking the front yard asked.

Stone shrugged his shoulders and threw his hands up. "Damned if I know. He seemed more intent on finding out what we were doing than anything else. Seemed to want to search the place more than we do. Looks like I've got one more to add to our list that needs to be checked out. Weird little motherfucker, wasn't he?" Stone waved at the tech as he walked toward his car.

Stone drove toward the Sacramento Medical Center. This was always the hardest part of sex crimes, especially brutal ones. To put victims through the torture of remembering every detail seemed cruel and inhuman punishment in itself. He arrived at the Center at 11:30.

Lunch was the furthest thing from his mind as he entered the emergency room. He showed his badge to the nurse at the admitting desk.

"You have a Heather Williams here. Should be with a deputy. She's being checked... ." He let the last of the sentence trail off.

"Too bad you're back here again. Under these circumstances, I mean," the nurse smiled at him.

"Pardon?"

"I saw you and your partner, Detective Wayne, when you were here with those two poor girls. I'm Gretchen Mitchell," Showing more friendliness than the situation would normally receive, she extended her hand to the surprised detective.

"I'm sorry. I guess I had my head somewhere else. I remember you. You were talking to Greg when I got here the last time. Nice to meet you, though I wish it were under different circumstances. Looks like I've got another."

"That's really too bad. Your deputy and Miss Williams are in the cafeteria. I'm going that way. Mind if I walk with you?"

"My pleasure. Add a little sunshine to my rainy day," she laughed at his awkward line and gave him a wide, bright smile. He returned it, embarrassed for a moment at the rush of enchantment he felt. She was almost as tall as he, big boned, like she could wrestle him to the ground, laughing all the time. He tried to look sideways to check out her figure, but when he did, she caught him and gave him another smile, which, just as before, he returned like a goofy kid.

"Not bad, not bad at all," he thought to himself. "The white uniform makes her look good and she's even prettier close up."

She wedged into his expansive thoughts with a question. "It is the same person attacking all the girls, isn't it, Sergeant Stone?"

The weight of her question made his spirits and shoulders sag. "We think so. A lot of similarities," glancing back, seeing her open, accepting gaze, no kind of accusation that he was not doing the best he could, he added, "It's Jim, by the way."

"Jim?"

"Jim. My name. Please call me Jim, not Sergeant."

"I'm sorry, Jim. I thought you meant the rapist's name was Jim," she laughed.

"It may be, for all I know."

"I can laugh a little at this thing. What else can you do? But I live in Rancho Cordova with a girlfriend. Just the two of us, and I have never worried before. Pretty much come and go as I please, but this has got me down. It really makes me nervous at night. Maybe you can give me some things to do to protect myself sometime."

"Sure, anytime. But it's really simple. The big thing is to keep your doors and windows locked and don't take chances." As he said the words, he felt how inadequate they were. This asshole could get into any house just by breaking a window. You could put the best locks in the world on your doors, and he could get in anytime he wanted. Force, enough of it, is a terrible weapon.

"Well, there's your deputy and Miss Williams. It was nice meeting you, Jim. Drop in and I'll buy you a cup of coffee."

"Love to," Stone did not want to leave her cheerfulness for the miserable interview ahead, but he did not want to embarrass the nurse or himself by making too much of her offer of coffee, so he nodded in her direction and crossed the large, empty cafeteria to the interview he dreaded.

Deputy Firlotte and two young women sat at a formica topped table that was much too cold and slick for the intimate conversation they were having. Firlotte looked up from the report he was writing as Stone approached.

"Hi, Jim," he said, making a clumsy, halfhearted effort to stand, but smiling as he did. From his crouched position, he shook Stone's hand.

"Sergeant Stone, this is Heather Williams and her friend, Mary Copeland."

"God help me," Stone thought. He smiled in spite of his thoughts, and shook hands with the two women who, like Firlotte, remained seated. Heather's handshake was strong and firm, but Stone could see her foot and leg bounce in rhythm to the terror she had to be feeling inside.

"Can I get you something to drink?" the detective asked to give some semblance of normalcy to the undertaking.

They all gave a polite smile of declining and he quickly bought himself a cardboard cup of watery coffee and returned to the quiet table.

"Heather," he said, as he sat, "We need to talk. I know you have told Deputy Firlotte everything, but I need to go over it again. We can use one of the offices here at the hospital, if you like."

It would be so nice to go back and talk to the nurse. So much easier than going through this painful conversation, this lousy intrusion of her most intimate privacy.

"It's okay. The worst is over. Mary knows about it all so we can talk here."

Chapter Fourteen

Stone looked around the empty cafeteria, and though he felt ill at ease, he figured it was just as good a place as any, and he started.

"Did you get the doctor's report, Bill?"

The deputy held up a file. "Got it right here, but..."

Heather interrupted. "I showered at Mary's before I called the police. I couldn't stand it. I just felt dirty and I had to scrub myself."

"I understand, Heather. That's normal and we can work around it. Why don't you start by telling me what he looked like."

"I don't really know. I guess he was about twenty-five years old. His voice sounded like he wasn't a kid, if you know what I mean. He always talked in a whisper. He was wearing a mask so I didn't really get to see his face. One time I saw his shoe when my blindfold moved. It was black leather."

"Okay, let's go through what happened step by step."

The young woman took a deep breath, holding her hands in front of her on the slick surface of the cafeteria table. Stone felt a rush of admiration for her bravery.

"I was alone in the house, and I went to sleep. I woke up and he had his hand over my mouth," she started in a matter-of-fact way. "He turned me over onto my belly. I tried to scream, but he told me to shut up or he would kill me. He tied my hands behind by back real tight and wrapped cloth around my eyes. He stuffed a cloth in my mouth and tied a piece of towel, I guess, around my face to hold it. He made me get up and he took me by the arm and led me down the hall. We had to duck down and I could feel ropes against my back. I didn't have any clothes on because I sleep in the nude."

"Did he say anything or touch you, fondle you in any way before he took you down the hall?"

"No, he just said 'Get up,' and we started walking. When we were walking down the hall he told me to duck down and then we went outside. He told me to lay down and he put me on a rug on the patio. He said he had dreams about me and always wanted to fuck me. One time he told me if I screamed after he left, he would hear me because he just lived down the block."

An image of Tracy Earle went through Stone's mind.

"He put me on my back and I heard a noise and I think he was, you know, playing with himself, masturbating. And then he told me to play with it, his thing, and he put it in my hand and moved back and forth for awhile. After that, he put my legs in the air and then on his shoulders... ."

Stone watched a tear gather at her left eye, fill, and then slowly roll down her cheek.

"...and he stuck it in. And he came. He got up and I guess he went into the house. Then he came out and he did it again and later he told me to play with it again and then he raped me again and came again," the tears were flowing freely down her cheeks and onto her blouse, but she continued to talk, not once sobbing, just letting the hurt, the frustration, the fear flow from her body. Stone had seen this scenario too many times in his career. Each time the urge to stop the interview, stop the hurt, was there, but he knew from experience he must let her continue.

"I think I heard him carrying paper bags out of the house. He tied my feet and dragged the rug over to the post on the patio and tied me to it. He took my rings off my fingers and I didn't hear him open the gate, but I guess he left then. I got my blindfold off, spit the cloth out and untied my feet from the post. I couldn't get my hands untied. I tried to cut the ropes when I got in the house, but I couldn't, he cut the phone cord so I couldn't call for help. I didn't know what to do so I waited about two hours until Mary rang the doorbell. When I let her in, she cut me free and we went to her house and I took a shower while she called the police. I guess I shouldn't have taken a shower, but I just had to. I still feel filthy. I still smell him. I'll always smell him."

Stone wanted to tell her that the smell, the memory, the nightmare, would go away with time but he knew it never would. He waited for her to settle back into herself.

"Did he say anything else?"

"Yeah, he said something about needing money for a fix or something and I better have some money for him. He told me he would kill me if I screamed. He took short breaths and he always whispered, real angry." Stone watched Mary reach out and put her hand over Heather's to try to stop the pain she knew her friend was feeling.

"Do you ever visit any of the military bases?" Stone asked.

"I've gone dancing at Mather Air Force Base for the last couple of years. Why?"

"It might fit something we are working on."

"I hope it's something that will catch him."

"You never know. I wish I could be more encouraging. Do you think you could go back to your house and walk us through this? I know it's tough, but we have to work together."

CHAPTER FOURTEEN

"I think I can do it, if Mary can come with me," she let go of her friend's hand that she was holding long enough to wipe away the tears that were running to the corners of her mouth.

"Sure. Bill, could you take them over? The techs are there ready to process and I don't want anything missed. I need to stop by the office," he stood and looked down at the young woman who was looking at her hands. He fought an impulse to pat her on the shoulder.

"I'll see you back at the house," he turned to leave.

"Thank you," Heather said.

"Sure," he answered back, thinking, "What in the hell does she have to thank me for? Or anyone for that matter. Society owes her an apology for allowing scum like this to run loose."

Stone walked into the empty detectives' bay. On weekends the office was always lifeless and cold, like the cafeteria in which he had just left Heather. It was full of life during a major crime with phones ringing and detectives yelling across the room to each other, people adjusting shoulder holsters, ripping pages from typewriters. All in motion as if something was happening, as if some progress was being made against the bad guys, something was being done that mattered.

This Saturday afternoon Stone was alone in the huge room that was only full of a grid of desks. It was only a rape he was working on. Only a rape. A young woman, once terrified, now being brave after her attack. Only a rape. It will get past "only" after the newspaper and the television clowns sensationalize it. A murder makes it to the front page if its particularly gruesome, or if it is somebody famous. A rape might make the fourth or fifth page, if at all. Stone knew this rapist was going to make the front page headlines before he was through. He knew that the whispering man in the mask was going to go front page soon.

He went to the file cabinet and unlocked the top drawer. Already five cases had been filed and evidence cross filed for reference. He reached back in the drawer to get the two cassette tapes...one was Walter Hamilton's interview. Only two minutes of the tape were necessary for victims to listen to and possibly identify the young man who was the neighbor of Rose Scott, who fought the rapist off to save her two daughters. The other tape was a placebo, a recording of a detective. It had been used many times with many victims as a comparison. Stone put the tapes in his pocket, picked up a portable tape player from his desk and headed back, to again meet with the latest victim.

Driving back to the house, Stone's thoughts of Hamilton, the little bastard who lied about not having guns, turned to Tracy Earle. He was just as weird as Hamilton. Something off with that little asshole, too. Why in the hell would he show up at Heather's door with a bag of jewelry? He wanted to see what was going on. Curious? Maybe. Stupid? Hell, yes. Could the stupid son of a bitch be her rapist? Stranger things have happened to break crime waves. We don't catch crooks because we are smart. We catch them because they are stupid. Christ, a break right now would be nice. The second coming of Christ seemed less remote.

At 3:30, Stone arrived back at Heather Williams'. She was in her bedroom talking to the crime scene techs. She seemed more composed now, more comfortable in her home. Strange, most victims of this type of crime had to force themselves to go back into their homes. He watched her from the doorway and tried to imagine the terror she must have felt and wondered how he would handle something as vile as being raped.

He excused himself for interrupting and the techs gave him a nod and disappeared into another part of the house. Stone remained standing while Heather sat on the edge of her bed.

"I have a few more questions I have to ask you. Do you feel up to it?"

"I guess. I know we have to. I just feel numb."

"I know. First do you know a Tracy Earle?"

His questioning brought a jolt of terror to her face, but it passed as quickly as it appeared.

"He's a neighbor. That's his house there," she pointed out her window with the plant hanging in it. "Why?"

"He was here earlier. Could he be the one who attacked you?"

"I don't know. I don't think so. Maybe. He's about the right size, but I don't think he would do anything like this. But he does know my family and he did know my mom and dad were going to be gone for the weekend and I was going to be home alone."

"What kind of car does he drive?"

"A little green Chevy Vega."

Stone felt his stomach respond with some kind of primitive pleasure.

"I have two tapes I want you to listen to. See if either of the voices sound familiar," Stone took her into the kitchen where they listened to the tapes. As she listened, she tightened her face in concentration during the first one. Hamilton's.

"I'm not sure," she said.

"Try this one," Stone said as he started the phony tape.

"That might be him. It sounds like Tracy."

"It's not Earle's voice, Heather. Listen carefully to them. It might help if you close your eyes."

Stone rewound the tape. She listened, nodding as the voice went on. As the tape went its way, her nodding became stronger.

"That could be him. That could be him, but he would have to whisper. Now that I listen, it could be Tracy. Is it Tracy?"

"No. Be careful now. Don't identify the wrong guy. It is definitely not Tracy. The worst possible is that you identify the wrong guy. The lawyers would have a field day with that. Don't worry about who the voice belongs to. Just let me know if it sounds familiar. If it sounds like the person who was here."

"Sorry."

"Nothing to be sorry about. I know this is hard on you."

"The first tape sounds like maybe it could be him. I'm not sure, but I need to hear it whispery. You know."

The pleasure grew. Hamilton was still in the picture.

"Heather, I have to go back to the office. Here's my card. If you think of anything, give me a call. Anything you remember, write it down in case you forget. People do that all the time, even people who have not gone through something like you just did. I'll call next week, if not sooner, and I'll keep you advised of any progress. Are you going to stay here tonight?"

"No. Not on your life. I'm going to Mary's. My dad will be home tomorrow, so I'll come back then."

"I'm afraid the techs will be here for quite awhile, so you can make arrangements for them to lock up if you want. That way you won't have to wait for them to finish."

"I'll do whatever it takes."

Stone took one last look around and left.

Monday morning, Stone walked into his boss's office. As always, he was apprehensive.

"God, it would be nice if we could just do our job without going through all this bullshit," he mused. "Fuck politics, promotions and the big picture," he thought as he walked into Lieutenant Burns' office.

"Mornin', boss. If we don't get this bastard, the media is going to crucify all of us. The long, the short, and the tall."

Burns shrugged his shoulders, indicating that he knew all there was to know about the problem, and he would be happy to straighten Stone out as soon as he got the chance.

"You sure it's the same guy, Jim? We want to be damned sure before we start jumping to conclusions. No sense getting our balls in an uproar if we don't have to."

"Gimme a fuckin' break. Ski mask. Tied up with shoelaces and torn towels. Same throaty whisper. Same fucking neighborhood. Just four or five blocks apart. This is the same guy, no doubts and the newspapers are going to ream us a new asshole, and I think you and the Sheriff better be ready."

"We're ready, but what have you got that's news for us? What have you got that will do us any good with the reporters?"

"We got Hamilton. The little fart lives right by Rose Scott. He's still looking good."

"You got anyone on him?"

"Of course. We're watching him like he was Lee Harvey Oswald's brother."

"Make sure you keep somebody on that son of a bitch and let's either catch him or eliminate him."

"Right. As good as this bastard looks, we got another problem."

"I don't need to hear problems. I need to hear solutions."

"This may be both. We got another suspect. A good one. Lives next door to this latest victim. His bedroom faces Heather Williams' bedroom and he can scope her out when she is sleeping naked. And she does sleep naked. On top of that, she leaves her curtains open."

"Doesn't mean she should be raped."

"Didn't say that. Didn't mean to imply it. Just that he's sort of nutty and he would be even nuttier watching a nude from his bedroom window. He also fits the description the victim gave us."

"Do what you have to do, but do it. Put a team on each of them."

"I have. Just wanted to hear you say it. I plan on working them six p to six a and see what happens."

"Any pattern? Any idea when he'll hit again?"

"He started out every four to six weeks, but it seems something turned him on. He only waited four days on the last one."

"Give me a copy of your new duty schedule so I can make sure the boss supports it. We have to get something out of this. Make sure you include something for Patrol. Keep their asses out of the coffee shops."

"They want this guy as bad as any of us. They're shorthanded, too, and the beat cops are taking this whole thing personal."

CHAPTER FIFTEEN

THE TERROR DISAPPEARED. Secure in the knowledge that "it couldn't happen to me," people slept once again. The highly individual paranoia lessened. The feeling that *he* might slip through the curtains vanished. People forget to lock doors. Windows are left open to the night breeze. Women once again walk alone. Porch lights are turned off. Normalcy once again returns to the Sacramento area.

The sun is lower, the season changing. Though the oncoming of a California fall is not as dramatic as the change further east, the nights are cooler, the wind is sharper, the trees are starker against the sky. Witches might be seen against an October sky, especially in California. A wind can come down from the Sierras that will put goose bumps on your arms and footsteps on your grave.

Sometime around midnight, Sunday, October 17, 1976, a gate swung open as a figure passed from the green belt paralleling the American River into a backyard. The sound of the gate hitting against the fence in the autumn night makes such a private noise that only the owner of the house might respond to it.

The man in the house hears the sound that is only strange because of its time in the middle of the night. Should it be heard in early evening when the sounds of life reverberate through the neighborhood, it would never register.

Hearing the sound, the owner of the house quietly got out of bed, not waking his sleeping wife. As he spread the curtains and looked out his bedroom window, he sees the open gate, turns and climbs back into the warmth of the bed.

Two and a half hours later, the sharp, incessant barking of a small dog brings him once again out of his deep sleep. The man stirs to the sound, his movement waking his wife. Half asleep, they both hear the last sharp bark of the dog.

Silence.

They drift back to sleep the way a drowned body slowly rolls under the surface of a slow, lazy river. Just before they are completely under, a woman's scream pulls them back to the edges of reality. The sleep is too strong and they sink once again into the current of sleep. In all the houses of the neighborhood, no one else stirred.

Except in one house.

Ten year-old Timmy Parker was slowly drawn from his deep sleep by the sharp staccato barking of his dog. He was almost awake as he climbed out of his bed to let the dog into the backyard to go to the bathroom.

The silent figure hears the dog bark inside the garage. He stops, window screen in his hand, and stares from the dark mask toward the barking. In the murky darkness of the house, a line of yellow light appears at the bottom of the boy's bedroom door. The figure moves away from the screenless kitchen window, leaning forward just enough to watch the boy walking down the hallway. Wearing only a t-shirt, a black mask, and tennis shoes, the figure stands naked from the waist down in the cool night air.

He watches the boy go through the kitchen to the garage door. He's just going to calm the dog and take him to his room...but he doesn't. He goes to the sliding glass door, the small dog following close behind. The figure moves back, away from the house, toward the darkness of the trees.

The backyard is flooded with light as Timmy turns on the porch light and opens the sliding glass door. Suddenly wide awake, Timmy sees the half naked figure. As the small dog bounds, barking, toward the masked figure, he quickly closes and locks the door. He stands, in shock, as he watches the figure run to the fence, climb and sit, watching the barking dog. His heart pounds and his legs grow weak as he watches the monster looking down at the dog. He watches as the half naked figure slowly lowers himself to the ground, ignoring the dog as it makes furious but harmless fakes at his tennis shoes. Embarrassment joins fear as Timmy sees the monster's privates below the t-shirt.

Timmy watched as the figure moved toward the house. He could not get his breath and he could not form thoughts. He wanted to scream for help, but he could not get enough breath. He watched as the figure walked past the barking dog toward the open kitchen window. Mesmerized at first, he watched the masked head appear through the window. Heart beating so hard his chest hurt, Timmy's legs finally took him toward his sleeping mother. Above the boom of his heart, he heard the sharp isolated sound of a plate hitting the floor in the kitchen.

CHAPTER FIFTEEN

He burst into his mother's room. Sobbing, he yelled, "Mom! Mom! Mom! ...A man!" He could not get the right words. He could not get the breath to say them.

"A man...a man...the window," Timmy slammed the door against the terror that was sure to follow.

Joyce Parker came awake immediately, her heart sending a mother's pounding energy to her brain and her body. She left sleep in an instant. The sense of dreams, the fog between sleep and waking nonexistent. In one alert motion, she turned on the bedroom lamp and swung her feet over the side of the bed and met her son as he rushed to her. She pulled him to her as he sobbed into the body.

"What is it?" she asked as she rubbed his back to soothe away the effects of what she thought was a bad dream.

"A man...a man...the kitchen window. A man is coming through the kitchen window," as her son stammered the words, she realized it was not a dream. It was reality. The boy had seen something terrible. The monster was real...the monster was in the house. She leaned over her son and grabbed the phone and frantically dialed "O." It rang once, twice...fifteen, sixteen times. Above the phone's constant ringing she heard a loud thump in the kitchen as if someone had jumped from a high place to the kitchen floor. The operator still did not answer. She slammed down the receiver and dialed again, this time the number of her neighbor, her best friend, but the pounding in her head, the fear that numbed her brain covered the numbers and the access to them. In her panic, she could not remember the number. She, like her son, could not form words. A new sound emerged. Footsteps running down the hall toward Joyce Parker and her son. Her bedroom door opened.

The worst image in her life stood before her. An image she could never have formed, even in her worst nightmare. A man, naked from the waist down, staring at her through a hideous mask, the small dog barking harmlessly at his naked legs. She saw the large, heavy knife in his right hand. And then she screamed. Terror tore from her throat as she pulled her son to her body.

His voice came across the room in a low, sinister hiss that could easily have come from a snake.

"Ssssshhhhut up!" he moved toward them in a way a snake moves to a pair of helpless animals. He brought the monstrous knife to her neck and pressed it against her throat, where her pulse pounded uncontrollably.

"Do exactly as I tell you or I'll kill you. I'll butcher you all to pieces," the dog kept yapping at his heels. "I'm going to kill you if you don't get him," he hissed. "Shut him up!"

Without taking her eyes off the half naked monster, she picked up the dog which growled softly in her arms.

"It's all right. Be quiet," she said, surprised at her composure. "I'll put him in the other room. He'll be quiet in there," holding the shivering, growling dog against her chest with one arm, and holding her son with the other, she moved slowly to the door and across the hall to the spare bedroom. She felt the blue eyes on her as she put the dog down and closed the door. She returned to her own bedroom and sat on the bed, wrapping her arms around her son to protect him. He pressed his face into her bosom.

The man in the mask slowly whispered, "Who else is in the house?"

"Just my four year old daughter. Please don't hurt her," she pleaded. The image of her little daughter sleeping in the other room, so close to this monster, sent shivers of fear throughout her body. To trade a significant bit of information so he would not think of the sleeping child in the other room, she blurted, "My husband is out of town," Now he knew the worst, the most dreadful thing he could know. Now she was at his complete mercy. She was alone. He had a knife. He was naked. She knew he would harm her, rape her. But that did not mean anything. She could survive anything he might do to her as long as her children were unharmed. What made her chest tighten against her breath was the clear sudden knowledge that he would happily harm her children. She felt it, she knew it. He would tear flesh and smear the walls with their blood. He could. He would.

He walked away from her to the telephone and yanked it out of the wall in a violent gesture that suggested how he would treat all of them. Without looking back at her or her sobbing, shivering son, he left the room, only to return with a towel in his hand. Using his teeth, knife, and hands, he ripped the towel into thin, efficient strips. His motion was violent. He jerked her arms, pulling her to him, away from the boy. Spinning her around, he pinned her arms behind her and tied her hands together. She felt the cloth bite into her flesh and watched in horror as the man picked up her son and laid him on the bed. She could not let herself think of what he might do to her tiny son. Too frightened to move, she watched the black and white gloved hands find her son's hands and tie them to the headboard. Moving with practiced skill, she watched him move to the boy's feet and fiercely tie them together. Joyce watched in horror as blood ran instantly from a cut on his foot. She had to be stronger. For the children. For herself.

"If you move," the voice that came from the mask hissed, "I will kill you."

"I don't want to die, Mommy," Timmy whispered.

Without acknowledging the boy's pleas, the man threw a blanket over Timmy's head and then turned to Joyce. He spoke in stuttering whispers.

"Don't move. If you do, it will take s-s-seconds off his life. If you do what I s-s-say, you won't get hurt. I'll be gone in a little while. If you don't do as I s-s-say, I'll k-k-kill you all."

He took her by the arm, pushing her forward. She stumbled clumsily and he led her out of the bedroom and into the family room. She was relieved that he went past her daughter's room and that he had left Timmy.

"Sit down," he ordered. She sat on the couch, her legs stretched out in front of her.

"Where's your money?"

"There's some in an envelope in my purse. It's for the heart association. That's all I have," as she spoke he knelt in front of her, the intimacy of the position sending shivers through her body. Using strips of towel, he tied her ankles together. He left the room and she heard him going through drawers in the other rooms, ransacking, opening cupboards. Soon he was back in front of her.

He leaned close to her face.

"You're beautiful," he whispered. She could see the darker hairs on his arms and legs from the light shining in from the patio.

"Please don't hurt me. I'm pregnant," she pleaded.

He ignored her and she felt a blindfold tighten around her head. Then a sweet smelling cloth was forced into her mouth and a third cloth tightened around her head, holding the cloth in her mouth. A wave of revulsion rose in her stomach and she realized she could not vomit with the gag in her mouth.

She felt his hands on her feet and felt the ties around her ankles loosen. Her feet were free as he lifted her and prodded her into a standing position. She swayed in the darkness of her blindfold and fought to keep balance. He led her by the arm, and at the first step she knew he was taking her back to the bedroom. She felt herself pushed onto the bed, the bed with her little boy tied to the headboard. She heard him ransacking the drawers in her dresser and then once again was engulfed in panic as she felt his hands on her arms as she was pulled from the bed and led from her son.

Back in the living room he ordered her to sit.

"On the floor," he whispered.

Her arms were tied behind her back and she stumbled in her darkness, falling to the floor. She was roughly pushed backward and she toppled onto her side and then rolled onto her back. She felt his gloved hands slowly unbuttoning the shirt she wore, one of her husband's old dress shirts. It slid open, exposing her breasts to the eyes behind the mask. His hands were on her waist as she felt her hips being raised as her panties were slipped down her legs, over her feet. She shuddered convulsively, her eyes wide behind the blackness of the blindfold.

"You have a beautiful body," he whispered. "Do you lay out in the sun?" She shook her head. She felt his mouth move across her body, moving slowly lower.

Her mind was racing. She could tell he was no longer wearing his mask or gloves as he moved over her body. She felt him between her legs as he forced her knees apart, his hands on her thighs.

"This is not happening. This is not happening," she screamed in her mind as she felt his cheek against her thigh as his face lowered. She felt his tongue explore her for a brief moment and then he was again at her feet, tying her ankles. She regained her ability to think without the pressure of her stomach rising in her throat, without the terrible thoughts of her children being torn apart. He was ransacking the kitchen again. Time once again turned to black tar as she waited, waited for the next terrible thing to happen.

He was back at her side, the cool blade of the knife against her cheek.

"You lied," he hissed. "You said there was no more money. I'm going to k-k-kill you for lying. There was m-m-more m-m-money in the desk." She could not answer because of the gag, so she shook her head. She did not know the money was there. She felt the point of the knife slide down her body and the fear intensified as the blade crossed her stomach, out to each side of her hips, and back up her body to her neck. Slowly the knife slid back and forth across her neck.

"If you don't do as I say, I'll kill you and the kids," she felt hands roll her onto her stomach, and she felt his wet, gooey penis in her hand.

"Play with it," he whispered. She was surprised at how small it was. Even through the fear, she sensed the lack of size. He moved back and forth in her hand as he untied her gag, then removed the cloth from her mouth. Through the clashing images of fear for herself and her children, she knew she had to endure.

"If you scream or do anything, I'll kill you. You better not fight me," he hissed.

She knew a fate worse than death would soon approach, yet death must not occur. Her son and daughter must be spared.

Fingers were pulling on her rings, but they wouldn't slide over her swollen fingers. She felt his anger as he tugged and twisted.

"I'll cut your fuckin' fingers off," he hissed.

"Get some soap," she cried. Three times she tried to make him understand that soap would help the rings slide off her fingers. She heard him at the sink and then she felt the soap being rubbed on her hands. Still the rings remained as her fingers had swollen to the point of bursting from the ties around her wrists. She felt the bindings being cut.

"Take the rings off or I'll kill you," she struggled and they broke free and again her hands were tied behind her back.

"Your body is beautiful," he whispered and she felt herself being lifted to a sitting position. She felt another cloth being tied around her eyes and then a hood slipped over her head.

"Suck on it," he ordered and she felt the hood being raised and felt his penis against her lips. She felt him rocking against her face and then he pulled away. He rolled her onto her side and she felt his body next to her. Again his penis entered her mouth. She felt the knife against her back and the humility and disgust were overwhelmed by her fear. She felt him leave her mouth again and now he was in her, penetrating her.

In desperation, she thought of what to do to end this nightmare. Maybe psychology would work.

"You're such a good lover," she lied. He pulled from her.

"No one ever said that before," he replied. "Most people just laugh at me."

"Do you like to be complimented?" she asked.

"Yes. People make fun of me, especially since something happened to my face. I need to know what time it is," he demanded. "Where's your clock?"

"In the kitchen."

She heard him in the kitchen now. Cupboards opening and closing, the refrigerator door being opened and the glass bottles so neatly arranged in the door shelves bumping each other. And then silence.

She felt him pushing at her rectum with his penis.

"Oh, God, you're hurting me!" she cried. She felt herself being taken to the couch and placed on her knees on the floor, her head resting on the cushion. This time she felt him enter her rectum, just for a brief moment and then he was out. She felt her leg being tied to the coffee table and again he was gone. She heard his voice down the hall.

"You better not move or I'll kill your mother."

She didn't hear him over her, but she felt his presence. She knew he was there. She knew he was standing over her, watching her through the mask.

"Now he's going to kill me," she thought. "We're all going to die." And she knew she was helpless. She was at his mercy. They were all at his mercy.

"When will your husband be home?" he asked through clenched teeth. "You better tell me the same as your son or I'll kill you all. Don't lie to me."

"He won't be home until Friday," she replied.

She felt him enter her rectum again and push against her. Again just for a second, and then he was gone, only to return a short time later to have her once again copulate him. She felt his face against her thighs, his tongue entering her. Her mind was numb, her head swimming as she felt his penis enter her vagina.

She was cold now, cold and near to hysteria.

"I'm cold," she managed to murmur and a short time later she felt a blanket being placed over her. Again she felt him enter her mouth and she fell limp onto her back. He was pressing against her vagina, entering her as her thoughts blurred.

The house was quiet as she slowly re-entered reality. She listened—nothing. She worked her hands, moving them against the cloth ties. She felt the pressure subside and her hands were free. Frantically she worked on the cord tied to her ankle. She left her blindfold on until she was completely free.

"If he is still here and sees me without the blindfold, he'll kill us," she thought.

Detective Michael Tripp sat in his county vehicle watching Walter Hamilton's house. For nine nights now he had parked down the street from the Hamiltons'. Three times he had followed Walter to the corner store where he met a group of young men. He watched them drink beer in the parking lot and then he followed Walter Hamilton home, and he sat until 6:00 a.m. each morning. Tonight was like the other eight nights. As he watched through his binoculars, he caught glimpses of their prime suspect wandering throughout his house until the lights went out. Tripp drank the hot coffee from his thermos, sitting alone in the darkness as the hours dragged on. He picked up his portable radio.

"You still awake, Phil?"

"Yeah, all quiet here," Detective Philip McDonald replied. "I haven't seen any movement for the last two hours. I saw him enter, haven't seen him since," McDonald had been sitting on Tracy Earle's house for nine days also.

"Something better happen soon because my wife is starting to wonder what I'm doing all night. How you doing?"

"Barely making it. This is the toughest time of night for me. I finished my coffee and need to hit a restroom real soon," Tripp replied.

"It's five thirty and nothing moving here. Want to call it a night and meet at Denny's?" McDonald asked.

"Let's give it another fifteen minutes and make it Corky's. I can't take Denny's coffee this morning."

"You're on. Countdown," McDonald returned.

"30A1, 10-63...261 just occurred, Carmichael area," the dispatcher's voice over the police radio brought the two detectives wide awake. 261, the California Penal Code for rape.

"You get that, Phil?" Tripp yelled into his portable.

"Yeah, let's hit it."

Both detectives bolted from their cars and within seconds were banging on the doors of Walter Hamilton and Tracy Earle.

Tracy Earle, sleep still in his eyes, opened the door to be confronted by Detective McDonald.

"This is your lucky night, Tracy," McDonald remarked as he turned from a mystified Tracy Earle and walked back to his car.

Michael Tripp was met by a wide awake Mrs. Hamilton.

"What do you want?" she demanded.

"I need to talk to Walter, Mrs. Hamilton."

"I told you people before to stay away from Walter, now get out of here."

"There's been another rape. I need to talk to Walter so we can eliminate him as a suspect. If he's here, we won't bother either of you again."

"Walter's in bed and he's not going to be disturbed. My lawyer said I could get a restraining order against you people for harassing Walter and if you don't leave us alone, I will. Now get off my property," she screamed as she slammed the door in Tripp's face.

"Damn," Tripp muttered. "Now what in the hell do I do?"

"You there, Phil?" Tripp asked into his portable.

"Yeah. Our man here is eliminated. How about you?"

"Met with a nut and came away with the shell. Mrs. Hamilton said Walter was sleeping and she wouldn't wake him. Slammed the door in my face. I don't know. I saw him earlier and he didn't leave. His car is still in the driveway, so he couldn't have left without me seeing him."

"Okay. I'll meet you in the office. We might as well head in."

CHAPTER SIXTEEN

THE HEADLIGHTS SWEPT ACROSS the well manicured lawn as the pretty nineteen year old turned into her driveway. Her small dog sat quietly in the back seat of the fourteen year old car. Julie Lowe turned off her headlights and her car engine. The streetlight in front of her house illuminated the interior of the car and she turned to talk to her pet.

"Good girl. Want to go in and eat?" Without looking she reached to open her car door and held it partially open with her left foot.

"Okay, Muffy, let's go in the house," she began to turn toward her door when she felt the hand grab her head and felt herself being pulled toward the open door. As she turned to face her attacker, she looked into the eyes staring at her through the wool mask. Out of instinct she fought the hand, trying to break free, trying to escape from the fear that engulfed her body. The gloved hand continued to pull as she began swinging her hands at the gray hideous mask. She felt the knife blade at her throat and felt the sting as it drew blood.

"Stop fighting," he hissed. "I only want your car. I won't hurt you."

She knew she couldn't win and the fight left her. Only the fear remained.

"Get out," he ordered and she slid from the seat. He closed the car door and walked her toward the side of the house.

"Turn around," he demanded and she felt her hands being drawn behind her.

"Please..." she began.

"Shut up," he hissed.

She felt her wrists being tied and felt the cord cut into her flesh.

"Don't look at me," he ordered. "Do you have any money? All I want is money and your car keys. I'm not going to hurt you."

"I've just got a dollar in my wallet," she replied.

"Shut up," she felt the knife dig into her chest. She could hear him going through her purse and she kept her head turned away.

"Please don't hurt my dog," she pleaded. "Let her go."

"Shut up. I'm not going to hurt your dog."

She was being led back to her driveway. He held her arm in a tight grip as they moved across the lawn, past her neighbor's house, toward the corner of her block. She stumbled as they turned into the backyard of a neighbor's home. As she stumbled, she saw his shoes, brown desert boots. They went through the open side gate. She could see that there were no lights on in the house and it appeared the people were away. He grabbed her by the blouse.

"Sit down," he ordered, and she felt herself being pushed to the ground. His grip on her blouse kept her from falling. She saw the strips of cloth by her feet; three strips neatly arranged as if in preparation for her appearance. She watched as his gloved hands tied her ankles with a piece of white cord. The knife lay on the ground, the blade glistening in the moonlight. The cement sidewalk was cold under her, but the fear running through her was the cause of her shivering. She watched as he picked up a piece of cloth. Blindfolded now, her mind focused on her fears. She felt the cloth being forced into her mouth and she began to move her head in protest, whimpering as the terror gripped her.

"Shut up," he hissed, and again she felt the knife dig into her ribs. She was lying on her side and felt him straddle her. She felt the cloth around her face, holding the gag in place.

He was standing over her. She could feel him looking at her. She knew he was trying to decide, but what was he trying to decide? What was her fate? The sound of her car keys jingling above her slowly found its way into her mind, momentarily dispersing her fears as she focused on the sound.

"I'm going to leave for five minutes," the voice hissed. "If you move, I'll slit your throat and cut your guts out. If you move, blam, blam, blam."

She knew he would kill her if she didn't do as he ordered. Her fear was that she didn't know if he would kill her if she did as he ordered.

She didn't hear him leave, but a short time later she heard her car start. She listened, but didn't hear it drive off. And she waited. When he didn't return, she began to struggle.

October 16, 1976. 10:30 a.m.

"Robbery. Can I help you?" the secretary asked into the phone.

"This is Sergeant Phillips, Patrol. Is Sergeant Stone in?"

"Just a minute, Sergeant, I'll get him for you," she pushed the intercom button. "Sergeant Stone, line one is for you."

"Sergeant Stone."

"Hi, Jim. Doug Phillips. Thought I better let you know we found the vehicle from last night's attack. It was parked over on El Segundo. The keys are missing and the victim's dog was locked in the trunk. Seemed to be all right. The car's being processed for prints."

"Find anything in it that might help us?"

"Doesn't look like it, but they're still working on it. We did a canvass of the area. Not much luck, but one neighbor on El Segundo had a prowler in her backyard two weeks ago. She didn't report it so nothing to follow up on."

"By the way, Doug, Lowe probably wasn't his intended victim. She said she hadn't been home alone in a long time and her brother and father usually get home around the same time. He already had the pieces of towel laid out at a neighbor's, so have your fellows keep an eye out. He should hit again soon, especially where he didn't rape."

"Any idea why he didn't rape her?" Phillips asked.

"Speculation only, but I think he got frustrated when his intended victim, whoever she was, didn't show up. Seems he likes to follow a pattern and maybe he just doesn't want to take a chance on trying something different. The people who live in the house where he had the ties laid out are elderly and don't fit at all. Don't really know. He raped the one earlier that day, so many times he may have been unable to get it up. I can't figure the bastard out. Anyway, thanks, Doug. Call me if you hear anything."

Stone went to Lieutenant Burns' office, stuck his head in and waited for his boss to lift his head from the paper work.

"They found the car from last night's attack over in Rancho Cordova. Processing it now, but don't expect anything. Keeping our fingers crossed. He probably had his car parked near where they found the victim's car. I'll have our team do a neighborhood canvass."

Sacramento Bee, November 4, 1976

MAN HUNTED AS SUSPECT IN EIGHT RAPES

Sheriff's detectives today disclosed an extensive hunt has been underway for a man who has attacked and raped eight women the past year in the areas east of Sacramento.

Sheriff's spokesman Richard Shelby today said the same man is believed to have raped four women in Rancho Cordova, two in Del Dayo, and two in the Crestview area.

He said the first case occurred in October last year. He said the man did not strike again until June. Four of the attacks were last month.

Shelby said the man is also believed to be responsible for a case in which a woman was molested and another in which a rape attempt was thwarted.

Sheriff's officials previously had asked the news media to hold back on reporting the case, saying publicity would ruin any stakeouts aimed at capturing the suspect.

But the series of rapes came to light last night at a Del Dayo Parents Club meeting. The meeting, conducted by deputies, was to have been on crime prevention in general but the series of rapes was disclosed after questions about rumored rapes from some of the 500 persons attending.

Shelby said the suspect is white, has a pale complexion, may be between five foot eight inches and six feet tall of a medium build, 25 to 35 years old, and has dark hair which hangs over his ears to his collar.

The attacks have been committed between 11:00 p.m. and 6:24 a.m. He frequently commits repeated attacks on individuals over a period of three hours. He has entered the homes through a window.

Investigators describe him as a "cat burglar" type who finds out if a husband is at home.

He has worn a mask, but descriptions are vague as to what kind. He has worn military-type boots and black tennis shoes. His weapons have included a revolver, knife, a stick, and a club.

He has cut and beat his victims, but none seriously.

"We completed all we could on the neighborhood canvass, Jim," Detective Greg Andrews parked his skinny ass on Stone's desk.

"Come up with anything?" Stone sat back hoping for the one break they needed.

"Well, quite a few people weren't home, so we left our cards and asked them to call. One neighbor four doors down saw a strange car in the area. Said it was an older white Chevy with chrome wheels. He remembered the first three letters on the plate as TOR. One of the patrol deputies recognized the description. Says it's usually driven by a local doper by the name of Paul Munoz. We've had him before on burglary and forgery, but nothing recent. Personally, I don't think he really fits. He's a real scum bag."

"Give Narcotics a call. See if they have anything on him. Maybe they know why he was in the area," Stone knew it wasn't their rapist, but better to be sure.

"Jim, you better get in here," Lieutenant Burns called to Stone from his office. Burns was on the phone scribbling notes on a yellow pad and motioned to Stone to a seat.

"Okay, thanks, Dick. Appreciate the call," he hung up and looked at Stone, tapping his pen on the pad.

"That was Shelby over in Burglary. Looks like the cat's out of the bag as far as the press is concerned, Jim. They had a crime prevention meeting over at the Del Dayo school. Patrol had two of their female officers there to talk about burglaries, so Dick was asked to go along for support. They had quite a crowd and questions got around to the rumors about the rapes. Dick had no choice but to tell them that there was a rapist on the loose. He gave them a real basic answer to the questions, but the press was there and they had to print it. They've played ball with us and kept it quiet until now, so it's our turn to play ball with them. Fred Knowood from the *Bee* called me this morning and said they had no choice but to print the story and now he wants to have an interview. I called the boss and he says to go ahead and talk to him. Says to use our own judgment and wants you in his office to brief him on what we have. The meeting is at 9:30 in the conference room, so he wants us in his office now. You ready?"

"Yeah. I read the article. Not bad. They gave a description and times he hit. Mentioned he beat his victims and cut them. At least nothing negative about us," Stone turned to leave.

"Not yet," echoed behind him.

Greg Andrews looked up as Stone and Burns walked past.

"Dead end on Munoz, Jim. Narcotics says they're on top of him. He's dealing small time dope in the Lowes' neighborhood. Not only that, he was in jail for six months. Just got out three weeks ago."

"Figures," Stone replied.

November 10, 1976. Citrus Heights

"Kim, we're leaving for the hospital now. You sure you don't want to go?"

"No thanks, Dad. Tell Tim I'll be in to see him tomorrow," Kim Alcone replied.

"Okay, honey. We want to get there by seven. You know how your brother is when we're late. Lock up if you leave and don't forget curfew."

"Don't worry. 'Night."

Kim Alcone heard her parents leave the house and she continued to watch TV from the family room couch. The family poodle sat quietly in her lap and Kim unconsciously scratched its head.

"Come on, Gidget. I'm going to get a glass of milk. Want a treat?" The poodle was thirteen years old, three years younger than Kim. They had been companions almost all of Kim's life. As she walked to the kitchen, her poodle padded along behind.

Kim poured herself a glass of milk and gave her dog a piece of hot dog that it swallowed without chewing.

"Come on, let's watch TV," she went through the living room to turn off the stereo, then sat back down on the couch. Her dog took its usual place on her lap.

"What was that?" Kim exclaimed. A loud bang from somewhere in the house had startled her. Her dog began barking and shaking.

"It's all right, Gidget. Quiet. Mom? Dad? Is that you?"

He was in front of her before she heard him. It was as though he had jumped into the room. She started to scream.

"Shut up or I'll kill you," she felt the knife at her throat and she looked into the eyes in front of her. Eyes staring at her through the slit of the leather hood.

"Shut that dog up or I'll kill it," he ordered through clenched teeth. He was in front of her, close, breathing through the slit for his mouth. She could smell him. Body odor or bad breath, she couldn't tell, but then it really didn't matter.

"Get up," he ordered. She was doing what he wanted now. Scared into submission. A sixteen year old can be so brave surrounded by friends, yet so vulnerable alone.

"Turn around," he hissed. She could see the black shoelaces in his gloved hand and then she could feel them biting into her wrists as he tied her tight. He led her outside and sat her down on the concrete walk. She saw the black shoelaces hanging neatly from the handle bars of her yellow bike. She watched as he removed them. She was thinking now. Thinking and watching. Her fear was in her throat as he knelt in front of her. She wanted to scream, but she knew a scream meant death. She could see it in his eyes, feel it through his presence.

"Maybe he'll go away if I do what he tells me. Maybe he won't touch me. Oh, God, I'm scared. Please God, please help me."

She felt him tying her ankles and she watched the leather hood. His gray sweater covered the bottom of the hood. He stood over her in his army fatigue pants and black square toed shoes.

"Don't move or you'll be dead and I'll be gone in the night," he ordered, and then he was gone. She saw him go back into the house only to return a short time later. She watched as he replaced the screen on the living room window and then he was in front of her, kneeling, looking at her. A face hidden behind a mask.

"Where's your money?"

"I don't have any," she managed to whisper.

"Where's your parents' money."

"I think they took it with them."

"Damn, no money. Ah, man, no money," again he ran back toward the family room door, returning a short time later.

"Do you like to fuck?" he hissed.

"Oh, God," she thought. She closed her eyes and didn't answer.

"Do you have a boyfriend?"

She could only nod yes, her voice wouldn't respond.

"Does he fuck you?"

She watched as her ankles were untied and felt herself being lifted to her feet. They were leaving the backyard now, toward the canal that ran behind her house. The canal where she used to play with her little friends. A place with good memories. A place where she laughed and whispered shared secrets. A place of innocence.

She heard the neighbors' dogs barking after them and prayed a neighbor would see them and take her from the monster walking behind her. But no one arrived and the dogs fell into silence as their attention soon diverted from the two figures disappearing into the darkness of the canal.

"Please let me go," she pleaded.

"Shut up," he hissed through clenched teeth. "If you don't shut up you'll be silent forever and I'll be gone in the dark."

She knew they were approaching the weeping willow tree, she could see its outline in the darkness. Her favorite spot–before tonight.

"Sit down," he hissed. She felt the cold ground through her jeans as she watched him kneel in front of her and tie her ankles together again. She watched him walk a short distance away only to return to untie her ankles. Her hands were numb and cold as the bindings bit into her flesh, cutting off all circulation. Again he tied her ankles and walked away. When he returned, she saw the knife in his hand as he walked behind her. Fear heightened as she felt her hands being pulled back. She felt the bindings fall free and almost felt relief. Temporary relief, as her wrists were again tied tightly. He was in front of her now, cutting at her jeans with the knife. Her legs were bare as the knife tore through her jeans. His hands were on her thighs and she tried to wiggle free, but his hands tightened, holding her firm.

"This isn't working right," he muttered. Her jeans were off now and his face close to hers. His eyes looking into hers.

"I know you, don't I?" he hissed.

"No," she replied.

"Do you go to American River College?"

Again she replied, "No," she felt the knife against her neck.

"You're lying," he accused. "What's your name?" She made up a name and he didn't respond. He stood in front of her.

"I have to wait for my parents to leave so I can go home," he muttered. Was he talking to her or was he playing a game, she wondered.

"I'm going to take off in my car," he was in front of her and she watched as he reached down and pulled up his socks. She could see in the dim light that his legs were very pale with brown hairs.

"Within the next twenty minutes make one move and you'll be silent forever and I'll be off in the dark," he hissed, and then he was gone.

She managed to slip her hands down and under her feet and easily untied her ankles. Her wrists were tied too tight to untie. She ran toward her house, her nakedness forgotten as fear drove her toward safety.

"We had our ninth one last night, Mike," Stone greeted Lt. Burns. "This one was lucky. Sixteen year old over in Citrus Heights. He stripped her, but for some reason didn't rape her."

"You sure it's our man?"

"Yeah, it's him. I think he got the wrong victim and it screwed up his plans. Looks like he thought she was someone else. We think he was after the neighbor woman. They look alike. He wore a leather hood with small slits this time. Took her from her house down into the canal, stripped her, and left. She said he seemed to be a little confused when she told him she went to San Juan High School. He seemed to think she went to American River College. The neighbor attends A.R.C. Strange thing is this one, even at sixteen, fits the mold. She's pretty, five foot seven, hundred fifteen, hundred twenty pounds."

"Okay, Jim. What do you have going?"

"Well, patrol is working on one lead. Probably isn't anything but one of Charlie Manson's family members lives around the corner on Dewey Drive. They say she gets a lot of weird visitors. They're going through their files to see if they can come up with some names. Intelligence is checking for us also. Apparently this bitch moved here from L.A. two years ago. The F.B.I. keeps tabs on her, I guess."

"That makes me fuckin' sleep better. The F.B.I., a bunch of bean counters. Even if they did have something, they wouldn't tell the real cops," Burns threw his hands in the air.

"I've got Kelly checking out some welding supply shops. The way she described the mask, it looks like it may be one a welder wears. Something has to turn for us," Stone continued.

"Something better. Between the community and the press, we are going to be on the hot seat in a big way. The Sacramento Bee has played it close to the vest for us, but it's out of the bag now and we can't expect anything but grief," Burns stated.

"Maybe it's for the best. Someone might come forward."

"The best for us is to catch the son of a bitch before he kills someone. Christ, I'm even beginning to check my window and door locks two or three times before I go to bed, and I live alone."

"You're not his type, Mike. You're too fuckin' ugly."

Burns laughed as Stone left the office.

"I sure hope so. I don't want to have to tell some young deputy that this bastard tied me up and blew in my ear."

CHAPTER SEVENTEEN

JIM STONE POURED HIMSELF his fourth cup of coffee of the morning, lit his fifth cigarette, and sat on the edge of Greg Wayne's desk.

"Well, partner, the lieutenant said he would give as many of our cases as he can to the other teams. He wants us to put all we can into the rapes," Stone began. "The news media picked up on all the rapes so it's out of the bag and the heat goes on."

"You sure we can't get out of this? I think our asses are going to be dragging before it's over," Wayne shook his head to show his disappointment.

"Look at it this way, Greg. If we do our job, we could save a lot of women from this bastard."

"Yeah, and if we don't get real lucky, real soon, somebody's going to take big bites out of our asses and I don't know about you, but if you haven't noticed, I can't afford to lose any ass."

"Think positive, Greg. We're going to nail this one."

"We better be quick, Jim. I don't think he wants to quit."

"Sgt. Stone, line one's for you," the Investigative Division secretary called.

Stone lifted the receiver and punched the button. "Sgt. Stone."

"Yeah. Uhhh. I don't want to give my name, but I think I know who raped those girls," a male voice stammered.

"What girls?" Stone asked.

"You know, the guy who wears the mask. He raped all those women. The newspaper described him."

"Who do you think it is?" Stone asked, preparing himself for another wild goose chase.

"Look, I work with him, so I can't let him know I'm talking to you guys. I don't have to give you my name, right?"

"We'll talk about that later. Why don't you give me his name and tell me why you think he's a rapist," Stone urged.

"We work for the phone company. He's on the road a lot, covers from Redding to Reno, but our office is here in Sacramento. His name is Vaughn Black. I know he's been arrested for making phone calls to women. You know, talking dirty. He doesn't like women, says they are all whores."

"How old is he? Where does he live?" Stone asked.

"He lives in Rancho Cordova. I don't know the address. He's twenty eight years old and lives alone. He's been seeing a shrink for a couple of years because of his problem with women."

Shit, Stone thought. Maybe this is something.

"Run down Black's description," Stone asked.

"Dark hair, mustache, about five eleven, maybe one eighty."

"Okay, look, in case I need to follow up on this, it's best if we have your name. I won't put it in the report and it will be between us."

"No dice, Sergeant. Oh, by the way, I think his shrink is a Doctor Frieden over on Seventh Street. I don't know why I know. Maybe he said something once. I don't know. Good luck," the phone went dead.

"What do you have, Jim?" Wayne asked.

"Another name to eliminate."

Stone picked up his Pacific Bell yellow pages and turned to the psychiatrist section. "See Physicians and Surgeons," so he thumbed back to the physician section. He found psychiatry and followed the list down.

"Shit, no Frieden," Stone muttered to himself. "Not even one close," He turned to the psychologist section and again scanned the names. Again no luck.

"Damn, maybe the asshole had the name wrong. Now I'm talking to myself. I'm going to need a shrink myself. Seventh Street. Seventh Street," as he scanned the list. His fingers stopped walking when they came to a Seventh Street address. FREVELE, Robert. Licensed psychologist. Stone copied down the phone number and sat looking at his notes, shrugged, and picked up the phone.

"Dr. Frevele's office," the phone was answered on the first ring.

"I'm Sergeant Stone, Sacramento County Sheriff's Office. I'm working a case that the doctor may be able to help me on. I know there's a confidentiality issue, but if I could I would like to talk to the doctor."

"He's with a patient right now, but he should be through in about fifteen minutes. I'm sure he would be happy to talk to you, Sergeant. If you'll give me your phone number, I'll call you as soon as he's free."

"That would be fine. I'll be here for about an hour if you could have him call," Stone gave his number to the secretary and hung up.

Ten minutes later Stone's phone rang and he picked it up on the first ring. "Sergeant Stone, Robbery, Homicide."

"Sgt. Stone, this is Doctor Frevele. I believe you called."

"I did. Thanks for calling me back. I'm working a case and a name was given to me that you may have had contact with. I was hoping you could confirm it and maybe give me some insight."

"Well, I might be able to help. You realize of course that my hands are tied to a certain extent. What is the person's name?"

"Vaughn Black.."

"Yes, I have seen Mr. Black. Interesting gentleman. What did Mr. Black do? Or can you tell me?"

"Well, I don't know if he did anything but I received an anonymous call that he might have raped someone."

"Oh, dear. I've been seeing Mr. Black off and on for about four years. Maybe you should meet me here in the office, Sergeant. I'm free from 10:45 until 11:30 if that's convenient?"

"10:45 is fine. I'll see you then. Thank you, Doctor," although Stone tried to keep his hopes down, his pulse quickened as he hung up the phone and leaned back in his chair.

At 10:30, Stone parked his county car in front of the Seventh Street address. He entered the plush office and approached the receptionist, a thirtyish redhead with a figure that made the office dull in comparison.

"Sgt. Stone to see Dr. Frevele," Stone made every effort to keep his eyes from straying from the dark blue eyes to other parts of the receptionist's well endowed body. The receptionist seemed to find great pleasure in holding his gaze on her eyes.

"Oh, yes, Sergeant. The doctor will be with you shortly. He is still with a patient. Can I get you a cup of coffee?"

Coffee was the last thing he needed, but the desire to watch her walk across the room was stronger than his promise to cut down on his caffeine intake. "Black, please."

He watched as she moved from her desk, her short skirt barely covering his imagination. A short time later he watched as she moved toward him with a cup of coffee. As she bent forward to hand him his coffee, all he could do was try to keep his hand from shaking as he reached out, his fingers touching hers as he took the cup from her hand. Still in a world of dreams as she turned to go back to her desk, he thoughtlessly raised the cup to his lips as his eyes followed the long, beautiful legs. His mind returned to reality as he took a mouthful of coffee. Hot coffee. Coffee that scalded his mouth. She turned to face him as she slid into her chair, just as his eyes filled with tears. It's tough looking cool with a mouthful of hot coffee, tears of pain, and no place to spit.

The roof of his mouth was still raw and paining and his thoughts were no longer on the receptionist when the door to the doctor's office opened.

"Sergeant Stone?" Stone looked up to see a balding fiftyish male smiling at him.

"Why don't you come into my office and I'll see what I can do for you. Would you like some more coffee?"

Stone shook his head and raised his cup as if to say he was well taken care of. In reality, he was afraid to try to speak. He wasn't sure his voice would work yet. He followed the doctor into a room filled with leather furniture and sat in an overstuffed chair that the doctor pointed out to him.

"Sgt. Stone, I'm Doctor Frevele," he reached out to shake Stone's hand. "What can I do for you?"

"Well, I don't know, really. I'm working some rape cases and your patient's name was given to me as a possible responsible. I was hoping you could give me some insight as to the type of person I'm looking at. Understand, he's not a suspect at this time, just a name. As a matter of fact, one of many given to us by concerned citizens."

"Well, I want to cooperate as best I can, so you must understand that anything I tell you is strictly off the record."

"No problem"

"I've been treating Vaughn Black for approximately four years. He's a schizophrenic and has had problems in the past relating to women. I think we have overcome that problem. Lately he's been extremely hyperactive and agitated; however, this does not alarm me at this time. He has no deep seated hostility toward women and to be honest, if he had any thoughts of rape, he would have discussed it with me. No, I can say in all confidence that Mr. Black is not a rapist. A disturbed young man, but not a rapist."

"Thanks, Doctor. I'm sure you're right, but for the record, could I have his address?"

"Certainly. I'll have my receptionist get it for you. Good luck finding your man, Sergeant. I've read about your case in the paper. He seems dangerous."

"He is. Very. Thanks again for your help."

If she had noticed his predicament with the hot coffee, she was professional enough not to laugh at him as she handed him a piece of paper with Black's address. "Here you are, Sergeant."

"Thanks. 'Bye now." Another name added to the growing list of possible suspects. A list that would grow into the thousands over the next few years as names would be checked and eliminated.

Stone drove back to his office, his mind on Vaughn Black. A gut feeling that most cops acquire after a few years on the job told him that Black was not his man. He would still go through the motions of elimination, but the excitement of the hunt was no longer there.

A cop worth his salt could look at someone and know whether that person was "dirty," but the courts had been very clear in telling cops they couldn't act on gut feelings. Because of that, many of society's dregs continued to walk the streets preying on innocent victims.

Greg was just hanging up his coat when Stone walked in.

"How'd it go, Jim?"

"A dud. I'll check it out further, but doesn't look like our man. At least the good doctor assures me that he is not a rapist."

"Well, stand by. The nuts are coming out of the woodwork. I've been on the phone for the last forty-five minutes talking to a woman who says her ex is the rapist. Says in 1975 she saw him loading his car with rifles and handguns. Says he got real angry when she confronted him. He told her he was going to L.A. and Santa Clara to get a job. Says he was only gone a couple of days and came back with a bunch of expensive engagement rings. Told her he got them from the janitor at the high school. She says the rings disappeared a couple of days later. Anyway, she says he tried to molest her ten year old sister and ten year old cousin. Showed them pictures of sexual intercourse and asked them if they wanted to see how it felt. She kicked his ass out. One interesting thing. She says he was a reserve deputy with us. Had a full uniform, scanner, and a large spot light. Said he would leave the house to ride with our patrol deputies. I checked. No record of him being with us in any capacity."

"How long ago did this happen?" Stone asked.

"She kicked him out a year ago and according to her, he was still a reserve."

"We better take a look at him. You never know. She give you an address?"

"He's not our man, Jim. The wife says when he gets aroused he's got a big dick. Says that's the only good thing about him."

"Lucky him. Does that eliminate him as a cop or a rapist?"

"Yeah. Had another one earlier. Mother called and said her son was the rapist. Eighteen year old with a lisp and a below normal mentality. Her IQ wasn't much better."

"We better get lucky pretty quick, Greg. He hasn't missed a month so he's due again. I don't know if it's a schedule he's on or if it just looks that way," Stone mused.

Chapter Eighteen

FOR THE PAST THREE WEEKS fifteen year old Nancy Hauser had been receiving hang-up phone calls. All the calls had been in the evening, possibly from a boy from school, too shy to start up a conversation. Boys don't mature as fast as girls and sometimes their games border on childishness. Then sometimes it's not immature young boys.

Christmas was only a week away. A festive mood prevailed throughout the Sacramento area and only a few really feared the rapist who had attacked nine times since June. Only the victims and their families knew how much terror they could endure.

Nancy Hauser's parents left to attend a Christmas party at 6:15 p.m. Nancy Hauser, ill with a cold, remained at home.

Darkness arrived three days before the longest night of the year and the dark shadow scaling the fences in the quiet Fair Oaks neighborhood dropped noiselessly onto the soft grass of the Hausers' neighbor's yard. Soft piano music drifted from Nancy Hauser's house as a masked figure pushed on the common fence between the two yards. The fence gave way under the dark figure's weight and slowly fell over, making a sharp cracking sound in the still darkness. The figure remained motionless as the piano music ceased to permeate the backyard, then, as music resumed, moved slowly toward the house and the music.

Nancy Hauser enjoyed playing the piano and as her fingers effortlessly moved across the keyboard, she hummed as she played: "Hear Comes Santa Claus, Here Comes Santa Claus..." A noise from outside caught her attention and she stopped playing. Listening, she calmed herself. She always heard noises when she was home alone. She started playing again, ignoring the sound, once again lost in her music.

A sound to her left caused her to turn. She felt the knife at her throat almost before she focused on the masked intruder.

"Make a move and I'll kill you," he hissed. "Do you have any money in the house? You better not lie to me."

"No," she was able to whisper.

"When are your parents coming back? You better tell me so I'll know how much time I have."

"I don't know."

"Get up," he ordered through clenched teeth. "Get moving. If you say anything or flinch, I'll push this knife all the way in and I will be gone in the dark of the night."

She felt herself being pushed toward the door leading to the garage. She saw him remove cord from his pocket and felt her hands being tied behind her back. Again she was being pushed, through the garage and into the backyard.

"You'll be okay, I won't hurt you. I'm going to tie you to a post. If you try and look at me I'll kill you."

He pushed her onto a picnic table and tied her ankles together. She saw him remove cloth from his pocket and tried to struggle as he forced it into her mouth.

"If you flinch or move, I'll kill you," she stopped struggling and a second piece of cloth was tied around her head, covering her eyes. "I'll be watching you every ten seconds from the window," she heard him enter the house through the door leading into the den and heard him opening and closing cupboards.

"Oh, damn," she heard him mutter several times.

"Have you ever fucked a guy?" His voice startled her.

"No."

"You better not be lying to me or I'll kill you. Have you ever felt a guy's dick? I want you to play with mine."

She felt his penis in her hands and she knew he was naked as he pushed his penis back and forth until she felt a wet and sticky substance in her hands.

He pulled her to her feet and she felt her pants being unzipped and pulled down to her ankles. The chill she felt was from fear of what she knew was going to happen, not from the cold evening air. His hand was under her blouse and she felt the knife cut through her bra. She stood helplessly as her blouse was torn from her body.

"8P6...10-63. A 261 just occurred," The dispatcher's voice broke the stillness. Deputy George White felt a wave of both fear and anger as he reached for his radio mike. The rapes had been the topic at patrol line up and he knew before he answered that this was the bastard.

"8P6, 10-4," and he waited for the address.

Stone and Wayne were sitting in their car in the Citrus Heights area when they heard the call go out to the patrol unit. They too felt the anger, knowing that once again, they had lost.

"Son of a bitch," Stone yelled in frustration as he drove toward the scene of the tenth attack.

As Stone and Wayne arrived they saw that two deputies and a patrol sergeant were already on the scene. Sergeant Poplin was just leaving the residence and contacted Stone.

"Hi, Jim. Greg. Merry Christmas."

"Same to you, Frank. What've we got?" Stone asked.

"Looks like our man again. Young fifteen year old home alone. Ski mask, white shoelaces, knife, and rape. She's in with her parents and White is getting a statement. Pretty shook up but holding up so far."

"You been over the scene, Frank?"

"Yeah. Ransacked. Don't know yet if anything is missing. Fence is pushed down in the backyard and the girl's clothes are in the neighbor's yard. Told the neighbors not to touch anything until the techs get here. I had Radio call them. As soon as White gets a prelim, the parents will take her to the med center. I'll have Anderson meet them there to collect the clothes and rape kit. I've got four units in the area and one knocking on doors for you. Want to take a walk through?"

"We better. Got a name?"

"Last name is Hauser. I didn't get a first."

Stone and Wayne followed Poplin into the house. As soon as he entered, Stone could again feel the presence of the rapist. It was such a strong feeling that Stone felt if he ever came across the rapist in the shopping mall, he would know him. Other investigators would get the same feeling over the coming years.

"Hi, Sarge," White greeted Stone. "I'm ready to let them leave for the hospital. You want me to go with them, Frank, or stay here?"

"Why don't you stay here. I'll have Anderson meet them there. You can run the scene down to Jim and Greg and show the techs through when they get here."

"Okay. Mr. and Mrs. Hauser, Nancy, this is Sgt Stone and Detective Wayne. They're the detectives that will be working with you," Stone and Wayne shook hands with the parents and nodded at Nancy, who remained seated at the table.

"I'm sorry we have to meet like this," Stone offered. What can you say at a time like this? "I'm sure Deputy White explained what needs to be done. I'll meet you at the hospital and go over some things with you. I need to check here first but a deputy will meet you there," Stone watched as the young girl and her parents left the house.

"God damn it, Greg. How does a young girl like that ever shut something like this out of her mind?"

"I don't think she ever does, Jim."

"Well, that shoots down our theory that he only rapes women with long hair. She's the first one with hair above her shoulders," Stone noted.

"Yeah, I noticed that, too," Wayne responded.

"May not mean anything, but all the pictures of her show her with long hair. There's quite a few of them around the house," White interjected, "And her picture hanging on the wall in the hall was moved according to the parents."

"I wonder when she got it cut?" Stone wondered aloud.

"Okay, George, what do we have so far?" Stone began.

"Well," White began, "the parents left the house around six fifteen this evening to go to a Christmas party. The daughter hadn't been feeling too well all day so she stayed home. Nancy put a pizza in the oven and was playing the piano when she heard a noise outside. She didn't think too much about it and continued playing. The next thing she knew she had a knife at her throat. Said she saw he was wearing a dark jacket and a dark red ski mask. Says he was about six feet tall, regular build. Kept telling her he would kill her if she didn't do what he wanted. He tied her hands and took her into the backyard. Said he had the white shoelaces in his jacket pocket. Odd thing, Jim, it seems he took the shoelaces from the older sister's tennis shoes so he must have been in the house for awhile before he contacted her."

"Or he was in the house before and set it up," Stone replied.

"Yeah, could be. One thing's for sure. The bastard has balls."

"Yeah, maybe somebody will castrate the asshole," Stone replied.

"Tied her to a post," White continued, "on the patio and had her lie on the picnic table. She said he had her masturbate him with her hands tied behind her back and then he took her in the house and raped her on the parents' bed. Took her back and forth three times and raped her three times, once on the bed and twice in the family room. He turned on the gas fireplace and put a knife to her throat and made her tell him she liked it."

"Real romantic," Wayne growled.

"I guess. We found her clothes in the neighbor's backyard. No idea why he threw them there. You can see where he entered the yard. Pushed the fence down instead of going over it for some unknown reason. You can see a tennis shoe print on a piece of the wood, Zigzag pattern. Couple of other things. We found a white shoelace hanging from a tree in the neighbor's yard and the Hausers say that he moved the living room furniture. Maybe it was to give a better escape route. I don't know. Nancy said he always spoke in a loud whisper and tried to sound tough. About the masturbation, he must have used some type of lotion because she could smell it on her hands."

"How did we get the call?" Stone asked.

"She was able to dial her neighbor and told them she had been raped. They came over and cut her free. The neighbor daughter is the same age as Nancy, so maybe he was watching both of them. Both kids have been getting hang-up phone calls for the last three weeks. You've got some brown and black shoelaces and pieces of torn towel on the family room floor and a strip of towel in the bathroom. The parents didn't have time to check to see if anything was missing, and I didn't want them to disturb anything. They'll make a list later and give us a call."

"Okay, George, I think the techs just arrived so we're going to head for the hospital. Good job," Stone and Wayne turned to leave.

"One more thing, Jim."

"Yeah?"

"She was a virgin."

"Hell of a way to become a woman," Wayne shook his head.

"Son of a bitch deserves to die," White added.

Stone and Wayne parked near the emergency entrance at the Sacramento Medical Center. Stone showed his badge to the woman at the counter. "I'm looking for a couple and their daughter, the Hausers. Should have arrived about forty-five minutes ago. Should be a deputy here also."

"The deputy is at the nurse's station and the daughter is still with the doctor. The parents are in the cafeteria. Do you want me to get the nurse for you?" she asked.

"No, that's all right. We'll talk to the parents for awhile. Thanks. Let the deputy know where we are if you would," Stone started toward the cafeteria.

"It's him, isn't it?"

"I beg your pardon?" Stone turned back to the lady.

"It's him. The rapist the paper wrote about. The one with the mask."

"We're not sure yet," Stone shrugged his shoulders.

"Poor girl. Such a pretty little thing. It just isn't right, a little girl like that."

Stone and Wayne walked to the cafeteria in silence, each deep in his own thoughts.

Chapter Eighteen

The Hausers were sitting at a table looking at their full coffee cups, not talking. Their red, swollen eyes showed that their inner thoughts were similar.

"Mr. and Mrs. Hauser," Stone interrupted their thoughts.

"Hello, Sergeant, Detective. I guess Nancy will be with the doctor for a little longer," Ted Hauser beckoned to the empty chairs at their table. "Elizabeth and I have just been trying to figure out why it happened and what we should have done. We should never have left Nancy alone."

"I know it's hard to do, but you can't blame yourselves. Rape Crisis people will be talking to Nancy and I think you might benefit from them, also. I know this is a tough time, but I have to ask you some questions," Stone knew this was the hardest time for them.

"We understand. Nancy didn't want her mother with her while she was with the doctor. She said she would be too embarrassed," Tears started to well in Ted Hauser's eyes as his wife placed a hand on his arm. "It's all my fault. All I could think of was the Christmas party. I should never have left her alone. She's only fifteen years old and I wasn't there when she needed me."

"Ted, you can't blame yourself. It's a terrible thing, but it's not your fault," his wife gently squeezed his arm.

"I know you feel bad, Mr. Hauser, but your wife is right. You couldn't prevent it. Maybe tonight you could have, but not tomorrow or the next night. We don't know why he picked your house or why he picked Nancy. All we know is, he did pick your house. It wasn't just random. If he didn't succeed tonight, he would have tried tomorrow, or the next day. It wasn't your fault. It wasn't Nancy's fault."

"I know. It's just so hard to deal with. I'm sorry. You wanted to ask some questions?"

"Have you noticed anything different lately? Any strange cars in the neighborhood, noises in the backyard? Anything that may be different?" Stone asked.

"No, I don't think so. At least I haven't. Have you, Elizabeth?"

"No, I don't think so. We have been getting a lot of hang-up phone calls lately. For the last three weeks, we have been getting three or four a night. Nancy seems to think it was one of her friends from school, a boy who might be a little shy. We won't let her date yet, but you can't stop the boys from calling. I guess there's a lot of things you can't stop, isn't there, Sergeant?" She still had lots of tears left and was unable to hold them back.

"We have reason to believe that the person who attacked Nancy has done it in the past. We think he is the one that the newspaper has written about. There are a lot of similarities. We need you to go through your things at home to see if anything is missing or moved. Jewelry, money, anything. Here's my card and I want you to call me if you have any questions or anything you think might help."

"I'll go through the house in the morning," Hauser stated.

"By the way, I noticed Nancy's pictures show her with long hair. When did she get it cut?" Stone asked.

"Two weeks ago. Why? Does it have anything to do with this?" Mrs. Hauser asked.

"Probably not. We're just trying to cover all the bases," Stone shrugged and looked at Wayne.

Stone looked up to see Nancy Hauser enter the cafeteria with Gretchen Mitchell, the nurse he had met the last time he was here with Heather Williams, the sixth victim. Funny, they all eventually become a number. You don't forget their faces or names, but they all get a number.

As the two approached the table, Gretchen smiled. "Hello, Jim."

"Hi, Gretchen, Nancy," Stone stood up to offer them a chair.

Greg Wayne stared at them as if to say, "Jim, Gretchen? How do you two know each other?"

Stone ignored him. "Nancy, I know you're tired and have probably talked all you want to tonight. I need to sit down with you and go over some things. Maybe Monday if you feel up to it."

"Okay. I'm going to Bible camp Tuesday and I'll be gone for two weeks," she looked at her mother as if to say, "Can I still go?"

Mrs. Hauser gave her a light nod to let her know it was all right.

"Okay. I gave your dad my card so if you need me for anything, just call that number and tell Dispatch you need to talk to me. If you think of anything, just write it down so you won't forget. Things will come to you when you don't expect it and that's normal. I'm sorry this all happened, Nancy. We'll do everything we can to catch him."

Stone and Wayne shook hands with the family and watched them leave.

Stone turned to Gretchen. "Well, Gretchen, this is getting to be a bad habit, meeting this way," Stone grinned.

"Yes. There are other things, you know," she grinned back.

Wayne just looked at them.

"You remember my partner, Greg?" Stone asked.

CHAPTER EIGHTEEN

"Sure. Hi, Greg."

"I think I'm missing something here," Greg looked from one to the other. "I didn't know you two knew each other."

"Old friends," Stone smiled at Gretchen. "What did the doctor find out?"

"Well, she was attacked, all right. Trauma and slight bleeding, but something strange," Gretchen responded.

"What's that?"

"She was a virgin and there was sexual intercourse, penetration, but her hymen is still intact."

"What exactly does that tell us?" Wayne asked.

"Well, it probably means that he was under-endowed, at least lengthwise," she answered.

"Well, that fits anyway," Stone looked at Wayne.

Gretchen glanced from Stone to Wayne with a questioning look on her face.

"All the victims have said that he does have a small penis. Very small. Guess they were right," Stone explained.

"What do you say we call it a night, Jim?" Wayne remarked. "Nothing more we can do now and I doubt if our boy is going to hit again tonight."

"Yeah, you're right."

"The short hair, do you think the son of a bitch had been in the house and saw the picture before tonight?" Wayne asked.

"I don't know. I think he had been in the house. I just don't know if he goes after long hair or it's just a coincidence. Anything's possible. Maybe he was after the neighbor girl and because the parents were home, he went after this one instead. We need to talk to the neighbor, but why a fifteen year old? Why rape? Shit, there's enough of it being given away out there," Stone mused.

"Yeah, if we had the answers we could bottle them and make a fortune. Even shrinks don't have the answers."

The Sacramento Bee, 12-30-76

Sacramento County Sheriff's Department officers are investigating the possibility that the rape of a fifteen year old girl December 18 was committed by the same man referred to as the "East Area Rapist."

According to Sheriff's reports, the rapes occurred in the northeast area of the county.

The Dec. 18 rape occurred in the early evening, while the others took place in the late evening or early morning hours, said Will Tillis, information officer.

But "The MO (method of operation) to some degree fits the East Area Rapist," Tillis said. "He is a suspect."

However, Tillis declined to give out any other information, saying that too much publicity would hamper the investigation.

"He [the rapist] is not going to quit. If there is a lot of publicity, he will go underground for awhile and then rape someone else. More women are going to be raped before this guy is caught," Tillis said.

The last known attack by the East Area Rapist occurred in October.

CHAPTER NINETEEN

THE SACRAMENTO COUNTY SHERIFF'S DEPARTMENT Investigation Division, as with most law enforcement agencies, functioned at half-staff over Christmas and New Years. Crimes were dealt with, however, the most serious received the attention of the investigators, and even these were only given basic contacts.

For the next two weeks, a festive mood would prevail, the seriousness of "the job" forgotten as individual officers' thoughts turned toward their families. All except Sergeant Jim Stone. The thoughts of the masked rapist would never again be far from his thoughts. Yet this holiday season, even Jim Stone didn't realize how intense these thoughts would become over the ensuing years.

January 19, 1977. 0830 hrs.

"Jim," Lt. Mike Burns called from his office.

Stone looked up from his stack of papers listing suspects who had been eliminated as the East Area Rapist.

"You better come in here."

Stone slid his chair away from his desk, glanced at the papers spread over his desk, shook his head, and walked toward Burns' office.

"Yeah, Mike?"

"Just got off the phone with the P.D. Our man hit them last night. Raped a twenty-five year old Oriental and stole her car."

"God damn it! Why didn't they call us? I've been working with their detectives for the last two weeks. I've given them everything I had and they were supposed to call me if they got a hit," Stone stood, shaking his head in disgust.

"Well, you know how things go haywire when the shit hits the fan. Anyway, why don't you go on over and see what they have."

"Okay. They say what time he hit?"

"Yeah, around eleven last night. Stayed in the house for about four hours. Must be terrifying for a woman to have that son of a bitch terrorize them like that."

At eleven a.m., Stone and Wayne met with Detective Sergeant Brian Fallow at the Sacramento Police Department. They learned that the victim had been home alone as her husband was out of town on business.

"Well, Jim," Fallow started, "looks pretty much like the ones you're working on. The victim said she was sleeping and for some reason sensed someone in the room. Said she opened her eyes and saw a bright light shining in her face. She asked who was there and he told her all he wanted was her money and he would leave. He tied her hands behind her back and blindfolded her. Raped her twice and ransacked the place. He took some of her jewelry, some money, and a digital clock."

"Did she get a look at him?" Stone asked.

"Not much. Figures he was a white male, five foot eleven, one eighty, ski mask pulled down to his neck. She can't remember if it had holes for the eyes and mouth or if it was open. He was wearing polyester pants that he never took off, leather gloves, and a light jacket. She can't remember the colors."

"How'd he get in?" Wayne asked.

"Broke a small hole in one of the windows facing the backyard, removed a wooden dowel, and slid the window open. Oh, by the way, the woman is five months pregnant. She told him but it didn't seem to make any difference to him."

"Nothing seems to matter to the asshole," Stone fumed.

"I don't know if this is part of his M.O. or not, but he cut her picture out of a photograph she had of her and her husband and took it, also."

"No, that's a new one. What did he use to tie her with?"

"Electric cords he cut up. He also cut all the phone lines and for some reason took a bunch of knives into the living room and broke the blades on some of them. Strange."

"What about the rape? Anything out of the ordinary?"

"Yeah. She said when he was standing in the bedroom she heard a popping noise. He asked her what it sounded like. She told him it was a can of spray paint he was shaking. He told her to keep guessing. She said he got real mad and told her to keep guessing. She realized he was massaging his penis with some kind of lubricant. He put it in her hands and told her to massage it. Rolled her over and got on top of her and told her to put her legs up around his back like she does with her husband."

"The lubricant and masturbation fits his M.O. She say anything about the size of his cock?" Stone asked.

"Yeah. I remembered you said all the victims mentioned he was small. She says he was large compared to her husband. About five inches, she said. He also tried to get her to copulate him. Told her not to bite or he'd kill her. Matter of fact, he told her several times during the night he would slash her or cut her up. Says she heard the garage door open and her car start up. She got her feet untied and ran to her neighbors. They called us."

"Find the car yet?"

"Nope."

"You will. Won't be far from the house. I can't figure this bastard out and it's driving me nuts. What hospital did you take her to?" Stone asked.

"Kaiser. I'll get a copy of the doctor's report to you along with a copy of our reports."

"Thanks."

"We've got a team out canvassing the area. Maybe... .," Fallow let the comment drop.

"Yeah," Stone and Wayne shook hands with Fallow and left.

The Sacramento Police Department's canvass of the victim's neighborhood located nothing that would help locate the suspect. It did, however, uncover information leading investigators to believe that the rapist had been prowling the area for several days and had been seen by several people.

At approximately five p.m., the victim's vehicle was located within the apartment complex on Great Falls Way, a few blocks away. The vehicle was locked and the keys were missing. A tennis shoe impression was located nearby. Nothing else of value was noted.

One week prior to the attack a neighbor had seen a prowler wearing dark clothing, peering into a window. He called the police department and reported it as a possible burglar. He stated no police cars came to his residence nor did he observe any in the area.

On January 12, 1977, a woman saw a white male, early twenties, in her front yard. The next evening someone removed the light bulb from her porch light. She did not report it to the police.

January 21, detectives received a call from a female who lived near the victim. She related that the night of the rape, she had been a victim of a prowler around eight thirty. She heard a dog barking and looked out her front window. She saw a male subject walk toward her side gate. She went into her garage to make sure her doors were locked. She looked through the side garage window and saw the person in her side yard looking at her house. When the subject saw her, he immediately ran off and jumped her back fence. She described him as approximately thirty-five years old, five eleven, one seventy-five, medium build, and extremely agile and fast. She felt his hair was blondish and noted he was under-dressed for the cold weather, as he was wearing a light wind-breaker and dark pants.

She stated she had called the police, however, they told her they weren't interested if the prowler had already left. When she heard about the rape, she didn't call the police because she was upset about their attitude.

She was subsequently taken to the Hall of Justice where she viewed the Miracode Photo System. She picked out eight photos that were similar looking to the prowler. None proved out.

CHAPTER TWENTY

CALLS INTO THE SACRAMENTO SHERIFF'S DEPARTMENT investigation increased one-hundred fold as paranoia reached more and more of Sacramento's citizenry. Some calls seemed promising, at least temporarily until an investigator worked the lead to elimination. Some simply added some much needed levity into an otherwise somber investigation.

Stone looked at his watch. Eleven fifty-five in the morning. "Time for lunch," he thought as he reached for a cigarette as his phone started ringing.

"Sergeant Stone," he stated.

"Yes. I know who the rapist is," the female voice on the other end began.

"Which rapist, ma'am?"

"You know, the one the T.V. described. The east area one."

"Oh. Tell me what you know," Stone continued.

"I don't know his name but I know where he lives. He's about thirty years old and he walks from place to place and he wears rubber milk boots all the time."

Stone took the phone from his ear and looked at it in amazement.

"Milk boots?" He knew he should hang up and go to lunch, but he continued.

"Yes. His father is a Seventh Day Adventist minister. One day one of the other minister's wife came home and found her bra and panties on the doorknob and a note that said he was going to rape her. He was committed to a hospital right after that, and when he got out he moved to Napa with a family. Well, the wife called a friend here in Sacramento and said that she and this fellow are having a wonderful relationship. She says after her husband goes to bed they go down into the basement and pray together."

"Pray together?" Stone wondered where this was going to end. "Why do you think this person is the rapist?"

"Well, the newscaster described the rapist and when he did I could tell he was describing this man and he did leave a note saying he wanted to rape a woman."

"Well, thanks for calling and we will surely look into this. I don't suppose you want to give me your name? I mean, you don't have to."

"I'd rather not."

"I don't blame you. I mean, I understand. 'Bye now," Stone hung up.

"Fucking nuts. I'm surrounded by fucking nuts. Those that should call, don't. Those that shouldn't, fucking do."

On January 24, 1977 a Citrus Heights neighborhood in the unincorporated area of Sacramento, a lone twenty-five year old female was awakened by a masked intruder grabbing her shoulders.

Although she was raped twice over a one and a half hour period, she felt that the rapist had not climaxed. She described her attacker, who smelled of body odor, as a thirty to forty year old white male with a very slender four or five inch penis.

As in previous rapes, the victim was asked to describe what she thought he was doing when he lubricated his penis and masturbated. He did not seem interested in her body as he only briefly lifted her gown to expose her breasts.

After rummaging through the house, the rapist left after drinking two cans of beer and eating the victim's food. During the incident, the rapist used the victim's first name several times.

Responding deputies found the victim tightly bound and still blindfolded after she had managed to call the telephone operator. She told the deputies that the rapist seemed very angry and several times had threatened to stab her with an ice pick he placed against her neck.

As in other attacks, numerous tennis shoe impressions were located in neighbors' yards and the victim's side gate was left ajar. Entry was made either through the sliding glass door or the door leading from the garage into the house. Both had been pried.

Two prime suspects were eliminated as being the rapist when detectives immediately responded to their residences and confirmed that they had been home all evening. A third suspect was also eliminated when detectives responded to his work place and learned he had been at work since midnight with three other employees.

A bloodhound brought to the victim's residence followed a scent for two blocks, indicating that the attacker had a vehicle parked at that location.

Sacramento Bee, 1-24-77

Rapist Strikes Again. Twelfth Time In Fifteen Months.

The so-called East Area Rapist attacked and raped a young woman resident of the Madison Avenue-Sunrise Boulevard area early today in the twelfth assault attributed to the man in the last fifteen months.

"It was exactly the same as all the rest," said a sheriff's detective.

Officers said the rapist gained entrance to the twenty-five year old woman's home shortly after midnight, bound her with rope and raped her "several times."

The woman told officers she was asleep when the man entered her home, apparently through an unlocked door. Because it was dark, she was not able to provide a full description of her attacker. However, she did say he threatened her with an ice pick. She also said he wore gloves—as the suspect has in most of the other attacks in the east area of the county and city dating back to October, 1975.

Officers said the victim is separated from her husband and was home alone. In other attacks, the rapist always has struck when the women, most of them married, were alone in the early morning hours.

It was the second attack by the man within a week. Last Wednesday morning a rapist forced his way into the home of a pregnant woman.

Sheriff's officials have assigned six detectives to the investigation full-time. City police have three detectives working full-time on their case.

Following the assault in the city last week, police and sheriff's detectives met to coordinate the search. According to authorities, the rapist always has struck between eleven p.m. and six forty-five a.m. Detectives say there are indications some of the victims' homes were watched before the attacks.

January 25, 1977 at 8:20 p.m., the Sacramento Sheriff's Department received a call from Dick Cable, the newscaster for KXTV Channel 10, a Sacramento television station. Cable advised that the television station switchboard operator received an anonymous phone call from a male subject stating that the East Area Rapist was a Jack Neal. The subject immediately hung up. No information of any kind could be located on a Jack Neal by the investigators.

On January 26, 1977, three two-man teams made up of Sacramento police and sheriff's detectives were given the task of contacting the twenty-three pawn shops in the city and county areas of Sacramento in an attempt to locate the missing jewelry taken during the rapes. By January 28th detectives had exhausted all leads.

On January 28th, Stone and Wayne contacted Dr. Jutz of the Sacramento Medical Center Crisis Clinic, to get a personality profile of the East Area Rapist. Stone gave Dr. Jutz a flow chart of the rapist's activities and discussed the cases.

Based on Dr. Jutz' prior knowledge and statistical data compiled on known rapists, the detectives obtained their first psychological profile.

"Well," Dr. Jutz began as he leaned back in his easy chair and looked across his expansive desk at the two detectives. "I believe I can give you some pretty basic and fairly accurate characteristics of the man you're looking for. For starters, it's pretty safe to say he's a loner and it would be unlikely he would work in a group or even with another person."

"We felt that, also," Stone interjected. "That's been a problem in catching him. If no one is close to him, then he won't be talking to anyone about the rapes and we don't hear from a snitch."

"Precisely," Jutz continued. "I see him as very methodical and ritualistic in his crime patterns. Although we see some differences, he still basically follows a plan. When he is forced to deviate from the plan, he tends to lose it and, as you show on your chart, will abandon his attack altogether. I think you will find he is immature, insecure, and, from a legal standpoint, probably a mentally disordered sex offender."

"You mean he's been arrested for some type of sex crime?" Wayne asked.

"No, not necessarily, although he may have been arrested for prowling or as a peeping tom as a juvenile," Jutz replied. "He probably has no normal relationships and feels uncomfortable in sexual relationships. The rape itself is probably more to relieve than it is to have sex. When he must concentrate on sex only, he seems incapable of doing so. That's why we have the leaving, returning, and focusing his attention on other things. He probably has had some homosexual experiences. Distant from his father—never close, and a mother who has been married several times. He is potentially violent and if pushed too far will probably revert to violence. He appears to be remorseful after a crime and consciously or unconsciously wants to be caught. I would say he masturbates a lot to relieve tension and would be the type to frequent massage parlors or adult bookstores. If he is caught, he will be suicidal and probably would confess if he were questioned. That, gentlemen, is it in a nutshell, figuratively and literally speaking."

"Well, that part is for sure, he is a nut. Now if you can give us a name," Stone shrugged and made a face.

"I wish I could," Dr. Jutz stood and extended his hand to indicate that the meeting was over.

"Well, what do you think?" Stone asked when he and Wayne were outside.

"Interesting, but I don't believe the crap about him wanting to get caught. For some reason, these shrinks think everybody wants to get caught. Bullshit. The son of a bitch enjoys it too much."

Detectives and patrol deputies with the Sacramento Sheriff's Department were well aware that all the rapes were committed by the same man. They knew they were dealing with a serial rapist. The problem was that there were no real studies done on serial rapists. General profiles dealt with the psychological make-up of a rapist with no distinction between a one-time rapist and one who raped and raped and terrorized and raped.

Did a serial rapist evolve from the promiscuous sixties? From the enlightened seventies?

It was not until the 1980s that real in-depth studies, studies conducted through one-on-one contacts with convicted serial rapists, would provide findings that would enable law enforcement officers the ability to enter the mind of a serial rapist. The conclusions formed by the detectives after investigating the East Area Rapist were amazingly close to the conclusions formed after the in-depth studies by teams of psychiatrists and other experts. One in-depth study concluded that 68 percent of the serial rapists studied had begun with window peeping while in adolescence. Over 95 percent chose their victims, not by physical characteristics, rather by availability, and the victim in 80 to 90percent of the rapes were strangers to the rapists.

Sergeant Stone had a firm belief that the East Area Rapist spent many hours, sometimes many days, searching neighborhoods for his victims. Outside activities that were obviously associated with Sacramento's serial rapist were presented by detectives to all the patrol deputies at their line-ups. Deputies were told to watch for strange cars in their neighborhoods as the bloodhounds would lose the scent within blocks of the attacks. They were told to watch for suspicious males walking in neighborhoods, listen for barking dogs, and watch for the one thing that remained consistent throughout the many rapes over the coming years—open side gates. For some reason never understood, EAR would open side gates and leave them open.

Because of the newspaper articles the calls to the Sacramento County Sheriff's department had doubled and then tripled. Some were legitimate leads from citizens who had become more and more paranoid. Most were from good citizens who would never really fully understand life as it had become. And then there were those who, seeing a man in the mall who looked like a rapist or who saw someone drive by them on the freeway who looked suspicious, would call the hot line phone number or the "Secret Witness" phone number in the hopes of collecting the $2,500 reward.

CHAPTER TWENTY-ONE

"**SERGEANT STONE,** line one is for you," the Division secretary called.

"Sergeant Stone, can I help you?"

"Yes, Sergeant. I've been reading about the rapist you're looking for and I have some information you might be interested in," the female voice replied. "It happened over a week ago. I believe it was December twentieth."

"What happened, ma'am?"

"Well, around two or two-thirty in the morning, I was stopped at a stop sign at Oakcrest and Dewey Drive. I looked to the left to check traffic and saw a person wearing dark clothing and a ski mask crawling on his hands and knees toward the front door of a residence. I checked to the right for traffic and when I looked back to the left, he was standing next to my car knocking on my window."

"Was he still wearing the mask?" Stone asked.

"Yes. It scared me, I mean, really scared me, so I drove off real fast. I slowed down and watched out my rearview mirror and saw him go to some bushes and pull a bicycle out. He got on it and started toward me so I drove off real fast."

"Did you report this to anyone at the time?" Stone asked, his pulse beginning to quicken.

"Yes, when I got home I told my boyfriend."

"Did he call the Sheriff's Department?"

"I don't think so. You know, we really didn't want to get involved, but I thought, you know, that you would want to know."

"Well, we really appreciate you getting involved, but it would really help if you had gotten involved a little sooner, say that night," Stone was getting frustrated with leads that were coming in too late, or leads that were too ridiculous to help.

Each morning Stone and Wayne checked the daily reports, pulling out rape and suspicious circumstance reports, eliminating those with no connections to the East Area Rapist and following up on those that may have a connection. And each day they became more discouraged.

"He can't be that good, damn it. He's just lucky," Wayne looked at Stone.

"Well, his luck better run out, partner, or we better get lucky," Stone replied. They would learn that neither would happen.

February 21, 10:15 a.m.

"Hey, partner, I'm ready to hit the road with some of these leads. What have you got for the day?" Wayne asked.

"Got a composite to have the porn shops look at. I don't expect anything, but we'll see. I didn't realize we had so many in the area. Then I'm going to see Francis Woods. She said she saw someone walking toward Greenback. She drove by him twice and said he looked like the person that raped her. She called and Patrol responded, but he was a g.o.a. I just want to touch bases with her and let her know we are still involved."

"Okay, I'll catch you back here around four unless something comes up," Wayne grabbed his coat and left.

"I'm Detective Wayne, Sacramento Sheriff's Department," Wayne showed his badge to the woman sitting at the front counter of the welfare office. "A Mr. Johnston called me."

"Oh, sure. He's in the second office. Just go ahead in."

As Wayne entered the small office, he saw a thin, older man with hair parted just above his left ear and combed over his head in a poor attempt to cover his baldness. Wayne never could figure out why men vain enough to worry about baldness made themselves look so stupid.

"Mr. Johnston? I'm Detective Wayne. You said you might have some information on a rapist?"

"Good morning, Detective. Yes, I have a client who comes in once a month and after reading some articles in the paper about your rapist, I thought I better call. His name is Tim Irving."

"What makes you think he might be a rapist?"

"Well, he's real strange and somewhat disoriented. He's about five foot eleven and around a hundred and sixty pounds, like the paper says, and he's twenty-one years old. Anyway, he speaks ill of all women. He says that women are made from the devil and he relates women to food, for some reason. He admits to masturbating excessively and he either takes a bus or walks until he's tired and then sleeps wherever he is," Johnston folded his hands in front of his chin and looked at Wayne as if to say, "See what a good guy I am?"

"That's it?" Wayne asked, wanting to say, "You stupid bastard. I hope he breaks into your house and cuts off your god damned hair," Instead he stood up and thanked Johnston for all his help, stating that he would certainly look into Mr. Irving and left.

Jim Stone wasn't having any better luck with the porn shops. One owner said that the composite looked like someone who had been in around Christmas time looking for books on bondage. He had only been in once and the owner had no idea who he was.

Stone drove toward his office, half listening to his radio. "That suspicious subject on Moorbrook watching women is the mailman on his mail route," he heard a deputy advise Dispatch, "In full uniform and driving a mail truck," The disgust in his voice mirrored the frustration Stone felt.

Somewhere out there, in or near Sacramento, lived a man who walked, drove, ate, slept, talked to neighbors, maybe talked to fellow workers or family members. And at night he prowled, watched, and when the urge became great, he terrorized and he raped.

Stone slapped his steering wheel in frustration.

"What am I missing? Who is this son of a bitch? There has to be a clue I'm overlooking," he spoke to no one, and no one gave him his answers.

February 7, 1977. Carmichael, California.

Patricia Lacer, a thirty year old housewife, awoke and lay in the darkness of her bedroom, listening to her husband Roy's rhythmic breathing. She looked at her clock on the night stand.

"Five o'clock," she muttered to herself. "I need a cigarette." Still she lay, hesitant to leave the comfort of her bed and the warmth of her husband's body next to hers.

After a half-hour of staring into the darkness, she finally worked up the courage to swing her legs out from under the covers, shivering as her feet touched the cold of the bedroom floor. She reached for her jeans and slipped them over her naked body, fastened her bra, and walked barefoot and silent from the bedroom as she buttoned up her blouse. She turned on the kitchen light, catching a glimpse of the outside darkness through the kitchen window, lit a cigarette, and settled into a swivel chair in the living room.

At six o'clock she woke her husband and returned to the kitchen to fix his breakfast and his lunch to take to work. Later they sat at the kitchen table, while her husband Roy ate and she smoked her second cigarette of the day. She walked her husband to the door and kissed him good bye. As she started to close the door, her husband called from the sidewalk, "Lock the house up real tight, Patty, there's a white van parked in the school yard that doesn't belong in the neighborhood," he was thinking of the burglary they had experienced a month ago.

She closed the front door, turning the thumb screw on the dead bolt, checked the door leading into the garage, and the sliding glass door in the living room.

Five or ten minutes later, as she stood in front of the kitchen sink, she felt a sensation of someone being in the house. Thinking to herself, "Roy is back," she turned and stared into the unblinking hazel eyes watching her through a slit in the dull green, tightly fitting ski mask.

"Don't scream or I'll shoot you. I just want your money, I don't want to hurt you," he whispered through clenched teeth.

She stood trembling, looking at the barrel of the gun pointing at her belly, thinking of her seven year old daughter sleeping in her bedroom.

"I'm going to tie you up. Do what I say or I'll kill you," the masked intruder hissed. "Sit down in the chair."

She watched him as he removed shoelaces from his jacket pocket and her arms were pulled behind her and her wrists tied. She began to whimper, softly, deep in her throat. She felt the knife at her throat before she saw it. "Shut up or I'll kill you. Get up."

"No," she heard herself saying, the safety of the chair her only security.

"I've got a gun. I just want to tie you to your bed," he spoke through clenched teeth, his lips barely moving. In a daze she found herself walking down the hall, past her daughter's closed bedroom door. "He must have closed it," she thought to herself. "It was open before. Please God, let her be all right."

Again she felt the knife at her throat, felt the pressure against her skin.

"On the bed," he ordered and then she felt her ankles being tied. She heard cloth tearing.

"I'm going to cover your face."

"No!" she yelled, "Get the fuck out of here!" She rolled onto her back, trying to swing her feet off the bed. He was sitting on top of her now, holding his gloved hand over her mouth.

"Shut up!" He hissed.

She moved her tied hands to her side and felt the gun in his pants pocket. She was struggling now, squirming under his weight, pulling on the gun. It was out of his pocket. She struggled to get her finger on the trigger. She fumbled, her hands going numb from the tight bindings, yet she fought. Now he was fighting her for the gun as he realized she was gaining control. He was punching her in the head with his free hand, once, twice, three times.

"Shut up or I'll kill your daughter. I'll cut off her ear and bring it to you," she felt blackness envelope her. Near unconsciousness, she felt cloth being tried around her eyes, the gun forgotten. She felt cloth being stuffed into her mouth.

"If you move, I'll kill you," she felt the knife being drawn across her cheek. "I'll cut up your face."

She heard him leave the room. Frightened for her daughter, survival her only goal, she moved her feet until the laces fell from her ankles. As she tried to swing her feet to the floor, she felt hands pushing on her chest. Again she heard the harsh whisper, "If you move I'll cut off your toes. One for each time you move," She felt her jeans being pulled off her hips, down her legs, her nakedness exposed to the monster above her. She tried to talk through the gag. She needed to tell him that she had just had an abortion and he could hurt her.

"Shut up," he hissed and she felt the point of the knife pressing against her naked belly.

He was standing beside the bed and she could hear him masturbating, the slapping sound of lotion on his penis heightened her fear. She felt his mouth on her vagina, his tongue entering her opening. He pulled away and again she felt the knife as he ran it up and down her legs. Now he was on her, between her legs, and she felt his penis inside her. The thought of how small it was entered her mind. He was moving inside her and she heard a small groan and felt him leave her body. The room was very quiet and she sensed that something was wrong. She sensed the presence of her daughter in the room.

"Go into the bathroom. I'm going to tie you up," he hissed.

"No-no-no, you're going to kill us," she heard her daughter scream.

She tried to scream through the gag to make him leave her daughter alone. She felt the weight of her daughter as she was thrown on the bed. Again she felt her ankles being tied, this time as tightly as her wrists. And then, silence, only the quiet sobbing of her daughter shattering the stillness.

"Mommy, do you think he's gone?"

Sacramento Bee. February 7, 1977

Another Woman Molested

A housewife was attacked and raped early today at her home near Madison Avenue in what authorities say could be the fifteenth assault in the past fifteen months by the East Area Rapist...

Anything come out of the neighborhood canvass on the Lacer rape, Greg?" Stone asked as he watched Wayne thumbing through a stack of papers.

"Normal. Some sightings could be our man but, as usual, no one reported anything until after the attack. A school teacher saw someone running fast near Kelly School. She said he ran into the Park area. Said it was around seven-thirty yesterday morning. Five foot eight to ten, medium build, blue jacket, mid-twenties. Another neighbor saw a white male staring at her when she was working in the yard on the sixth. Said he gave her a weird, creepy feeling. Mid-twenties, short blond hair. How about you? Anything interesting?"

"Yeah," Stone leaned back in his chair. "The techs removed some cigarette butts from an ashtray in the Lacers' kitchen. They smoke Marlboros and there were several. One was a Vantage. The Lacers say they don't smoke Vantage and none of their friends do. That probably tells us that the bastard smokes, anyway. I'll check later to see if they come up with prints."

For the next week Stone and Wayne, with the help of other detectives and patrol deputies when they could be spared, worked through the mounds of paper work, eliminating hundreds of suspects. Elimination factors were few, so the process was slow. Still no fingerprints that could be traced to the rapist and frustrations mounted.

Valentine's Day. Memories of childhood days, of passing out valentines to all the kids in the class, in later years, giving that special Valentine to that one special person. Stone's memories stuck on the Valentine's days he had spent with his wife. Most of them were good times, especially the first couple. She would spend hours looking for just the right card for him. Funny how some memories remain, but others disappear. The bad seem to fade into obscurity. Does rape?

Stone was jolted back to reality with the ringing of his phone.

"Sergeant Stone," he unconsciously picked up his pen and pulled a note pad in front of him.

"My husband is the East Area Rapist you're looking for," the slightly intoxicated female voice began. "He told me two weeks ago that he was."

"Can I have your name, ma'am?" Stone broke in thinking to himself, "another nut."

"This is Mrs. Gates."

"Why did your husband tell you he was the rapist, Mrs. Gates?"

"One night two weeks ago he was out late and when he came home he said he was the rapist. He stays out all night lots of times and I don't know where he goes. We separated last week and he has some man living with him. He told me he wanted a divorce. We had a good sexual relationship but he had some homosexual experiences when he was a kid, so I don't know. I don't think he is into the gay thing, but most of his friends are."

"Did your husband ever beat you or tie you up before you had sex?" Stone asked.

"No, but he said he would like to tie me up to see what it felt like. He never did, though."

"I don't mean to get personal, Mrs. Gates, but I need to ask you a question. Is your husband under endowed?"

"What do you mean?"

"His penis. Is it normal size, large, small.... ."

"Oh, it's real big. Bigger than anybody I know."

"Shit," Stone thought to himself. Once more a suspect is eliminated because he was born lucky.

February 16, 1977. 2230 hours, Sacramento.

"Frank, did you hear that?" Bess Carmichael asked as she got up from the couch and hurried toward the kitchen.

"What?" Frank asked.

"That noise. It sounded like someone bumped into your smoker in the backyard," She turned on the light in the backyard. Frank and their seventeen year old son, Bill, ran to the kitchen. Frank grabbed his flashlight and followed Bill into the backyard.

"There he goes, across the court," Frank yelled as Bill sprinted from the backyard and across the court toward the neighbor's fence that the prowler had just scaled.

"I hear him, Dad," Bill yelled. "He jumped this fence." Bill was at the fence before his father had crossed the court. He grabbed the top of the fence and pulled himself up, throwing his leg over the top. He heard the gun being cocked before he saw the dark figure crouched beneath him. He started to fall back when the shot hit him just above the bellybutton, throwing his body backward.

He hit the ground screaming, "I've been shot," He felt his father's body shelter him as a second shot shattered the darkness. He felt himself being dragged to safety, his father crawling, pulling, expecting the next shot to tear into their bodies.

Frank held his son in his lap, praying, pleading until the ambulance arrived.

The suspect was described as a white male, approximately twenty years old, five foot ten, one hundred and seventy pounds with straight blond hair. He had been wearing a blue watch cap, blue sweatshirt, dark pants, and white tennis shoes.

A spent casing and a live 9mm round were found at the scene.

Bill Carmichael was operated on and was in stable condition in intensive care with ten holes in his intestines, three holes in his bladder, and two holes in his rectum from the single gunshot wound.

February 18, 1977, 1115 hours.

Detective Frank Lawson was sitting at his desk in the Investigation Division when his phone rang.

"I know who the rapist is," a female voice blurted. "I'm pretty sure."

"Can I have your name, ma'am?" Lawson asked reaching for his pen for the umpteenth time.

"I can't tell you because he'll know. I won't tell you."

"Okay, just tell me what you know," Lawson sighed.

"His name is Mike. I don't know his last name, but it starts with an S and his birthday is November 5, 1940. He lives in Rancho Cordova and used to work at a grocery store but he was fired for giving away beer. He belongs to the Banayo family. They're Mafia back east."

"Is he Mafia?" Lawson broke in, calculating in his head as he spoke: 1940, 1977. Thirty-seven years old. No fuckin' way, Jose.

"I don't think so," she continued. "He owns a van and does yard work. He's married and his wife is out of town a lot."

"Why do you think he's a rapist? Did he tell you?"

"No, not in so many words, but he talks a lot. He says he doesn't get enough sex from his wife. He's obsessed with sex. He has a lot of fantasies and says he would like to tie someone up and have unusual sex or something. He's very gentle during sex, though."

"Is this Mike your boyfriend, or something?" Lawson asked. "You said he was married."

"No, I just now him. I'm married."

"Okay, okay. Tell me more," Lawson rolled his eyes at Stone, who was watching him.

"Well, he is five feet nine inches tall and weighs about a hundred and sixty pounds. He's real attractive and he's got a real small penis but it's real rough like it's been used to death."

"You did say that you're married?" Lawson closed his eyes tight and rubbed his forehead.

"Yeah. He also tried to have sex with my daughter, but I told him to stay away because she's only sixteen. He came over when my husband wasn't home. My husband called him and told him someone would think he was a rapist he was so obsessed with sex. Mike said he didn't want anyone to say that because it would blow his cover."

"You don't want to give me your name?" Lawson crossed his fingers and looked skyward.

"No. My husband doesn't even know I'm calling."

"Okay. Look if you have anything else, you be sure to call."

"I will. You won't tell Mike I called, will you? He'll know it was me."

"Don't worry. Mike will never know. Thanks for the information. 'Bye now," Lawson hung up.

"Anything?" Stone asked.

"Right out of the twilight zone. Where do these fuckers come from, for Christ's sake?"

Over the next two weeks, detectives were busy following up on leads. A man called stating that on February 6 at approximately eleven p.m. a car was parked on Aslin Way. The driver had been acting real strange and the man attempted to get a license number. He got a partial number off the Chevrolet. Greg Wayne checked it out through the department of motor vehicles and contacted the family. The owner was in jail for drunk in public. His brother said he was "fruity" and wandered around at night. He wore a size ten and a half shoe and had type B blood. Eliminated.

Another subject was contacted at his residence after a phone call from his wife. He had told her he was EAR and enjoyed bending peoples' spoons. He told the investigator he told his wife that because he was pissed at her. He says a friend told him that a deputy sheriff said EAR liked to bend spoons. He denied any knowledge of the rape activities.

Stone contacted a subject because of an anonymous tip. A subject was seen at a McDonald's "lustingly" looking at women and left after one, leaving his full cup of coffee. The Lutheran minister was embarrassed. Although the woman he was looking at was beautiful, according to the minister, he did not physically resemble the rapist.

A judge called regarding a phone call from a female. Her husband had struck her in the face. He then killed her dog. She had stated that he was a sex deviant and wore women's clothing at night. Last night he was wearing a rubber band around his wrist and penis. He told her to tell her friends that he was the rapist. The wife said that he had molested their sixteen year old daughter and a young man at work. Eliminated as a fifty year old fat man. Information was given to the Juvenile Division for follow up on the molest of the daughter.

The Sacramento County Sheriff's Office received a letter from a man stating he knew who the rapist was. He saw him at Sambo's Restaurant. The subject was suspiciously hungry. Everyone became suspicious over his "hungriness" so he must be the rapist, the letter writer stated. He also said further results would be forthcoming when President Ford got his letter.

A real estate agent called stating he and his associates have all shown houses to a subject who gives a promissory note and then cancels the next day. Described as scruffy, twenty five, twenty six, one glass eye, and face scales.

The next day Detective Wayne received a call from a real estate agent. Subject was at the agency. Upon contact, Wayne was told the subject was a truck driver who lives in Yuba City or Folsom. Wayne contacted a brother who stated that the brother was on disability from a motorcycle accident. He has a metal plate in his forehead and a glass eye that bulges out.

The same day, two female real estate agents called and said they had shown houses to the subject. One said he only wanted to talk about sex with three women at one time in his truck. Said his wife was pregnant and he was horny. The second agent said the subject told her he was a Hell's Angel and told her of making it with women in his truck. He told her that when he first got married, his mother-in-law came into the bedroom where he and his wife were. The mother-in-law was nude and wanted to have sex with him. The agent said he had a bumper sticker that read, "Looking For a Dirty Old Woman."

And on it went, one brick wall after another. Before the American Civil Liberties Union got involved, most of these people would be in an institution. Now they were everywhere.

Friday, February 25, 1977.
Sacramento Sheriff's Office, Investigations Division

"Hey, Stone!" Lt. Burns yelled from his office.

"Yeah, Mike," Stone replied as he leaned over his desk to look into Burns's office.

"Come here. Bring Peg with you."

Stone looked at Peggy Vickers and nodded his head toward Burns's office as he got out of his chair, carrying his third cup of coffee of the morning. Vickers followed.

"Yeah, boss?" Stone inquired.

"Sit down. Both of you. I just got off the phone with the Youth Authority. We've got a meeting with them Monday morning in their office," Burns folded his hands in front of his chin, put his elbows on his desk, and dropped his chin onto his hands. "I want the two of you there along with Wayne. I'll be there also. They'll have one of their directors from Los Angeles along with three Ph.D.'s, one from L.A., two from Sac. Maybe we can learn something about our rapist from them. They feel that their specific involvement with Youth Authority oriented offenders could provide us with a useful criminal-oriented overview of the EAR's psyche. It's going to be an open discussion. Theories, hypotheses, findings. I'm going to have one of our patrol units drop off copies of our reports today so they can review them."

"Good. Maybe they can tell us who the son of a bitch is. Be nice if they just let someone out that has a similar M.O.," Stone replied.

"Anything coming together, Jim?" Burns asked.

"Nothing. Still following up on leads. Most of them from nuts, some look good at first but they peter out in the end. Seems to be quiet since the kid got shot. Maybe it was enough to scare him off. The EAR units are still active, making a lot of car stops, taking pictures and prints of the ones that look good," Stone shrugged.

"What about you, Peg? Anything?" Burns looked at her wrinkling his forehead in question.

"Nothing. The lab is still working on semen and blood. None of the fingerprints have worked out. Some of the victims have called with updated inventory lists and lots of questions that I have no answers for.

They're scared to death he'll come back and I can't tell them that he won't."

"Yeah. Real shitty. Anyway, make sure Wayne knows about Monday morning. We need to be there by nine so we can go together from here. Give us a chance to discuss what we want to ask," Burns unclenched his hands and shrugged.

"If we don't hear from this motherfucker over the weekend, you mean," Stone added.

"This is important. If he hits, I want you at least to be at the meeting, Jim."

"Okay, boss. I'll keep my fingers crossed," Stone and Vickers left the office.

"I hope he doesn't hit. I've got a date for the Napa Wine Train Sunday," Stone muttered to himself.

Vickers grinned. "Gonna take the dinner ride?"

"It's supposed to be pretty nice. Get to see the wine country. Beautiful scenery," Stone replied.

"Should put her in the mood for something," Vickers laughed.

"Hope so," Stone headed for the conference room. Butcher paper lined the walls. Each victim was listed separately. Dates, times, addresses, ages, anything that might help was written for each attack. Stone leaned back and scanned the information and then began to write on a tablet. On the top he wrote "M.O.," and then:

1. *Suspect enters, pries door or window. May break glass.*

2. *Goes to victim's bedroom. Shines light into eyes. "Shut up or I'll kill you...I just want money and food"*

3. *Has knife in hand. Sometimes gun. Ski mask and gloves.*

4. *Ties female. Uses shoelaces or cut electrical cords.*

5. *Sometimes brings laces with him.*

6. *Ransacks bedroom and then rest of house.*

7. *Dishes on back?*

8. *Eats. Drinks beer.*

9. *Cuts towel in strips. Blindfolds.*

10. *Lubricates penis.*

11. *Assaults. Sodomy. Oral cop. Both ways. Straight sex.*

CHAPTER TWENTY-ONE

Stone looked at the tablet, rubbed his temples, and at the bottom of the list wrote, "small penis!!!" He pushed his chair back, left the notebook on the table, and went back to his desk.

> Monday, February 28, 1977.
> California Youth Authority near Florin Perkins Road.
> 0900 hours.

Introductions were made and the discussions began.

"We went over the reports you gave us," the Director started, "and we have come up with some deductions. As you listed, he's a white male adult, eighteen to twenty-two, five foot nine or ten, one sixty-five with dark or dirty blond hair. We don't think he is married at this time."

Dr. Gohen, the L.A. psychologist broke in: "We feel that the suspect is unable to maintain any normal, heterosexual relationship with a female. As a consequence, he is capable of harboring deeply rooted feelings of inadequacy which manifest themselves in the rape crimes. It is through the crime of rape that he is finally able to establish dominance over the female; asserting his masculinity and perhaps repaying all of womanhood for causing him such anxiety."

"Is he homosexual?" Stone asked.

"It is thought," Dr. Roth answered, "that as a result of his sexual inadequacies, that he would be constantly combating a fear that he will become involved in some sort of homosexual encounter. He is basically a loner and avoids relationships. We don't know yet whether he attempts to prove his manhood to his male peers."

"Where did he come from? I mean, he didn't just start rapeing, did he? Family life, criminal background. Do you have any feeling on it?" Wayne asked.

"Good question," Dr. Abrahms remarked. "If there is any past involvement with the authorities, it would probably be in the area of indecent exposure or peeping tom. The time he entered the house without his pants on would indicate voyeurism. As far as family, he was probably the youngest male member. Although he may have an older brother in the service, we feel that he probably has an older sister and an unusually domineering mother. Probably a total lack of any assertive male influence in his early years."

"We've had some indication that he may be in the military or just got out. Any idea on that?" Stone asked.

"I probably feel strongest about this," Dr. Gohen remarked. "I doubt if he has had any prolonged exposure to military service. My colleagues feel he may have attempted to enter the service and was turned down or did not make it through basic training."

"He probably comes from a middle class family environment. This is mainly based on his apparent change of attire, including shoes and various shapes and colored masks. The basic theory is that an individual in a lower income bracket would have the tendency to wear the same clothing," Dr. Abrahms interjected. "He's probably not addicted to any hard drugs, but may be a pill popper. We also feel he doesn't smoke or drink. He is probably pouring the beer down the drain because no one has mentioned smelling it on his breath. Probably a strong religious tie inherent in his upbringing. The fact that several victims themselves are functional religionists could prove slightly more than coincidental in their selection. We don't feel you should dwell on this aspect, though. It is possible that he lives in the area of Rancho Cordova, or used to and just moved to the east area of the county. He knows the area, that's obvious."

"How about a break before we get into how dangerous your man is and what you need to be aware of," the Director broke in. "We've got coffee and donuts coming. If you need to use the restroom, it's just out the door and to your left."

During the break, Stone asked, "Have you encountered any cases with a similar M.O.?"

"You'd be surprised how many are similar," Dr. Gohen responded. "None exactly like this, but several similar. Is he one of our parolees? I don't know."

"Any questions," the Director asked, "before Dr. Gohen talks about how dangerous this individual really is? None? Okay, doctor, it's all yours."

"We detect an increasing aggressiveness in the suspect's degree and method of attack. This is indicative of what we term 'de-compensation.' He is a very dangerous individual who would kill himself and any law enforcement officer, or person, attempting to take him into custody," Gohen caught Stone look at Burns and start to say something. "Hit a nerve, Sergeant?"

"We had a young boy shot while chasing a prowler. We didn't give you the report because we haven't determined yet if the prowler is the rapist," Burns began. "I don't think it was, Jim disagrees. The kid chased him over a fence and the prowler was waiting on the other side. Shot him in the stomach. We haven't told the press that we're looking at it."

"It does fit the profile of this type of individual," Gohen remarked, "but we would have to look at it further to make any kind of guess. Following the commission of a crime, or its attempt, the psychological profile suggests that the suspect harbors extreme guilt feelings from his acts and any thoughts of public exposure or ridicule would fully justify his self-destruction. Only when the suspect is planning and preparing for the crime does he feel himself to be a 'whole human being.' As a consequence, the overall planning and preparation are the main impetus sustaining his paranoid schizophrenic personality. The actual assault on the victim is probably secondary in the overall scheme. When he is planning, prowling, concealing himself in underbrush, evading detection, etc., he is at the height of his paranoic fantasy. Once inside the house, however, he has reached his peak and rapidly starts to decline. His reaction to any field contacts with law enforcement personnel will be dependent upon interception being made before his entering the house or after leaving it. If the contact is made before he enters, his overall demeanor will be cunning and cooperative during the field interrogation. His mannerisms should be exceptionally calm, yet acutely alert since at this time he will be feeding on the schizophrenic excitation made possible in the planning stage. If, on the other hand, he is intercepted in the process of leaving the area, it is likely that a nearly explosive resistance will be immediately encountered. In the event that he exhausts such efforts as running, jumping fences, etc., to effect his escape, then he should resort to homicide and/or suicide as the ultimate means of preventing apprehension. Your young teen that was shot would fit under this scenario. Any field interrogation of this subject should be approached with knowledge of certain psychological thought patterns prevailing the paranoid schizophrenic."

"You mean we need to have a psychiatrist in each patrol car so we can interview him?" Stone asked.

"Not a bad idea. Impossible, of course, but it is something you need to consider. Not one in the car but a psychiatrist on call. It could be really important. Also your patrolmen and investigators need to be aware of the approach they need to take. They must know that the paranoic will be both calm and calculating during the planning phase, thus any attempts toward detention or solicitation of information during this stage will only serve to stimulate the excitation. As a result, he could prove most cunning and confident in his replies while simultaneously demanding that he know the reason for his detention.

"This is where the key lies. The schizophrenic must have information to perpetuate his fantasy, thereby allowing him to remain intact during the charade. Conversely, if the information is denied, then similarly his fantasy is denied and the onset of 'non-integration' would become apparent in the contact. From apparent calmness the suspect would begin to display erratic behavior. Some agitation and fidgetiness would be the early manifestation as he starts to realize that he is not controlling the situation.

"From that point, he would rapidly deteriorate in front of the officers. With this information, it is suggested that initial contact, if the suspect is found serene, be viewed as stated. The officers should then delay the individual while simultaneously withholding as much information from him as possible. This will cause the suspect's inherent schizophrenic tendencies to begin working against him. With no information to work on, and without the officers' active participation, the suspect will not be able to perpetuate his fantasy. This results in increasing amounts of frustration serving to exaggerate those pre-existing doubts and anxieties which are a fundamental makeup of the paranoid schizophrenic.

"Another thing. When he has a well developed plan, he is able to be effectively meticulous in his actions. If the plan goes awry, his actions demonstrate more anxiety and frustration. He seems frightened to touch breasts and is preoccupied with masturbation. I think he has thoughts of killing, probably associated with thoughts he has had of killing his mother to resolve his home situation. He overcomes this fear of killing someone by tying them up and raping them."

"Well, that covers our part," the Director commented as the doctor returned to his seat. "If we can be of help, please keep in contact. All we can say is 'good luck.' I'm afraid you're going to need it."

Burns stood. "We want to thank you all very much for your time and insight. Our first job, obviously, is to train our patrol deputies. Our second step is to catch this bastard."

CHAPTER TWENTY-TWO

"**JOHN,**" the thirty-two year old Sacramento housewife whispered to her husband. "when I passed the living room window, I saw someone looking in. I think he had a woman's nylon stocking over his head."

She watched as her husband hurried to the hallway, turned on the porch light, and opened the front door. As he looked toward the area of the living room window, he could see the bushes moving as if someone had just left. Closing the door, he turned to his wife, who had followed him.

"Well, we scared him off, whoever he was," he remarked as he turned off the light and returned to his place in front of the television.

And at night, a lone figure dressed in dark clothing, prowled the Sacramento neighborhoods. Only he knew why he prowled, and only he knew what he was looking for. And the most frustrating thing to the cops was ... only he knew when he would again rape and terrorize.

"What have you got there, Jim?" Lt. Burns stopped at Stone's desk and looked at the array of shoelaces, ropes, and string neatly laid out on the desk.

"These are the ties used in the rapes, Mike," Stone replied. "I thought I would check the knots to see if there was a pattern to the way he ties his victims."

"And?"

"None I can tell. I picked up this book, *The World Book Encyclopedia,* from the library so I could check on the knots. It seems he just ties them without worrying too much about the type of knot. So far, I found granny knots, square knots, and overhand knots. The book gives a list of all users of different knots, from sailors to surgeons to housewives. They forgot one, though," Stone shook his head as he looked at Burns.

"Oh? What's that?" Burns asked.

"Rapists ... They forgot rapists."

Sacramento Bee, 3-8-77

A thirty-seven year old woman was tied up and raped in her home early this morning. "The M.O. [method of operation] is the same as the East Area Rapist," said a sheriff's office spokesman.

The woman, who was alone in her home, said she was asleep when she was attacked and never saw the rapist. She told authorities he blindfolded and gagged her. She told officers the rapist rummaged through her house for as long as three hours.

The victim was separated from her husband and had a small child who was staying elsewhere Monday night. The East Area Rapist has never attacked while there was a man in the home, although occasionally there have been children.

His attacks have always occurred between 11:00 p.m. and 6:45 a.m. His victims range in age from sixteen to the late thirties.

Stone threw his copy of the *Sacramento Bee* on his desk and looked at his partner.

"Well, Greg, now we'll find out if the son of a bitch reads the paper."

Wayne was just opening his briefcase, preparing to begin his shift. He and Stone were working the afternoon shift almost exclusively as they worked the rape cases.

"How's that?"

"Well, the paper printed the rape last night and said he never hits a home with a man in it. That throws out a challenge to the bastard."

"Either that or a lot of men are going to get real lucky sleeping over with some single ladies. Could be cheap protection," Wayne grinned. "Matter of fact, maybe I should put an ad in the paper that I'm available."

"Yeah, and with your luck, he'll take the challenge, break into the house you're in and prove to you he really is gay and shove it up your ass," Stone laughed.

"Well, at least they say he's under endowed so it won't hurt too much."

"I read over the reports from the rape. Looks like our boy had staked out this one for awhile. They found tennis shoe impressions under her bathroom window that matched ones in her backyard. Said the impressions were at least a week old. Seems her bathroom curtain is hanging in such a way you can see into her bathtub and also into her bedroom."

"That fits," Wayne remarked.

"Yeah. Also a lot of dogs barking in the neighborhood over the last week. No one called in though, as usual."

"Anything we can go on?"

"Not yet, but a sixteen year old girl saw a yellow older truck in the area. Peg Vickers is going to set up a hypnosis session to see if we can get a license number."

March 18, 1977, 1615 hrs

"Sacramento County Sheriff's Office, can I help you?" the PBX operator answered the non-recorded line.

"I'm the East Side Rapist," the male caller stated, laughed, and hung up.

March 18, 1977, 1630 hrs

"Sacramento County Sheriff's Office, can I help you?"

"I'm the East Side Rapist," the same male voice stated, laughed, and hung up.

March 18, 1977, 1700 hrs

"Sacramento County Sheriff's Office, can I help you?"

"I'm the East Side Rapist and I have my next victim already stalked and you guys can't catch me," Again the phone went dead. The voice, definitely male, without accent or speech impediment, sounded as though the caller was holding the phone away from his mouth. All three calls were made by the same person.

At 2130 hours, Linda Klein was peering out her living room window at the Janik residence across the street. A street light played with the bare branches of the large maple tree in the Janiks' front yard. A shadow stepped from the darkness and moved from the sidewalk toward the front door. She could see that the figure was that of a male, average height, but as the lighting was poor, she could not make out the features. She watched from the darkness of her living room as the subject turned toward the side of the house and passed through the side gate, disappearing into the darkness.

Frightened, the fifteen year old closed the drapes and moved to the comfort of her bedroom.

2230 hrs, Rancho Cordova

Sixteen year old Erica Janik pulled into her driveway. She had just finished her shift at Kentucky Fried chicken, her chicken dinner on the seat beside her. As her parents were out of town, she would eat and then call her friend June Kirk to let her know she would be leaving to spend the night with her.

Janik noticed that the front porch light was off and the thought crossed her mind that her parents had forgotten to turn it on when they left. The sixteen year old unlocked the front door, entered, and walked toward the kitchen, placing her chicken dinner on the counter. She reached for the phone and dialed her friend June's phone number. She listened to the first ring and turned toward a noise behind her.

Her eyes fixed on the green handled ax raised above her head and she tried to scream, knowing the ax would come crashing down on her head.

"Don't scream or I'll kill you," the voice hissed.

She looked at the dark green canvas mask surrounding the two eye holes. A hand grabbed the phone cord and it separated from the wall as the phone was wrenched from her hand. She felt her body being pushed toward the family room. Her knees were weak as she stumbled forward, directed by the gloved hand on her shoulder.

"Get on the floor," the voice hissed and she sank to the floor. "On your stomach," he commanded and she felt her hands being pulled behind her back and felt the brown shoelaces cutting into her wrists.

He left her then, and she heard him moving throughout the house. She heard the sliding glass door to the backyard open and then there was silence...a minute, two minutes, then she heard the living room drapes being opened and closed.

The phone in the bedroom was ringing and the masked intruder fell silent. The ringing stopped and he was beside her.

"My car is just a block away. If you don't do as I say, I'll kill you," he hissed.

She watched him as he cut strips off a towel with scissors. She thought he was going to gag her, so she spit out the piece of Doublemint gum she was unconsciously chewing. His eyes were fixed on her as he walked across the carpeted room.

"Please don't hurt me," she pleaded.

"I'm not going to hurt you. I just want your money."

"Really?" she asked.

"Just do as I tell you."

She felt the strip of towel being tied around her mouth and a second strip tied around her eyes. The house was quiet and she could hear him as he rummaged, occasionally returning to her side, each time clicking the scissors near her ear or pressing the hatchet against her neck.

The phone was ringing...once, twice...she found herself counting the rings...twenty-nine, thirty, and then it stopped. She realized she hadn't been breathing and she tried to gasp for air. She felt the gag being loosened.

"When's your family coming home?" the voice hissed.

"My sister's at a friend's house and my parents are in Lake Tahoe," she replied. "Please don't hurt me."

"Shut up," he commanded. She felt the bindings on her ankles being loosened.

"Have you ever fucked, Erica?"

"No, please," she begged.

She felt her pants being pulled down over her feet and then her underpants.

"You have a beautiful body, don't you, Erica?" he hissed.

When she didn't answer, "Don't you!" he demanded.

"Yes," she replied.

She felt her legs being spread and then his face against her thighs. His tongue was inside her and her tears wouldn't stop.

"The operator received three calls tonight. Each time the caller said he was the East Side Rapist. On the last call, he said he had his victim all picked out and we couldn't stop him," Detective Vickers stood in front of the patrol division's night shift line-up. Nine deputies that made up the East Area Rape units looked at each other and their hearts quickened as one. It was 2355 hrs, March 18th.

"We have no reason to believe it wasn't our rapist," she went on. "The newspapers have been printing a lot about the rapes as you all know, so it could be a prank. We do know that all three calls were made by the same person."

"Exactly what do we look for?" one of the deputies asked.

"Anyone suspicious. Any cars or trucks that seem like they are out of place in a neighborhood. Vehicles that don't fit. He seems to park within two or three blocks of his attacks. Write down license numbers. Another thing. He seems to like to go into the backyard through the side gate and always leaves the gates open. Keep an eye out for that. He also likes to climb fences. Listen for dogs barking."

"What does he look like. Anything new on him?" another asked.

"Just what you have in front of you. He always wears a mask during his attacks, dark clothes. Somewhere between five foot eight to six feet, medium build. And his victims all say he has a small penis. We think he must be a cop," Vickers joked.

"And how many have you eliminated by memory?" a deputy retorted.

Sergeant Gonzales, one of the patrol sergeants, entered the room.

"We just had a rape in Rancho Cordova. A sixteen year old alone. Unit 12P4, Rich and Craig, are on the scene and got a preliminary report, however the victim doesn't want to talk to a male officer. They're requesting that you respond, Peg. They're transporting her to the Sac Medical Center. Said to meet them there. We've got a dog enroute."

"Okay," Vickers replied. "I'll call Lt. Burns and Stone. Stone can go directly to the scene. The rest of you, hit the area and start a canvass. Maybe we'll get lucky."

Units X1, X2, X3, X4, X5, and X6 were dispatched to the area to assist in the search.

Upon arrival, Stone met with the patrol officers on the scene.

"What've we got, fellows?" he asked.

"Sixteen year old home alone. Just got home from work and was going to her friend's to spend the night. Parents are in Tahoe. Her friend got worried when she didn't hear from her and had her father bring her over. Scared the bastard away, but not before he did a real number on the little girl. Raped her several times, orally coped her, and made her play with his cock. Just like all the rest, Jim. Only thing is, she was a virgin. The bastard came on her with an ax, for Christ's sake. Tied her up, blindfolded her, threatened to kill her, and kept telling her to shut up. We found the ax on the back fence. No one has touched it," Craig advised Stone.

"She get a look at him?" Stone asked.

"Somewhat. WMA, twenty-five to thirty, five foot nine or ten, wearing dark green nylon jacket, dark green canvas type mask with eye holes, dark shoes, no heels. She was on the phone calling her friend when he came up behind her with the hatchet over his head. Told her if she screamed he would kill her. She said he talked in a harsh whisper. Tied her up with shoelaces and an electrical cord he cut from an iron."

"This son of a bitch is driving us nuts. Why can't the bastard get run over by a fuckin' truck?" Stone growled.

"Yeah. We're all as nervous as a cat burying shit. I'll tell you nobody's sleeping on duty. Oh yeah, she said he remarked about his eight inch dick. Victim said it felt about the size of a hot dog. She didn't have anything else to compare it to. Said every time he went by her he clicked scissors near her ear and he placed the ax against her neck a couple of times. Looks like he drank some Dr. Pepper. He covered the lamp with her pants to cut down on the light, but you can see that when you go in. The bastard even had her sit on his lap and raped her. He needs to die, Jim. He really needs to fuckin' die."

"Yeah, I know. By the way, radio received three calls around four or five o'clock. Caller said he was the rapist and he had his next victim stalked and we couldn't catch him," Stone remarked.

"They told us. I'm telling you, Jim, my neck's sore from swiveling back and forth. He's got us all paranoid and we still can't catch him."

"Luck's got to change. I've got a dog on the way. Maybe he can tell us something."

Officer Benton and his dog, Prince, arrived at 0014 hours, 3-19-77, and immediately picked up a scent from the backyard. The dog followed the scent to the side gate and across several front yards to Ellenbrook Drive, where the dog began to vector back and forth across the street. The dog could not relocate the scent. When a K-9 is searching on a track and he begins to vector from the track, it's an indication that the trail ends at that location. This is where EAR probably had his vehicle parked.

Shoe impressions were located in the damp ground of the victim's backyard. They showed a herringbone or zigzag pattern, same as found at other rape locations.

At 0300 hours, Erica Janik underwent a rape examination at the Sacramento Medical Center. Erica had never had intercourse before and was experiencing bleeding from the assault. She was first counseled by a member of the Sacramento Medical Center Crisis Center, briefing her on what would be happening to her. At 0330 hours, Erica Janik was transported back to her residence by her parents who had arrived at the hospital from Lake Tahoe.

Detective Vickers talked to Mrs. Janik and learned that for the past six months she had been receiving hang-up phone calls. On three occasions, Mrs. Janik blew a whistle into the phone.

Missing from the residence were Erica's driver's license, her sister's school identification, and two of Erica's rings.

A canvass of the Janik neighborhood by uniformed officers was conducted during the day shift. Each occupant interviewed was asked four predetermined questions:

1. *During the evening of 3-18-77, did you observe or hear any vehicle or person which were suspicious or did not belong in the area?*

2. *During the past month or more, has any vehicle or person been suspicious enough to attract your attention?*

3. *Have you in the past several months been the victim of a burglary or prowler at your residence?*

4. *Have you received phone calls which you thought to be suspicious in the past month or more?*

Some residents were not home. Some were home but could offer no information. Some were home and the information was depressing. In the middle of an area where pervious rapes had occurred, where people checked out every noise, every strange vehicle, every movement, very little had been reported to the Sheriff's Department.

Even more depressing were the times when information was given to the patrol deputies and no reports were turned in. Unfortunately, this became an all too familiar occurrence during the reign of terror.

On 3-13-77, a neighbor of the Janiks', one with two teenage daughters, had left their residence for approximately two hours. Upon returning, they found a bedroom window wide open. Pry marks were found, yet no signs of entry was noticed. A deputy responded to take a report. Records Division had no report on file and no case number had been requested by the deputy.

A neighbor, between 2030 hours and 2100 hours the night of the attack, noticed his small dogs growling toward his backyard. He looked out and did not notice anything. His backyard adjoins the Janiks'.

A neighbor near the area where the K-9 had lost the scent advised that he had seen a 1966 or '67 Chevrolet Belair station wagon, grey in color, parked near his residence on numerous occasions during the past month. The vehicle would disappear for several days, and then return. No subject was ever seen and the vehicle had not been seen in the last three days. No license number was recorded.

A sixteen year old neighbor arrived home approximately 2305 hours on 3-18-77 and sat in his vehicle for a short time. Approximately five minutes after arriving, he observed a 1972 or newer Chevrolet station wagon pull away from in front of a residence. It did not leave in a particular hurry, nor did he see the driver. The vehicle was not familiar to him.

Another neighbor received numerous hang-up phone calls from mid-January until late February. The calls came at all hours of the day and night.

And then there was the next door neighbor who finally told of the incident that occurred in February where she saw a prowler wearing a nylon stocking over his face, looking in her front window.

As in many of the rapes, a bottle of Vaseline Intensive Care hand lotion was found on the victim's roof in the backyard. The bottle did not belong to the Janiks.

In the days following the rape, leads were checked, license numbers run, and more dead end streets; more brick walls; more headaches; more frustrations. Detectives contacted all the high schools in the area. An EAR profile was given to the very cooperative faculty members who promised to look through yearbooks of the past two years.

Stone again laid out the shoelaces and ties to check knots. This time he checked them against *The Complete Boating Encyclopedia*, Editor, Morris Weeks, Jr. The rapist had used overhand knots, granny knots, square knots. Eliminate sailors.

CHAPTER TWENTY-THREE

April 1, 1977

ORANGEVALE is a Sacramento County community situated between Interstates 80 and 50. A Siberian husky begins barking in the backyard of one of the homes in the four year old tract. A light brightens the backyard and a man's voice carries in the cool night air.

"Quiet. Lay down!" The barking stops and the light disappears into darkness once again. Ten o'clock in the sleepy neighborhood and a car's throaty muffler reverberates in the distance and then it too disappears. The night grows colder and the neighborhood sleeps.

At midnight the Siberian husky once again begins its barking. Other dogs in the neighborhood begin to answer. For a half-hour the dogs continue their conversation and then, one by one, their conversation is over. They grow silent.

Dana Forsyth, her boyfriend Lee Kwok, and Dana's two young children pull into the driveway of her Orangevale neighborhood home. Her two small children are sound asleep in the backseat. It had been a long night. A double feature at the Thunderbird Drive-in Movie and both children had stayed awake through them both: "Earthquake" and "Airport 77." Airport 77 had ended around 1:30. At 1:35, both kids were sound asleep. Dana and Lee were also tired and it had earlier been decided that Lee would stay as he had several times before since Dana's separation from her husband.

Both children were already in their pajamas, eight year old Barry in blue, seven year old Danielle in pink. They never stirred as they were carried into the house and put in their beds.

Dana and Lee were fast asleep by two o'clock.

A bright light burned through the closed eyelids of the sleeping Dana Forsyth. Dreams can be so real. As her brain focused on the bright light, she slowly floated from her deep sleep. The dream vanished, but the light continued to burn into her mind and she slowly opened her eyes. She stared toward the open bedroom door, past the light, and focused on the white mask.

"Don't make a sound," the voice hissed through clenched teeth. "Do you see this gun?"

"Yes," she replied, although she didn't, she was still staring at the white mask outlined in the light of the flashlight. Two dark holes stared back at her.

"Wake him up," the voice hissed.

Dana gently shook Lee's shoulder.

"Someone's in the bedroom," she whispered and nodded toward the intruder. The light was directed into the eyes of the now fully awake Lee, who started to move from the bed.

"Stop. Don't move. Lay on your stomachs. I have a forty-five with fourteen shots and two clips. I want your money. Exactly where is your wallet. If you don't tell me the truth I'll kill you. Don't make any sudden moves. Lay still or I'll kill you like I did some people in Bakersfield," the voice ordered.

"It's in my pants on the floor," Lee answered.

"All I want is your money. If you cooperate I'll be out of here in a couple of minutes. Get on your stomach and put your hands behind your back," Lee complied, his heart beating so hard the bed seemed to move with each pounding.

"You! Tie your husband up."

"With what?" Dana asked.

"With the rope on the bed," The flashlight beam moved down the bed until it picked up the white shoelaces neatly stretched out.

"Do exactly as he says," Lee cautioned.

"Shut up. Don't talk. Point your hands apart. Tie up your husband," the intruder hissed. "Tie the rope tighter," He went to Lee's pants, picked them up, and returned to the bed.

Lee felt the barrel of the gun against his head.

"Don't look up. If you see me I'll have to kill both of you," He backed away and they heard change rattling in Lee's pants. "After I take the money I'm going down to my camp by the American River."

Lee felt his ankles being tied together then felt his wrists being tied again, tighter. Dana felt her wrists being tied and then felt herself being pulled from the bed.

"I'm going to tie you up in the hallway so you can't untie each other," he hissed.

She was guided out of the bedroom and felt something sharp against her back as she was prodded into the family room. She was only dressed in her bikini underpants and through the fear, she also felt the humiliation of her nakedness in front of the masked intruder.

"Lie down," he hissed, "on your stomach."

She felt her feet being tied then felt a towel being wrapped around her head, covering her eyes. She heard him in the kitchen, dishes rattled, and then he was back.

"Where's your matches?" he whispered.

"I don't know. I don't smoke," she sobbed.

"You better not lie to me or I'll have to kill you."

She felt a cup and saucer being placed on her bare back.

"If you move I'll hear you and I'll have to come back and kill you."

She heard him back in the kitchen again and then things were quiet. "Did he really take the money and leave?" she prayed to herself, and then she saw the glow from the candle through her blindfold.

"I'm going to go get your purse out of the car," he whispered.

"How did he know?" she wondered. She felt his presence back in the room and then the cup and saucer were removed from her back.

"Hold my cock. Be gentle with it," he hissed. She felt his penis in her hand as he rocked back and forth. He was off her then and she felt herself being rolled onto her back. Her ankles were being untied and her underpants were pulled down and off. She lay naked, only a towel around her head remained.

"You have to tell me the truth and if you don't, I'll find out and kill you both," he threatened. "Did you fuck tonight?"

"No," she whispered, fear rising as she felt the blood pounding in her head, so hard now she could hear it. She felt his mouth on her vagina, his tongue exploring. He stopped and she felt him placing a pair of high heeled shoes on her feet. He was on top of her now, spreading her legs as he entered her.

"Make it good and I'll leave you alone," he panted. She felt him ejaculate and then he was gone.

Her feet weren't tied and she fought the urge to run. She could not see and in high heeled shoes, he would catch her. He would kill her. He could kill her children, Lee, all of them. She lay quietly on the floor. She could hear him now, back in the kitchen. She could hear him eating, munching food loud enough so she would know.

He was back then, penetrating her once more and then he was pulling her arm.

"Get up," he hissed and led her to a chair. She felt herself being pulled onto his lap and again she was violated. She could feel the hair on his legs against hers, coarse, like face whiskers, and she felt his jacket against her back. He moved back and forth and then pushed her to the floor. Once again her ankles were tied. She lay still, listening, straining.

She could not hear him now. Had he left? She felt something against her leg and jumped involuntarily. It was her poodle. She didn't dare call out for fear he would kill her children. She was freezing, her naked body overcoming the fear enough to feel the cold creeping into the room through the open door to the backyard. As she lay on the floor, her mind wandered from her children to Lee, to the rapes. She even remembered that although she was naked, he never touched her breasts with either his hands or mouth.

"Dana?" she heard Lee calling, "Are you all right?"

"Have Michael go out the bedroom window and get Jerry next door," she cried. She felt Lee untying her feet and slipping the towel from her face. Lee was still tied and had hobbled to the family room.

At 0800 hours Lt. Mike Burns was awakened from a sound sleep.

"Yeah, hello," He fell back on his pillow.

"Mike, Peggy Vickers."

"Shit, Peg, don't ruin my Saturday," Burns begged.

"Sorry, Mike. He did it again. Orangevale this time. I called Stone, but there was no answer. Wayne's on his way, but we've got this pretty well covered. White mask, skin tight gloves, flashlight, same as before except this time there was a man in the house, her boyfriend."

"Well, I guess we can be sure of one thing then, can't we?" Burns broke in.

"What's that?"

"We know he reads the paper. I knew the news media would challenge this bastard to hit with a man present."

"Yeah, I was thinking the same thing. Another thing different. He put a cup and saucer on the man's back and told him if he heard it rattle he would come back and kill him. Apparently checked on him four or five times during the hour and a half he was there. He put a cup and saucer on the victim for awhile also. Told her the same thing."

"They all right? The victims, I mean."

"Yeah. They're doing pretty good. The female was scared to death. Still shaking when I got there. It was cold as hell in the house when I got there. We found out later he pulled the plug to the furnace out of the socket for some reason and cut the cord to the television. Same description as the others: five ten, medium build, no pot belly, white male, light complexion. She says his thighs were larger than usual, penis smaller than usual. Said he talked as though his teeth were clenched. Threatened them with a .45 auto. Two kids around seven, eight, but he didn't seem to bother them."

"I'm getting a headache, Peg. This has got to stop. How long before patrol got there?"

"About five minutes after the call. They searched the neighborhood but as usual, nothing. Oh, there is one other thing. She has a poodle. Nosiest little bastard I've ever seen. She had put it in another room while I talked to her because it wouldn't shut up. She says the son of a bitch told her if the dog barked he'd kill it. She says it never made a sound the whole time EAR was there. Don't know if the dog was afraid of him or what. Anyway, I've got a bloodhound enroute and the victim was seen at the Sac Med Center for the rape kit."

"Okay. I'll talk to you Monday. If you come up with anything, give me a call. I'll be here and I'll call the captain and run it down to him."

"Yeah. Just before he left he told the male, 'next place, next time.' Maybe he's going to leave. Mentioned he had killed some people in Bakersfield."

"You got anything else you'd like to fuckin' add? Or do you think you've pissed me off enough? Did he take anything this time?"

"He took money from the male's wallet and from the victim's purse, but then he left it on the kitchen counter."

"Good night, Peg."

"Good night, Chet," Vickers chuckled.

At approximately 0730 hours, the handler and his dog arrived, took up the scent from the articles EAR had touched, and was off and running. As in the past, the scent was lost not far from the scene near a main thoroughfare. The rapist's car had been parked in such a way that it was not in front of anyone's house.

Monday morning at 0730 hours, Vickers was briefing Stone on the rape.

"Anything good from the neighborhood canvass, Peg?" Stone asked.

"Oh, yes. Didn't do us much good though, as usual. But it convinced me that most people are fuckin' stupid or in some time warp. Next door neighbor looked out her window at six o'clock because her dog was barking. She says a dark colored vehicle was backing out of the victim's driveway. Loud exhaust, full size. Didn't see the driver. Really don't know if there is a connection, because the bloodhound followed the scent for three blocks before he lost it. Same as the others. Another neighbor said that about three weeks ago she saw what she thought was a police officer near the victim's house. Says it was late at night. Victim says she never talked to any deputy. The neighbor also says she was bur-glarized two months ago. Entry was through an upstairs window. Said they called the department, but no one showed up to take a report.

"Another neighbor chased a prowler about three months ago. Says the prowler was in a neighbor's backyard and she was single. He chased him over some fences and lost him. White male, twenty-five to thirty, five nine or ten. He didn't call the Department. Another one received a bunch of strange phone calls. Just breathing on the other end. I took the victim to the Med Center."

On August 18, 1977, the Crime Lab concluded that saliva was found on some bubble gum located at the scene and on several spoons, pos-sibly used by EAR. These were checked for blood group factors and a reaction giving that of a group A blood factor was found on two of the spoons.

Phone calls to the Sheriff's Office increased as the information of a serial rapist became wide spread throughout the Sacramento area. Stone and his detectives spent every waking hour, and more and more their restless sleeping hours, thinking of the masked rapist. Nerves be-came frayed as each lead faded into nothing. The detectives pressured their informants to bring back information. Patrol deputies hounded their informants, offered deals, offered money. Nothing.

On 3-24-1977 at 0100 hours Deputy Timmons was working the Rancho Cordova area, cruising neighborhoods, his patrol car head-lights out most of the time, looking for strange vehicles, vehicles not known to him. Timmons was one of the Patrol Division EAR Task Force deputies, a unit developed to focus on the EAR cases.

"1Z1," the dispatcher's voice broke the silence.

"Z1," Timmons responded.

"Z1, meet the man at Dunkin' Donuts on Folsom Boulevard. He wouldn't give his name, but says you'll know him."

"Z1, 10-4."

Timmons pulled into the parking lot of the donut shop and im-mediately Tom Blackwood, a confidential informant of Timmons', ap-proached the patrol car.

"I've got some good shit for you, man," Blackwood whispered, "about the rapist."

"Get in the car, Tom."

Blackwood slid into the passenger seat.

"Your rapist is a burglar named Roy Morris. He's a two-bit thief, been arrested before."

"How do you know he's a rapist, let alone our rapist?"

"I got suspicious 'cause Morris lives in Vallejo and every time he comes to Sac, I read in the paper about another rape. His father's a real estates salesman who's been locked up in a mental ward and his mother's dying of cancer."

"How old is Morris? What's he look like?"

"He's twenty-one, blond hair, maybe five-nine, not too big. He drinks a lot of beer and he got arrested a week ago for prowling. He gave a phony name and I think they just gave him a ticket. He doesn't have any girlfriends."

"Where's he stay when he's in Sac?"

"I don't know. He's adopted. Might stay with his mother. She lives in some apartment on Garfield."

"Thanks, Tom. I'll let you know if anything works out. Keep digging, okay?"

"Yeah, sure. Look, you don't have five dollars you could lend me, do you? I haven't eaten at all today."

"Here's three dollars," Timmons said reaching into his shirt pocket. "That's all I got."

"Thanks, man. I'll catch you later," Blackwood slid out of the patrol car and was gone in the darkness.

At the end of his shift, Timmons stopped in Investigations to give the information to Stone. Stone contacted the apartment manager of the Garfield Apartments and learned that a Phylis Morris lived in Apartment 201.

"I'm Sergeant Stone, Sacramento Sheriff's Department," Stone introduced himself to the frail looking woman who answered the door. "I'm trying to contact a Roy Morris. Would he be your son?"

"Yes, but I can't help you. I haven't seen him in several weeks. You might talk to his sister. She lives over on Fair Oaks Boulevard. What's he done now?"

"We just need to talk to him. He might be able to help us on a case we're working. Do you know your daughter's address?"

"I'll get it for you. She goes by the name of Hart. Mary Hart."

Upon contact, Mary Hart told Stone that her brother had been in a motorcycle accident three years ago and has a pin in his shoulder and a bad knee.

"Do you know who his doctor was?" Stone asked.

"No, but he had his operation at Kaiser."

"Do you know where I could find your brother now?"

CHAPTER TWENTY-THREE

"He lives here in Sacramento sometimes. I think he works for the State."

Stone checked and found out that Morris had worked in the Student Loan Department for the State and had access to all the files. He was not liked by his fellow workers and had been terminated during probation. His attendance had been horrible and he had not worked on any of the nights that the EAR had struck. His supervisor related that Morris walked with a noticeable limp and continually complained of his shoulder hurting.

Morris was never located and was not eliminated, however due to the activities displayed by EAR, Morris was not considered a "good" suspect.

The Crime Lab returned a report to Investigations regarding a band-aid with blood that was found on a picnic table used by EAR during the attack on fifteen year old Nancy Hauser on 12-18-76. Hauser had Type A blood. The blood on the band-aid was Type O.

At 1640 hours Greg Wayne contacted Deborah Hilliard at her residence in Carmichael. On 3-24-1977, she had observed a prowler in her backyard. She described him as five foot nine, one hundred and fifty pounds, twenty-five years old. A neighbor had reported the prowler; however he had disappeared before the deputy had arrived. Hilliard said another neighbor had seen the same prowler about a month ago. The neighbor's twelve year old daughter had seen the subject jump their back fence around 6:30 in the evening. The subject had walked to the patio and stood looking into the house. The daughter called her mother at work and watched as the subject walked around the house. He did not try to break in. Hilliard was asked to contact Investigations to set up an appointment to do a composite of the subject.

On 4-11-1976, at 0930 hours, Carmichael resident Sharon Gregson, eighteen years old, stood in front of her bathroom mirror, curling her hair getting ready for work. Nineteen year old Damon Vista was sitting on the edge of the bathtub watching his pretty fiancee.

"What was that?" Sharon asked, turning her ear toward the front of the house.

"What?" Damon asked, looking in the same direction.

"I heard a noise."

"I didn't hear anything."

"I did," Sharon left the bathroom, walked down the hall and into the living room. She looked toward the large window facing the back-yard. The lined drapes were open, however transparent nylon-type curtains remained drawn. A man standing outside the window seemed to be looking down at the locking device and did not notice Sharon.

"Damon!" Sharon yelled and the male subject looked up. Startled, he turned and started running toward the fence. "There's a man in our backyard!"

Damon ran to the front door, exited, and scrambled for the backyard. The subject had disappeared.

Although several neighbors had been working in their yards, no one saw or heard the subject run from the area.

The prowler, a white male about five ten, tall with dark blond collar-length hair, had disappeared.

Earlier studies of serial rapists done by the Federal Bureau of Investigations suggest that many rapists practice a variety of sexual perversions. Sixty-eight percent of serial rapists used in one study admitted that they began with window peeping while in childhood or adolescence. Most reports describe "peeping" as a nuisance sexual offense and generalize that "peeping toms" are non-dangerous. Recent studies tend to conflict with the generalization, as many "peeping toms" have graduated to rape and murder.

4-15-1977, Carmichael, California

Today everybody's thoughts will be on the government, the Internal Revenue Service. The post office will be the busiest place in town as those taxpayers who have waited until the last minute to mail their taxes will flood the parking lots, stand in long lines, shifting from one foot to the other. This will also be the day that the little old lady at the head of the line, God bless her, will want fifteen five-dollar money orders, pay for them with pennies that aren't rolled, ask a dozen questions not related to anything, and then decide to buy stamps with the purse full of pennies she has left over. Or does that only happen in my line?

One person's mind is not on taxes. One person's mind is focused on a mission: a mission that has been planned for days, maybe weeks.

A dark figure silently passes the house where Sharon Gregson and Damon Vista are sleeping soundly. They are so accustomed to Sharon's father snoring in the master bedroom that it is like the ticking of a grandfather clock. It lulls them into a deeper sleep.

The dark figure silently passes a house that was burglarized a week ago and moves toward a house a block away near Madison and Manzanita. The figure moves from one yard to another. A dog barks from inside one of the residences. It had barked at the same time the night before. One more fence and then the figure moves into the shadows. Watches. Listens. The neighborhood is quiet as the figure approaches the rear sliding glass door. The noise echoes through the night air as the figure pries on the lock and the door slides open. Again the figure stands silent, listening, and then slides into the house.

Karen Vosper and Cameron Wilsey were sleeping soundly when a beam from a flashlight played across their faces. They began to stir.

"Don't look over this way or I'll kill you," a voice broke the stillness. "Roll over on your stomach. Do you know what a .45 magnum is? I'll blow your brains all over the room with it if you don't do what I tell you," the voice growled through clenched teeth.

Wilsey caught a glimpse of the gun pointing at him as he rolled to his stomach.

"All I want is your money and nobody will get hurt. Tie up your husband," Vosper saw the black shoelaces as the light moved slowly across the bed. She tied Wilsey's wrists and laid back on the bed. She felt the intruder pull her hands behind her back and tie them. She felt him lean across her body and tie Wilsey's wrists again.

"Don't move or I'll kill you," the voice hissed.

They heard nothing for about fifteen minutes.

"Come with me. I can't find your purse," the voice broke the silence. "If you move one inch, I'll cut her throat."

Wilsey heard them leave the room. A short time later they were back. He felt his wrists being retied and his ankles were tied with some type of wire cord. They were leaving the bedroom again.

"Don't move or I'll kill her."

Wilsey's heart was pounding. He was afraid for Vosper, he was afraid for himself. The intruder was back in the room. He felt dishes being placed on his back.

"If I hear the dishes fall, I'll kill her first," the voice whispered.

Wilsey heard the intruder talking to Vosper. "Do what I say or I'll kill him," Then they were both gone.

His hands were becoming numb, his fingers swelling, and he tried to loosen the knots to give himself relief. The dishes fell from his back, crashing onto the bed. He felt a gun against his head and heard it being cocked. He waited for the bullet to go crashing into his brain.

"You do that again and I'll kill you," the intruder hissed as he replaced the dishes and then he was gone again.

Twenty minutes passed. Wilsey moved and the dishes fell. The sound rang through his head. He felt a sheet being pulled over his head and again the dishes were placed on his back.

"Don't move or I'll kill her," the voice hissed.

Wilsey's hands were throbbing with excruciating pain. His muscles ached. He tried to concentrate on the dishes, to keep them in place.

"Cameron, Cameron!" he heard Karen calling him. "I've got a knife," She was beside him now, crying, fumbling with the cord and shoelaces on his wrists. His hands were loose and he quickly took the knife from Karen and cut the cords from his ankles and Karen's wrists. He reached for the phone next to the bed. Nothing. The cord had been cut. He was in the kitchen reaching for the wall phone. The cord dangled uselessly from the wall.

"I'm going next door to call the sheriff," he shouted as he ran from the house.

At 0515 hours, Vickers received a call from dispatch. A 261 P.C. had just occurred in Carmichael. At 0537 hours, she arrived on scene and met with Stone and Lt. Burns, who were outside the residence. Vosper and Wilsey were inside sitting on the couch. They were introduced to Vickers by Deputy Thaxter, the first one on the scene.

"She would like to go directly to the Medical Center for examination so she can get cleaned up," Thaxter advised Vickers.

Karen's mother, who had also arrived, drove to the Medical Center with her daughter and Vickers. Karen was taken to the Crisis Center at the hospital prior to the rape examination. At 0647 hours, she was examined by a doctor. At 0730 hours, they left the Center and at 0845 hours, Detective Vickers began her interview of Karen Vosper.

Vosper couldn't recall seeing a mask, but feels the rapist was wearing one when he woke them. She did see the green khaki colored nylon jacket and army boots that were laced up, his dark colored pants tucked inside the boots. She knew he wore gloves, as she could feel them. As with previous victims, he held a knife to her throat at times and she had felt the barrel of a gun against her head. During the rape she could feel the gun in his jacket pocket hitting against her body. He had her take his penis in her hands and masturbate him, questioning her until she called it a cock.

"I need to tell you," Karen looked at Vickers, "he kept going to the kitchen and I could hear him getting into the refrigerator and eating. I checked and we had a half gram of coke in the refrigerator and it's gone. He also took a pill bottle that had two beans in it and a little bit of marijuana."

"Well, we're not here to investigate drug use, so don't worry about it. I am glad that you told me, though. It gives me something else to look at."

At 0416 hours, earlier that morning, X-RAY 5, a two-man patrol car working the EAR detail, was patrolling their area when they received the call of the rape. The officers drove to their prearranged position, the Sunrise Bridge, and parked on the shoulder of the southbound lane of Sunrise Boulevard. The time was noted as 0425 hours when they began writing down license numbers of cars passing by.

At 0427 hours the deputies observed a yellow, two-door Datsun being driving by a white male, twenty-five years old. The driver matched the description of the East Area Rapist and a traffic stop was initiated on the on-ramp to westbound U.S. 50.

Deputy Richards approached the vehicle and observed a plastic squeeze type container of hand lotion in plain view on the front passenger seat. A white surgical type mask was on the dashboard. The driver of the vehicle, who was extremely quiet and cooperative, was asked to sit in the backseat of the patrol car. He was not given his constitutional rights and was not questioned at this time. Deputy Garfield removed the keys from the ignition and opened the trunk of the vehicle. Several large duffel bags and overnight type bags were observed. A hunting knife and handgun were in plain view in one of the bags.

Stone arrived and spoke with the driver, who was still cooperative and gave Stone permission to search the trunk. Rope, shoelaces, leather bindings, and two pairs of shoes, size nine, were also located. The handgun was determined to be a pellet gun. The subject, who stated he was on his way to work as a janitor, agreed to accompany Stone to his residence, where a thorough search was conducted. Nothing was located to connect the subject to any of the rapes. He was fingerprinted, photographed, thanked, and allowed to leave for work.

At 2200 hours, 4-14-77, deputies Rankin and Lee were parked near a residence on Garfield Avenue. They were also part of the EAR Trap Force and were watching the movements of a possible EAR suspect.

At 0416 hours, 4-15-77, they also received the rape call. They immediately left their vehicle and contacted the suspect's mother, who answered the door. She told the deputies that her son was asleep. The deputies told her that a crime had just occurred and her son could be a possible suspect. They needed to visually confirm that he was home so they could clear him. The mother led the deputies to the bedroom and woke her son. It was apparent he had been sleeping for some time. And thus another suspect had been cleared.

During the processing of the Vosper residence, two empty Miller beer bottles were found on the rear patio. None were consumed by the victims. Black shoelaces were found throughout the residence and a bottle of Rose Milk lotion was on the living room floor. A lamp covered with towels was on the floor where Vosper had been sexually attacked. Cords cut from several electrical appliances were also strewn about the residence, as were pieces of towel torn in strips.

The central heating unit was still plugged in, however the rapist had turned the thermostat down to 68 degrees.

A subsequent interview by Stone of Vosper set the time of the attack at 0243 or 0233 hours as Vosper had glanced at the clock upon being wakened. Although the attacker's penis was dry when he placed it in Vosper's hands, it was wet with lotion when he had placed it in her mouth. She had heard a popping sound just prior to the rape, a noise made when the attacker kept pushing the dispenser on the lotion bottle.

Vosper stated that when compared to a dollar bill, the rapist's penis was just a little shorter and less than an inch in diameter. A dollar bill is six inches long.

In checking the knots in the shoelaces, one was an overhand, the rest were granny knots.

The victim's residence was five blocks from a major thoroughfare and three miles from the freeway.

CHAPTER TWENTY-FOUR

Sacramento Bee. April 15, 1977

The East Area Rapist early today attacked his eighteenth victim, a nineteen year old woman who was raped in her home near Madison and Manzanita Avenues. The woman was assaulted between 2:30 and 4:00 a.m. and called Sacramento County Sheriff's Officers shortly afterwards, a Sheriff's spokesman said.

"It's the same M.O. (method of operation) as the others," he said.

The rapist forced his way into the women's house, but the spokesman refused to say what kind of force was used or when the entry was made. In the other seventeen rapes attributed to the East Area Rapist since October, 1975, the victims have been attacked between 10:45 p.m. and 6:45 a.m. by a masked or hooded man who forced his way into their homes.

The rapist has tied and gagged his victims before sexually assaulting them. He has never attacked while there was a man in the home, although he has raped some of his victims with children present. The women have ranged in age from sixteen to late thirties.

Six of the rapes have occurred in a relatively small area between Folsom Boulevard and the American River, north of Watt Avenue. All have been in the Carmichael, Glenbrook, Del Dayo, and Rancho Cordova areas.

The rapist has been described as 25 to 35 years old, white, between 5 feet 8 and 6 feet tall, clean shaven, with dark, neatly cut hair.

After this morning's rape, Sheriff's officers in the area stopped a car nearby and took the driver to headquarters for questioning. After a lengthy investigation, they released him.

CHAPTER TWENTY-FIVE

May 3, 1977

SACRAMENTO POLICE DEPARTMENT OFFICERS Marvin Craig and David Watts were working the East Area Rapist detail in the area of Folsom Boulevard and Julliard Drive. At 0442 hours they were dispatched to the scene of a burglary with the victims being tied up. At 0445 hours officers arrived at the scene, approached the front door, and knocked.

"Help, help! I'm tied up!" came from inside the residence. A moaning could also be heard in the background. Watts tried the door and found it to be locked. Both officers drew their weapons and as Watts kicked the door, just below the doorknob, Craig ran to the backyard. As the door splintered near the lock and slammed open, two more officers arrived on the scene. Watts moved toward the male voice still yelling for help as a second officer joined him. They found Leonard Terranian sitting on his bed, his hands tied behind his back and his ankles tied, both with shoelaces.

Two of the assisting officers found Sandra Terranian in an upstairs breakfast area. Lying on her back with only a pajama top, her hands tied behind her back and ankles tied with shoelaces, Sandra was moaning with fear and pain. Humiliation is not a thought that crosses the mind of a woman violated and terrorized by a monster.

Both victims were cut free of their ties and Sandra was given a blanket to cover her nakedness while they waited for detectives and a bloodhound team to search the area. The bloodhound lost the scent near the levee behind the victims' residence. A tire track and a shoe impression were found in the wet earth near the area. Casts were taken for possible future comparisons.

At 0718 hours Sandra and Leonard Terranian arrived at Sacramento Medical Center where Sandra would undergo a rape examination.

Stone was just beginning to close his door to leave for his office when the ringing of his phone stopped him. Leaving the door open, he hurried back into the kitchen and picked up the phone on its fourth ring.

"Hello?"

"Jim, this is Gretchen," Gretchen Mitchell answered. "I'm just getting off duty and the P.D. just brought in a rape victim. It looks like one of your EAR cases and I thought I better call to see if you knew."

"Nope. Nobody called me. Do you know when it happened?" Stone asked.

"I think around three o'clock. I guess they got free around four thirty. Husband and wife with two small kids."

"I don't know if anyone called our Dispatch. I'll call and find out. Thanks."

"Jim?"

"Yeah?"

"Don't tell anyone I called. I could get in trouble. I just thought you should know."

"My lips are sealed. I appreciate it and I'll call you later this afternoon," Stone hung up and then dialed the Sheriff's Dispatch.

"Sheriff's Radio. Is this an emergency?" the dispatcher answered.

"This is Sergeant Stone. Who's the supervisor on duty?"

"Good morning, Sergeant. Liz Campbell until eight. Do you want to talk to her?"

"Yeah. Please."

"Good morning, Sergeant. This is Liz. What can I do for you?"

"Liz, did we get a call from the Police Department about a rape earlier this morning? Around four or so?"

"No, we didn't hear anything. EAR hit again, Jim?"

"Apparently, and the bastards didn't call us again. Thanks, Liz."

"Sure. Anything you need us to do for you?"

"No. I'll take care of it when I get to the office. Talk to you later."

At 0930 hours the doctor finished the examination of Sandra Terranian. Investigators who had been talking to Leonard stood up when she entered the cafeteria where they had been waiting.

"Sandra, I'm Sergeant Fallow. This is my partner, Detective Johnston. We're sorry to have to bother you at a time like this, but we need to ask you some questions about this morning."

"I understand. What do you need?"

"Leonard told us what you were doing all day up until the time you went to bed. We need you to tell us what you can that happened after that."

"Where do you want me to start?"

"Well, we'll have to go into it in more detail later, but for now, why don't you start just before you went to bed. Did you hear anything, get any phone calls? Anything suspicious?"

"I told your officers everything this morning. I really can't think of anything else," Sandra looked drawn out. She was still frightened;

however humiliation, anger, and questions about self blame had begun to creep into her thoughts.

"I know, but I need you to go over it again for me. I'm sorry, but it really is important," Fallow urged.

"Well, our two boys went to bed at ten o'clock, right after the television program, "Noah's Ark" finished. Len and I stayed up and watched some more television and Len went to bed around midnight. All our bedrooms are on the first floor, and I went upstairs to do my exercises. While I was doing sit-ups I heard what sounded like a thump. A sound like my sons make when they jump the fence when they come back from the levee into our backyard. I looked out our picture window but didn't see anything unusual. I pulled the shades and went downstairs to go to bed. I checked all the doors to make sure they were locked and then went to bed."

"About what time was that?"

"Around one, I guess. Len was already asleep and I think I fell asleep right away. I guess it was about an hour later that I woke up. I don't know if it was a voice or a noise that woke me, but I saw him standing there in the doorway. He had a small flashlight in his left hand. I woke Len. The person seemed real calm and spoke in a calm voice, real soft. He told us not to move, all he wanted was our money. He said he had a gun and he shined his light on it. He said he could kill us and easily get across the levee to his camp.

"He said, 'I got a .45 caliber military automatic. I'll kill you if you move,' He said it twice, and then he pressed the gun against Len's head. He told me to tie Len's hands behind his back and he gave me a shoelace. He said if I didn't tie him tight he would kill me and everybody else in the house. He told Len that if he moved he would kill him and if I looked at him he would kill me. He made me lie on my stomach and then he tied my hands real tight and then checked Len's hands to make sure I tied them tight. He said he wanted money for cocaine and Len told him his wallet was on the dresser. He said 'This can't be all your money. You better have more money or I'll kill you both.' He asked me for more money, and I told him my purse was upstairs. He started to shiver like he was an addict, but he stopped, so I think it was a put on."

"He told me that if I tried to grab him he would kill me and everybody in the house, then he'd flee to his camp on the river," Leonard broke in. "Then he tied my hands again, real tight, and my ankles. He said something about wanting big money because he needed a fix."

"He told me to roll over on my back and get up," Sandra continued. "He helped me and then he shoved his gun in my back to make me move."

"Did you see him at all? At any time?" Fallow aksed.

"I really didn't see him. I guess I was too scared," Sandra related.

"What about you, Leonard? Can you think of anything else about him?"

"Well, like I said, I know his clothing was dark and I know he had a .45 automatic. His gloves were heavy construction type. I think his mask was brown, but I still can't remember if it was a ski mask or a stocking."

"Any eye holes? Holes for his mouth?" Fallow pursued.

"I don't know. I really couldn't tell."

"Okay, after he had you sit up, Sandra, what then?" Fallow asked.

"He took me upstairs to show him where my purse was."

"Before they left," Leonard broke in, "he put a jewelry box on my back. Said if I made a noise he would kill everyone in the house."

"He told me to lie down on the floor near the bathroom and he tied my feet," Sandra continued. "He went into the bathroom, then he put a shower cap over my face. I heard him go downstairs but he was only gone for about five minutes and then he was back. He untied my feet and said he was going to tie me to a table leg. He was just wandering around the kitchen and family room. I heard him unzip something. It sounded like a large zipper, like a gym bag. I heard him open and close the refrigerator and then he told me to sit up. He started to masturbate. He was making a greasy, slimy sound like he was jacking off. He said, 'Do you know what this sound is? If you don't tell me, I'll kill you.' He made me massage his penis with my hands behind me. He said, 'Do it like you're doing it to your husband.' Then he raped me. He said, 'You know, you're big. Bet you like big cocks, too.' Every time he said something he wanted me to answer. He got mad and called me a bitch. Called it more than once. After he raped me he tied my feet again and told me to lie on my stomach. Then he put some glass things on my back and said if he heard them move or fall he would kill me. I really thought he was going to kill us all, Sergeant. My little boys, Leonard, me," She began to cry.

"It's all right, honey," Leonard soothed her. "it's over and everybody is safe."

"I know," she sobbed. "He left for a long time and I thought he was gone but then he came back and pressed the gun against my neck and he said, 'You don't want to die, do you?' Every time I tried to answer he told me to shut up. When I started to cry he got mad and told me to shut up. I heard him in the kitchen. He said he was going to eat. I don't know when he left. I just heard Len talking to someone and then the officers were there."

"Have you noticed anything unusual lately? Dogs barking late at night, the gate to your backyard open? Anything at all?" Johnston asked.

"No, not really, except that we have been getting hang up phone calls around midnight after I return home from college. It would ring once or maybe just a half ring. No one would be on the other end. It's been happening for the last week," Sandra answered.

"One more thing and then we'll get you back home," Fallow looked down at his hands and then into Sandra's eyes. "Can you describe his penis? Size, I mean."

"It was small, real short," Sandra shrugged.

"Is there anything else you can think of? Either of you?" Fallow asked.

"When he was going through my closets he asked me if I was in the Service," Leonard responded. "I told him yes, and he asked me which one. I told him the Air Force. He said 'I got thrown out'."

"He say which Service?"

"No, just that he got thrown out. One time when he checked on me, he said if I moved while he was eating he would hear me. He sounded like he had something in his mouth. When he wanted to make a point, he would breath real heavy and talk like he was nervous. I think it was fake because he sounded like he had been through it all before. He sounded like an actor reading from a script."

"God damn it, Mike!" Stone was standing in front of Burns' office. "The bastards got hit again and they didn't call us. We've had fuckin' meetings, we've given them all our reports, and the sons of bitches don't even call when they get hit."

"I know, Jim. It's a real fucked up way to work, but we can't force them to cooperate. Just stay on top of them and maybe...." Burns' voice trailed off.

"Fuck them. We can work that way, too. Tell them shit," Stone fumed.

"We don't want to get into a pissing match. The only one's who lose are all of us. Especially the victims. Just keep hammering. I'll make a few calls."

"Yeah, I know. Make a hell of a headline in the newspaper, though, wouldn't it? 'Sacramento Police refuse to cooperate with the Sheriff. EAR keeps on hitting'."

"This is only their second one, Jim. Maybe the ones working it didn't realize it was EAR. Give them a call and see what you can find. Maybe they have something."

"Okay, Mike. I'll get back to you," Stone walked back to his desk shaking his head.

"Greg, call that ignorant fuck over at the PD and see if you can get anything on their rape last night. If they'll admit they had one."

Sacramento Union, May 4, 1977

New Attack by Rapist.

A man whose method of attack closely matches that of the East Area Rapist entered a College Greens home early Tuesday, bound a man and woman, and raped the woman, police said. The man entered the home after prying a sliding glass door and awakened the couple while holding a gun on them. He was wearing a ski mask.

It was revealed Tuesday that it was the second in a series of attacks attributed to the East Area Rapist where a man has been in the house. It had been reported in previous cases that the woman victims were alone or in their homes with only their children.

"Greg," Stone asked when he arrived for work Wednesday morning, "Did you get anything from the PD on their rape or are they keeping it a secret?"

"I've got copies of their report. Fallow apologized, said they got so tied up in it they just thought someone had called us. Nothing new, really. Same MO, same acts, same threats, same small cock. He didn't cut any electrical cords, used shoelaces to tie them. Must have been in the house awhile before he woke them because the shoelaces all belonged to the victims. Took them out of their shoes from the closet. Two small boys in the house but he didn't bother them. One thing, though. He got mad at her and called her a bitch several times. Fallow says she was scared to death. Said she knew they were all going to die."

"Well, they all think that. My fear is that sooner or later, one of them is going to be right. He's getting braver and he's going to have to do something more to get his thrills," Stone remarked.

"Well, he's hitting places with men present, so he's getting his confidence up. Hate to think of the next step," Wayne replied.

"Jim, Greg," Burns called from his office, "Come here. The boss went in front of the Board of Supervisors yesterday afternoon with the CAO. He got us unlimited funds to work this case, so we're going to put together a full Task Force. We think we can get an office away from here. Patrol is putting fifteen deputies on it, and they're to coordinate with us. I've been put in charge and you two, along with Vickers, Bonnell, and Merton, will be the investigators. The Sheriff wants us all in the patrol briefing room at two for briefing. Let the other three know. Sac PD will be there also with some representatives. They indicate they will give one or two investigators to the Task Force."

"Gonna be some pissed off detectives, Mike. They'll all want to be on this," Stone stated.

"Well, they'll have to get pissed on again because that's it."

"You're the boss. That's why they pay you so much. Thanks, Mike. For us, I mean," Stone replied.

"Yeah. Well, if we don't catch him we may all want to be somewhere else."

CHAPTER TWENTY-SIX

May 5, 1977, 0240 hours, Orangevale

STONE WOKE UP to the ringing of his phone. He reached and picked up the phone. "Yeah?"

"Sergeant Stone?" the female voice inquired.

"Yeah?"

"This is Dispatch, Sergeant. We just got a call of a rape in Orangevale. You're the first one on the call out list. It says all EAR rapes are to go to the Task Force and Patrol says it's him."

"We just got together yesterday. Is this a test? Christ, EAR just hit yesterday. He wouldn't hit again this soon."

"No test, Sarge. The real thing."

"Okay, give it to me and I'll be on my way. Call Lt. Burns and let him know and call Jerry Merton and Peggy Vickers. Tell them to meet me there as soon as they can."

"Will do, Sarge. We called the Crime Lab. The Corporal requested them and a dog is on the scene."

"Thanks. I'll be there in forty-five minutes."

At 0315 hours Stone arrived at the scene. Burns was standing outside the residence talking to a deputy.

"Hi, Jim. I just got here. Timmons was the first one on the scene. He was just going to run it down for me."

"Hi, Dan," Stone greeted the deputy. "You sure this is our man? He just hit one in the city day before yesterday. He's never hit this soon before."

"It's him, all right. No doubt about it. He confronted them outside in the driveway but everything else is classic EAR. The ransacking, same sex acts, same statements. Walk into the house and you can feel the bastard," Timmons stated.

At 0330 hours Vickers arrived. She was briefed by Timmons and then went inside to contact twenty-five year old Sue Barger and her friend, thirty-four year old Phil Raines. Upon entering, Vickers observed several dishes and cups on the floor in the dining room. Several kitchen drawers were left open, and the phone cord had been severed. Both victims were seated on the couch in the living room. Both were obviously shaken.

"I'm Detective Vickers. Peg," she introduced herself. Raines introduced Barger and himself.

"I'm going to have to ask you some questions," Vickers began. "but I need to separate you. Sergeant Stone will talk to you, Phil. Deputy Timmons said you told him that the attacker wore gloves at all times?"

"Yes, he had them on every time he touched me, at least," Barger stated.

"If he touched you with his bare hands, we have a method of developing fingerprints on the skin. It's called iodine fuming. It's an iodine-silverplate transfer. If you're sure he always wore gloves, there is no need to try it."

"No. I know he always wore gloves," Barger stated.

"He did with me also," Raines stated.

"Okay. So you will know what's going to happen, let me explain. We're pretty sure it's the same person we've been after."

"You mean the East Area Rapist?" Raines asked.

"Yes. So we need to follow a procedure. I need you to be examined at the Sacramento Medical Center. They know the procedure we need to follow. We need to get you there as soon as possible to preserve any physical evidence. I'll drive you there and we can talk after the examination."

"I have my two dogs here with me. I can't leave them, and I want Phil to go with me," Barger replied.

"They can ride with us and Phil needs medical attention, also. His hands are purple and swollen from being tied so tight. Sergeant Stone can meet us there later."

At 0500 hours both victims were attended to by a staff member from the Crisis Center at the Medical Center. At 0600 hours, Barger underwent a rape examination and Raines was attended to by medical staff. He had temporarily lost feeling in both hands, however the damage was not permanent.

At 0700 hours the examination of Barger was completed.

Stone interviewed Raines in the Medical Center cafeteria. Vickers interviewed Barger in the office of the University Police assigned to the Medical Center.

Sue Barger and Phil Raines worked together and had been friends for approximately six months. This was the first time Barger had been at Raines' house. She had met him to discuss a job interview she had been on earlier that day. Although they were good friends, the relationship was purely platonic.

She had arrived at Raines' house at approximately 10:30 p.m. with her two dogs. They discussed her interview and watched the last of the Richard Nixon interview and the start of the basketball game. Barger had said she had a very uneasy feeling while driving to Raines' and when they let her dogs into the backyard, she and Raines had stood just outside the door. She again had the feeling someone was outside the house and her dogs wouldn't stop barking. When they went inside, she still had the feeling they were being watched.

At approximately 0015 hours, she decided it was time to leave. The dogs were the first to go out the door and immediately turned to the right and began barking. She could see the hair on the dogs' backs stand straight up. All of a sudden, the attacker was there in front of her wearing a ski mask and holding a gun pointed at her. The mask was beige, knitted, with holes for the eyes, nose, and mouth. The first thing she had seen was the gun, then the mask. He wore light brown gloves with tiny air holes, a dark blue navy type jacket, and a brown pullover sweater. Sue, who is five foot eight, felt the attacker was no more than five nine.

He told them to turn around and go back into the house. If they didn't do what he said he would blow their brains all over the house. He told them to lie on their stomachs and threw some shoelaces at Sue and told her to tie Raines. He kept telling her he would shoot her if she didn't do what he said and he would blow her brains out. He told her to keep her dogs quiet or he would kill them all. The dogs were barking and snarling, but made no attempt to bite the attacker. After tying Raines' hands and feet, the intruder told her to put her dogs in the bedroom. He kept telling them not to look at him or he would kill them.

He had her lie on her stomach again and ordered her to cross her ankles, however he did not tie them. She felt the attacker had turned off the lights, but she couldn't be sure as she had her eyes closed so tight. She knew she was going to be killed and didn't want to see when he pulled the trigger.

He put dishes on their backs and told them if he heard them click he would kill them. He said all he wanted was their money and he would leave. Raines told him he would give him anything he wanted. The attacker put a knife to his neck and told him to shut up. He took Barger to a back bedroom and told her not to move. He threatened her with the gun and put the knife against her throat.

He unbuttoned her blouse and cut her bra with the knife. He blindfolded her and she heard him masturbating with lotion before he raped her.

"You better swear to God you didn't see a van down the street," he said it three times and made her repeat it. She heard him go to the kitchen and open and close the refrigerator. He told her she had better not make a sound while he was eating and drinking or he would kill her. Barger stated that the rapist seemed to be trying to disguise his voice by talking through his teeth and keeping his lips together.

The man's penis was about five inches long and a little larger around than a quarter. He seemed to get very frustrated as he couldn't keep an erection.

Barger's clothes were collected and sent to the Crime Lab. On November 29, 1977, two semen stains found on Barger's sweater were tested for ABO blood group activity. No ABO activity was detected. This result is consistent with the stains originating from a person who is a non-secretor of ABO substance. The ABO blood group of such individuals cannot be determined by testing of their secretions. This test confirmed that the attacker was included in 20 percent of the population. Eighty percent of the population was now eliminated.

Black, blue, and white shoelaces were used to tie the victims. These were all brought to the scene by the rapist.

After Vickers dropped Barger, Raines, and the two dogs off, she met Stone at Denny's restaurant for coffee. Vickers told him that Barger had been raped three times and had been orally copulated by EAR.

A canvass of the area by the X-Ray units (Patrol Division's EAR Trap Force) provided very little pertinent information.

One neighbor three houses from the scene of the attack had observed a subject sitting in a vehicle outside her residence on Tuesday evening. She described the vehicle as a metallic gray Plymouth with the first letter of the license as a "D." She had reported the incident and a uniformed deputy had responded. The subject was GOA.

Sacramento Bee, May 5, 1977

East Area Rapist Attacks 20th Victim in Orangevale

The East Area Rapist attacked his twentieth victim early today after confronting a couple in an Orangevale driveway at gun point and ordering them back into the house, Sheriff's deputies said. It was only the second time in the 19-month series of rapes the victims have been confronted outside their homes. It was the third time couples have been confronted by the rapist.

CHAPTER TWENTY-SEVEN

"**TOM, WAKE UP!**" Beth Rideout touched her husband's shoulder, pushed it gently twice. "Tom. Tom."

"Huh? What?"

"Someone's on the roof. Listen!"

"What in the hell is going on?" Tom Rideout sat up in bed, listening to the footsteps on their roof.

"Dogs are barking in the neighborhood. Something's going on," Beth's heart was pounding.

"The footsteps have stopped. Whoever it was must have left," Tom laid back, listening.

"You better check, Tom. Someone was on our roof."

"I'm sure he's long gone now. It's all right."

0100 hours, two blocks north

"Mary, wake up. Listen," Dean Walker shook his wife.

"What?" Mary Walker growled, coming out of a sound sleep.

"Listen. Someone's on our roof. I hear them walking. Hear them?"

"Oh, my God, Dean. What are we going to do? Why would some-one be on our roof?" she whispered.

"I don't know. Call 9-1-1 and have them send a deputy. I'm going to check on Jimmy," Dean slid out of bed to check on their fourteen year old son. When he returned, Mary was still on the phone with the dispatcher.

"Yes, I still hear him up there," she told the dispatcher.

"Jimmy's sound asleep," Dean told her.

"They're sending a deputy right over," Mary told him. "They want me to stay on the phone with them until he gets here."

Four minutes later they could still hear someone on the roof. Approximately one minute later the dispatcher advised Mary that a deputy was outside. A short time later, Dean answered the doorbell and spoke with the deputy.

"I've checked all around your residence and I couldn't find anything or anybody. You're sure it sounded like someone was on your roof?" the deputy asked.

"Not sounded like. It was. My wife and I both heard him," Dean replied.

"Well, it looks like he's gone, then," the deputy replied. "I'll cruise the neighborhood for awhile."

Dean locked the door and returned to the bedroom.

"Did he find anything?" Mary asked.

"I guess not. Maybe it was the wind."

"Someone was on our roof, Dean. We both heard him."

"Well, I guess whoever it was got scared off by the deputy."

No report was ever filed on the incident.

0200 hours

"Dean, wake up! Someone's outside our door! They're trying to get in!" Mary shook her husband's shoulder.

"What the hell is going on?" Dean yelled. "Get my gun," He jumped out of bed and ran toward the sliding glass door leading to the backyard. He turned on the outside light, pulled back the curtain, and looked into the backyard. Nothing moved. No sounds, no dogs barking.

"Whoever it was is gone again. I'll check the yard in the morning to see if I can find anything. I'll leave the outside light on," Dean went back to bed.

"You're not going back and sleep and I think you should bring Jimmy in here with us for the rest of the night."

"He'll be all right. I'll stay awake, but I'm sure whoever it was won't be back again. We heard him twice, so I'm sure we scared him off. He thinks I've got a gun," Dean laid back on the bed.

The neighborhood canvass continued by the Sacramento Police Department investigators. Six homes in the area of the Terranian rape had received hang-up phone calls over the past three weeks, two neighbors had been burglarized.

One neighbor advised that sometime around Christmas she had found a plastic bag under her window. The plastic bag had contained a pair of cotton gloves and a flashlight.

In the meantime, Greg Wayne received a call from a female who suspected her ex-fiancee of being EAR. He met her at her apartment.

"I'm Detective Wayne," he introduced himself. "You called about your boyfriend?"

"He's not my boyfriend. Not now, anyway. I broke off our engagement in March. I've been reading about the rapes in the papers and I thought I better call."

"What's your friend's name?"

"Greg. Greg Glass."

"Why do you think Greg might be a rapist?"

"Well, I saw a ski mask at his house and he laughed and said he was EAR. Later he said the ski mask was for riding his motorcycle. Anyway, he used to beat me real bad. On March 17th, he put me in the hospital and then on the 18th you had a lady get raped. He came back today and wanted to get back together. I don't want anything to do with him. I used to find pieces of jewelry and women's underpants at his house. I figured it was from girls he had there when I wasn't. He used to brag about burglarizing."

"What about his sexual habits? Anything you feel might be different?"

"Yeah. He was a sex fiend. He likes to use lotions to lubricate his penis. At times, he couldn't reach a climax, but he insisted on sex twice a day while we were together. Toward the end he wanted me ten times a day. When I got too sore, he masturbated. He was crazy. I mean, everybody likes sex, but he was nuts."

"Yeah," Greg replied, wondering how anyone could get it up once with this one, let alone ten times a day. "I know this may sound strange, but how big is his penis?"

"Big. Real big. That's why he had to lubricate it."

"How tall is he? How heavy?"

"He's six feet, weighs about two hundred pounds, I guess."

"Okay. Look, thanks. If you can give me Greg's address, we'll check him out."

Other Task Force officers were canvassing the Greenback Lane area of Orangevale. A female on Viceroy told them that approximately two months ago a white male in his thirties had knocked on her door and stated he was with the American Pet Association. He asked her if she had any pets she needed registered. When she told him no, he left, but paused in front of her garage and appeared to be examining the door lock. She became uneasy and checked outside for him, but he was gone. She checked with a neighbor who saw him and said he only had gone to her house. The woman had checked with the Better Business Bureau and was told there was no such association in Sacramento or California.

On May 10th, around two in the morning, she awoke and thought she saw a light go out. She did not check further and had no further incidents.

An appointment was made for her to contact the Sheriff's Department to complete a composite of the individual.

CHAPTER TWENTY-EIGHT

May 13, 1977, Citrus Heights.

THE DARK FIGURE slipped into the backyard of the Merlindale residence, a black gym bag hanging from his shoulder. It was a familiar area to him now. He had been here several times over the last month. He looked at the roof he had climbed onto the night before and then silently scaled the fence into the next yard. He knew no dogs would be lying in wait as he silently moved from one yard to the next. His destination was set. Another house, another familiar roof. He had hid in the darkness behind the fence when the deputy had checked around the house. He hadn't even entered the backyard. Just shined his flashlight around for a brief moment. Shortly after he had watched the deputy drive off. He had stayed crouched next to the fence and when the deputy had not returned and the lights had been turned off in the house, he had approached the sliding glass door. He had tried it and heard the man and woman yelling inside. He had left the neighborhood then.

Tonight he was back. Tonight he carried his black zippered bag. Tonight this house was not his destination. He moved to the next yard and he was there. His destination.

He watched them through the window as he sat in the darkness. The light from their television flickered off the walls, bathing the couple on the couch in its subdued light. The evening was cold, but his heavy jacket and the knowledge that he was the master, the one in charge, kept him warm. He watched his victim doze, her head falling on her husband's shoulder. He watched the German shepherd puppy lying at the feet of its masters.

The movie was over, she was awake. Soon they would be in bed. He watched as the man approached the television...and changed the channel. A basketball game flashed on the screen and the man settled back on the couch.

The dark figure moved away from the window to the back of the yard. He could still see the couple as he sat, his back against the fence. Only occasionally did he shift his position or check his watch. The game was over. He checked his watch again. Two o'clock. He crept closer as the couple left the room, the female first as he saw the light from the master bedroom glow faintly through the drape-covered window. The television was off, and the room disappeared into darkness.

The night was his as he saw the soft glow from the bedroom extinguished. The house now was as dark as his world, and he quickly approached a window. The screen easily slid from its frame, metal against metal sounding in the stillness. He heard them!

"I hear something! I hear something!" the female voice broke the silence.

"It's just the cat in the litter box," the male voice replied.

"I heard something at the side of the house," the female voice again.

"It's just a tree brushing the house in the wind," the male insisted.

The dark figure leaned the screen against the house. Silence from within. No lights. No movement. The dog was also silent.

May 14, 1977

It was three o'clock as the figure worked on the window, the screw driver forcing the lock as the window slid open. The figure knelt beside his black bag and removed a nylon stocking, pulling it down over his face, distorting his features from the tightness. He lifted the bag, reached through the open window and dropped the bag on the bed inside the empty bedroom. The silence, the darkness, they were his allies. He again reached into the bag and removed a flashlight, a knife, and a blue steel .45 automatic. He was safe now as he silently moved across the floor toward the sleeping couple in the master bedroom. He watched them, his eyes accustomed to the darkness, as he stood in the doorway. The light from his flashlight began to slowly play across the sleeping couple's faces. She was the first to stir, then the man.

"You make a sound and I'll kill you. I have a .45 and I'll kill you if you move," he hissed through the mask. He knew they could see the gun in the light of the flashlight. "I'm going to take your money and I want some food and then I'll leave in my van. Get on your stomachs. I'm just going to tie your hands and legs," He removed shoelaces from his jacket pocket and threw them on the bed beside her. "Tie his hands," He could see her fumbling, tying bow ties. "Do it over. Tie them tighter. In a knot, or I'll kill you."

He pushed her to the bed, grabbing her hands and pulling them behind her back. She moaned with pain as the laces bit into her wrists.

"Don't hurt her," the man growled.

"Shut up or I'll kill you."

"My kitten. It's in bed!" she cried.

"Shut up!" he commanded.

He lifted the blankets from their feet.

"Cross your ankles," he ordered. He tied her feet first and then he retied the husband's hands, watching the laces bite deep into the flesh. Then he tied his feet. He pressed the gun against the man's neck.

"Where's the money?"

"On the dresser."

He turned toward the dresser and saw the bottle filled with pennies. He hit the top of the bottle with his gun, breaking the neck of the bottle. The dog sat watching the dark figure searching through the closet, its head cocked to one side. He picked the dog up and carried it into another room. He could feel the dog shivering in his arms. He placed the dog on the bed and closed the door.

"Is there any money in the green box?" he asked.

"It's blue. No there isn't," the man answered.

"You better not be lying or I'll kill you."

"There's just insurance papers," the man explained.

He pried the lock with his knife. Only papers. He threw them on the floor. The glass coffee mug on the dresser caught his eye. He removed the Canadian coins and put them in his jacket pocket.

"I have to take a break now," he whispered to them and stepped into the backyard through the sliding glass door. The night air cooled his body. He lifted the nylon off his mouth and breathed deeply.

"Do you have a purse?" he asked as he entered the room and closed the door.

"It's in the family room," the male answered.

He left the room and walked down the hall to the family room. He saw the woman's purse sitting on the bookshelf and then he walked into the kitchen, ignoring the purse. He picked up a cup and saucer from the counter and carried them back into the bedroom.

"I can't find your purse," he hissed as he placed the cup and saucer on the man's back. "If I hear this move, I'll slit her throat, cut off her ear, and bring it to you," he threatened the male as he untied her feet with one pull of the slip knot and swung her to her feet over the edge of the bed.

"Walk and don't look at me. If you don't do as I tell you I'll kill you both," He pushed her in the back with the gun as he walked her to the family room. As he left the bedroom he glanced at the clock on the night stand: 0445 hours.

"On your stomach," he ordered her. "Cross your legs." He knelt behind her and tied her ankles. He took her purse from the shelf and emptied it on the couch. He put the money in his pocket and walked back into the kitchen. He opened the refrigerator and took out a beer, removing the cap with his gloved hand as he walked back into the family room.

"Please God, don't kill me. Please!" He heard her whisper to herself.

"Shut up," he ordered her. "You better cooperate or I'll kill you."

He went back to the bedroom to check on the male. He put the gun against the man's head.

"You move and I'll kill you," he threatened. He took his knife and pressed it against the man's neck. "I'm going to rest now and have a beer," he whispered as he left the room.

He walked down the hall and into the bathroom and opened the medicine cabinet. He removed a bottle of Vaseline and closed the cabinet door. He removed a towel hanging from a rack. He saw his face in the mirror, illuminated by the light of his flashlight, his features distorted, his eyes staring at himself and then he was back in the family room.

The woman was still praying, pleading for her life. He stood and watched her and then tore the towel in half. He walked to the television and placed half the towel over the front of the set. He placed a candle holder on the towel to hold it in place and then turned on the television with the sound off. The subdued light from the picture tube washed the room with a faint glow.

He placed a cup and saucer on her back.

"If you move, I'll kill you," he hissed as he tied the other half of the torn towel around her head, covering her eyes.

He unbuckled his belt and unzipped his fly, letting his pants fall around his ankles. She was crying now, deep sobs.

"No. Just leave me alone and go," Her voice was wracked with fear.

"Be quiet or I'll kill you. I'll slit your throat."

He removed the top from the Vaseline jar and felt his penis begin to harden as he removed one glove and spread the Vaseline over his penis. He began to massage himself as he approached the woman lying on her stomach. He knelt over her, placing his penis in her hand.

"Massage it. Play with it," he hissed as he moved back and forth in her hand. He moved from her, watching through the nylon stocking. He reached down, rolled her over, and untied her feet. He slid her pajama bottoms down over her feet and reached for her underpants. He pulled them down, feeling her resistance. He stared at her nakedness, then lifted the nylon mask off his mouth and knelt between her legs, his tongue exploring. He lifted his head, spread her legs, and entered her.

"You are beautiful," he whispered. "I'm going to take you in the van with me. How would you like to be in the river?" Her body was shaking with fear under him and she again started to cry.

"Shut up. Don't make a sound or I'll kill you," he hissed.

He pulled out of her and stood up. He rolled her over onto her stomach and replaced the cup and saucer on her back. He watched her as he dressed. Her diamond ring caught his eye and he reached for her hand, pulling on the ring. She was resisting, trying to pull her hand from him. The bindings prevented her from tearing her hand away.

"No, please don't take them. Please don't take them off," she pleaded. He put the gun to her head.

"Shut up or I'll kill you," Her body shook with each sob that came from deep within her chest. Cries of fear, of desperation, of humiliation as the rings slid from her finger.

He picked up his bag and walked to the back door. He turned and looked at her, her naked body trembling in the glow from the television. His night was over as he entered the backyard, climbed the fence, and disappeared into the darkness.

It only took him three minutes to get to his car parked on the street next to the neighboring apartment complex. Greenback Lane to U.S. Interstate 80 took less than seven minutes. He was now one of the many commuters traveling through Sacramento at 5:30 in the morning.

At 0557 hours the first call went out to the patrol units. A rape in the Citrus Heights area. As the beat officer responded to the scene, other officers took up prearranged positions copying down license numbers of cars passing by, stopping those that could possibly be the suspect. Somewhere a subject in dark clothing carried his zippered bag into his residence, unconcerned with the activity going on behind him.

Deputy Phil Money arrived at the scene. Upon entering the residence he noted brown shoelaces lying on the floor beside a pair of light pink bikini panties. The victim's purse was on the couch, its contents spilled on the floor. A plastic bottle of Vaseline Intensive Care lotion was next to the purse, its top off.

Janet Pace and her husband, Randy, were seated on the couch near the purse. Janet Pace was still sobbing, her head on her husband's shoulder. Deputy Marilyn Waddell, a female member of the Patrol EAR

Trap Force, arrived a short time later. Iodine fuming of the victim's body for prints by Waddell proved negative.

At 0710 hours Janet Pace was transported to the Sacramento Medical Center by Detective Vickers. As with those before her, Pace spoke with a member of the Crisis Center prior to the rape examination.

Janet and Randy Pace had lived at their current address for approximately three months at the time of the attack. On 5-14-77 at 0900 hours Greg Wayne was contacted by Nancy Martingale, the previous owner of the residence.

"The reason I called," Martingale advised, "is that when I was selling the house I had a real strange realtor tour the house. He said he was from the Brannigan Realty Company, although a realtor from that company had previously toured the house. He seemed more interested in the outside. He asked real weird questions that frightened me. He asked about my husband, where he worked, why my daughter wasn't home. Things like that. His eyes seemed to glare at me and I was real uneasy with him there."

"What did he look like? His age, height?" Wayne asked.

"I guess five ten. Maybe twenty-five years old, medium frame, brown hair, dark complexion."

"Did you get his name?"

"I think he said it was Frank Boham. The other realtor was a Mr. Barker."

"Did you see his car?"

"Yes. I was real nervous so I watched him when he left. His car didn't match his appearance. It was a ratty brown color, older car. He was well dressed."

"When did you move out of the house, Mrs. Martingale?"

"February seventh. Before I moved I got several hang up phone calls. It's probably nothing, but I thought I better let you know just in case."

"We really appreciate it. You did the right thing and if we come up with anything we will let you know," Wayne concluded the call.

Wayne contracted the Brannigan Realty Company. Neither realtor worked for them. He started calling Realty Companies and at one o'clock he found that both realtors had worked at the Branford Realty Company on American River Drive. Frank Boham had recently moved to South Lake Tahoe. Barker still worked for Branford. He was sixty-two years old.

Wayne contacted the South Lake Tahoe Police Department to inquire if Boham was known to them. He left his phone number with the dispatcher. At three o'clock, Sergeant Williams returned the call.

"You wanted to know about Frank Boham?" Williams asked.

"Yeah. We're working a series of rapes down here and his name popped up. Have you had any contact with him?" Wayne asked.

"Yup. We had a rash of apartment burglaries and assaults on women up here. On several of the attacks, he would be the first one on the scene after the call was put out. Boham would say he chased the suspect on foot and lost him. At the time, he was a security guard for an outfit up here. We found out he had a police scanner. Anyway, I talked to him. Couldn't come up with anything concrete. All this happened in 1975 and he said he was moving to Sacramento to work. Said he was born in Sac and lived there until he joined the Service."

"Well, apparently he's back up there," Wayne replied. "He worked here for a realty company but quit in April."

"He's a stone alcoholic, or at least he was when we were checking on him," Williams stated.

"You said he was suspected of some rapes?"

"Not rapes. Attempted but none completed. Nothing like the ones you have going. Read about them. Glad it's you and not us."

"Thanks. Think he could be our rapist?"

"Well, he's a coward, but he might be capable if he was armed and the woman asleep. Don't know about if there was a man present. Doesn't sound like him."

"Well, we were hit around three this morning. Think you could do some checking and see if he is working there and if he was there early this morning?" Wayne asked.

"Sure. By the way, don't know if this helps, but he's got two pretty deep scars near the corner of his mouth."

"No one has seen his face. Always wears a mask."

"Okay. Let me work on this. I'll get back to you one way or the other."

"Thanks for the help. Talk to you later," Wayne hung up.

The Sunday Union, 5-15-77

The East Side [Area?] Rapist invades Home No. 22

A twenty-second rape was attributed to the East Side (Area) Rapist Saturday, the fifth straight time he has struck with a man in the house. The rapist entered the home through a sliding glass window in a house in the vicinity of Greenback and Bird Cage Walk.

A sheriff's spokesman said that he didn't want to give out too many specifics because it might inspire "copycats" and disrupt the thousands of hours of investigation which officers have put into the case.

The spokesman did say that the rapist "has committed all sorts of perversions" in the attacks. Officers can't find a time pattern for the series of rapes. Some will be a month apart.

CHAPTER TWENTY-NINE

"**DISPATCH. IS THIS AN EMERGENCY?**" the Sheriff's dispatcher answered the call on the first ring.

"Yes, my husband's got a robber, he's holding him," the female voice quavered.

"Does he have a gun?"

"No, he's just holding him. Please hurry."

"Okay, ma'am. I'll have a deputy there as soon as I can. I want you to stay on the line with me until the deputy arrives. Are you and your husband all right? Is anyone hurt?"

"Not yet, but I'm afraid of what my husband might do if he tries to get away."

"Okay, just take it easy. The deputy is on his way. He'll be there in about three minutes."

At 2218 hours, Deputy Goods arrived at the scene and met Mildred and John Peters. John Peters had a white male by the arm in the middle of the living room. The male, identified as Scott Barnes, was five foot nine inches tall, one hundred and sixty pounds, brown hair, and blue eyes.

"What happened, Mr. Peters?" Goods asked.

"I noticed my wallet was missing from my dresser in the bedroom. Went outside to look and didn't see anything. Came back in and saw this asshole just leaving the spare bedroom. I caught him and he had my wallet and money in his pocket," Peters shook his head in disbelief.

"Okay, I'll take him from you. I need a statement and some information."

"What are you going to do?" Barnes asked as he tried to pull his arm from Goods' grasp.

"Just turn around and put your hands on top of your head. You try that again and you and I are going to have a little problem," Goods searched Barnes and handcuffed him. After placing Barnes in the backseat of the patrol car, he told him he was under arrest for burglary. Goods closed the car door and got his statement from Peters.

"X-Ray 2," Goods keyed his mike.

"X-Ray 2," Dispatch responded.

"X-Ray 2. See if you can reach Sergeant Stone. I have one in custody. Might be the one he's looking for."

"10-4," the dispatcher responded.

"X-Ray 2," Dispatch called two minutes later, "I have Stone on the land wire."

"Tell him I have one in custody and ask him if he can meet me in Investigations. I think he needs to talk to him."

"10-4. He says he's on his way into the office now. He and Detective Wayne will meet you there."

"Thanks."

Goods arrived at the office just as Wayne was pulling into the parking lot.

"What do you have, Bob?" Wayne asked.

"Victim caught him in the house. Had the victim's wallet. Resembles EAR, same area. Thought you better admonish him. I didn't want to screw it up," Goods advised.

"Good. Vickers is inside. Let's see what we can find out."

A short time later Wayne stated, "Got his name, address, and phone number. Lives at home with his mother. I'll start a search warrant, Peg. See if you can get his mother on the phone. Try to learn something about him. Could be our man. Wearing the same type of boots as in the Vosper case, military lace-ups."

Vickers hung up from talking to the mother.

"His mother says Barnes is really a juvenile. 5-11-59, and shouldn't be in jail. Said he was in the army for three months from 10-10-76 to 12-12-76 in Kentucky. Went AWOL and was discharged. He's been living with her for the last three months. Fired from a roofing company two months ago and is working for a carnival in Lincoln."

"Yeah. I just ran a record check on him. He's got three birth dates listed. 57, 58, and 59. Record check shows he's been picked up by Lincoln P.D. a few times. Give them a call to see if they can help us," Wayne stated.

Stone arrived as Vickers was hanging up from talking to the patrol sergeant in Lincoln.

"What have we got, Greg?"

"House burglary. Owner caught him in the house. He's in the interview room with Goods. I'm putting the search warrant together in case we need it. Could be our man. He's a little young, but looks older. Mother says he was in the army when three of the victims were hit. We'll check it out Monday."

"Just talked to Lincoln," Vickers stated. "They know Barnes. Served a search warrant on him in the past. Said his mother is real domineering and his father is real laid back. Lets the mother run the house. Mother has told all the kids to never cooperate with the cops. They stopped his car in the park. He had a bottle of Vaseline and a jar of moisturizing cream. Sergeant said they didn't come up with anything else on him. They were after him for burglary, but I guess the district attorney didn't file. He said he'd get back to us Monday if he can dig up anything else."

CHAPTER THIRTY

"**13P4,**" the dispatcher's voice broke the silence.

"P4," answered Deputy Dan Timmons. He knew before the dispatcher keyed her mike that this was another one.

"13P4, a 261 has just occurred. More information is coming in, but it looks like EAR," the dispatcher began. "Meet the victim on Del Dayo, Carmichael."

Timmons and Phil Money were working a two-man car in the American River and North River Drive area about a mile and a half from the scene of the attack. At 0352 hours they arrived at the scene. Two white males were standing outside the residence. One, Frank Rossali, the husband of the victim, was wearing light blue pajamas and had a white shoelace tied to his left wrist.

"What's the hurry?" he yelled, a combination of broken English and Italian. "He's gone, just come in."

"13P4, we need a cover car and a supervisor code two. And it is an EAR attack," Money replaced the mike in its holder and followed Timmons into the house.

The victim, twenty-six year old Joan Rossali was sitting on the couch with two other females, neighbors who had heard Frank Rossali screaming and came to their aid. An older male subject was sitting in a chair next to the couch. He was later identified as Frank Rossali, Sr. He was visiting from Italy, spoke no English, and had been here for ten days.

Several pieces of white shoelaces were lying on the floor in front of the couch. Two plates and a cup were also on the floor.

Joan Rossali kept mumbling half to herself, "He had a ski mask and a gun. It's horrible. He's crazy."

Corporal Robinson, who had arrived and observed the scene, returned to his patrol unit and called dispatch. "This appears to be the East Area Rapist. Notify those on the call out list."

"10-4," Dispatch replied.

Robinson returned to the residence and followed Rossali into the master bedroom. A saucer and a broken plate were on the bed. Several more pieces of white shoelaces were on the bed and on the floor. The plate had been broken by Rossali's father and was used to cut the laces from Frank Jr.'s wrists.

X-Ray units began arriving and performing their prearranged assignments, securing the residence, taking names of all those at the scene for fingerprint elimination and future questioning, canvassing the area, and keeping those not involved away from the scene.

Corporal Robinson stayed with the victim, attempting to calm her down prior to the arrival of the detective units. Stone and Detective Cerezo, Sacramento Police Department's Task Force member, arrived at 0435 hours. They interviewed Frank Rossali in the master bedroom after checking the rest of the house.

"Joan and I went to bed around midnight after watching the first guest on the Tonight Show. Our two boys were already in bed asleep. My father went to bed earlier also. At exactly one thirty-six I woke up and saw a male standing in the bedroom doorway. I looked at the clock and I knew it was the East Area Rapist. I closed my eyes and feigned sleep. The fellow said 'Wake up. Wake up. I've got a gun. Don't move.' When we didn't move, he started banging on the door with his hand and telling us to wake up.

"Joan shook me and said that there was a man in the room. I started to get up and he shined a light in my eyes and told me to lie down. He told both of us to get on our stomachs. He said, 'I'm going to tie you up. I'm going to take all your money and jewels.' He told Joan to tie my hands and then he retied them and tied my feet and then he tied Joan. He asked Joan where her purse was and when she told him, he told her to go with him to find it and if it wasn't there, he would kill her. Before that he went through all the drawers and closets in the bedroom. Then the bastard took Joan. He came back in and put that saucer and bowl on my back. Said if he heard the dishes fall or any noise, he would kill Joan."

"Did he use Joan's name then?" Stone asked.

"No, he just said he'd kill my wife. He kept coming back into the room and checking the closets and drawers and every time he said if I made a noise, he would kill me. The last time he came in, he seemed real angry. He stuttered some when he talked, but this time he said, 'You tell those fucking pigs that I could have killed two people tonight. If I don't see that all over the papers and television, I'll kill two people tomorrow night.' After that he said he was going into the kitchen and cook and eat something. Said if he heard any noise he would kill my wife.

"When I thought he was gone I yelled for my father and he cut me free. I really thought he would kill us if we didn't do exactly as he said. It was like he wanted to kill us."

"Can you give us any description?" Stone asked.

"Male adult, maybe five eight. He was wearing a grey or beige ski mask and leather gloves. He put that gun to my temple several times. Felt like a large caliber," Rossali answered.

"What about speech? You said he stuttered. Anything else?"

"Well, he took deep breaths all the time and seemed to talk in a whisper like he had his teeth clenched. He seemed real nervous."

At 0445 hours, Vickers arrived. After talking to Timmons, she met with Joan Rossali and explained the procedures. Rossali remembered Vickers from the public presentation she put on at the Del Dayo School earlier in the year. Rossali said she wanted to go directly to the Medical Center for examination so she could try and clean herself as soon as possible. Rossali was transported to the Center and after talking to the Crisis Center staff worker, she went through the rape examination.

At 0705 hours, Vickers began her interview of Joan Rossali.

"I know this is going to be hard on you, Joan, but it's real important we get everything that happened, everything that was said, by you, by Frank, by your attacker," Vickers began.

"I know. It's just hard, so scary. Where do you want me to start?"

"Let's start last evening. Later on we'll talk about your daily routine. What were you doing before you went to bed? If I need to clarify something, I'll ask. Okay?"

"Well, after dinner we watched television and talked. Around ten o'clock the children and my father-in-law went to bed. Frank and I went into the study and talked and went to bed a little after eleven. Johnny Carson was on and we kind of watched him for a little while first. The next thing I knew, a light was shining in my eyes and I saw a shadow of a man standing by our sliding glass door. He had the light in his left hand and a big square gun in his right hand. I could see he was wearing a ski mask. I pulled the covers up over my head."

"Could you see if the mask had eye holes or a hole for his mouth?"

"No. I was so afraid I pulled the covers up over me."

"Okay, what happened next?"

"He said, 'Look at me.' He stuttered kind of. He said it like l-l-l-look at me. Then he said, 'Do you hear me? I have a .45 magnum.' He told me to pull the covers down off me. Frank was pretending to be asleep trying to plan how he could overcome him, but he ordered us to roll onto our stomachs and then he threw some shoelaces on Frank's back and told me to tie him. He kept telling me to tie him tighter and then said he was going to kill everyone in the house if I didn't do what he said. He said if we didn't move or yell he wouldn't hurt anyone in the house. Then he tied my feet and hands. He put the gun against Frank's head and said something but I couldn't hear it.

"Frank started to say something and the fellow got real excited. He told Frank to shut up and if he said one more thing he'd kill. Then he said, 'She's dead. She's dead.' He went outside the sliding door and it sounded like he was putting something in a tool box. When he came back in he put a coin bank on Frank's back. He went through the drawers and closets and then said he was going to get something to eat and get everything he needed. He said if he heard anything, he would kill everything in the house," Joan was shaking, remembering the fear and tears were running down her cheeks.

"I know this is hard," Vickers said. "Do you want me to get you something to drink?"

"No. I'll be all right," She wiped the tears from her face with the back of her hand and rubbed her finger under her nose while she sniffed back her fear.

"He was gone for about thirty minutes, but we could hear him, and then he came back and said he couldn't find my purse. He seemed real mad. I told him it was on the refrigerator. He said if I was lying he would kill me, and then told me to help him find it. He untied my feet and helped me off the bed. He told Frank he would kill me if he moved. He said, 'She's dead. The first thing you'll hear is two shots.' I showed him my purse on the refrigerator, and he took me into the living room. I noticed my afghan draped over the lamp. He told me to lie on my stomach and he tied my feet again. He put a blindfold over my eyes and then I heard him in the kitchen again.

"I heard him open the knife drawer and then he came back and put the knife against my throat and he said if I did everything he asked me to, he wouldn't hurt me. Then he went back into the kitchen. I heard him in the refrigerator and it sounded like he was eating. He came back and put the knife against my throat again and said he wanted more money. He said he knew we had more, and I told him that there were coins in Frank's den. He seemed real angry and said if they weren't there he would kill me. When he came back he straddled me and put his penis in my hand. I could feel hand lotion or something on it and he told me to masturbate it."

"Did he say masturbate?"

"No, he said 'rub me.'"

"Can you tell me how large his penis was?"

"I don't know. Maybe five inches. After awhile he made me sit up and then he put it in my mouth and told me to suck it. He said if I didn't he would kill everyone in the house. He kept calling me Joan. He said, 'Oh, Joan, that feels good. I like that, Joan.' I think he got my name from my purse. Then he untied my feet and he raped me. I knew he would kill all of us if I didn't do everything he said," She could not stop the tears and the sobs came from deep inside.

Vickers reached across the table and took her hands and squeezed them gently.

"It will get better," she said. "It really will."

"I don't know. I don't think it will. I thought he was going to kill us. All I could think of was our two little boys and I thought he was going to kill them."

"I know. You did the right thing. Can you go on or do you want to take a little break?"

"No. He went into the kitchen and I think he was eating some more. Then he came back and he tied my feet real tight. He said he was going to get some beer and food and go into the backyard and eat and drink for about an hour. He put some dishes on my back and said if he heard the dishes, he would come back and kill for the first time. He got real excited and whispered, 'Those fuckers, those fuckers, those pigs. I've never killed before, but I'm going to now. Listen, do you hear me? I want you to tell those fuckers, those pigs. I'm going to go home to my apartment and I have bunches of televisions. I'm going to listen to the radio and watch television and if I hear about this, I'm going to go out tomorrow night and kill two people. People are going to die.' He was stuttering when he talked. I didn't hear him for about ten minutes and I thought he was gone. I tried to move to get my hands untied, but they were too tight. All of a sudden, I could hear him breathing through his mouth, walking around me but not saying anything. Then all of a sudden his face was close to mine, and he said, 'Those fuckers, those fuckers, those pigs, those pigs, those fuckers. I'm going to kill them, too.' I thought he wanted me to say something so I told him I would tell them tomorrow. He said, 'Okay, tell them I'm going to kill those fuckers.' Then it was real quiet. I heard Frank yelling in Italian to his father. They checked on the boys and then they cut me free."

"You did real good, Joan. If you hadn't done what he told you to, we believe he would kill someone," Vickers explained.

"I put on my robe and picked up my underpants from the floor. I was too embarrassed to leave them there and have anyone know what he had done to me."

"I understand," Vickers said. "Is there anything else you can think of?"

"One thing I can't forget. He said, 'I'll kill everything in the house and then I'll leave in the night.' I know he meant it. Another thing. We have a dog in the backyard, in a dog run on the side of the house. Usually the dog barks at all strangers, but for some reason, he was real quiet when the man was there. Even when he went in and out of the house several times."

Vickers transported Rossali back to her home. Going back into the house was probably harder on her than talking about it.

Detective Cerezo talked to the Rossalis' neighbor. Two to three weeks ago the neighbor heard someone in his backyard. The next morning he found a window screen had been pried off. He also heard his dog barking frequently and thought he had heard unusual noises to the rear of his residence. He did not call the Sheriff's Department at any time.

Stone accompanied the bloodhound and handler. The dog entered the house, became excited, and left through the rear sliding glass door area. It followed the suspect's scent throughout the rear yard and to the area where he had eaten. It followed the trail into the garage and to the victim's vehicle and then back to the rear yard. The scent took them through the gate and to the corner of Sandbar Circle and Canebrake Circle. The scent was lost at that point, less than two blocks from the victim.

During the canvass of the neighborhood, faith in humanity continued to drop. One neighbor heard her dog barking furiously around eleven thirty. The dog was running frantically from one side of the yard to the other. He did not check and he did not call the Sheriff's Office. Another neighbor saw a subject around nine thirty at night on May sixteenth shine a flashlight into the yards near the victim's residence. At the same time, she heard dogs barking. She notified no one.

CHAPTER THIRTY

Sacramento Bee, 5-17-77

East Area Rapist Attacks No. 23

The East Area Rapist attacked his twenty-third victim this morning in a Del Dayo home and said he would kill his next two victims, sheriff's deputies reported. The rapist told his victim and her husband he would kill the next time he strikes, but he gave conflicting reasons for the threats.

Deputies released a composite sketch of the suspect by piecing together bits of a description from the 23 women the man has attacked since October, 1975. Although rumors about the rapist and his attacks are rampant, he has never disfigured, cut, or beaten any of his victims.

Stone sat in Burns' office. His eyes were red from lack of sleep and his hand shook as he raised his coffee cup to his lips.

"Well, is he going to hit again tonight?" Burns asked.

"Fucked if I know. He's really got me baffled. Just when you think there is a pattern, he fucks us up. I hope it's just idle threats, but he's getting more violent. It seems he has to escalate the attack to get his rocks off. If he does kill, this county is going to go nuts," Stone shook his head.

"Well, the media had agreed to keep the threats out of the paper for awhile, but apparently they figured it was too big to sit on. Can't really blame them this time," Burns remarked.

"Yeah, well, the son of a bitch either doesn't know what he's doing or he's playing head games big time. Told the husband it better not be on the news and then tells the victim it better be. At least we can be pretty sure the bastard has been reading the papers or watching the news."

"Well, we might find out tonight. Maybe some deputy will blow the fucker away," Burns sighed.

"Or some victim waiting for him in the dark. Gun sales are way up. Pawn shops are doing a hell of a business. That reminds me, Greg checked with Juvenile Hall. That little burglar, Scott Barns, that was caught in the house a week or so ago?" Stone raised his eyebrows.

"Yeah, what about him? The Hall let him go just before the rapist hit?"

"Nope. He was still in custody. He's eliminated."

"You look like death warmed over, Jim. You better head for home and get some sleep. What do you have going tonight?"

"I've got a couple of areas to stake out. Neighbors say dogs have been barking. At least some people are calling in. Dispatch says calls have increased to three thousand a day. The people are scared, Mike. So am I. Nothing on the street, nobody knows anything, but I think the bastard is using disguises during the day and evenings when he's not going to hit. Too many reports of strange males roaming the streets. Beards, afros, mustaches, redheads, blonds, and when we do get the calls, they're gone. Wouldn't be so strange except the calls all come from areas near main roads or the freeway.

"I think he's checking the areas out and then comes back to them a week or so later. Anyway, the composite the paper printed might get us something. I've got Wayne, Bonnell, and Merton sitting in homes tonight that we think he might hit."

"What time are they going to get in the houses?" Burns asked.

"Around six or six-thirty. The people fit the profile and they have all reported prowlers. I'm going to hit the sack. I'll be back around eight and stay on it until six tomorrow. I'll call if anything happens," Stone got up and walked back to his desk. "Better go home and get some sleep, Peg. Tonight could be a big one."

"Soon as I finish my statement, Jim. You look like I feel, by the way," Vickers replied.

"You know what's really fucked up? Dopers pay good money to feel like I do. Strange world. Never did figure out my ex-wife," Stone shook his head.

Detective Cerezo was sitting at his desk when the phone rang.

"Task Force. Can I help you?"

"Yes. I work at the airport and I saw the picture of the rapist in the paper. I'm acquainted with someone who resembles it. His name is Richard Morton. He lives in Sacramento and works as a milkman."

"How old is Richard?"

"Twenty-one. He's six feet tall, brown hair, hazel eyes. Weighs maybe one sixty. He graduated from Rio Americano High School and went to Chico State for two years. He spent some time in the military, but they discharged him for smoking dope. He's got a real temper. In school he got mad when people called him Dick. Most of the time he's soft spoken and polite, but he can't take a joke. He has trouble keeping girlfriends and most won't date him more than once. He doesn't get along with his mother. I know she tried to get him psychiatric help."

"Where does he live?" Cerezo asked.

"Well, I talked to another friend today, and she said he was in Oregon but I know he's in Sacramento. He told me he has a job in Stockton and commutes. He's real intelligent but he doesn't have much ambition."

"Okay. If you can find anything else, let us know. I'll see what I can do to follow up on what you gave me. Can you give me your name and number? I won't tell him you called if we find him, and we may be able to eliminate him without talking to him."

Cerezo got the information and hung up.

Later another woman called, said that at one o'clock in the afternoon on the 16th she was on the American River levee burying a snake when she saw a person peering into backyards. She saw him looking into the Rossalis' backyard and he resembled the composite in the paper.

Lt. Burns received a call from a detective in the Youth Division. The detective had received a call from a Mrs. Conway who he knew from previous contacts involving her children. She said that her niece babysits for her and she believes the niece's boyfriend is the EAR. The boyfriends works for the Department of Motor Vehicles in the license department and bought a .45 caliber handgun just before the first time the rapist had used one. She said he is five foot nine, lives in Orangevale, and told her he was the rapist. She told the detective his name was Jerry Neiko.

Sacramento Bee. 5-18-77

East Area Rapist Issues Death Threat.

The East Area Rapist, said by psychiatrists to be "in a homosexual panic" because he is sexually underdeveloped, attacked his 23rd victim Tuesday morning. The rapist for the first time made death threats, telling the victim and her husband he would kill his next two victims, but gave contradicting reasons for the threat.

A sheriff's spokesman told a press conference that although the rapist has caused no serious physical injuries, they fear he may harm someone soon. The rapist told his victims to "tell the pigs" that he would kill two people if the rape received press coverage. However, he told her husband he would kill if there was no coverage. Anybody who enters a home where people are sleeping with a gun or a knife is a potential killer, the spokesman stated.

After first asking the press to withhold coverage of Tuesday's attack, the sheriff's office, considering the contradicting nature of the rapists threats, called a press conference and released a composite sketch and a psychiatric profile. According to the profile, the rapist is probably "a paranoid schizophrenic" of above average intelligence, most likely from a middle class or upper middle class home, raised by a domineering mother and a weak father.

The psychiatrists said he is probably operating in a "homosexual panic" because of "his inadequate endowment." Several victims have told investigators that the rapist has a very small sex organ. The phrase "homosexual panic" is used by psychiatrists to describe not an overt homosexual, but someone with the unconscious fear of being homosexual. He panics when that fear comes close to consciousness, they say.

Sacramento Bee, 5-18-77

East Area Tense But Rapist Fails to Carry Out Threats

Sacramento law enforcement breathed a sigh of relief this morning as dawn arrived with no indication that the East Area Rapist had carried out a death threat issued Tuesday. Porch lights burned through the night. Private homes became armed camps. But the rapist's threat to kill two people during the night apparently was not carried out.

There has been a run on weapons the last two months as the rapist has attacked with increasing boldness and frequency. A chief deputy said 2,600 guns had been sold in Sacramento County since January 1, about double the usual number.

"These people are crazy," said a local gun shop owner. "They want anything they can aim that will blow a hole in something." One woman, whose home is two blocks from one of the rapist's victims, said "I'm scared to death of guns, but my husband sleeps with a gun next to him and my son has one." She says she has lain awake most of the night for the past two weeks, watching intently through the open drapes of her bedroom for any sign of the rapist. "I take two hour naps in the afternoon [to catch up on lost sleep]," she said.

CHAPTER THIRTY

Sacramento Bee, 5-19-77

WANTED

CB radio owners to help gather information relative to the EAST AREA RAPIST

The total community reward now stands at $15,000.00. It will take concerned citizens, business and professional leaders, civic organizations, and church groups involved in a community wide effort to apprehend the criminal. For further information, call

EARS Patrol
555-8855
East Area Rapist Surveillance Patrol

Sacramento Union, 5-19-77

Police Donate Own Time Hunting East Area Rapist

Sacramento police are spending hundreds of off-duty hours as are sheriff's deputies and highway patrolmen, in the search for the East Area Rapist, the police chief told Sacramento Lion's Club yesterday. "It's the first time in 21 years I've seen so many policemen dedicated to a case on their own time."

Sacramento Union, 5-20-77

CBers to Hunt East Area Rapist

Three hundred persons with citizens' band radios say they will start prowling the streets tonight looking for the East Area Rapist. Both the police and the sheriff's departments wish they'd stay home. A new group, the East Area Rapist Surveillance Patrols (EARS), announced Thursday its intention to help. Law enforcement regulars feel they will only be in the way.

Sacramento Union, 5-22-77

Women Moving Out Because They're Scared

"He's got women moving out of Sacramento because they're scared," a Sacramento Rape Crisis staff member stated. "He's

getting off on a power trip. He's got a lot of power in his hands now with the police and the media."

"The East Area Rapist, not known to use violence to mutilate or injure his victims, instead employs 'psychological violence' against his targets. He threatens to kill and harm his victims throughout the attack," the staff worker stated. "In a strange sense, the victim of the East Area Rapist has an advantage over other rape victims. They know they aren't the only ones who were attacked. They don't have to carry that guilt that others in isolated rapes burden themselves with." The staff member said relationships between the Center and the police and sheriff's departments have been spotty.

"While some deputy sheriffs will call the center for assistance in rape cases, the official line from the top echelon of the sheriff's department is 'not to cooperate with us,' the spokeswoman said. The psychiatric consultant for the Sacramento Rape Crisis Center said the police are wrong in their assessment that the attacker is homosexual. She stated that his main goal is to hurt and degrade women, has difficulty relating to them, and was probably an abused child. The increased frequency of attacks, together with the conflicting threats of death and violence to future victims, mark a volatile change in his personality," she told a Sacramento Union reporter. "He's proud of his notoriety, but his aggressive element is growing quickly. His braggadocio, his adventuresomeness, probably will be the thing that gets him caught. Those attacks with men show a 'rivalrous' attempt to compete with other males."

CHAPTER THIRTY-ONE

"WELL, IT'S BEEN A WEEK since the last attack," Burns stood in front of the EAR Task Force. "Maybe he's satisfied for awhile. Anyway, the Sheriff went in front of the Board of Supervisors today and asked for more money. Our overtime budget is depleted and he got us another hundred thousand."

Several of the detectives gave each other "high fives" accompanied by, "All right!"

"The Sheriff showed the Board figures that blew them away. So far, deputies have volunteered four thousand, eight hundred, ninety-six hours of their own time in working this son of a bitch. That computes to around seventy seven thousand dollars. The Sheriff realizes the hours the Task Force has put in without compensation.

"A Supervisor also suggested that the County allocate fifteen thousand to the *Sacramento Bee*'s Secret Witness program, but the Board Chairman got it voted down. Said the *Bee* already has fifteen thousand in the program and the East Area Rapist Surveillance Patrol has ten thousand in it. He said he thinks the community is so offended that no money is necessary for a reward. He says even the crooks will help."

"I wonder what he'd say if it was his wife or daughter that got fucked by this asshole?" Bonnell muttered.

"Well, at least he voted for the hundred thousand," Burns remarked, "Although he did say he had reservations."

"Politicians," Jim Cereza, the Sacramento Police Department officer stated. "People in the city are up in arms over the vice-mayor's comments about sprucing up our vice unit to stop prostitution around his law office downtown. We had a fifteen year old girl raped and murdered, and he's worried about his prostitutes. That's where he gets most of his fucking clients," he fumed.

"Play on words there, Jim," Vickers laughed.

"Excuse my French, Peg," Cerez apologized. "I just get so damned fed up with politicians."

"Frank Rossali called me this morning, Mike," Stone remarked. "Said his father wants us to give him the name of the person who raped his daughter in law. Said he would see that we didn't have to take him to court and said he'd make it worth our while. Apparently, he's a godfather or something big back in Italy. The thing is, he's serious."

"I'm not sure I wouldn't give it to him if we had it," Burns remarked. "Sure save the County a bundle."

"That's about what I said. He said his offer stands if we get it."

"I can't believe some of these stupid fuckin' citizens," Burns continued. "We've had a number of calls complaining about the Highway Patrol helicopter. Some of the calls have been from neighbors of some of the victims. They're complaining about the noise and the lights shining into their homes. Said they're losing sleep."

"Bullshit," Wayne replied. "I flew with them for three of the nights. We made sure we didn't shine the light into windows. Those Chipper pilots know what they're doing. One thing for sure, it's faster getting from one place to the other."

"Yeah, I flew two nights," Merton stated. "We spent most of the time looking for open gates. These people would be the first to bitch if they got hit. Some people can't be pleased. These pilots are great."

"Well, I know we have a County full of scared citizens," Burns said. "Gun shops are doing a booming business and citizens are staying awake all night waiting for this bastard to break in. Maybe we'll get lucky and one of them will do the job for us."

"Anybody had contact with this EARS patrol group?" Stone asked.

"Patrol has. Driving them nuts. I talked to Timmons the other night. He says every car he's stopped is a CBer. He said he hopes EAR catches one of them and butt fucks him," Bonnell said.

"I guess they mean well," Burns stated. "The Sheriff met with them and told them absolutely no guns, got to ride in pairs, and they're not to leave their cars. So far it seems to have worked. Burglary says their cases are down seventy percent since the CBers started patrolling. That's one hell of a drop."

"Maybe they'll scare him off. We sure haven't done anything to deter him," Stone stated.

"Well, there's more than a hundred running around, so it should do something," Burns stated. "What do you have going tonight, Jim?"

"We've got six of the X-RAY units sitting on houses we think he might hit and two more sitting on suspects. Jerry's going with the helicopter, so he's supposed to meet them at nine. Bill's going to sit in a house in Del Dayo. Pretty good idea EAR's been in their backyard and the woman fits the profile. She found a towel in the bushes in her yard and her gate was open. We left the towel in place just in case he does check back," Stone replied.

"What time do you plan on getting there, Bill?" Burns asked.

"Jim's going to drop me off a couple of blocks from the residence around six on his way home," Bonnell nodded his head toward Jim Cerezo. "I'll walk from there in case EAR's out and about. He'll pick me up around six in the morning if nothing happens."

"Okay. Peg? Greg? Anything special?"

"We're off at six tonight. We'll both be on pager. I'm not going anywhere anyway," Wayne answered.

"I'll be home also," Vickers stated.

"Okay. Good luck. I'll be home after nine," Burns stated. "I'll be on pager until then. What about you, Jim?"

"I've got a date with a hot tub," Stone grinned.

"Come on, Jim. I've seen her. I know she's hot, but I don't think you should call her a tub," Wayne laughed.

"Don't stay in the water too long, Jim. Something might shrivel up," Vickers joined in.

"You mean shrivel up more," Wayne continued.

"Never heard you complain, Greg," Stone laughed as they headed for the parking lot.

CHAPTER THIRTY-TWO

5-28-77, 0410 hours.

DEPUTIES BRIAN BRETT AND RICHARD KENT were working the County area near Florin Road and Highway 99 when Dispatch gave them the bad news. EAR had moved to the southern end of the County. A 261PC had just occurred and the rapist had been wearing a red ski mask. The deputies arrived on scene exactly four minutes later and took up positions, Brett at the front of the house, Kent at the rear. Kent heard a woman's voice from inside. The patio door was open and Kent announced his presence and entered. He found the victim in the living room lying face down, her hands tied behind her back and her ankles tied.

"I've been raped by the East Area Rapist," she stated. "My husband is tied up in the bedroom."

Kent cut the bindings, made sure that the victim was all right, and proceeded to the back bedroom. The victim's husband was sitting on the bed, his wrists and ankles tied with brown shoelaces. He cut the bindings and noticed that the phone was off the cradle.

"Someone from the Sheriff's Office is on the phone. I called them."

Kent picked up the phone. Sergeant Brown, Sacramento Sheriff's Department Communications, was on the other end. "It's an East Area Rapist attack," Kent advised the sergeant.

"Ten four. The X-RAY units are responding from Rancho Cordova and you've got two other units on the scene with you," Brown replied. "We're calling the detectives now. Anyone hurt?"

"Nothing physical," Kent replied. He noticed the plates on the bed as he scanned the room. Sitting outside the closet were two pairs of shoes with the laces missing. Kent took the male subject to the living room and had him sit with his wife on the couch.

"It's all clear outside," Brett called from the backyard.

"Okay. Secure the back and have someone secure the front until the X-RAY units get here," Kent replied. "I'll stay here."

"I'm Deputy Richard Kent," he introduced himself.

"I'm Harry Britmore," the male replied. "This is my wife, Gayle."

"We've got units on the way that work these details," Kent said. "They'll need to interview you both and take Mrs. Britmore to the hospital to be checked. Did the attacker touch either of you with his bare hands?" he asked.

"I think he had his gloves on all the time he was near me," Harry Britmore said.

"He wore gloves most of the time, but I don't know if he touched me with his bare hands," Gayle answered.

"We've got a female deputy responding. She'll do an iodine-silver-plate transfer test to try and get fingerprints, just in case," Kent advised. "We also have a female detective responding to talk to you, ma'am. Can either of you describe the attacker?"

"Vaguely. He was about five nine or ten, maybe one sixty, one seventy, wearing a red ski mask with eye holes and a mouth hole. He was wearing a bulky dark colored jacket and dark pants with black gloves. He was carrying a military type .45 automatic. I'm in the Marine Reserves, so I know it was a .45 auto," Harry replied.

At 1430 hours, Deputy Sharon Breedlove arrived and did an iodine-silverplate transfer on Gayle Britmore's arms, buttocks, and shoulders with negative results.

At 0435 hours, X-RAY 5 arrived on scene from the Rancho Cordova area. Deputy George White and Deputy Greg Andrews relieved Brett and Kent.

White stayed with Harry Britmore while Andrews checked the exterior of the residence. Torn strips of towel and two lengths of brown shoelaces were noted by White on the living room floor. Andrews located a green wine bottle and two packages of sausage on the patio.

"Mr. Britmore, I need you to tell me what happened, but I'd like you to talk to me in the patrol car. It's best if we talk to you separately so you won't be putting images in each others' minds. If there are discrepancies, like different colored hair or statements, we can discuss it later," White explained.

"I got home from work around midnight or a little after," Britmore began after he and White were seated in the patrol car. "I work swing shift. I had a beer while I watched the late show. Gayle and our son were already in bed. After the movie ended, I went to bed. Must have been around two. I dozed off pretty quick and I guess Gayle woke me. We were engaged in some foreplay and I had my back to the sliding patio door. I heard a rattling noise at the door and turned over to see what it was. When I did, I saw this person coming through the door. He had a small two cell flashlight in his left hand and was carrying a .45 auto in his right hand. It was a blue steel military type. He said, 'Lay perfectly still, don't make a move and don't look at me. Put your hands where I can see them in front and don't move a muscle.' He had some shoelaces and told Gayle to tie my hands."

"Did he use your wife's name?" White asked.

"No, he just told her to 'tie the man up.' He kept telling her how to tie me and told her to tie it tight. Then he tied Gayle's hands. He said he was hungry and he was going to get food and money and then leave. He was rummaging in the closet and several times he would swing the light back on me. He said 'I'll kill her and your son if you don't keep your face down.' I heard him taking laces out of shoes and then he put the gun to my head and told me to lay still. He retied my hands and then tied my feet. He rummaged some more in the bathroom and then he put some glass things on my back. He said, 'Don't move. If I hear that sound, I'll kill everyone in the house.' He tied Gayle's feet and then he left the room. I could hear him in the kitchen, opening and closing cupboards. When he came back into the bedroom, he put some dishes on my back. He put a knife to my neck and said, 'Don't make a move or I'll kill everyone in the house. As I promised, I'm only gonna get food and money and then go to my van and eat it. If I hear that sound I'll come back and kill everyone in the house.' He then took Gayle out of the bedroom. A little while later he came back and shined the flashlight around and then closed the bedroom door. He was only gone about five minutes and then came back in. When he left, I heard Gayle moaning. It didn't last long and then he was back in the bedroom. After awhile, I heard him open the other patio door. I waited a few minutes and then knocked the dishes off my back. When he didn't come back in, I knocked the receiver off the phone and dialed with my hands behind me. I got the operator and she connected me to your office."

Stone had arrived while Britmore was talking, so he just leaned into the car and listened.

"Did you notice anything about his voice?" Stone asked.

"Just that he seemed to speak in a whisper all the time," Britmore replied.

"I noticed a For Sale sign on your lawn. Are you moving?"

"No, we just bought this house. We moved in three weeks ago. The salesman was supposed to pick up the sign. Why? Does that mean something?"

"Probably not, but we have noticed For Sale signs near similar attacks. Could be a coincidence," Stone replied. "By the way, I'm Sergeant Stone, Investigations."

"This is Harry Britmore, Jim. His wife, Gayle, is in the house. We're just waiting for Peg to get here. Harry, Sgt. Stone is the lead investigator," White explained.

"Peg should be here any minute," Stone advised. "There's her car now. Harry, she's going to take your wife to Sac Medical for examination."

"Deputy White explained the process," Britmore replied. "I just felt so useless. I keep thinking I should have done something."

"You did the right thing," Stone replied. "If you had tried to do anything, you might all be dead."

"He kept saying he was going to kill us if we moved. I think he wanted to kill us."

"He didn't, and that's the important thing," White replied.

At 0505 hours, Peg Vickers arrived and contacted Gayle Britmore. After explaining the procedure, she transported Britmore to the Sacramento Medical Center where she was examined. At 0730 hours they arrived back at the residence where Vickers conducted the interview.

"Last night I was doing my laundry and had to make several trips to the garage. That's where my washing machine is. On one of those trips I noticed that the side garage door was open. I closed it thinking that the wind had blown it open. I locked it and didn't think any more about it. You don't think he was in my garage, do you? If he was there, why didn't he attack me then?" Gayle began.

"I don't know, unless he knew when your husband usually got home and wanted to wait. Or maybe he was afraid he might get home early. I really don't know," Vickers answered.

"Anyway, my son fell asleep on the couch and I carried him to bed and then watched television until eleven thirty, and then I went to bed. I don't know when Harry got home, but when he came to bed we were engaged in sexual activity for several minutes before we realized he was there. He told us to lie still or he would kill us. He kept saying that all the time, he would kill all of us. He said all he wanted was something to eat and money. He told me to tie Harry up."

"Did he use Harry's name?"

"No, he said to tie the man up. He threw some shoelaces at me and kept telling me to do it right. I was trying to tie him loose, but he tied Harry up after I did. After he tied me, he went in and out of the bedroom several times. One time I heard him in the bathroom with a bottle of lotion or something. I could hear it make squishing sounds. He left and then he came back and put some dishes on Harry's back and told him not to move or he would kill everybody. He took me into the living room and told me to lie down. He had pieces of my towels on the floor. He had torn my good towels into strips and he tied one of them around my eyes. I heard a zipper and then some kind of snapping or slapping noises. I don't know what they were and then he got on top of me."

"Did he roll you over?" Vickers asked.

"No. I was still on my stomach. He entered my vagina for a short time, and then rolled me on my side and entered me again. After that he put it in my anus but just for a second. It didn't hurt because his penis was so small. When he pulled out, he put his face right next to my ear and he told me to tell the police they were wrong the last time."

"The last time?" Vickers asked.

"Yeah, when he said he would kill someone."

"Oh. Can you remember exactly what he said?"

"Yeah. He made me repeat it. He said 'I have something for you to tell the fucking pigs. They got it mixed up the last time. I said I would kill two people. I'm not going to kill you. If this is on the T.V. or in the paper tomorrow, I'll kill two people.' Then he said, 'Are you listening? Do you hear me?' He stuttered when he said 'listening', like l-l-l-listening. I think he may have stuttered other times, too, but I'm not sure. Then he said, 'I have T.V's in my apartment and I'll be watching them. If this is on the news, I'll kill two people.' Then he kind of sobbed and said, 'It scares my mommy when it's on the news.' He said it twice, and I thought he was going to cry when he said mommy. Whenever he said "pigs," he got real mad. Then he left."

"Did he touch you? Sexually, I mean? Fondle your breasts, anything like that?"

"He touched my breasts, but really didn't fondle."

"Did he try oral sex at all?"

"Nope, not at all. He attacked me that one time and never tried again."

"Do you feel he climaxed?"

"I don't think so. The whole thing didn't last long enough, really."

"Did he ask you where your money was or demand more money or ask for drugs or pills?"

"No, not to me anyway."

"Anything about his voice that you can recall, other than the stuttering?"

"No accent, if that's what you mean. He just seemed to talk in a whisper. Real harsh like loud breaths. Real hyper and maybe high pitched."

"Okay. I think that's enough for today. If you feel you might be up to it, we would like to have you hypnotized to see if we can find out something else. Something you might see clearer under hypnosis. Harry said he would be willing. In a few days, of course."

"Sure. No problem if you think it might help."

Sacramento Bee, 5-29-77

East Area Rapist Hits South, Victim 24

Sheriff's deputies are convinced that Saturday's intruder was the East Area Rapist. Why did the rapist move south? "Possibly it could have been due to all the publicity the EARS Patrol has been receiving," a sheriff's spokesman said.

The EARS chairman said Saturday that up to 75 members of his group were patrolling Friday night. The reward for information leading to the capture of the rapist has been increased to $30,000.00 and issued an appeal for more volunteers. The sheriff's office has increased patrol using cars and helicopters and has been allocated $100,000.00 for overtime pay in the search.

Besides the overtime pay, many deputies are donating their time for added patrols and some Highway Patrol officers have volunteered their time. City police are also working special details.

"Dispatch called me at home yesterday," Wayne remarked to Stone as they started their Monday morning briefing. "Said they didn't want to disturb you. Anyway, they had me call a couple who said they had some information. Might be something to it. I called and talked to the wife. Says she and her husband work as security guards at the Mormon Church. On April 18th they saw a subject and she stopped him. Said he was nervous and made excuses for being there late at night. He reached for the woman's breast just as her husband showed up. The fellow began shaking and crying. Said he fell to his knees as though he was praying and then he jumped up and ran. They got a license number. I took a photo line-up over to them last night. They picked out the picture of Richard Morton. He's the one that the airport worker called us about back on the seventeenth. I checked with the gal at the airport and she gave me Morton's address. I drove by and his car was there. I sat on it for awhile, but there wasn't any movement. I didn't make contact."

"Good. Let's let the X-RAY units know. It's a place we need to sit on," Stone remarked.

Sacramento Bee, 5-31-77

Static Develops on Rapist Patrol From Other CBers

Leaders of organized citizens' band radio clubs today criticized East Area Rapist Surveillance (EARS), asserting the volunteer CB Patrol is degenerating into a "vigilante" action motivated by the $30,000.00 in reward for the man who has raped 24 area women...

Sacramento Bee, 5-31-77

Hatred of Rapist

Armed Women Attend Gun Class...

Sacramento Union, 5-31-77

CBers call rapist patrol "helter-skelter vigilantes"...

Chapter Thirty-three

RAPE IS A TERRIFYING ORDEAL and for most victims, a traumatic experience that leaves them terrified for the rest of their lives. This scarring touches not only the victim, it encompasses the entire family and sometimes the entire community.

EAR became a major preoccupation for the entire Sacramento area.

In 1976, the Sacramento Sheriff's Office and City Police investigated more than three hundred rapes. Estimates vary, however unreported rapes may fall somewhere between six hundred and twenty-five hundred annually. Official statistics show that there is a rape almost every day. Although investigators denounce the figure as over inflated, the Sacramento Rape Crisis Center estimates that seven other rapes daily go unreported.

The U.S. Law Enforcement Assistance Administration surveyed thirteen cities in 1975. They determined that in some urban areas, as many as 66 percent of all rapes were never reported. And of those that are reported, most are never solved. Only 44 percent of the three hundred and twenty-three forcible rapes reported in Sacramento County were solved.

Sacramento isn't alone. In 1976, nine thousand five hundred and fifty-two forcible rapes were reported in California. Only 45.7 percent were cleared. This calculates to only four thousand three hundred and seventy rapes solved. Although unsolved rapes remain high, media concentration on a single rapist can obscure the total picture and create fear in the minds of the entire population.

Although the East Area Rapist commanded the attention of the media, he was not the most active rapist in the area. In a twelve month period, EAR had raped twenty-two times. Approximately three hundred other rapes had occurred during the same time period.

Over a four year period ending in 1976, a rapist identified by law enforcement as the "Early Morning Rapist" attacked and violated at least thirty-six women. He disappeared in 1976 and was never identified. Although a number of the Early Morning Rapist's attacks occurred in the same unincorporated area as the East Area Rapist attacks, the offenses were not widely reported and very little panic ensued.

It is felt that possibly the absence of publicity with the Early Morning Rapist was due to the fact that many victims were on welfare, divorced, and from lower income groups, therefore lacking political clout.

During the East Area Rapist's attacks, another serial rapist, nicknamed "Wooley" due to his wet wool odor, was invading Sacramento apartment complexes. Wooley's M.O. was to place the victim in a closet and tell them to count to one hundred backwards before emerging. In one rape, he tried to confuse law enforcement into believing EAR had committed the rape. He placed dishes on the victim's seventeen year old brother's back and then after the rape, returned to his familiar M.O. He placed the victim in a closet. Still wanting to "confuse" law enforcement, he ordered the victim to count backward from fifty. It took the Wooley Task Force less than a month to make an arrest.

Sacramento was not unique in being unfortunate to have serial rapists terrorizing communities.

During this same period the Los Angeles Police Department was actively pursuing the "Pillowcase Rapist," a psychopath who had raped approximately fifty-four women in South Central Los Angeles. His trademark was placing a pillowcase over the heads of his victims. In January of 1997, two of the Pillowcase Rapist's victims traveled to Indiana for the start of a trial to put Reginald Muldrew, age forty-nine, back in prison. Muldrew, the Pillowcase Rapist, was investigated in as many as two hundred sex crimes in the Los Angeles area from 1976 through 1978. He was released from a California prison in December 1995 after serving sixteen years of a twenty-five year sentence. At the time of his release, he was determined to still be a danger, but had completed his sentence, shortened for good behavior. On August 5, 1997, he attacked a Gary, Indiana woman.

In Berkeley, California, a Rapist Task Force was searching for a serial rapist known as "Stinky" due to his foul breath, body odor, and oil and gasoline scent. Stinky raped at least forty-seven women before leaving Berkeley to continue his career in the nearby city of Oakland. Stinky was never caught, although Berkeley P.D. investigators were sure they knew who he was. The Alameda County District Attorney's office refused to file charges due to "insufficient evidence."

The "Car Key Rapist" attacked more than forty women in Los Angeles in 1977 before being caught. He earned his nickname by raping women in their cars then fleeing with the car keys, dropping them a block away.

San Diego police arrested the "East San Diego Rapist" after thirty women had been raped.

Police in Dallas, Texas investigated the "Friendly Rapist" for two years before finally arresting him, but not before he had violated more than fifty women. He was nicknamed "Friendly" because victims described him as "polite." Friendly was a former journalist who learned police tactics while covering the crime beat for a newspaper.

EAR remained on everyone's mind throughout the summer months, not because of continued attacks, as there were none, but through the articles that appeared weekly and sometimes daily, in one or both of the major Sacramento newspapers. Many of these were anti-law enforcement due to their inability to capture the rapist. Rumors that the rapist was known to investigators as a police officer and therefore had not been arrested because officers were reluctant to turn in "one of their own" was alluded to in several articles.

Tensions arose between elected members of the Sacramento Board of Supervisors who voted not to add money to the *Sacramento Bee*'s reward program. One female supervisor stated, "When I think of all the unsolved crimes in the area, including the north area's murder, I don't see how this body can become involved in setting priorities for catching criminals. It would set a precedent to which there would be no end."

On June 9, 1977, the Sacramento Police Department formed their EAR Task Force.

Although days stretched into weeks in which no EAR attacks occurred, and weeks into months, investigators remained active. Thousands of calls were received and thousands of leads dissolved into nothingness. Like the call Greg Wayne followed up on.

Jane Smart called on 6-10-77 to say she believed her husband, Forrest, was the rapist. She told Wayne that her husband couldn't decide if he was a boy or a girl and had been wearing girls' clothes for years. She said he became enraged every time a rape occurred. She also said he was well endowed. Wayne ran Smart's criminal history. He had been in jail 10-31-74 until 5-30-75, and 9-17-76 until 12-7-76. Eliminated.

Of the call that Vickers received on 6-13-77 at 1920 hours: Candy Tori, Citrus Heights, stated she had been hitchhiking and was picked up by a white male in a tan van. The man spoke to her "through her mind" and said he was the East Area Rapist. She told Vickers she was a strong believer in mental telepathy. She did not see the license plate of the vehicle, but her telepathy told her it was YLIC198. The man gave her his business card for a Jack Somebody, an encyclopedia salesman, but she threw it away.

The EAR Task Force also received a call from a Fair Oaks resident who stated that on May 22nd she and her husband arrived home around 7:30 p.m. A male subject was sitting in a vehicle parked at the Harry Dewey School. They watched the subject, described as a white male twenty to thirty years old, five foot nine, one hundred and seventy pounds, brown hair and wearing an army fatigue uniform with a webbed belt and a knife in a scabbard, leave the car, enter the schoolyard and return a short time later. The subject then drove off. She described the vehicle as a dark green Chevrolet Capri and gave investigators the vehicle license number.

On June 9th, a surveillance began of the registered owner. The subject was eventually eliminated as an EAR suspect due to having type O blood, an 8 ½ shoe, and not being under-endowed.

Since 1949, persons convicted of certain sex offences have been required to register with the local law enforcement agency with jurisdiction over the place where they intend to live after being released from jail, prison, or a state hospital. Every time the sex offender relocates, they must re-register with the new jurisdiction.

The Department of Justice files contain approximately 65,000 registered sex offenders. Of these, the department estimates that about 10 percent are serious habitual sex offenders who have committed multiple crimes on either children or adults. Research indicates that these offenders will continue to commit crimes as long as they are not in custody. Rehabilitation is not an alternative. An Emery University (Atlanta, Georgia) study found that offenders over eighteen years of age who continue to commit assaults have similar characteristics:

They are almost always male

They begin their deviant behavior before the age of fifteen

They commit an average of 380 crimes in their criminal careers

They commit all types of offenses from peeping in windows and "flashing" to the most brutal offenses as rape, sodomy, and murder

Due to the estimated age of the East Area Rapist, the Task Force felt that EAR fit the profile of the Emery University study. The Department of Justice was contacted and a list of all registered sex offenders living in the Sacramento area was obtained. During the summer months thousands of registered sex offenders were eliminated as EAR. Race, height, weight, age, physical disabilities, and incarceration dates were used as basic elimination factors. Person to person contact was used when necessary for elimination purposes.

Handgun sales in Sacramento County soared about five times the normal rate in May when County residents bought more than 1200 new pistols. More than 3400 handguns had been purchased in the County since the first of the year. Normally about 250 guns were purchased each month.

Yet as paranoia increased and more and more citizens armed themselves, the number of forcible rapes reported to the Sheriff's Office increased by 68 percent over 1976. So far in 1977, 113 forcible rapes were reported, compared to 67 for the same period in 1976. Speculations among Sheriff's investigators was that the activities of the East Area Rapist may be spurring other disturbed persons into sexual assaults.

Superior Court Judge John Boskovich appointed three psychiatrists to determine if James Kevin Dobson, twenty years old, who pled guilty to five rapes, was a threat to the community because of mental defect. Dobson had raped two fifteen year olds, two fourteen year olds, and badly beaten a twenty year old who fought him in a fruitless attempt to preserve her virginity.

One psychiatrist stated that Dobson's sexual assaults occurred after he had been discussing the activities of the East Area Rapist. "He feels that he didn't have any violence or aggression toward these girls or women in general," the psychiatrist related.

Dobson was ruled a mentally disordered sex offender and committed to Atascadero State Hospital. Dobson married eighteen year old Laura Guerrera in a judge's chambers after his guilty plea.

"He ain't no sex fiend or some sort of weirdo," the new Mrs. Dobson told reporters. "What he did hasn't affected me or us. I don't hold it against him."

CHAPTER THIRTY-FOUR

"JIM," LT. MIKE BURNS CALLED from his office. "Better get in here."

"What's up, Mike?"

"Just got a call from Rick Garth, a lieutenant with Stockton P.D. Looks like our fellow moved. At least on the surface it sure looks like EAR."

"You're kidding. What in the hell is he doing in Stockton? You really think it's our man?" Stone asked.

"Preliminary. Ski mask, early morning, flashlight, threats to kill the husband and wife. Said all he wanted was money and food. Threatened to cut off the kid's ears if they didn't do what he said. Gun and knife. Shoelaces. Need more?"

"Damn," was all Stone could muster.

"Look, why don't you get a hold of Peggy and meet with their lead investigator. Garth said it would be Sgt. Peter Michaels and you could meet him at their investigations division around one o'clock. He said they should have all their info by then and would appreciate any help we can give them," Burns said.

"Yeah, okay. I know Michaels from our robbery, homicide meetings. Seems like a pretty nice fellow," Stone replied.

"Garth said Michaels asked him to call us. He has a sister who lives here in Sac so he is up on the news articles," Burns shrugged. "Maybe we got too close to him and he decided to move."

"Maybe, but Stockton? Nobody goes to Stockton. I didn't even know they had women there."

"Forty miles down I-5. Maybe he is on his way to LA. This is the second one south. Maybe he's been in that area all summer. Better check that one with Michaels also. Maybe it's not their first and they just didn't put it together," Burns replied.

At 12:30 p.m. Stone and Vickers met with Michaels and Sgt. Andrew Rock, the detectives in charge of the assault.

"Nice meeting you again, Jim," Michaels began. "This is my partner Andy Rock."

"Peter, Andy. This is Detective Peggy Vickers. She does most of our female victim interviews," Stone and Vickers shook hands with the two Stockton investigators.

"I think he is your man, Jim. I've talked to my sister about EAR many times. She lives in your area and to tell you the truth, she's scared to death. Wish you had chased him in a different direction," Michaels remarked.

"Well, run it down to us, Pete. Maybe it's not EAR," Stone and Vickers followed the two detectives into the interrogation room.

"About 3:30 this morning dispatch got the call. I was on call, so they got me at home. Got there a little after four. Patrol had secured the scene and were transporting the female to County for examination. I talked to the husband who said he and his wife were asleep and she woke him up. When he turned over, a flashlight beam was in his eyes and he heard a male voice tell him not to move or he would kill him. He said the suspect repeated it several times and then told him to roll over on his stomach. The suspect told the wife to tie her husband's hands behind his back. The suspect retied him and tied his feet then tied up the wife. Told them all he wanted was money and food for his apartment. Asked where the husband's wallet was and if anyone else was in the house. They have two kids, five and six. The suspect said if he or his wife caused any trouble he would chop up the kids and bring them their ears.

"The suspect left the room but came back in a short time and told them to shut up. He put a knife to the husband's throat and threatened to kill him. Then he took the wife out of the room and came back in and put plates on the husband's back. Said if he heard them rattle he would kill him. The husband said that the suspect had some sort of doctor's bag. He could hear it rattle whenever he put it down. He also said the suspect put a gun barrel to his head and cocked it. He also put the knife to his throat a couple of times.

"When we checked the house, we found a Pepsi can in the backyard, peanut butter jar on the kitchen counter. Husband said the suspect removed them from the fridge.

"He tied them up with shoelaces taken from the husband's shoes. Also a blanket was draped over a lamp in the living room. They heard him closing all the drapes earlier. Apparently the wife was naked in bed and when he took her out of the bedroom she asked for a robe and he draped it over her shoulders."

"How did he get in? Do you know?" Stone asked.

"Victims think the sliding glass door in the bedroom was unlocked. There were pry marks on the screen door, but not on the slider."

"Did he get a look at the suspect?"

"Not a good one. Thinks he was about five nine. Said he thought he was wearing a hat or mask," Michaels replied. "Also said the suspect seemed to be trying to disguise his voice. Always talked low except when he was excited. Then he would speak in a high pitched voice. Also said he was wearing gloves. He felt them when he was being tied."

"You talked to the female?" Stone asked.

"No, Andy talked to her and then Julie Ott, one of our detectives, talked to her. We haven't talked to Julie yet, so we don't know if she learned anything else," Michaels replied.

"She was real upset," Rock began. "She heard the suspect open the slider and he told her to shut up. She saw him place a doctor type bag on the floor. He was shining a light in her eyes and when she woke her husband, he told them he would kill them if they moved. She pretty well said the same as her husband about what happened in the bedroom. He held a knife to her throat when he walked her down the hall. Raped her twice and apparently climaxed both times. She said she heard him masturbate both times before he raped her. Funny thing is she says she feels he used a rubber penis also. Said it felt like two different things. The rubber penis was stiff, the suspect's penis was small and not real hard. He made some remarks about seeing her in the store and he wanted to fuck her. Said he only lived a few blocks away and needed things for his apartment. Soap, towels, portable television. She said he had bad odor. BO or something. Said it was just a dirty smell. Both victims said they heard a Volkswagen start up and leave after the suspect left."

"Did she say that the suspect used any kind of lotion before he raped her?" Vickers asked.

"Yeah. Said she heard a sloshing noise when he masturbated. We found a bottle of Fuller Brush lotion on the bathroom sink. Victim said he must have removed it from the medicine cabinet," Rock replied.

"Did the suspect have the victim masturbate him?" Vickers asked.

"She didn't say anything about it to me. Is that something he usually does?" Rock asked.

"Sometimes. Not always," Vickers replied.

"Did either of them say he was wearing a mask?" Stone asked.

"Both said they couldn't be sure," Rock answered.

"Did your canvass come up with anything?" Stone asked.

"Dogs barking in the neighborhood. A few strange cars. Nothing else yet but we're still out there," Michaels replied. "As soon as we get the reports I'll get them to you."

"Do you think it's EAR, Jim?" Rock asked.

"Looks like it or a damned good copycat. Any chance of talking to the victims later?" Stone asked.

"Our town is yours, Jim. Any help you can give us will be appreciated. We don't want to go through what you have. Help us chase him back your way. As to the victims, just let us know when you're ready. I've already told them that we would be asking for your help and they're willing to cooperate," Michaels replied.

"Okay. Thanks, Pete, Andy. Anything you need, let us know. Our files are open to you. No sense reinventing the wheel," Stone said.

"I'll give you a call when I've talked to Julie, if she has anything," Michaels replied.

Friday, 9-9-77, 8:30 a.m.

"Hey, Jim. A call for you from a Detective Ott, Stockton P.D. Line one," Wayne called to Stone.

"Sergeant Stone. Can I help you?"

"Sergeant, I'm Detective Ott, Stockton. Sgt. Michaels asked me to call you regarding the Sanford rape."

"Oh, yes. It's Julie, right?"

"Yeah. Look, I talked to Jennifer Sanford again last night and got some more information. Pete said he ran the case down to you, but last night Jennifer said she talked to her six year old daughter, Danielle, who saw the suspect in the hall. I interviewed the daughter, who seems real sharp. She got up to go to the bathroom and the suspect was standing in the hall near the kitchen. She said he was wearing a purple t-shirt, brown ski mask, and black knit mittens. She said he wasn't wearing any pants, but he had on a belt with a sword in it and a gun in a holster on the left side. Later she wasn't real sure if it was on the left or not. The knife could be a hunting knife. I asked her if she said anything to the man, and she said no, she woke up and had to go to the bathroom. He told her he was playing tricks with her mom and dad and asked her to come and watch. She didn't answer, said she went to the bathroom and went back to bed. I asked her about jewelry, and she said he was wearing a watch on his right wrist."

"Interesting," Stone remarked. "Anything on the neighborhood canvass?"

"Lots of reports of dogs barking within a week of the rapes. Quite a few shoe impressions in the victim's yard and several neighbor yards. All appear to match and seem to be a size nine and a half. We checked with Sport Sity Shoes and they said it was definitely a Converse All Star tennis shoe. We also checked with the sales rep and he said the All Star is the only shoe with these markings. There were also some phone calls, hang-up types, in the area over the last week or so. A couple of them were fuck and suck type calls.

"Oh, also Jennifer said she found a pair of her pantyhose in one of the drawers the suspect had ransacked. One leg had a knot in it and there was a finger size hole in the crotch. She says they weren't that way before. We found a knife at the foot of the bed the morning of the rape. The husband said at the time it was his but called us later and said he found his knife under the bed. He said the one we found definitely wasn't his."

"Anything missing from the house?" Stone asked.

"Five silver dollars, wedding and engagement rings, cufflinks, tie pin, and a man's onyx ring. Seven dollars in Michael's wallet wasn't taken. They've also had hang-up phone calls since the rape. We're attempting to get a trap on the phone now," Ott finished.

On November 26, 1977 Jennifer Sanford was hypnotized at the Sacramento County Sheriff's Office. During hypnosis Jennifer recalled the suspect placing a gun to her head and cocking it. He continually stated he would kill her or her children if she didn't do as she was told. She was sure that the rapist had used an artificial penis during his attacks. She also heard what she described as a Volkswagen motor shortly after the suspect left. Several neighbors, her husband, and her daughter also had heard a VW leave the area.

Danielle Sanford, the six year old daughter, under hypnosis, remembered a tattoo, one that investigators determined to be the Schlitz beer bull, on the rapist's arm.

Sacramento Bee, 9-7-77

Police Certain East Area Rapist Struck in Stockton

STOCKTON - Police here are certain a sexual assault on a twenty-seven year old North Stockton housewife was committed by Sacramento's notorious East Area Rapist.

CHAPTER THIRTY-FOUR

"We tried to convince ourselves it was somebody else, but there's just no way to do it. It's him," a Stockton police sergeant said after an extensive conference with detectives from Sacramento. The method of operation employed in the Stockton rape early Tuesday was "identical" to that attributed to the East Area Rapist and the details of the sexual assault itself "leave absolutely no doubt" that it was the same man who assaulted 22 to 24 women in Sacramento County.

...The last reported attack by the rapist in Sacramento occurred May 28 in the south area of the county. Newspapers called it the 24th assault since October 1975, but sheriff's deputies say it was the 22nd rape by the man. Two earlier rapes attributed to the "inadequately endowed" sexual psychopath were not committed by the same man, deputies said.

Chapter Thirty-five

"SHUT UP. DON'T MAKE A MOVE or I'll kill you. I want your dope. I know you have some andI'll look until I find it."

Harvey Westcott heard the male voice and turned toward his bedroom door. He saw the flashlight in the man's left hand, saw the nylon-covered head and saw the revolver in the intruder's right hand. The flashlight beam played between Harvey Hays and his shot gun leaning against the wall near the bed. Back and forth the beam slowly moved and finally settled on the eyes of Hays.

"Roll over. Get on your stomachs," the voice hissed and Hays saw the shoelaces land on the bed as he rolled over.

At 0340 hours Stone groped in the darkness for his phone. Even before he was awake he knew the ringing phone meant another attack. It seemed even the phone knew. The ring was somehow different, or so it seemed to Stone, like the sound of a distant train whistle. Sad.

"Hello," Stone closed his eyes as he spoke, waiting for the news.

"Jim, Colin Bryant here. You've got another hit over in Rancho Cordova. Looks like he didn't leave our area for long," the patrol lieutenant on duty began.

"Good morning to you, too, Lieutenant," Stone replied.

"Sorry to wake you, Jim. I called Burns and he asked me to call you. Said he'd pick you up in half an hour. He's got the info. Young couple, boyfriend-girlfriend, looks like. Everything fits. Vickers is on her way, too."

"Thanks, Colin. Dogs on the way?"

"Already on the scene, Jim."

"Okay, talk to you later," Stone hung up.

At 0440 hours Burns and Stone arrived at the Rancho Cordova address and contacted Deputy Rich, the first unit on scene.

"Morning, Merle," Stone greeted Rich. "What do we have?"

"Seventeen year old female and her twenty-one year old boyfriend. Vickers is already with the female inside. Ganon's got the boyfriend next door. He's my partner tonight. We're working the 05P4. Got here four minutes after the call. Didn't look good to me at first. I didn't think he hit duplexes, but everything inside fits. Mask, gun, knife, same words, same threats, shoelaces, dishes, lotion, masturbation," Rich explained.

"Let us talk to Vickers for a minute and then we'll talk to the male. Got names?" Burns interjected.

"Female is Margarita Lopez, male is Harvey Westcott. One other thing that doesn't fit. He's a biker type. A little lower on the food chain than EAR's been used to," Rich replied. "I'll have Ganon bring Westcott over for you."

Burns and Stone met Vickers as she was exiting the house with the female victim.

"Morning, Lieutenant, Jim," Vickers greeted them. "Just leaving for the Med Center. This is Margarita Lopez. Margarita, this is Lieutenant Burns and Sergeant Stone. They will be in charge of the investigation."

Burns and Stone nodded at the crying seventeen year old.

"We'll meet you later, Peg," Stone stated as Vickers and Lopez continued down the walkway.

Lopez had undergone an abortion just two days prior to the attack. Although she had previously lived with Westcott, three weeks ago she had moved to an apartment with a girlfriend. After the abortion, she stayed with Westcott as she had not been feeling well.

On the night of the rape, she and Westcott had argued violently and he drove her back to her apartment. They talked and decided to return to his place around 11:30 p.m. and went to bed. After falling asleep, Lopez was awakened by a light shining in her eyes by a male she described as twenty-one to thirty-five years old, five foot nine inches tall, one hundred and seventy pounds with a nylon stocking over his face and wearing a dark knit type cap on his head. The intruder was carrying a flashlight and a revolver.

Prior to tying the victims and placing dishes on Westcott's back, the attacker had played his flashlight beam back and forth between Westcott and his shotgun leaning against the bedroom wall, tempting Westcott to reach for it. Westcott didn't. Later, crime scene technicians found that the shotgun had been unloaded and the shells lined up in a row under the bed. EAR, probably while the victims had been out of the house, had unloaded the shotgun. Would he have shot the victims if Westcott had reached for the gun? Was he looking for a reason to kill? Would that have been the justification he was looking for? We will never know. We can only speculate.

Several times during the ordeal the attacker placed the barrel of his gun against the temple of Lopez and Westcott, cocking the weapon, terrorizing the victims.

Westcott's seven month old pit bulldog jumped on the bed while EAR searched the house. When he returned, the dog growled once but did not bark. EAR picked the dog up and walked out of the room.

Twice he raped the seventeen year old, holding a knife to her throat and threatening to slit it if she didn't help him.

Sacramento Bee, 10-2-77

East Area Rapist Returns to District, Assaults Teen-Aged Girl in Duplex

Sacramento sheriff's investigators say the East Area Rapist struck Saturday for the first time in this area in four months when he assaulted a 17 year old girl visiting her boyfriend in his duplex home east of the city limits.

The number of attacks attributed to the East Area Rapist has been revised downward because two assaults which occurred in October 1975 and 1976 have been dropped from the list.

CHAPTER THIRTY-SIX

THE HANG-UP PHONE CALLS over the past two weeks did not alert Sandra Belton to the possible danger lurking in her neighborhood. Two days ago her thirteen year old daughter had returned from school to find the door leading into the residence from the garage ajar. A family member left it open, thought Belton when her daughter told her.

None of this entered the minds of the husband and wife enjoying the intense pleasure that only those secure in their relationship find when making love. Never again, after tonight, will they ever lose the paranoia that will cut through their minds when something, even minute, appears out of place. Never again will they feel secure locked in their home. Never again will they feel safe. Not in this lifetime. Not on this earth.

Sandra Belton, sound asleep, felt a presence in the room. Not a noise. Not a voice. An evil presence. She awoke to the feeling and turned toward the bedroom door. A light flashed across her eyes. She could see the flashlight in his left hand, the gun in his right hand, and the hideous mask covering his face.

"Don," she said as she nudged her husband. "There's a burglar in the house."

As Don rolled over from his stomach, he heard, "I have a .357 magnum. If you don't do as I say, I'm going to blow your fucking head off."

Shoelaces landed on the bed. "Tie him up. If you don't tie him up tight I'm going to blow your fucking head off. Put his hands behind his back and be sure that you tie him tight."

They could hear the intruder rummaging throughout the house. When he returned she heard the dishes rattle as they were placed on her husband's back. She knew then that he was the rapist.

"Please, God," she prayed to herself, "don't let him put dishes on my back. Please."

She felt herself being pulled from the bed and she knew her prayers had been answered. She would be the victim, not her thirteen year old daughter.

After the attacks on her body, her circumcised rapist stuttered, "Tell the p-p-p-pigs I'll be b-b-b-back New Year's Eve," She heard him crying, sobbing, after the second attack.

Although the attacker repeatedly put the knife to her throat and threatened to kill her and had placed the gun against Donald Belton's head several times and threatened to cut his fingers off, the victims remained composed. Because of their closeness, they will cope. They will survive.

At 0500 hours Sergeant Stone received a call from Lieutenant Colin Bryant, the on-duty patrol watch commander.

At 0530 hours Stone arrived at the scene and transported Sandra Belton to the U.C. Davis Medical Center. Vickers met them at 0605 hours to conduct the interview. Stone returned to the scene and met with Greg Wayne and the Task Force personnel. It was a routine that everyone knew. Each officer was well into his assignment.

Sacramento Bee, 10-21-77

Foothill Farms

Rapist Gets 25th Victim

By Warrent Holloway and Thom Akeman, Bee Staff Writers

The East Area Rapist shifted to the Foothill Farms area today to attack a sleeping couple, ransack their home, and leave them to be untied by their two small children, sheriff's deputies reported.

The rapist entered the home northeast of the Elkhorn Boulevard and Diablo Drive intersection about 3 a.m., sheriff's deputies said. He wore a ski mask and carried a pistol and a knife to overpower the couple in their bedroom, deputies said.

It was the 25th attack in 16 months attributed to the rapist. Twenty-two have occurred in the north or east area, one in the south area, and one in Stockton. The rapist last struck October 1 when he raped a 17 year old girl who was visiting her boyfriend in the LaRiviera-Folsom Boulevard area. In today's attack, the rapist forced open a side door on the garage, then broke through a kitchen door to enter the home. This is one of the few forced entries of the East Area Rapist. The man has more routinely entered the homes of his victims by snapping open sliding glass doors. Neither of the doors in today's entry were secured with deadbolts.

The rapist awakened the sleeping couple, tied the man on the bed, then led the woman to another part of the house where he tied her and repeatedly raped her, deputies said. It is the same pattern the rapist had followed in his last nine strikes.

"As sure as we can be, this was the East Area Rapist. He had the same M.O. [method of operation]. Sure the attacker was gone, they awakened their children and had them untie them." They called the sheriff's office at 4:35 a.m. The spokesman refused to reveal further details of the rapist's activities in the home or to say if the attacker left any messages for the police or press, as he has done in other strikes.

The rapist first struck June 18, 1976. His first 16 attacks were against women who were either home alone or with their small children. The invader awakened and tied up the children in at least one case.

The last nine attacks attributed to the East Area Rapist have involved couples. His pattern is to awaken them as they are in their bedrooms, point the gun and knife at them, order the woman to tie the man, place dishes on the man and tell him his wife will be killed if the dishes rattle, lead the woman into another part of the house, rape her, tie her in a chair, ransack the house, then return to rape the woman again.

Only two of the rapist's attacks have started outside the victims' homes, with one woman and one couple confronted at gunpoint in front of their homes. The other 23 have occurred after the rapist broke into the homes of his sleeping victims.

The rapist has been described as a "paranoid schizophrenic" acting in a homosexual panic caused by feelings of sexual inadequacy. That was contained in a psychological profile released by the sheriff's detectives in May.

The terrorist has attacked irregularly since then, striking in the south area May 28, in Stockton September 6, back in the east area October 1, and in the north area today.

Chapter Thirty-seven

AT 0445 HOURS on 10-26-77, Harold Baines was leaving his Whitney Avenue residence for work. He observed a white male, twenty to twenty-five years old, five foot eight to six feet tall, medium build with medium brown hair, walking past his residence in an easterly direction. The subject was walking slowly and appeared to be looking at the various houses. As the subject walked past Baines' yard, he was illuminated by the bright light over the garage. He looked directly at Baines, not changing his facial expression or pace. Three houses down, he stopped near a large palm tree, looked back at Baines, then vanished. Baines checked the area, however did not see the subject again. After arriving at work, he called his wife and advised her of the incident. Although the weather was cool and very brisk, the subject had not been wearing a jacket or sweater.

Thursday, 10-27-77, at approximately 5:00 p.m., Margaret Hayworth picked up her ringing telephone only to be greeted by silence.

At approximately 2:00 p.m., 10-28-77, a white male, twenty-five to thirty years old, was seen driving on Wooden Avenue in a large four-door vehicle, dark in color. The vehicle was described as possibly a Dodge or Plymouth and the driver appeared to be checking the residences.

At approximately 6:30 p.m., a 1963 or 1964 Ford Falcon was seen driving slowly on Woodson Avenue. The vehicle had been seen twice before in the area; however no description of the driver could be given.

At approximately 7:30 p.m., Eric and Margaret Hayworth left their Carmichael area residence and drove to Ricco's Pizza. Darkness had already arrived before the Hayworths drove off.

The dark figure blended in to the shadows, unseen, unheard. The figure approached the rear of the Hayworth residence, checking the sliding glass door and bedroom windows. He returned to the sliding glass door and began to pry near the lock. The lock held and he quietly moved to the bedroom window. He could see the bedroom was unused as he pried the screen free. Again he pried and a small piece of glass broke free near the latch, enough to unlock the window. Quickly the dark figure slid through into the bedroom. He went directly to the master bedroom and unlocked the sliding glass door. He opened drawers, looked, then closed them, leaving everything intact. He opened the nightstand drawer and removed the .357 magnum Colt Trooper revolver, opened the cylinder and the six cartridges fell quietly into his gloved hand. He placed the gun back into its hiding place and silently exited, carefully closing the unlocked sliding glass door. He returned to the broken window and replaced the screen, then once again disappeared into the darkness.

At 10:00 p.m. Margaret and Eric Hayworth returned, watched T.V., and around midnight went to bed. Having lived in their home for only two and a half weeks, the newness still filled their senses and sent tinges of excitement through their bodies.

At 1:45 a.m., 10-29-77, Eric Hayworth felt a steady tapping against his foot. As he re-entered consciousness, the ugliness of the real world stared at him from behind the bright light shining in his eyes.

"Don't move or I'll blow your fucking brains out. I know you've got a gun in a drawer in here somewhere, and if you move I'll blow your fucking brains out. I know you've got a gun in here somewhere," the intruder hissed.

"It's in the nightstand drawer," Eric replied.

At 0407 hours, 10-29-77, Deputy Brian Brett received the call.

"Rape just occurred ten minutes ago. Husband and wife tied up."

At 0412 hours Brett and his beat partner, Deputy Kent, arrived at the scene and met with Eric and Margaret Hayworth. A short conversation and observation confirmed the EAR attack.

At 0415 hours, EAR protocol was implemented by the Watch Commander. Sergeant Stone, detectives Wayne and Vickers, were notified. The neighborhood canvass team, bloodhounds, and the on-call criminalists were notified. The EAR Trap Team had taken position when the initial call was received.

At 0430 hours a female officer arrived and processed Margaret Hayworth's upper body for fingerprints with negative results.

At 0440 hours Stone arrived on scene and contacted Brett who introduced him to the victims. Upon arrival Wayne began his interview with Eric Hayworth and Vickers transported Margaret Hayworth to the U.C. Medical Center. After the rape examination was completed, Vickers began her interview.

"I heard voices and saw a light shining," Margaret began. "He said he would blow our heads off, but I think he was as frightened as we were of him because he didn't come near us for about five minutes. He threw me some shoelaces and told me to tie Eric."

"Did he use Eric's name?" Vickers asked.

"No. He just said 'tie him.' You know, I always thought that if I was ever attacked by the East Area Rapist, I would tie my husband's hands real loose, but when it happened, I just wanted to do exactly as he told me. I made a mistake and only tied one wrist and the rapist got real mad and said, 'Bitch, I'll blow your brains out if you try something like that again.' He threw me another lace and told me to tie him right. After that, he tied both of us.

"He rummaged for awhile and then came back into the bedroom and accused me of trying to untie Eric and then he cut the rope from my ankles and told me to get up. He pushed me down the hall and had his gun in my back and his knife at my throat. He said if I tired anything he would kill me.

"When we got to the living room, I saw strips of towel on the floor. He told me to lie down on my stomach and then he tied my feet and tied a towel around my eyes. He left for awhile and then he straddled me and told me to play with him and that I better make it good. I tried to tell him that I had no feeling in my hands, but he told me to shut up or he would cut off my ear.

"Then he told me to suck on him. I almost vomited because he had some kind of lotion on his penis. Then he got on top of me and raped me and then he put it in my mouth again. When he took his penis out of my mouth, he stood up and said, 'I'm sorry, Mom...Mommy, please help me, I don't want to do this, mommy.' He was sobbing and I think it was genuine. He repeated it over and over while he was sobbing and hyperventilating.

"He left for awhile, I guess he was checking Eric, and then he came back and did it all over again and then he started crying again. He seemed to be stumbling around and he said, 'Mommy, I don't want to do this. Someone please help me.'

"When he tied my feet the last time he said he was going to watch television and for me to keep my mouth shut. He constantly threatened me and kept calling me bitch and used the word 'fucking' a lot. At first he kept saying he only wanted food and money for his van and he would go. I told him we didn't have any money, but I would write him a check. He told me to 'shut my fucking mouth.' Before he left he put a cup and saucer on my back and took my wedding rings."

"Did you see him at all during this?" Vickers asked.

"Not really. I saw his legs from his knees down and I saw the tips of his fingers on one hand. It looked like black leather gloves. He was wearing blue tennis shoes with brown and burgundy socks. The shoes were dirty and worn and his legs were white with light colored hair."

"Can you describe his penis?" Vickers asked.

"I was surprised because the paper said it was small. It seemed big around but short."

At 9:30 a.m. Stone received a phone call from a female who ran a business on Whitney Avenue. She had arrived at her place of business a little after 4:00 a.m. and, as she had clients waiting, she went right to work. Shortly after, she saw several patrol cars in the area. A deputy came in and asked about the vehicles parked in front of the business. They all belonged to her customers.

At 6:30 a.m., she saw a man rise up from inside a dump truck trailer across the street from her business. She saw the man, dressed in dark clothing with a hood over his head, get on a bicycle and ride east on Whitney Avenue real fast. She said the truck is parked there by the owner at night during the week occasionally and every weekend.

The bloodhounds earlier had followed a scent from the Hayworth residence, losing it near the curb where the truck was parked.

On 11-14-77, a State Patrol officer living behind the Hayworth residence, called to report that his daughter had found a .38 caliber bullet in his backyard. During a further search, he had found another bullet, a wadcutter, in the same area. Eric Hayworth was able to identify the bullets as those taken from his gun.

Stone and the members of the Task Force followed leads. All tried and true investigative techniques were used and still they were no closer to finding the identity of the rapist than they were 6-18-76.

Even techniques shunned by the law enforcement community were researched. The Task Force contacted a psychic, one who claimed to have helped numerous law enforcement investigations. They attempted to have a biorhythm chart made of the rapist. While most of the investigators laughed when these were suggested, they all went along with the unorthodox ventures with the secret hope that something would help.

The psychic, who had initially contacted the Task Force, offered a tip that did not check out. The biorhythm chart was impossible to construct without the rapist's birthday.

Half of the overwhelming numbers of hours devoted to the rapist were spent tracking down rumors.

One thing common to all twenty-six attacks of the East Area Rapist, is silence. In each attack there were long periods of silence, a way of playing games with the victims' minds. It was not just a physical attack; it was mental torture. Being master over their minds once they were bound and secured was his goal, his "trip."

So little was known about the rapist, that investigators were unsure of whether he was basically a burglar who had turned to sex crimes or a sex pervert who had learned to burglarize. They did know that a typical rapist did not have such elaborate schemes.

During the quiet hours of the rapist's attacks, although he ransacked the homes, it was not to any great extent. It seemed to be another part of the mental trip.

The victims themselves had suffered more trauma after the attacks than during them. The biggest trauma was coping with the community. Terrorized by the rapist, then attacked by their friends and relatives demanding to know how they could just lie there and let all that happen. The victims themselves were the biggest supporters of the Task Force. They came to realize why the East Area Rapist was so hard to catch: the rapist's caution and skill and an extreme amount of luck had so far helped him elude capture; operating in the dark; people who had heard or seen something suspicious to only dismiss them and go back to sleep; an M.O. that had remained the same since the first attack, combined to keep the detectives also in the dark. The detectives knew it would not only take the right information to catch EAR, it would take an incredible amount of luck.

Sacramento Bee, 11-9-77

RAPIST

Profile Given

A sheriff's spokesman said the rapist is not abnormally sexually endowed. Rumors that he was were false. A study released by the sheriff's department that said the rapist is in a "homosexual panic because of inadequate physical endowment" were false. "After talking with sources at the office, I understand that he is average," she stated with a smile. To a question as to what would occur if the rapist was shot breaking into a home, the detective said "I'll tell you what. If you see a man in your living room wearing a ski mask and gloves, and you shot him, you will probably get a commendation and award."

CHAPTER THIRTY-SEVEN

At 5:40 p.m., 11-7-77, Greg Wayne received a call from Sergeant Ortiz of the California State Campus Police regarding a note written on the bathroom wall in a campus restroom. The note, according to Ortiz, concerned information about the East Area Rapist.

At 6:10 p.m., Wayne met with Ortiz in the library at the University. Wayne was directed to the men's room located on the main floor of the building. In the middle stall on the right hand side, written in pencil, was a message which stated, "The East Side Rapist was here / Will rape my first black girl tonight / Dumb cops will never find me."

Wayne photographed the message and left.

CHAPTER THIRTY-EIGHT

THIRTY-THREE YEAR OLD HEIDI McDOUGAL awakened from a sound sleep. A noise on the west side of their residence caused their neighbor's dog to bark loudly. Her husband got up and looked out the bedroom window.

"Nothing moving," he said as he got back into bed. The McDougals were a little apprehensive after Heidi had been awakened almost eight months ago by an unknown prowler shining a flashlight into the bedroom onto her. Several hang-up phone calls over the past several weeks added to the fear.

None of the incidents were reported by the McDougals.

11:00 p.m., 11-9-77. LaRiveria Drive, Sacramento

Donna Carl had just turned out her bedroom light when a sound was heard from the side of the house in the patio area. It sounded as though someone had fallen against her house. No other sound was heard and she was soon fast asleep.

12:05 a.m., 11-10-77. LaRiveria Drive, Sacramento

Jean Hoffmeister heard someone tampering with the sliding glass door. At the same time her dog began barking and growling. She turned on her outside light. Nothing was seen; she returned to bed.

3:00 a.m., 11-10-77. LaRiveria Drive, Sacramento

David Dorval was awakened by what sounded like someone trying to open the screen door to the bedroom sliding glass door. He turned on the outside light and looked out the window. Nothing was seen, so he returned to bed. At 3:30 a.m. his sixty-seven year old mother was awakened by pounding sounds outside the residence. She fell back to sleep.

3:30 a.m., 11-10-77. LaRiveria Drive, Sacramento

A loud banging noise made by the closing of the bedroom sliding glass door brought fifty-six year old Denise Kent from a sound sleep. She sat straight up in bed and was blinded by the light shining directly into her eyes.

"What do you want? I'm an old lady," She shouted.

"I won't hurt you or harm you. All I want is your money. Lie back down," the intruder whispered. "No, not that way. On your stomach," He tied her hands and then her ankles.

"My hands are tied too tight," she complained.

"Do you want me to cut off your fingers? Who else is in the house? If you lie to me, I'll slit your throat," he hissed.

"My daughter," she replied.

"I'm going to tie your daughter," He left her then. Later he returned and placed two plates on her back. "If I hear these plates jiggle you will be dead, bitch. All I want is your money and food. Do you hear me? Do you hear me? Do you hear me?"

"Yes," she replied.

"I need things for my apartment. Blankets. My car is parked out front and I'm going back to L.A.," he told her as he was leaving the room.

Later he returned. "I'm going upstairs and cook something to eat and if you make any sounds, your daughter will be dead. Do you hear me, bitch?"

"Yes," she whispered.

Thirteen year old Deborah Kent felt someone shaking her. "Leave me alone," she said, thinking someone was waking her because it was morning. She opened her eyes and saw the black ski mask with the holes for eyes and mouth.

"Stop joking around and let me go back to sleep," she muttered, still thinking it was a friend waking her.

"This isn't a joke," the masked intruder hissed. "Get onto your stomach and put your hands behind your back."

"No," she argued.

"Do what I say or I'm going to stick you with a knife. I'll slit your throat and watch you bleed to death," he ordered in a vicious whisper. She felt the knife beside her neck and felt it slide down behind her ear. "Do you want me to cut off your ear?"

"I don't care," She rolled over.

"All I want is your money," he said as he tied her hands and feet.

"I don't have any," she lied. If he couldn't find it, she wouldn't lose it, she thought to herself.

He left the room and she could hear him in the bathroom. She moved her feet and the ties came loose. She heard him returning and wished she hadn't loosened the ties.

"If you move again, I'll kill your mother," he threatened as he retied her feet.

He left her then and she could hear him rummaging. She heard him coming down the stairs. She heard the dishes rattle and she knew he was the East Area Rapist she had read about.

"Please put them on my back," she prayed to herself. She knew that if he did, she wouldn't be the one raped. Her hopes were dashed when she heard him go past her room toward her mother's.

He returned to her room. She saw the strips of towels in his hands. He tried to gag her but she stuck her tongue out to make sure it wasn't tight. Then he blindfolded her. He untied her feet and straddled her on the bed. She felt his penis in her hand.

"Grab it. Squeeze it," he demanded. "Do you know what this is?"

"No," she replied.

"Have you ever fucked before?" he whispered.

"I don't know," she answered.

"Do you know what that means?"

"No."

"Roll over," he demanded.

"Why?" she challenged.

"Roll over or I'll kill you."

"I don't want to," she challenged.

"Roll over," he demanded as he grabbed her and physically rolled her over. "Bend your legs."

At 5:30 a.m., Stone received the call from Captain Ward.

"Looks like a case for your Task Force, Sarge. We have officers preserving the scene for you."

"Thanks, Captain," Stone muttered as he wrote down the address. "I'll start the call-out."

Stone and Vickers arrived at the scene at the same time and met with Sacramento Police Officer Krenshaw.

"The mother and daughter both say there was no sexual assault," Krenshaw began, "but I don't think that's true. Everything points toward EAR and I think the thirteen year old was his victim. I didn't want to push it with her. Felt you would rather talk to her," Krenshaw nodded at Vickers.

"Thanks," Vickers replied. "I'll talk to her and get her to the hospital."

CHAPTER THIRTY-EIGHT

The strong willed young child had used all her wits to challenge the masked intruder. As with those before her, she had lost. EAR had assaulted his youngest victim.

Sacramento Bee, 11-10-77

East Area Rapist Attacks Girl, 13

The East Area Rapist broke into a Sacramento condominium early today, raping a 13 year old girl after he awakened and tied up the mother...

She was the youngest victim in the terrifying series of attacks, police said...

He has been the subject of the most intensive manhunt in the county's history, police have said. Detectives have checked out in one fashion or another more than 5,000 men reported as possible suspects. Still they have no idea of whom they are looking for or what kind of man he really is, detectives say.

CHAPTER THIRTY-NINE

HANG-UP PHONE CALLS can be a real nuisance. Sometimes that's all they are; sometimes it's more.

For the past three weeks, Roxanne McMeel had been receiving calls every day after 2:00 p.m. At first she felt it was girls calling her fourteen year old son. Then her son answered the phone twice; both hang-ups. Could there be a connection to the burglary of their home October 27th? Why would someone break into a house and steal two photographs from an album? The photographs were of her taken six years ago. Younger, slimmer, happier times in her marriage. And why did the burglar turn the thermostat off? The heat had been on when she left that day.

12-2-77, 8:00 p.m.

Greg Wayne was driving around the Carmichael area when he received a radio call to contact the Metro Division and talk to the PBX operator in the communications center.

"This is Detective Wayne. I'm supposed to talk to a PBX operator," Wayne advised when his call was answered.

"Just a second, Detective. Dale Masters is the operator and I'll get him for you."

"Dale Masters here. Is this Detective Wayne?" Masters asked.

"Yeah, this is Wayne. What can I do for you?"

"I just took a call, sounded like a male twenty to thirty years old, clear voice, no accent. He said, 'I shall commit another rape,' then he hung up. It sounded like he was reading or reciting the words."

"Damn. Is the call on tape?" Wayne asked.

"Should be. I'll pull it and hold it," Masters replied.

"Good. I need you to get a hold of Sergeant Stone and let him know."

"We tried. He's not home so we left a message to have him call."

"Nothing else? No background noise, anything else he said?" Wayne asked.

"Nope. That was it. Sorry."

"Okay. Have them hold the tape for me and I'll pick it up on the way into the office. And thanks for the call."

12-2-77, Revelstok Drive, Sacramento

The fog blanketed the Sacramento area, as it often does during the winter nights. The streets were wet and the yellow glow from the street lights illuminated the teenagers playing innocent teenage games across from Roxanne McMeel's house. They were loud and boisterous, but it was Friday night and they were just neighborhood kids. They didn't notice the figure dressed in black moving silently from backyard to backyard. They didn't notice the occasional barking that seemed to draw nearer to their location. Later, after midnight, they didn't notice the masked face peering at them through McMeel's curtained windows.

12-3-77, 2:30 a.m.

"3P4," the dispatcher's voice broke the silence, "Suspicious circumstance detail on Revelstok Drive."

Deputies Allan and Brett, working unit 3P4, arrived on scene one minute after receiving the call. The victim, Roxanne McMeel, was lying on the living room floor covered with a blanket when they entered the residence. A female neighbor was comforting McMeel who was crying and taking quick, shallow breaths of air.

A pair of scissors and several pieces of black shoelaces were near the victim's feet.

At 2:45 a.m., Stone, who was also patrolling in the area in his unmarked vehicle, arrived and took control of the scene. He entered the residence to find McMeel near hysteria.

"It's going to be all right," Stone tried to comfort her. "A female investigator will be here soon to work with you," He knew when he first entered the room that EAR had been in the house. The feeling, the presence, was heavy in the air. He could smell the evil. "Can you describe the man who tied you up?" Stone asked as he knelt beside the victim.

"No. I didn't see him. He shined a light in my eyes," she sobbed. "He told me to be quiet or he would kill my son. He thought my daughter, who was in bed with me, was a boy. He took me out of the room and tied me up."

"Detective Vickers will be here soon, Mrs. McMeel. I understand how difficult this is for you, but we do need your help," Stone stood. "May I use your phone?"

"It's in the kitchen," McMeel nodded toward the kitchen area.

"Hi, Radio. This is Stone. It looks like our man again. I need you to start the EAR protocol. I already talked to Vickers, but we need the Canvass Team and hounds right away."

"Okay, Sarge. Good luck," the dispatcher responded.

"Looks like that's the only thing we don't have–good luck. Lots of bad luck, though," Stone hung up.

At 3:30 a.m., Vickers arrived and took McMeel next door to the neighbor's for the interview.

"I went to bed at 11:30. My six year old daughter was in my bed because my husband left at 11:00 to go gambling with his friends. Just before I fell asleep I heard a noise at our bedroom door. I think it was our cat," McMeel began.

"Did you get up to check?" Vickers asked.

"No. I fell asleep shortly after. I don't know how long I was asleep and I don't know what woke me, but I turned over and the man was there shining a light in my eyes. He told me to get up and I asked him why. He said, 'Get up and come with me or I'll hurt your little boy.' He thought she was a boy because she has short hair. When I got up I saw he had shoelaces in his left hand."

"Did he have a gun or knife?" Vickers asked.

"I didn't see any. He told me to walk down the hall and when we got to the living room he told me to get on my knees. He always seemed angry and it was like he kept his teeth clenched. After I got on my knees, he tied my hands behind my back. He tied them real tight. The string cut into my skin. Then he told me to lie down on my stomach and then he took off my underpants. I knew he was standing over me looking at me for awhile and then he tied my ankles together real tight. I was crying and sobbing and he told me to be quiet or he would gag me. I begged him not to. I told him my daughter sometimes got up and if she did I could tell her to go back to bed if I wasn't gagged. He didn't gag me."

"Did he ever say he wanted money or anything?" Vickers inquired.

"No. He didn't say much. He was real quiet. There were a bunch of kids in front making noise and I think that made him nervous. He kept going to the window and looking through the drapes. One time he said, 'you think you're smarter, but I'm smarter than you are.' He sounded real angry," she sobbed.

"What did he mean by that?" Vickers asked.

"I don't know. I think he might have been talking about our house being burglarized. The Sheriff came out and was here a long time checking things. Maybe that was it. I kept hoping a neighbor would call about the kids outside because they were really making a lot of noise. I knew he was standing over me, but he didn't touch me," McMeel shuddered.

"He didn't sexually assault you?" Vickers asked incredulously.

"No. Never."

Vickers looked at her thinking she had to be lying.

"Did you see him? Can you describe him?"

"I kept my face in the carpet. I know he was wearing dark clothing. They didn't seem to be heavy clothes. Just a light jacket or something," McMeel answered.

"Did he touch you anywhere on your bare skin? Your shoulders or breasts?" Vickers asked.

"No. Never. When he took my underpants off, I thought he was going to, but he never did. I guess it was because of the kids outside."

"The only door that we found to be unlocked was the sliding glass door. Was it locked, do you know, before you went to bed?"

"I'm pretty sure it was. We always kept a key under the mat on the front porch. It has been missing for a couple of weeks. We just felt our son had misplaced it. He said he didn't, so maybe this person stole it," McMeel sobbed.

"Did he say anything when he left?"

"No. I really didn't know when he left. I heard a van leave at the side of the house. I know it was a van. I started moving and when he didn't say anything, I knew he was gone. I got to the phone and knocked it off the hook and called my neighbor. I counted the holes on the dial and dialed with my hands behind my back. When Howard answered, I yelled and told him what had happened. He came over and cut me free."

"Could you tell if he wore gloves?" Vickers asked.

"I could feel them when he tied me and I felt them when he took my underpants off, too," McMeel responded.

"I'm real sorry you had to go through this, Roxanne. I know how hard it is on you, but I really need to know everything that happened. He didn't sexually assault you in any way? Not have you touch his genitals or anything?"

"No. If he did, I would tell you. I've talked to my neighbors before and we all said we would tell if it ever happened to us," McMeel cried.

"Okay. I need to talk to Sergeant Stone for a minute. We need to take your underpants that he took off you. Maybe there is some type of evidence. You relax as best you can and I'll be right back," Vickers touched McMeel's shoulder and walked out.

"I don't know, Jim. She says she wasn't assaulted and remained adamant," Vickers told Stone when she met him outside the residence. "She says she thinks some kids playing outside scared him off. She also says he was wearing gloves, so there is no sense in trying to get prints off her."

"Maybe she wasn't. I talked to the neighbor who cut her free. He said she told him she hadn't been assaulted. He said she would be up front about it if she had. He also said he had a hell of a time getting through to us. He called the phone operator first and couldn't get an answer, so he called our PBX operator and told her he found a woman tied up. She said she would put him through to our Communications Center and he said the phone rang and rang so he hung up and called again. Same thing. So he called again and told her to stay on the line until someone answered the phone. She put him through on the emergency line.

"He said when he found McMeel he cut her free with a pair of scissors because he couldn't get the laces untied. He said she was hysterical, crying, sobbing. Said she told him she knew she would have been raped if it hadn't been for the kids outside. Says he heard them also and they were noisy."

12-5-77, EAR Task Force

"What do we have on the McMeel attack, Jim?" Mike Burns opened the Monday morning meeting.

"Not much more, Mike. We think EAR was a burglar earlier at their residence. Looks like he may have taken McMeel's photograph thinking they were recent. She frosts her hair now and looks older than the photograph. Maybe he changed his mind about raping her because of that or maybe it was the kids outside. She's thirty-six and that's the upper end of his age bracket for victims. He didn't ransack, didn't take any money or jewelry so maybe a combination of her age and the kids outside just fucked up his thought process enough to piss him off and he left. Peg thinks it was the kids and the age had nothing to do with it. Girl thing," Stone smiled at Vickers who politely gave him the finger.

"Crime Lab says no physiological fluid stains on the panties. They did find striation marks on the family room window when they removed the screen. Looks like that may be how he got in. The gate on the south side of the residence was unlocked. Victim says they always keep it locked. Greg was in charge of the canvass, so he can run that down," Stone nodded at Wayne.

"Just like most of the attacks. Lots of activity that was never reported. Two females who live in the area said someone turned off their electricity Thursday night. Didn't report it. Stranger than that, back in May they lived on Brett Avenue and one of them received a harassing phone call during the time we made our news release. The caller whispered three times, 'You are next.' They didn't report it, although they knew about EAR.

"Thursday afternoon another neighbor saw a male twenty-five, thirty years old walk from the Woodridge School area. She was working in her yard and the subject stopped and watched her for awhile. She got frightened and went into the house. Didn't report it because she says they have an alarm. Another neighbor who lives next door to McMeel saw a beige colored station wagon parked between the two houses. She couldn't recall the exact date but says she went out and looked at the plate. Couldn't remember what it was, though. A sixteen year old who lives down the street says he got home around midnight and saw a car parked across the street from his house. Says the windows weren't fogged up like the rest of the cars. Says it was a station wagon but doesn't know the make or model. Said he never saw it before.

"We also contacted all the kids who were playing outside that night. Nobody saw or heard anything," Wayne concluded.

"Peg?" Burns spoke. "Anything else from the victim?"

"Nothing. She insists she was not assaulted and says she'll take a polygraph. I set one up for the 7th at 9:00 a.m. I believe her, though. She was real shook up and scared and I think she would have told me," Vickers concluded.

(On 12-7-77, Roxanne McMeel took the polygraph examination. She was truthful).

"Anyone else have anything?" Burns inquired.

"Couple of articles in the *Union* today," Paul Pinnington, a Sacramento P.D. officer recently assigned to the Task Force spoke up. "One rapped us pretty good."

"I saw one headlined 'Teen Boys No Help In Rape Hunt' but must have missed the other," Burns stated. "Personally, I think the boys were a big help, at least to the victim. If I were her, I'd take them all to Disneyland."

"The other was a letter to the editor," Pinnington said. "Tells us to basically shit or get off the pot. Says where we can't catch him or deter him, we better ask for help from other agencies or start telling the public the full M.O. of EAR."

"Christ, if he read the *Bee* back in October he could have gotten a map of how to do it. What's their names? Hollaman and Akeman or something like that. The only thing they didn't do was tell you what shoes to wear," Vickers spoke up.

"Yeah, I saw that. Wondered how you felt about it," Pinnington continued. "Anyway, this fellow says it's criminal that taxpayers are forced into spending money to protect themselves by buying locks and alarms. Says voters should take a good look at the law enforcement officials next election. Did make one good suggestion, though. Suggested that the television stations periodically flash warnings that people make sure their windows and doors are locked."

"Okay," Stone stood up. "Better hit the bricks. Greg, how are we doing with the pawn shops?"

"They've all been updated with the missing property list, although I still think the motherfucker just throws the stuff away," Wayne shrugged.

"Hey, Jim," Jerry Morton, the other Sac P.D. officer broke in, "I just got a call from a lady in Folsom. She read about the last attack so thought she better call. Says back in May she put an ad in the paper that basically said she would put reward money in a bank account for EAR if he would turn himself in. Said he could use the money to start a new life after he got out of prison. She put a box number in the paper for him to respond. Anyway, she got one response that said her gesture was well intentioned but it was obvious that EAR is an animal. It was signed NOP, whatever that means. Anyway, I'm heading up that way to pick up the reply and get it to the lab for prints."

"Okay, Mort. Catch you when you get back," Stone replied. "Didn't take her long to call us did it? Par for the course."

No prints were obtained.

CHAPTER FORTY

JOAN ROSSALI, EAR's twenty-first victim turned from drying the dinner dishes to answer the ringing telephone.

"Hello," She placed the receiver on her shoulder and continued to dry the plate in her hand.

"Merry Christmas. It's me again," the male voice said in a hoarse whisper. She heard the click, click, click of the phone as the caller rapidly pushed the button and then the phone went dead. Rossali began to shake and the plate and phone crashed to the floor.

"What's the matter, Joan?" Her husband rushed into the kitchen to see his wife staring at the floor with her hands over her mouth. "You look like you saw a ghost. What's the matter?"

"It was him, Frank," she cried. "I know it was him. His voice. It was the rapist, Frank. Oh, God."

"What did he say?" Frank asked as he put his arms around his wife's shoulders and drew her to him.

"He said, 'Merry Christmas. It's me again.' Oh, Frank, what are we going to do? Why can't they catch him?" she cried.

"I'll call the Sheriff's Office and have them send an officer over," Frank shook his head.

At 5:50 p.m. Deputy Phil Money received the information from Joan Rossali and immediately called Stone.

"Thanks, Phil. I'll get hold of the Pacific Telephone Special Agent's office and get an emergency trap system in place. I'll call the Rossali's," Stone replied.

Stone called the San Francisco office and requested the trap. At 6:40 p.m. he was advised that the trap would be in place at 7:00 p.m.

"This is Sergeant Stone, Mr. Rossali," Stone began when Frank Rossali answered the phone. "Deputy Money called and told me about the call that Joan received. Are you two all right?"

"As good as can be expected under the circumstances, Sergeant," Frank replied. "Do you want to talk to Joan?"

"Please, if she's up to it."

"Just a second."

"Sergeant Stone, this is Joan."

"Joan, Are you okay?" Stone asked.

"I'll be all right after we calm down."

"Deputy Money called me about the phone call. Look, we have a trap set up on your phone, but before I get into that, tell me about the call," Stone asked.

"I know it was him, Sergeant. I know it's been seven months, but to me it's like yesterday. I'll never forget his voice. He just said, 'Merry Christmas. It's me again,' and hung up," Rossali replied.

"Okay. The trap is in place. I need you to log the times of all incoming calls. No matter who they are from, log the times. If he does call back, try and keep him on the line as long as possible. The EAR trap units have been advised and will be in the area to check on you. If you have a tape recorder, hook it up to the phone. If you don't, I'll get one over to you," Stone told her.

"We have one, thanks Sergeant. We'll be all right."

At 6:06 p.m., while Stone was working on the phone trap for the Rossali's, Lieutenant Burns received a call at the Task Force office. A woman had returned home from work to find that a light she had left on had been turned off by someone who had entered her residence. She found that the rear sliding glass door was unlocked.

Greg Wayne and Paul Pinnington were dropped off at the residence at 6:45 p.m. by an unmarked unit. They would remain in the house, hidden from view, throughout the night. If it was an EAR attack, they would be in position. If not, they would be picked up at 6:00 a.m. This had become a common occurrence by the Task Force investigators. So far with negative results.

9:19 p.m., 12-10-77

"Sacramento Police Department," the dispatcher answered the emergency line.

"I'm Michelle Nail and I live on Rossway. Five minutes ago I saw a man near the intersection of Sierra Oaks and American River Drive. He was wearing a ski mask and dark coat. He saw me looking at him and he jumped into an old Chev truck and drove away," the caller blurted.

"Can you describe him?"

"Like I said, he was wearing a ski mask and dark clothes. He was wearing gloves also. He was about five ten, one hundred and seventy pounds. I couldn't tell how old he was, but I know the rapist wears a ski mask and I thought I better call."

CHAPTER FORTY

"Thank you. We'll get a car in the area right away. You did the right thing. I'll have an officer contact you after they check the area."

9:50 p.m., 12-10-77

"Sheriff's Department. Can I help you?" Dale Masters, the PBX operator answered the phone.

"I am going to hit tonight. Watt Avenue," the male voice whispered and the phone went dead.

9:52 p.m., 12-10-77

"Sacramento Police Department. Can I help you?" the dispatcher answered the phone.

"I am going to hit tonight. Watt Avenue," the male voice whispered and the phone went dead.

Stone was paged by the Sheriff's Dispatch at 9:58 p.m. He returned the call at 10:04 p.m. and learned of the calls. He was also told that PBX operator Masters confirmed that the voice appeared to be the same as the caller on 12-2-77. The call was recorded on the console and on the master tape system.

The Sacramento P.D. trap units were advised of the call to their dispatch center at 10:10 p.m. Sergeant Duff, the detail supervisor, deployed four units south of the American River, three units north of the river, and one unit in the Bluff area. At 10:15 p.m., Duff contacted Stone and advised him of the call and deployment.

The Sacramento P.D. recording was taken to the Sheriff's PBX operator Masters at 10:20 p.m. Masters confirmed that it was the same voice as the two calls he had received. Patrol units with the Sacramento P.D. and S.O. were briefed. Swing shift units were held over on overtime to work with the graveyard units.

Although numerous traffic stops were made and field interrogations cards made out on hundreds of motorists and pedestrians, nothing materialized.

12-11-77

Letters, all on legal size onion skin paper and titled "Excitement's Crave" were received by the editor of the *Sacramento Bee*, the Sacramento mayor's office, and KVIE 6 television station. The letters were written poem form:

EXCITEMENT'S CRAVE

All those mortal's surviving birth
Upon facing maturity,
Take inventory of their worth
To prevailing society.
Choosing values becomes a task;
Oneself must seek satisfaction.
The selected route will unmask
Character when plans take action.
Accepting some work to perform
At fixed pay, but promise for more,
Is a recognized social norm,
As is decorum, seeking lore.
Achieving while others lifting
Should be cause for deserving fame.
Leisure tempts excitement seeking,
What's right and expected seems tame.
"Jessie James" has been seen by all,
And "Son of Sam" has an author.
Others now feel temptations call.
Sacramento should make an offer.
To make a movie of my life
That will pay for my planned exile.
Just now I'd like to add the wife
Of a Mafia lord to my file.
Your East Area Rapist
And deserving pest.
See you in the press or on T.V.

The letters were turned over to the EAR Task Force on 12-13-77.
The letters and envelopes were processed for prints and one latent palm
print was developed from the front side of the envelope addressed to the
Sacramento Bee.

Was the letter a legitimate message from EAR? Was there a hidden
meaning in the letter? The part where he mentioned "Mafia"? Was he
referring to the Rossalis? If nothing else, the legitimacy would hang on
this line. Nobody except the Rossalis, the investigators, and EAR knew
that the father-in-law was visiting from Italy.

Did EAR want to be caught for the publicity? Did he really think
he was in the same class as Jesse James or the Son of Sam? Stone and

the Task Force spent many hours thinking, talking, analyzing. Another piece of evidence to be stored away. Maybe someday...

Task Force and trap units from both agencies remained on alert working extra hours. Social lives suffered and with the Christmas season approaching, nerves wore thin. Many hours were spent updating search warrants to be served on various suspects that were not eliminated through regular procedures.

Every report was scrutinized and salient points recorded: statements made by EAR, victim profiles, suspect profile, tool marks, fingerprints, psychic profile, semen, blood, trace evidence, stolen property, stolen vehicles, area profiles, criminal acts, method of entry, weather, days of the week the attacks occurred, times and duration of attacks, shoe patterns, weapons.

At best, it was determined that EAR was a white male. Twenty to thirty years old, five foot eight to five foot ten, approximately one hundred and sixty pounds, dark brown hair, light complexion with an inclination toward sunbathing due to his legs being darker in summer months. His shoes, size nine, and masks seemed to be different for each attack. It also appeared that he had access to several vehicles.

After all this, the only consensus of opinion among investigators was that EAR's boldness or dedication to his attacks could be his undoing. On occasion he had caused havoc with the neighbors and victims' dogs and in spite of the obvious noise, he persisted in his efforts to affect entry into the victims' homes. So far, adjacent neighbors who were awakened simply returned to bed after looking out their windows.

"Well, Jim, any ideas? All the phone calls all of a sudden? Is he going to hit again or is he going to sit home and write a movie script of his escapades? That poem, if it was him, proves he's an egotistical asshole," Wayne asked Stone.

"I don't know, Greg. I think he wrote the poem and I think he made the calls. No one knew about Frank Rossali's father being here from Italy. And the phone call to Joan just two days before the poem arrived? It couldn't be a coincidence. Could it? Shit, I don't know any more. Something has got to happen with all this activity, and remember last year he hit December 18th. He said he was going to hit New Year's Eve this year and back in March he called three times and then he hit," Stone remarked.

"Look, I've got a feeling about all this. Throughout we know he has been making phone calls before his attacks and then the one to Rossali. I think he kept the phone numbers of the victims and I think he's going to make more calls. Let's get Merton and Bonnell and contact all the victims who still have the same phone numbers they had when they were attacked. We need to warn them about the calls and have them record their calls in case he does call," Stone sat back in his chair.

"Going to bring back memories that some of them are trying to forget, Jim. Been a year and a half for some. Maybe they would rather forget EAR and us," Wayne mused.

"I know, Greg, but it might be our chance to nail him and if we don't warn them, we may be doing them a disservice," Stone answered.

"Okay. I'll get the boys. How do you want me to handle it?" Wayne looked at Stone.

"I'll take the first ten victims. You three divide up the rest and let's see where it takes us," Stone shrugged his shoulders.

Twenty-eight victims and their families lived with a renewed fear over the holidays. Investigators, patrol deputies, and officers lived every day in apprehension.

1977 came to an end without the anticipated and promised attack by EAR.

CHAPTER FORTY-ONE

ON JUNE 18, 1976 Carey Frank of Rancho Cordova became known as victim number one. Although never forgotten by Sergeant Stone, her attack melded into only one of several EAR attacks. Eighteen months later Carey Frank was learning to live with the horrible past, as were some of the other victims. The phone call from Stone brought back the fears as memories once again surfaced, their focus as sharp as the attack itself.

1-2-78

Carey Frank faced the day as she arose. Funny, before she received the call from Stone things had almost returned to normal. Now as she reached for her hair dryer, the shudders returned as she remembered her attacker tying her up with the electric cord from the dryer. All the memories of that horrible night were back in vivid, terrifying color.

Carey Frank spent the day, first at the mall, exchanging gifts as we all do after Christmas. The "Clapper" we got from Aunt Millie, the hideous tie from Uncle Mel. The Chia Pet? Hell, it'll die within a week anyway. Keep it and throw it away later. The rest of the day she spent with a friend from work.

That evening as she absently sat in front of the television, the phone beside her rang. She automatically pushed the record button on her tape recorder and picked up the phone as she had been doing for the past two weeks.

"Hello?" she answered.

"Is Ray there?" the male voice asked.

"Pardon?"

"Is Ray there?"

"I'm sorry, you must have the wrong number."

"Sorry," The caller hung up and Carey clicked off the recorder.

Fifteen minutes later the phone rang again.

"Hello?" she answered as she turned on the recorder.

"Hi, Carey," a friend, and she turned off the recorder to continue the conversation.

The scenario repeated itself several times into the early evening.

"Hello?" Once more Carey went through the ritual. Silence.

"Hello?" she repeated as the silence stretched, and then the deep breathing began. Eight times she heard the exhale. Her heart pounded and she resisted the powerful urge to slam the receiver down. "Keep him on the line," she remembered Stone telling her should she receive a call.

"Gonna kill you....Gonna kill-l-l you...Gonna kill-l-l-l-l-l you," the male voice whispered. "Bitch...Bitch...Bitch...Bitch...Bitch," the whisper continued as the caller emphasized the "tch." "Fuckin' whore." Dead silence and then, click, click, click of the phone button and then the phone went dead.

Carey Frank dropped the phone onto the floor and recoiled from it as if it were a viper about ready to strike. Her father entered the room as her sobs began, at first shallow breaths and then heart wrenching cries from deep within her stomach.

"Carey? What's the matter?" her father asked as he took her into his arms.

"Dad. It was him. It was the rapist. Just like Sergeant Stone warned me. Oh, Dad, he said he was going to kill me," she managed to tell him through sobs.

He held her tight to his chest. "It's all right, honey. It's all right. I'm here and I won't ever let anything happen to you again. I'll call the Sheriff's Department," he picked up the phone and cradled it, also turning off the tape recorder that was still running.

Stone picked up the phone and turned down the music on the stereo. George Jones's "He Stopped Loving Her Tonight."

"Hello?" he answered.

"Sorry to bother you, Sarge. This is dispatch. A Carey Frank called and said she needs to talk to you right away. Said EAR called her," the female dispatcher said.

"Damn. Did she leave a number?" Stone asked.

"Yeah. Got a pen?"

"Go ahead," Stone copied down the number. "Look, I need you to get a deputy over there right away and have him wait there until I get there. Damn. I hope she taped the call."

"She said she did," the dispatcher replied.

"Do me a big favor and keep this under your hat. Tell the rest of the crew also. I don't want this getting out yet, especially to the press, until the boss hears about it," Stone advised.

"You got it, Sarge."

On 1-3-78, Peg Vickers picked up a copy of the Carey Frank call. At 9:30 a.m. she met with Joan Rossali at the Rossali residence. Frank Rossali was at work, due to return home at 6:30 p.m.

"Joan," Vickers began, "I want you to listen to a tape of a phone call made to another victim of EAR. I need you to listen real close and tell me if it sounds like the person who attacked you."

After listening to the tape, Joan Rossali tentatively identified the voice as the same as the person who called her.

"Sergeant Stone will come by tonight to have Frank listen to the tape. I need you to tell him that we have a tape, but don't tell him what's on it. We need him to listen with an open mind," Vickers advised.

"Okay. Tell Sergeant Stone that 8:00 p.m. will be fine."

At 10:30 a.m., Stone met with Sergeant Michaels and Jennifer Sanford, the victim in the Stockton rape. Jennifer listened to the tape several times and concluded that the voice on the tape was that of the East Area Rapist. She had also received a call prior to being contacted by the Task Force in December. Although the call was not recorded, she felt it was the same caller.

Stone arrived at the Rossali residence and was met by Frank Rossali at 8:15 p.m.

"Come on in, Sergeant," Rossali greeted him.

"Hi, Frank. Sorry to bother you like this, but we need you to listen to this tape for us."

"Joan told me that another victim had received a call. Why don't you come into the study where it's quiet," Rossali led Stone down the hall and into the room.

"Go ahead and set it up. I'll close the door and turn off the lights so it will be similar to that night," Rossali advised.

After listening to the tape recording one time, Frank Rossali turned on the lights.

"There's no doubt in my mind. That is the voice of EAR. When he said 'I'm going to kill you,' there was no doubt in my mind. It's difficult, Sergeant, to make others understand, you know, those that have never heard him themselves, what fear he puts in you. He speaks with a young sounding voice. I really don't think he's older than twenty-five or six."

"Can I come in?" Joan stuck her head in the room.

"Sure, come on in, hon," Frank responded.

"Sergeant, can I listen to the tape one more time?" Joan asked.

After listening to the tape Joan stated, "I know it's him. The inflection on 'kill' was the same as the night of the attack. He said it over and over. Also the clicking of the phone button at the end of the tape is exactly what he did when he called me on December 9th."

"Oh, by the way, Sergeant, I almost forgot. Joan found a gold St. Christopher's medal in her jewelry box just after Christmas. She thought it must have been mine, so she gave it to our son. When I came home I saw it and asked him where he got it. I had never seen it before and nobody has been in the jewelry box but us. We think EAR must have left it there. We just never checked it. Here it is, you better take it," Frank handed the medal to Stone.

"I never really went through my jewelry box since he took some of our jewelry in May. He must have placed it there," Joan added.

"In addition to all else, a packrat," Stone shrugged. "You two going to be all right?"

"We're fine, but thanks anyway. Good luck with this," Frank showed Stone to the door.

"Just so you know, we have an undercover officer in the area. He'll be around until we get a handle on this," Stone advised as he left.

10:50 a.m., 1-5-78

Stone and Vickers met with Julie Lowe. Lowe had also received a phone call in December. After listening to the Carey Frank tape several times, Julie stated that the voice sounded similar to that of the person who had called her. She said she could not be positive, however, that the voice on the tape was that of EAR.

At 6:30 p.m., Stone met with Denise Kent, the mother of EAR's twenty-seventh victim. EAR had called Denise "bitch" several times during the ordeal. She was asked to pay particular attention to "bitch" in the Carey Frank tape. Denise Kent stated that she could not identify the voice as the East Area Rapist. She stated that the night of the attack, EAR spoke in a high pitched voice and spoke much more rapidly.

8:25 p.m., 1-6-78

Edna Watson, a volunteer for the Contact Counseling Service, picked up the ringing telephone.

"Can you help me?" the male caller asked.

"What's the problem?" Watson asked.

"I have a problem. I need help because I don't want to do this anymore."

"Do what?"

"Well, I guess I can tell you guys," the caller stated. "You're not tracing this call are you?" he asked in a violent, angry voice.

"No, we are not tracing any calls," Watson remained calm.

"I am the East Side Rapist and I feel the urge coming on to do this again. I don't want to do it, but then I do. Is there anyone there that can help me? I don't want to hurt these women or their husbands anymore," the young voice pleaded. "Are you tracing this call?" the voice again becoming violent.

"We are not tracing this call. Do you want a counselor?"

"No. I have been to counseling all my life. I was in Stockton State Hospital. I shouldn't tell you that. I guess I can trust you guys," he continued. "Are you tracing this call?" Again the violence.

"No, we are not tracing the call."

"I believe you are tracing this call," the male angrily shouted and the phone went dead.

"Ralph," Watson called her director, "I just got a call from a male who said he was the rapist."

Ralph Manning, the director of the service, listened to Watson explain the call.

"Contact the Sacramento Sheriff's Office right away," he instructed Watson.

At 9:05 p.m. Stone learned of the call and immediately contacted the Stockton State Hospital. Although the hospital is State and County supported, most patients are from San Joaquin County. The Psychiatric Care Unit is divided into two major units, one for geriatrics, the second, known as T-2, for the general population. The average stay for a patient is around three weeks, however there are those who remain for two or three months. The patient discharge rate is five to fifteen a week, and the mental stability of the discharged patient is normally of the level that they would function, for the most part, normally in society. The age range in T-2 is from sixteen to sixty-three.

Without a name or date of admittance or discharge, staff could not be of assistance.

"Well, Jim," Burns handed Stone a cup of coffee. The cup had a picture of a fisherman casting a line, the hook caught in the seat of his pants, and a caption that read "Old fishermen never die; they just smell like it." "EAR hasn't hit in a month. Think he's gone?"

"No, he's been too busy making phone calls. It has to be him because no one else has the phone number of the victims and most of them agree it is the same voice," Stone remarked as he rotated the cup in his hand to read the inscription. "Kids give you this for Christmas?"

"Yeah, they got quite a kick out of it," Burns laughed. "Well, he hasn't gone this long since summer. Maybe he found God and quit."

"I wish God would find him and shove a cherry bomb up his ass. He'll be back, Mike. I just have the feeling. I think he's just fuckin' with us right now," Stone took a drink of coffee and leaned back in his chair.

"Then tell me where he's going to hit if you've been blessed."

"Just a feeling, Mike."

"Feeling, shit. You don't want him to quit or leave. You want him to stay so you can catch him and you know it," Burns put his hand on Stone's shoulder and walked toward his office. "The big picture, Jim. Told you not to get personally involved. Just wish him into another county."

"He needs to be caught. He's hurt too many of our citizens," Stone slowly shook his head.

1-14-78, Carmichael

Grace Shapiro, with a basketful of dirty clothes, opened the door leading into the garage. As she stepped through the doorway she saw a figure run from the garage. It startled her so much she did not get a good look of the subject. In checking, her husband Howard discovered tools missing from a tool box.

During the next two weeks, Dana Shapiro, age fifteen, and her sister, Elaine, fourteen, received four unusual phone calls from a man with a "funny" voice. Each time the caller asked if the mother was there.

Tuesday, 1-17-78, Burns called Stone into his office.

"Jim," Burns began, "Newport Beach arrested a rapist Sunday morning just after he raped a thirty year old Corona del Mar woman. They found jewelry when they served a search warrant and some of it is similar to stuff taken in some of ours. Anyway, I want you and Peg to fly down and talk to their subject. He's from Provo, Utah, so we are in his flight path and he's in the ball park as for age. Thirty."

"Okay, Mike. I'll get with Peg," Stone advised.

1-20-78

At 5:20 a.m. Denise Kent, the mother of Deborah Kent, the thirteen year old victim from the November 10th attack, reached for the ringing telephone beside her bed.

CHAPTER FORTY-ONE

"Hello," she said, her eyes still closed and not yet fully awake.

"I have not struck in awhile. You will be my next victim. I'm going to fuck you in the butt. See you soon," The phone went dead. Denise Kent came fully awake.

Sandra Terranian, EAR's eighteenth victim, reached for her alarm to shut off the morning buzz. She looked at the alarm clock, not believing it could be 5:30 a.m. already when the ringing of the phone startled her. Already half out of bed, she reached for the phone.

"Hello," she answered. She heard the oh-ahhh sounds and immediately handed the phone to her husband, Leonard, who did not speak. He did listen.

"I have not struck in awhile. You will be my next victim. I'm going to fuck you in the butt. See you soon," The phone went dead.

On 1-21-78 at 4:45 p.m., Stone met with Sandra and Leonard Terranian. They listened intently to the taped call made to Carey Frank. Leonard stated that it was not the voice of the East Area Rapist and also was not the voice of the caller the previous day.

Sacramento Union, 1-21-78

Newport Beach suspect isn't Sacramento rapist.

NEWPORT BEACH (AP) - A 30 year old Utah man charged with rape, child molestation, and two connected burglaries in which antiques were stolen, lost a bid Friday to have his $30,000 bail reduced but a judge also refused to increase it.

Two Sacramento County sheriff's investigators also questioned Gerry Branagan, 30, of Provo, Utah, earlier in the week about 28 rapes in Sacramento's east side. But Sacramento County sheriff's spokesman said that while methods used in the Newport Beach and Sacramento rapes are similar, "There is nothing to connect him with Sacramento."

CHAPTER FORTY-TWO

THE FOG SLIPPED into the Sacramento Valley each day around 5:30 p.m. and each morning the California sun did its magic and the fog disappeared, not dissimilar to the dark figure sliding in and out of the Carmichael neighborhood.

Dana Shapiro and her younger sister, Elaine, sat in the subdued light watching television in their living room. Their parents had left around 7:00 p.m. to attend a concert. Elaine, tired from a day of skiing at Boreal Ridge near Lake Tahoe's North Shore, dozed off and on. At 10:00 p.m. Dana shook her sister awake and the two went to bed, soon falling fast asleep.

A loud thumping sound brought Dana out of her deep sleep. Without turning on her light she got out of bed and peered through the curtains of her bedroom window. She saw nothing.

"Get all of your money or I'll kill you," she heard the whispered voice from the doorway. She turned and the flashlight beam blinded her seconds after she saw the dark masked figure with a gun in his right hand. Frightened, her heart pounding so hard it hurt her chest, she went to the headboard of her bed and removed her money from behind the picture of her cat playing with a ball of yarn. She saw his gloved hand reach for the money, two twenty dollar bills and a ten.

"Go wake up your sister. Don't make any noise or look at me," he ordered.

She walked past the intruder who followed her with his cold eyes from behind the frightening mask. He followed her to her sister's room.

"Elaine, wake up. Get your money," She shook her sister.

"Don't look at me. You look at me and I'll kill you. Get your money," he hissed.

Dana watched as Elaine got out of bed and walked toward the closet.

"Don't look at me," the masked intruder hissed. "Get on the bed. On your stomachs."

He tied their hands then behind their backs and placed a pillow over Dana's head.

"If you move I'll slit your throats and slip away in the fog," he hissed. "What time will your parents be home?" he demanded.

"Midnight," Dana whimpered.

"Don't lie or I'll kill you and when they get home I'll kill them, too," he hissed and placed a knife against Elaine's neck.

"Midnight," she whispered.

Dana felt the knife at the back of her neck and then he was gone.

They heard him rummaging, ransacking the house as drawers were opened and slammed shut. He returned then and they felt him climb onto the bed. His wet and sticky penis fell into Dana's bound hands as he straddled her. It moved back and forth and then he was straddling Elaine, his penis, still not erect, was in her hands. Seconds later he pulled her from the bed onto the floor.

He put a sweater over her face and then he was straddling her, pushing, pushing. Elaine groaned from the pain.

"Shut up," he hissed and left her to climb onto the bed once again. Dana felt her underpants being removed and then she was rolled onto her back and the pillow once again was placed over her head.

"Spread your legs," he hissed. "Relax," he ordered when he couldn't enter her. He was off of her then and climbed off the bed.

"Don't talk to each other or I'll kill you," he ordered and left the room. They heard him whimpering in a high pitched voice like that of a child.

"Where's your parents' money?" he cried.

"On my parents' dresser," Dana replied and he again left the room.

"It's not there," he whimpered when he returned. "I don't want to do this anymore. She's making me do it," He seemed angry as he left the room.

At 11:53 p.m. the call went out from the dispatcher. "261PC just occurred, Carmichael."

At fifteen minutes after midnight Stone and Vickers, who had been working the North Highland's area, arrived to take over the scene from the responding deputies.

Fifteen minutes after EAR's departure, Howard and Grace Shapiro, the parents of the two teenagers, had arrived home. After cutting the shoelaces from the hands and ankles of the girls, Howard called the Sheriff's Dispatch.

Although both victims had no experience with male organs, they described EAR as "small" and "not fully erect" during the attacks. EAR was described as five foot nine, one fifty.

Both girls were immediately transported to the Sacramento Medical Center.

Two small photographs of Elaine were missing and two dimes with small holes drilled at the top for earrings were missing from Dana's jewelry box. That and the money taken from the girls were the only things missing.

Sacramento Bee, 1-30-78

East Rapist
Assaults
Teen Sisters

The ski masked man who smashed through the front door of a home near American River College and raped two teenaged sisters was the East Area Rapist, Sacramento County Sheriff's deputies have concluded...

The rapist, who now has victimized 29 women and girls in Sacramento county and one in Stockton in the past 20 months, had never forced his way through a front door until the attack on the two sisters late Saturday night...

When the victims' parents returned about 11:30 p.m., the rapist was gone, but the girls were still tied in their room.

The rapist may have been scared away by the return of the parents. If the attacker left earlier on his own, it was the shortest period he stayed in a home he terrorized...

Detectives theorize the rapist knew the girls were home alone. Otherwise they doubt he would have brazenly—and noisily—kicked in the front door.

Sacramento Union, 2-5-78

Rapist Warned in Rhyme

Jack Young has a personal message for the East Area Rapist.

And it's pure poetry.

Young said he is "fed up with the rapes and murders going on in Sacramento so I decided to take out an ad in the newspaper."

Young sat in his truck and wrote a poem to the rapist, then came to the Sacramento Union to place an advertisement in the "personals" section of today's paper.

"It didn't take me no time to make it up," Young said. "I did it in about five minutes."

The poem runs:

East Side Rapist you are a fool
What you are doing is against God's rule
You are sick, sleezy and lower than a mouse
I'll fix you good if you come to my house.

Young, who has a wife and four daughters, also has a Chow dog he calls "a leg-eatin' dude." Young lives in North Highlands and he hopes the poem will make the rapist think twice before hitting another home.

"I just want him to worry, 'Is this the house?' next time he tries something."

Young paid $8.73 for the ad and said he will continue to run one every week until the rapist is caught.

"He'll get what he deserves if he comes to my house," Young said.

CHAPTER FORTY-THREE

ON 3-11-78 an old faded van was seen in the Rivera Drive area. The subject, a white male, twenty to twenty-two years old, was driving very slowly and looking at the homes. That evening a babysitter heard someone in the backyard of a Rivera Drive residence. In checking, she saw nothing.

Andrew Churchill and his common-law wife, twenty-four year old Eleanor Hickey, drove from their Meadow Avenue, Stockton, residence to Old Sacramento.

Old Sac, as it's affectionately known, is a quaint area of downtown Sacramento that has been remodeled to appear as an early century small town. Its wooden sidewalks and numerous antique and souvenir stores blend well with the restaurants and business offices.

Churchill and Hickey had a late dinner at the China Camp Restaurant and then drove home, arriving around 1:00 a.m. Sunday morning.

On 3-13-78 at 11:30 p.m., a young married couple with two children observed a white male, approximately thirty years old, walking near their Meadow Avenue residence. Two nights later they heard someone in their backyard.

On 3-15-78, a ten year old girl saw a figure at her bedroom window around 10:30 p.m. Her father checked the backyard of their Rivera Drive residence. No one was seen by the father. The mother had seen a faded VW van parked across the street from their residence several times over the past two weeks around 4:00 a.m. She also saw an older green Ford in the same location on occasion.

On 3-16-78, Andrew Churchill noticed that the lock leading from the garage into the kitchen was not working properly. Although it was locked, it could be opened by turning the knob to the left. He made a note to repair it.

That evening a twenty-eight year old mother of two children answered the phone.

"I need someone to talk to while I masturbate. Would you be interested?" the male voice whispered. She hung up.

At 9:30 p.m. someone was heard in the backyard of a Meadow Avenue home of a family that included a seventeen year old daughter.

Another Meadow Lane residence heard what appeared to be a chair hit the side of her house. No one was seen.

At 10:30 p.m., a twenty-six year old housewife heard a rattling noise at the side of their house.

At 11:30 p.m., a Meadow Avenue resident, arriving home, saw a white male, eighteen to twenty-five years old, get out of a small vehicle and take something out of the trunk. The subject was wearing a light colored nylon jacket. At 12:30 a.m. her seventeen year old daughter saw a flashlight beam shine into her bedroom window. Her father checked and found no one.

Sometime after midnight a twenty-four year old housewife woke her husband. Someone was at their sliding glass window. No one was seen.

No reports were made of these incidents.

"I won't hurt you, just be quiet. All I want is your money and food so I can live a little longer," the masked intruder whispered as he shone his light into the eyes of Andrew Churchill and Eleanor Hickey. "I won't hurt you, just be quiet," he repeated as he waved the gun in his right hand. "This is a .357 Magnum you see and I'll blow your head off."

The young couple stared at the hideous figure in the mask.

"Get on your stomachs. Turn your head," he hissed and placed the barrel of the gun against Churchill's head and cocked the weapon. "Put your hands behind your back and cross them. You. You, get up and don't look at me," he ordered Hickey. "Don't turn around. Tie him up," A brown shoelace landed on the bed near Hickey. "One move, one flinch, and I'll blow your fuckin' head off. Tighter. Tighter," he ordered her. A second shoelace was thrust in front of her face. "Tie him again. Tighter and go around again," he hissed.

"On your stomach," he ordered Hickey. "Don't you move. Don't flinch or I'll blow your head off," he pushed the barrel of the gun between her shoulder blades. "Put your hands behind your back and cross them," He tied her hands then. Tight.

He pulled the blankets off Churchill's legs. "Cross them," he ordered. "One hand under the pillow, one hand under the mattress and you're dead," he hissed as he tied Churchill's ankles.

"Where's your money?" he demanded.

"My purse is on the kitchen counter," Hickey answered.

"My wallet is on the coffee table in the living room," Churchill advised.

"One squeak of the bed and your dead," he hissed. They heard him tearing a towel in strips and then he was back.

"It isn't there, where's your wallet?" he demanded as he placed the gun to Churchill's neck.

"Maybe it's in the kitchen," Churchill replied.

"Oh, man," the masked intruder whispered as he left the room.

"Put your head up," he ordered Churchill when he returned and tied a strip of towel around his face.

"Don't cover my mouth," Churchill begged.

"Shut up."

"I have allergies and I'll die," Churchill continued.

"Get up and get away from him," the intruder ordered as he placed the gun in Hickey's back. "Don't look at me or I'll blow your head off. Walk and be quiet," He pushed her out of the bedroom, down the hall, and into the living room. "On your stomach. Turn your head and don't look at me or I'll kill you. Cross your feet," he ordered and tied her ankles loosely. "Pull your head up," he demanded and tied a blindfold around her face. "Don't make a sound or I'll kill you."

He was gone then, into the kitchen and then back to the bedroom. "If I hear these move, I'm going to kill your girlfriend," he hissed as he placed a dish and bowl on Churchill's back, placed the gun barrel to his head, and cocked the weapon.

He was back in the living room, straddling the sobbing Hickey.

"Do you like to fuck?" he whispered as he placed his penis in her numb hands.

Sacramento Union, 3-19-78

East area rapist hits Stockton

STOCKTON - Seven weeks after his thirtieth known attack, the east area rapist early Saturday entered a north Stockton home, tied a man and raped a woman.

Police said the rapist entered a home in the Park Woods area through an unlocked door leading from the garage to the home's interior at 1:00 a.m.

His victim, a woman in her 20's, lives with a man, and the couple was in bed when the rapist tied the man and raped the woman...

"We are sure it was the east area rapist," police said. "It was exactly the same M.O. [method of operation] he has used in all the others."

The rapist stayed in the house an hour and ten minutes...

His only other attack in Stockton was September 6 of last year when he woke a 24 year old woman and her husband in their bedroom, tied up the man and took the woman to another room where he raped her twice.

In 29 months of depredation since October 1975, the rapist has struck 31 times.

Officers say he has gained entry most often through unlocked doors, or easily unlocked patio glass doors.

The rapist has struck 12 times on Saturday mornings, including the last two attacks.

Monday morning, Burns called Stone into his office.

"Any more on the Stockton rape, Jim?"

"It was him, Mike. Not a doubt in the world. He pulled his sobbing act again and did the stupid fuckin' nylon stocking trick again. Tied one leg and poked a hole in the crotch area. He's getting weirder, if that's possible. Went the whole gamut with her and used sun tan lotion for a lubricant and tore up a towel for blindfolds.

"One time when she was crying he told her to shut up and said 'this is how me fuck.' After he was through with the victim, he placed a bowl and plate on her back and said 'one click, one small noise, and he's dead.' She said he was about three inches long erect," Stone shrugged.

"How was their canvass? Anything come up?" Burns asked.

"Same as all the rest. Lots of prowling, strange cars, strange males seen in the area. No two exactly alike, so we are sure he's using disguises. Of course, no one reported anything. One woman said she heard someone running around 3:30 in the morning. She looked out but didn't see anyone. Said she heard a car drive off. Loud mufflers, maybe a VW," Stone explained.

"Anything taken?"

"Took her driver's license, thirteen dollars in cash from her wallet, hundred and fifty dollars in quarters, dimes, and nickels in two jars, earrings, rings, watch, and a high school picture of the victim," Stone explained. "Oh, she also said when he was raping her she felt a shoulder holster hit her knee. Apparently drank two bottles of beer before he left."

"He didn't, by any chance, tell them he was going to stay in Stockton, did he?" Burns smiled.

"Nope."

"Get to work, buddy," Burns ended the conversation.

CHAPTER FORTY-FOUR

Sacramento Bee, 3-29-78

East Area Rapist Attacks His 32nd Victim

The East Area Rapist assaulted his 32nd victim today when he broke into a Rancho Cordova home and raped a 30 year old woman while her two children slept nearby, sheriff's deputies reported.

Experts on the case were at first hesitant to attribute the 3:20 a.m. assault to the rapist, but later evidence convinced them the assault could be added to his growing list of crimes...

He stayed in the house approximately 30 minutes, returning twice to check on his victim. Two children sleeping in another bedroom were not disturbed during the attack. The woman was divorced.

The woman later freed herself and called the authorities.

"Jim, the paper says we called the rape this morning an EAR attack. I thought you said no way. Change your mind since you talked to me on the phone?" Burns asked as he scowled at Stone.

"It wasn't a fuckin' EAR attack, Mike. He tied her up and raped her. Other than that, nothing else matches. I didn't smell the son-of-a-bitch, I didn't feel the son-of-a-bitch. He wasn't in the house and he didn't rape her. EAR has people so paranoid, they'll blame anything on him," Stone angrily retorted.

"Who talked to the press? Any of our people?" Burns asked.

"Peg and I were the only ones there from the Task Force and we sure didn't. I took some notes, but patrol wrote it. Sex Crimes unit was called and we left before anyone got there," Stone replied.

"You're the expert, so you better be right," Burns shrugged. "Anyway, I hope the bastard stayed in Stockton."

8:15 p.m., 3-30-78, Riverside Convalescent Hospital, Sacramento

"Hi," the young male spoke to Pauline Ness, the LVN on duty at the hospital.

"You shouldn't be in here," Ness responded. "Our doors are supposed to be locked."

"I need to talk to someone. I've got a sexual problem," the male looked at her.

"This isn't the place you need to be. There are places that specialize in certain problems," Ness responded.

"My name is Jack and I'm from Quincy. No one there can help me. I've been in for psychiatric treatment before. My father has a girlfriend but I don't."

"Look, Jack, I'm sorry but you're going to have to leave or I'm going to have to call Security. I can get in trouble for letting you in here," Ness pleaded.

"I like music. I'm a singer," the man started singing the Johnny Cash song, "I'll Walk the Line."

A delivery man entered the hospital and the young male left, singing.

CHAPTER FORTY-FIVE

VERNA HANCOCK and her fourteen year old daughter, Bernadette, were watching television together in the living room of their Casilada Way home. The two younger daughters were sleeping.

"What was that?" Bernadette asked as she looked toward the backdoor.

"Someone's out there," her mother responded. "Someone's on the patio."

Verna Hancock held her daughter's arm, too nervous to check. Her husband was not home. She did not check the backyard.

On 4-13-78, a neighbor of the Hancock's on Rio Lane heard someone at their side window at 11:00 p.m. It appeared to be a scratching noise that stopped when their dog began to bark. No one checked.

Another neighbor on Rio Lane noticed that her side gate was open several times over the past two weeks. Even with this, no call was made to the police department.

4-14-78

"Hi, Jean, this is Verna Hancock," she said when fifteen year old Jean Allen answered the phone. "I was wondering if you could look after Dawn for us tonight as Charlie and I would like to go out to dinner. The other girls are staying with friends."

"Sure, I'd be glad to," Jean replied. "What time would you like me to come over?"

"Around nine would be fine."

"Okay. Thanks Mrs. Hancock," Jean hung up.

At 9:00 p.m. Jean Allen arrived at the Hancock residence. Eight year old Dawn was home alone as her sisters had left just prior.

At 9:30 p.m. a young housewife on Casilada Way heard her dog barking in her backyard. Her husband was not home and she did not investigate. Shortly after, Verna Hancock's neighbor's German shepherd began barking, indicating that someone or something was in the backyard. The dog stopped barking. No one checked the backyard.

At 9:30 p.m. Jean told Dawn it was time for bed. The child did not argue and after covering her and turning out the light, Jean returned to the living room and started watching a movie special on Sacramento's Channel Three: "The Two Five."

Shortly after Jean left the room, Dawn saw two flashes of light on her bedroom wall. Ten minutes later she heard two "bangs" at the backdoor and then a man's voice, much higher than her father's. She remained quiet in the darkness of her bedroom.

The pretty fifteen year old turned toward the loud noise as a second "bang" followed and the door crashed open. She stood, fear so intense she could neither move nor scream as she faced the masked intruder running toward her. She saw the gun in his gloved hand, his blue plaid flannel shirt and dark blue windbreaker. His face was covered, her fear blocked out the type of mask.

"Don't move or I'll kill you. Don't talk or say anything," he hissed. "Lie on the floor on your stomach and put your hands behind your back."

The room darkened as he threw a baby blanket that had been on her lap over her head.

"There's a little girl in the other room sleeping and the dog's barking. Can I get him?" she asked, afraid that Dawn would wake and come out to see what was happening.

"No," he hissed as he grabbed her arms and tied her wrists. "Don't move or I'll stab you with my ice pick."

"What are you doing? What do you want? Are you going to hurt me?" she cried.

"I'm not going to hurt you. I'm just going to take money and I'll leave. Just don't talk or move," he ordered.

She could hear him opening drawers and cabinets in the kitchen and then she felt herself being lifted to her feet. The blanket was tied around her face as a blindfold as she was led to another room.

"Lay on your stomach," he ordered and then she felt her feet being tied, not as tight as her wrists. She heard him moving around the house, sounds of change hitting together as he went through her purse.

"Don't move. Be quiet," he hissed and she felt the gun barrel pressed against her head and then she felt herself being turned over onto her back. She felt her ankles being untied and her pants being unzipped.

"What are you doing?" she cried.

"Be quiet or I'll kill you," he threatened as he pulled her jeans and underpants down over her feet.

"Keep quiet," he demanded as he lifted her blouse. Her legs were being spread. "Relax or I'll kill you. I've wanted to rape you for a long time, Jean," he whispered. He attempted to enter her as the phone began to ring: eight, nine, ten times, and then, silence.

He left her for a short time, then returned. She felt him rubbing lotion on her and again he attempted to assault her. "Relax, don't scream or yell or I'll kill you," he hissed as he removed her socks. Again the phone began to ring and she felt herself being lifted to her feet and prodded toward the phone.

"Say hello," he ordered as he placed the phone to her mouth.

"Hello," she mumbled and he hung up the phone.

"Touch it," he demanded as he placed his penis into her hands. Again the phone began to ring. He walked her outside onto the patio and again he attempted to assault her.

She heard a car pull into the driveway and then she heard her father's voice.

"Who's there?" her father demanded.

"Dad!" she cried.

Her father was there, the suspect gone.

At 10:30 p.m., officers received the call. Upon arrival they determined that it was an EAR attack and the Task Force was called. Helicopter Seven was requested as was K-9 One in an unsuccessful attempt to locate the attacker.

At 10:15 p.m., Maria Vargas, who was fishing with her husband and nephew at the "Minnow Hole" on the Sacramento River, returned to her car. As she walked up the levee, she was startled by a white male, approximately twenty-five years old, five foot eight, medium build, mustache and brown hair, who was running along the levee.

"Did you catch any fish?" the male asked.

"No, I didn't get any," Maria answered.

"Oh, my wife is going to be mad," the man said as he ran off toward the apartments on Riverside Boulevard. The Minnow Hole is about a half mile from the Casilada scene and about one half mile to the Riverside Boulevard on-ramp to Interstate 5. The man did not appear to be a jogger as he was out of breath and was not dressed as a jogger.

At twenty minutes past midnight, Stone and Vickers arrived on scene. Jean Allen was immediately transported to the Sacramento Medical Center by Vickers for a rape examination. Because of Jean Allen's virginity, penetration had not been successful and no sperm was noted. Although, due to her innocence, she knew of no comparison, she did describe her attacker as being small endowed and not completely erect.

Sacramento Union, 4-16-78

Rapist attacks 15 year old girl

A 15 year old girl was raped Friday night while babysitting in a southwest Sacramento home, with her 8 year old charge asleep a few feet away.

In what officers believe was the 33rd attack of the east area rapist, the attacker kicked open a rear door to a room where the babysitter was watching television in a home near Seamas Avenue and Riverside Boulevard.

A sheriff's spokesman for the joint city police/sheriff's east area rapist task force, said the girl told them her attacker had something over his face and she thought he had a gun.

The man tied the girl's hands and raped her inside the house.

The mother of the 8 year old called the house to see that everything was all right and receiving no answer, called the babysitter's parents.

Her parents then called several times. Finally the phone was picked up and they heard their daughter's voice say "hello" strangely and then the phone was hung up.

The girl told officers her assailant picked up the phone, held it in front of her face and told her to say" hello," then re-cradeled the phone.

The girl's parents got in their car and sped to the residence.

By this time the rapist had taken the bound and partially clad, badly frightened girl into the backyard. Her parents drove into the driveway and the rapist fled over a fence.

Officers swarmed into the area immediately, stopping cars and pedestrians without success...

It was the second time the rapist has struck in south Sacramento. Most of his attacks have been in the Rancho Cordova, Orangevale, and other suburban residential areas east of downtown Sacramento. The rapist has struck twice in Stockton.

His last attack was April 6 in Rancho Cordova.

"Anything on the neighborhood canvass of the Sacramento attack, Jim?" Burns asked.

"A couple of things. One looks real good. A neighbor saw an older Cadillac pull into the driveway where the attack happened. Said it was about nine fifteen. When the neighbor drove by, the Cad left. Apparently it's been seen in the area a few times over the last month. I'll get something together for the patrol units," Stone stated.

"Let's get it out to all the Departments in the surrounding counties," Burns remarked.

"Good idea. Also Greg checked at the Convalescent Hospital. They've had a strange acting male drop in twice. The last time was on the tenth. He seems to be around twenty-five. Told them he had sexual problems the first time he was there a couple of weeks ago. The last time the nurse told him she would call someone for him to talk to. He told her he already had an appointment with a psychiatrist. Said he was polite at all times but weird."

Stone issued a crime bulletin for all agencies to stop and identify anyone driving a 1960 Cadillac, black vinyl over blue, ragged top, no body damage.

"Well, folks, we're getting close to May. Last year he hit us five times and then took a break. Got any thoughts?" Burns asked at the Monday morning task force meeting.

"If there's a pattern we sure as hell don't have it," Stone replied. "We tried everything. Months, weeks, days of the week, number of days between hits. The only pattern seems to be that he doesn't like Sundays and we're afraid to say that out loud, because the son-of-a-bitch will start hitting on Sundays. None of it makes sense. Last year he took the summer off. Maybe he's a college student. At least we know he can read, so he must have at least reached twelfth grade. I guess that's the grade they teach you to read in California now. The paper says he doesn't hit where there's a dog, his next hit is where there's a dog. The news says no man in the house, the next hit, a man is in the house. Hell, when the EARS Patrol was going strong and the news media was writing about them, he hit in the south area for the first time, two blocks from their patrol leader's office. He fuckin' knew where he was hitting.

"Last year the second week of June became a city-wide prayer week to rid us of EAR. The EARS Patrol's spiritual leader asked God for help," Stone rambled.

"Well, he took three months off. Maybe we need to pray a little harder this year," Wayne interjected.

"We need something of a miracle, that's for sure. Attitude has changed. I can feel it. People seem to be bored with EAR. Our calls have really diminished. Those college kids that tried selling t-shirts with our sketch of EAR and something about 'Get Him Before He Gets Us,' folded right away. It worked in New York when the Son of Sam was hitting, but this isn't New York. This is California where the average attention span is thirteen seconds," Stone went on.

"Well, I think he feeds on publicity and right now he's not getting it. Oh, there's a newspaper article when he hits, but it's just old rehash. Last year almost every day there were letters to the editor, editorials, all kinds of shit. I think he's going to have to do something to get the publicity back," Jim Cerezo spoke up. "and that really scares me."

"Last year over a hundred thousand hours were donated by deputies working on their own time. We're no different than the news media or the citizens. It's not news any more, so we don't see the volunteer hours. Boredom sets in, citizens realize that there are a million or more people he could hit. Chance of an individual being attacked is pretty slim, so they stop worrying. Like Jim said, this is California and our attention span is directly commensurate to the amount of sun we get. The more sun, the less attention span," Burns shrugged.

CHAPTER FORTY-SIX

THIRTY MILES SOUTH OF STOCKTON, CALIFORNIA on State Route 99, lies a small city in the middle of farm and ranch land. Modesto is a quiet city, more of a small town atmosphere, unassuming, low crime, and basically a nice place to live and work and play.

2:00 a.m., 6-5-78, Modesto, California

Tap, tap, tap. The incessant tapping brought Danielle and Howard Christie out of a sound sleep. Both looked toward the sound and saw a masked intruder standing in the doorway of their bedroom. The flashlight beam immediately hit their eyes.

"Wake up, motherfuckers. Get on your stomachs and put your hands behind your backs. I've got a .357 Magnum and if you flinch, I'll blow your fuckin' brains out," the intruder hissed.

The young couple, frightened to full consciousness, complied.

"Tie him up," he hissed and threw a shoelace near Danielle's face. "Tie him tight."

She tied her husband's wrists, trying not to cry. Fear knotted her stomach.

"Get on your stomach," he ordered and she felt her wrists being tied. He tied her feet and then he retied her husband. He placed the gun against Howard's head and cocked the weapon.

"Don't flinch. All I want is money and food to put in my van and then I'll leave," he hissed.

He was gone then. They could hear him rummaging.

"One move and there's going to be two dead people," he hissed and they knew he was still there.

"Get off the bed," he ordered and poked Danielle with a knife, the one he used to cut the shoelace from around her ankles. "If you make a move, I'm going to blow up your fuckin' kid," he hissed and once again placed the gun to Howard's head.

At 3:54 a.m., officers Ott and Fletch were dispatched to the Fuchsia Lane address to handle a residential robbery. The officers arrived at 3:56 a.m.

Sacramento Bee, 6-7-78

East Area Rapist Strikes in Modesto

MODESTO - Sacramento's East Area Rapist struck for the first time here Monday morning, raping a 27 year old married woman and taking $1,500 in cash.

Modesto and Sacramento law enforcement officers thoroughly reviewed the actions and words the attacker used before concluding it was the same man according to police.

The rapist, who now has victimized 31 women and girls in Sacramento County, two in Stockton and one in Modesto, has never taken such a large amount of money from a victim.

The woman and her husband were awakened about 3:00 a.m. by a man brandishing a knife and wearing a ski mask. The rapist was carrying a flashlight and kept it trained in the couple's eyes as he has done in previous attacks...

As the couple's child slept in another room, the rapist tied up the husband and placed dishes on his back.

The woman was taken to another room and raped and then tied up with shoelaces...

The couple told Modesto police officers that they heard what sounded like a hammer or a pistol being cocked and released...

Detectives from the Sacramento Sheriff's Department and police department say the attack was typical of previous East Area Rapist attacks and are convinced it was the same man.

The Sacramento detectives traveled to Modesto Tuesday to speak to the victims and police before concluding that the rapist had struck for the first time in Stanislaus County.

Chapter Forty-seven

3:50 a.m., 6-07-78, Davis, California

A PRESENCE IN THE ROOM awakened twenty-one year old Faye Carmichael.

"All I want is food and money or I'll kill you," the dark, nylon stocking-masked intruder whispered into her subconscious mind. She felt a sharp object pushing into her back. She knew now she wasn't dreaming; the pain wouldn't leave.

"It's my boyfriend," she thought to herself. "He's teaching me a lesson that I need to be more cautious." They had spoken just this evening about her future move to Berkeley and her upcoming job in Oakland. Both cities were much more dangerous than the quiet university town of Davis.

"Put your hands behind your back or I'll blow your brains out," he hissed.

Still it was just a joke and she put one hand behind her back. She felt the nail file pressed against her neck and her other arm pulled behind her, the pain screeching into her brain.

She yelled, "It's too tight. You're hurting me!" She felt the laces biting into her wrists and then she felt her ankles being tied. She saw the blunt end of a screw driver pointed at her left eye.

"All I want is food and money," he again hissed.

He grabbed her hair and lifted her head off the pillow, the screw driver pressed tightly against her neck.

"Don't move or you won't see any of your friends ever again," he whispered close to her ear.

She opened her mouth to scream and she felt herself being gagged as the masked attacker shoved a pair of panties into her open mouth.

He left her then and moved toward her dresser. She turned her head and saw his back. She could see he was wearing a dark t-shirt, but he had it on inside out. She could see the tag illuminated by her closet light. She could see his rough cord pants and the dark nylon stocking pulled down to the nape of his neck that was partially covered by the knit ski cap. She knew now it was no longer a joke, a silly prank. This was real and she must fight. She moved her feet and felt the ties come loose. Could she run? Should she run? Confusion kept her there.

He was back at the bed, pulling the covers off her legs. He pulled at her underpants, down and off over her feet. She kicked and felt her foot connect with his thigh. He was on her then, smashing his fist into the side of her face. He lifted her head with his right hand and she screamed. Four more times his fist smashed into her face.

"Don't move, don't scream, or you won't see any of your friends again. And I mean any of your friends," he panted.

He was off her then, rummaging. She could hear him in the kitchen and then he was back. She felt the nail file drive into her face near her left eye. Blood flowed and she again screamed. The nail file was now at her neck.

"I told you to be quiet or I'll kill you," he hissed through clenched teeth. He was on her back now, his penis in her hand. "Play with my dick," he ordered.

Her hands were numb, his penis was small and flaccid. Again he was off her and she could hear the bottle of lotion being squirted into his hands and then he was back on her, sitting on her buttocks. She was crying now, sobbing into her pillow.

"Shut up," he hissed and again she felt the nail file against her neck. He penetrated her then. She knew he was lubricated as there was no feeling of friction and then he was off her, off the bed. He never did achieve a full erection.

And then he was gone.

8:00 a.m., 6-8-78, Ear Task Force Office

"Jim, tell me about Modesto," Burns looked at Stone and raised his eyebrows.

"It's him, Mike," Stone began. "Everything's classic except why would he go to Modesto? I don't even go to Modesto. Hell, nobody goes to Modesto."

"Maybe he's leaving the area. Maybe he is going south," Burns crossed his fingers.

"I don't think so, Mike. I don't think you can go anywhere from Modesto. Isn't that the end of the earth?" Stone grinned.

"It will be for him if one of those Modesto rednecks gets hold of him. They'll shove that .357 up his ass and really give him an ejaculation. Those cowboys don't cotton to people fuckin' with their women," Burns joked back.

"Pretty close-knit community all right, but the detectives seem pretty cooperative. I don't think they're ready for anything like this, though. Of course, I don't think we are either," Stone shook his head. "But, it was EAR."

"Jim, line one is for you," Jerry Merton broke in. "Davis P.D. is on the line. They think they had an EAR attack Wednesday morning. They want to run it by you."

"Sergeant Stone," Stone picked up the line.

"This is Sergeant Brockington, Davis P.D. We had a hit Wednesday. Twenty-one year old was attacked in her apartment. I just got the report and thought of you right away."

"Apartment?" Stone asked. "Doesn't sound right, but your area sounds more right than Stockton or Modesto. Tell me what happened."

"Well, to begin with he beat the living hell out of her because she resisted. Stuck her in the face with a fingernail file several times. Cut her pretty good and broke her nose. They took her to the hospital in an ambulance," Brockington replied.

"Did he tie her up?" Stone asked.

"Shoelaces, belt from her bathrobe, and towels. Also says he put his cock in her hand and told her to play with it while she was tied behind her back. She said he never did achieve an erection and said he was small as penises go."

"Did he verbally threaten her?" Stone asked.

"Yeah, continually. Said all he wanted was food and money. Guess he lied," Brockington answered.

"Shit," Stone muttered. "Can I come over and meet with you and the victim?"

"Our town is yours and we can use your expertise," Brockington replied.

"I don't know about expertise, but I can tell you enough to scare the living shit out of you if it is him," Stone answered. "How about two this afternoon? Your office?"

"See you then," Brockington hung up.

"You look sick, Jim," Burns remarked.

"Don't know about this one, but I'll take a look," Stone answered. "Except for the apartment and the fact that she was alone, it looks like EAR."

CHAPTER FORTY-EIGHT

6-22-78, Modesto

BEN ARAGON was working as a cab driver, parked at the Modesto airport near the United Airlines terminal when a white male, approximately thirty years old, five foot eight or nine, medium build, light brown hair, approached him.

"Can you take me to the area of Sylvan and Coffee?" the man asked.

"Sure. Hop in," Aragon replied.

"Let me get my luggage."

When he returned, Aragon drove toward the destination. As he was northbound on Coffee approaching Sylvan, the subject told him to turn west on Sylvan. Almost immediately after turning, the subject stated, "This is fine. Stop here."

The subject exited the cab and walked north through a vacant field at the northeast corner of Coffee and Sylvan. Only homes under construction are near the area.

6-23-78, Modesto

"Shut the fucking dog up!" The hissed words brought Albert Montgomery out of a sound sleep. Montgomery looked toward the voice and could see the male with the dark knit ski mask pointing a gun at him. A flashlight beam searched out Montgomery's eyes, blinding him to the terror in his bedroom.

"Shut the fucking dog up!" the man repeated. "One flinch and I'll blow your fucking head off."

Montgomery reached across his still sleeping wife and picked up the three month old cocker spaniel that was growling and barking at the strange intruder.

"What's the matter?" Wilberta Montgomery asked, coming partway awake.

"Shut up. Roll over," he hissed.

Both husband and wife complied.

"Tie his hands behind his back," the intruder hissed through clenched teeth. "Don't flinch and don't try anything," The shoelaces fell in front of Wilberta's face.

"Tighter. Tighter," he demanded as she tied her husband's wrists. "Lay back on your stomach."

He was at the closet. They could hear him pulling laces from Albert's tennis shoes and then he was back at the bed, pulling the covers from Albert's feet.

"Lie still or you'll get your fuckin' heads blown off," he hissed. "All I want is food and money for my van," Albert felt his ankles being tied.

"If you try and kick me, I'll blow your fucking brains out," he hissed. "If you're going to make your move you better make it good because I'm going to blow your fucking brains out," Then he tied Wilberta's hands and feet.

Albert felt the gun at his head. "If you try anything, I'll kill your fuckin' wife and it will be your fault," the intruder threatened.

He was gone then, rummaging throughout the house.

They heard running footsteps coming down the hall. "Get away from him. You're trying to get him free," he ordered and pulled Wilberta from the bed after untying her feet.

"If you flinch, I'll kill your wife," he threatened. "And if you try anything, I'll come back and kill him," he threatened Wilberta as he pushed her from the room.

Soon he was back in the bedroom, rummaging, threatening, opening drawers. He found the .357 Magnum in the nightstand and again he was gone, only to return minutes later.

"I'm putting these dishes on the bed and if I hear them rattle, I'll kill your wife. I'll blow her fuckin' brains out," he hissed as he tied the torn piece of towel around Albert's face. Albert knew then that the masked intruder was the East Area Rapist.

CHAPTER FORTY-NINE

3:15 a.m., 6-24-78, Davis, California

"**DON'T YOU FUCKIN' MOVE.** Don't you fuckin' move," the whispers and loud breathing brought Marvin and Julie Webster out of a sound sleep. The light from the flashlight focused on their eyes. "Put your hands behind your backs and don't you fuckin' move or I'll shoot your fuckin' heads off. I have a .357 Magnum and I'll shoot your fuckin' heads off," he hissed through the ski mask covering his face.

They both rolled onto their stomachs.

"Don't move or I'll kill every person in the house. I'll kill every fuckin' person. I'll shoot you and splatter blood all over the walls. All I want is food and money. Food and money. I got to have money for gas. I got to have food," His threats drove to the marrow of their bones. "You, tie him up. Tie his hands up," he whispered.

Julie started to ask what she was supposed to tie her husband with when she saw the two shoelaces, neatly rolled in an oval shape, laying on her husband's back.

"Run it between his hands," he ordered as she attempted to tie her husband. Her hands shook so that she could not tie the knot.

"Between his hands," he hissed, angry because of her clumsiness.

Finished, she lay back on her stomach, trying to hide her naked breasts. She put her hands behind her back and felt him cross her wrists and tie them tight. They heard him in the closet, pulling laces from shoes and then he was back at the bed tying Marvin's wrists. He tied Julie's ankles, not tight like her wrists.

"Don't you say one fuckin' word or I'll kill everybody in the house," he warned and pressed the barrel of the gun into Julie's back.

"Maybe he's an escaped convict who had run out of gas and money for food," Julie thought to herself. "If we're lucky he'll take the money and food and leave."

"You. Where's the money?" he demanded as he hit Marvin's foot with the gun barrel.

"In my pants," Marvin answered.

"Where's your purse," he asked and tapped Julie's foot with the gun.

"It's in the kitchen," she answered, her voice quavering. "There's forty-five dollars in it," she added, trying to diffuse his anxiety.

"Shut up," he ordered as he left the room.

They heard him whispering in the hallway and they knew he was talking to their ten year old son who must have gotten up to go to the bathroom. They would later learn that the masked intruder had pushed their son into the bathroom and told him not to move or say a word. He placed a cup over the doorknob on the outside of the bathroom door.

"Oh, no. He's got the kids," Julie cried. The helpless, terrifying, agonizing feeling in her stomach was more than any mother should have to bear. To know that this creature was threatening her children and she could do nothing to protect them shattered every nerve in her body. She thought of the little league game in the morning and the other functions that were scheduled. "If I can only live to see those things," she prayed.

He was back in the bedroom and Julie felt the point of the knife in her back.

"That kid better stay in that bathroom or I'm going to push this ice pick into your back. He'd better stay in the bathroom. I'll kill every person in this house. I'll shoot all your fuckin' heads off. All I want is food and money," he hissed through clenched teeth, then he was gone from the bedroom.

"Do what he says," Marvin whispered to Julie.

"I wish he'd get to the part about the food," Julie whispered back.

They heard him rushing down the hallway to the bedroom.

"Don't talk to him," he ordered.

They heard him tearing a towel into strips and then they were being blindfolded.

"Move over," he ordered and hit Julie's foot with the gun. "On the floor."

She was mortified. Her naked body would be exposed to his scrutiny. She tried to quickly flatten herself into the carpet, but she felt his hands under her arms, lifting her to her feet. She felt the shoelaces fall from her ankles and felt herself being pushed from the room. In the living room she was gently lowered to the floor, her face pressed into the carpet. She heard lotion being pumped from the bottle of Vaseline Intensive Care and then he was squatted on her buttocks.

"All I want is to feel good. You'd better make it feel good," he whispered and she felt his penis, wet with lotion, in her hand. She knew he was the East Area Rapist and she focused on his penis. Was it like the papers said? He was not fully erect, and it seemed slender. He seemed circumcised. He was off her then and she felt herself being rolled onto her back.

"You'd better not bite me or this knife will go six inches into your back," he warned.

CHAPTER FIFTY

Sacramento Bee, 6-24-78

East Area Rapist's 36th Attack in Modesto

MODESTO - A young Modesto couple who told police they locked all doors and windows of their home before going to bed have become the victims of the East Area Rapist's 35th attack.

The rapist, who now has victimized 31 women and girls in Sacramento County, two in Stockton, and two in Modesto, awakened the couple at 1:30 a.m. Friday. Modesto police said.

As in the past attacks, the man wore a mask and shined a flashlight in the couple's eyes. Police said the man was armed with a knife and a revolver.

The rapist gained entry to the home in a newly constructed area in northeast Modesto through an aluminum sliding glass window which opens into the kitchen. The window had not been forced open and police said the couple are positive they had locked it before retiring.

The rapist spent about 45 minutes ransacking the home, after he ordered the woman to tie up her husband with shoelaces and then tied her in the same fashion.

When he finished going through the house, he returned to the bedroom and took the woman into another room where he raped her. The rapist was in the house about an hour an a half and left immediately after raping the woman, police said.

As in previous attacks, the rapist took articles from the house. The couple told police the rapist took their wedding bands and a revolver that he found in the house.

The couple untied themselves and called police after the rapist left.

The previous attack by the East Area Rapist occurred June 6 in Modesto when he struck only a mile from Friday's location, raping a 27 year old woman and taking $1,500.

Sacramento Bee, 6-25-78

Rapist Hits In Sequence Again - Modesto, Davis

DAVIS - The east area rapist reportedly assaulted a 32 year old housewife here Saturday morning and police believe it was the second time he has struck in Davis this month.

He also is believed responsible for beating and raping a 21 year old student.

Saturday's attack in Davis came only one day after a Modesto woman was raped by an intruder who used similar tactics.

Davis police said the department is working under the assumption that an attack on a 21 year old University of California at Davis student on June 7 and Saturday morning's rape were committed by the same man.

Both Davis rapes occurred one day after the rapist reportedly struck in Modesto...

The rapist, wearing a ski mask, apparently entered through an unlocked door or window to a house in one of the newer subdivisions west of Davis at about 3:15 Saturday...

The intruder was armed with a long bladed knife and said he had a handgun he would use if the couple did not cooperate...

At one point the couple's 10 year old son awakened and when the rapist spotted the boy he was ordered to stay in the bathroom... Two other children remained asleep during the attack.

The rapist took the woman into another room in the house where he raped her and then left the home after an hour. He took 17 rolls of pennies from the home.

The June 7 attack occurred during early morning hours in an apartment complex on the north side of the UCD campus.

The UCD student, who lived alone, suffered a broken nose, a mild concussion, and a blackened eye in the attack when she argued with and resisted the rapist...

Unlike previous attacks, when the intruder was armed with a gun or knife, the rapist carried a screwdriver and a nailfile. According to police the rapist stuck the nailfile in the woman's eye.

The woman was hospitalized after the attack. It was the first time a victim of the rapist was reported to have been extensively injured....

6-27-78, EAR Task Force Office

"Well, do we finally have a pattern?" Burns asked the investigators seated around the conference table. "Modesto, Davis, Modesto, Davis. And only twice before has he hit so close together."

"Well, Modesto called after their rape, but we didn't get a call from Davis until yesterday afternoon," Wayne replied. "Guess they still think they can make an arrest without help."

"You went to Modesto, Greg. Any question about it being EAR?" Burns asked.

"No question. He was there and there is no connection between the victim and Sacramento so he was obviously prowling around there. Still don't know why Modesto, especially with him coming back to Davis," Wayne replied.

"If it was him in Davis. I'm still not convinced it was him on the seventh. Too many differences. Just doesn't seem right to me," Burns shook his head. "Maybe he's still in Modesto."

"I went to Davis yesterday. Brockington called me at home. There may have been doubts before, but there are none now. It was EAR Saturday morning. Classic case even to the sobbing and crying after one of the attacks on the victim. Everything else fits. Dishes, threats, lotion, having her masturbate him. Not only that, it's in the same neighborhood of the last rape. I think this was the one he really wanted last time but he saw the one at the apartment while he was prowling and took her," Stone advised the group. "I think he's getting ready to move out of the area. Maybe we got close enough to him to scare him."

"Wishful thinking, maybe," Burns replied, "But I hope he goes somewhere."

"Well, one of the neighbors said that on the eighteenth she saw a male between her house and her neighbor's. She contacted him and he said he worked for a developer and they were interested in solar homes. Said after talking to him she didn't think he knew anything about solar. Also, the same neighbor found a jacket on her walkway by her gate Saturday morning. She knows it wasn't there the day before. Brockington said it was a "Golden Bear" brand made in California. Apparently it's made in San Francisco, so he's checking on it.

"Another neighbor saw someone looking over her fence around 8:30 Friday night. She didn't call the P.D. and said she wouldn't recognize him if she saw him again," Stone advised.

The manufacturer of Golden Bear Sportswear was located in San Francisco.

Davis detectives contacted the owner of the company who stated that the jacket was manufactured about five years ago. The jacket was a model 300 or 303 and because of the color, navy blue, did not sell well, therefore very few were made. She knew of only two stores that would have sold the jacket, one in Berkeley, one in Sacramento.

Independence Day, 1978

A day of picnics, fishing, boating, water skiing, drinking, and at night, fireworks. Many towns had parades: floats, bands, horses, fire trucks, clowns. Everything to please the children who lined the streets along the parade routes. The real children and the child in all of us.

Soldiers, sailors, airmen, veterans of previous wars marching behind the flag they fought so valiantly for. They marched for themselves and for their comrades who didn't return. And if they had time to look, they might even see an occasional person removing a hat and placing it over his heart. Not many, but some.

Does anybody under forty even know that July 4th isn't just a day of parades and fun and fireworks? The greatest secular holiday of the Untied States, the day of the Declaration of Independence, proclaiming the severance of the allegiance of the American colonies to Great Britain.

Gary Wells, a neighbor of Julie Webster, EAR's last victim, was enjoying the warm weather and a chance to relax. He also looked forward to the evening. He would enjoy the neighbor kids with their fireworks. Their bottle rockets, their sizzlers.

Near dusk, Wells watched a male subject about thirty years old, wearing a concho and walking with a cane, walk east on Buckleberry Road toward Arlington Boulevard. The concho and the beard that somehow didn't seem real caused him to call the Davis police department.

CHAPTER FIFTY

He had also seen a male on a bicycle cruise around the neighborhood and ride down Amador Avenue the previous night, he told responding officers who searched for the bearded man with a cane without luck.

CHAPTER FIFTY-ONE

2:00 a.m., 7-6-78, Davis, California

THE DARK FIGURE EMERGED from the vacant field at the end of Arlington Boulevard and quietly opened the side gate of a Westerness Road residence. He left the gate open and silently moved from one fenced yard to the next, coming closer and closer to the divorced housewife on Amador Avenue.

Quietly he approached the kitchen window, shadowed by a weeping willow tree between the house and the street light across the street. Silently he removed the screen and placed it behind the shrubs near the fence.

His gloved hand held the screwdriver on the glass near the lock. A quick, short slap on the end of the handle broke a small hole in the glass. He listened then, as he waited in the darkness, his ears and eyes attuned to the night sounds of the neighborhood. Only silence surrounded the house as he slowly slid the window open. The plants on the windowsill above the sink, he removed one by one and neatly lined them alongside the house. Slowly and silently he lifted himself through the open window and into the darkened house.

At 4:33 a.m. Sergeant Brockington received a phone call from the Davis P.D. dispatcher. A rape had just occurred on Amador Avenue and it looked like an EAR attack.

At 4:35 a.m. Brockington called Sheriff's dispatch in Sacramento. He requested that Sergeant Stone be notified immediately of the attack.

"Give me your phone number, Sergeant, and I'll have Sergeant Stone call you. He's on the air," the dispatcher advised.

"If he's on the air just ask him if he can meet me at the scene," Brockington answered.

Seconds later Stone was enroute to the city of Davis.

"Hi, Al," Stone greeted Brockington, who met him in front of the Singleton residence.

"Thanks for coming, Jim. Looks like one of your classic EAR cases. I haven't talked to the victim yet, as I had patrol take her to Davis Community for the rape examination. I talked to the officer who got here first and got some information. I thought you might like to sit in on the interview when she gets back," Brockington shook Stone's hand.

"I appreciate the call," Stone replied, "and I would like to sit in."

"I thought we might take a look inside to get your impression and then we can go get a cup of coffee and talk about it. There's a small coffee shop about a mile down Russell Boulevard. Dispatch will call us when the victim is ready to return," Brockington gestured toward the front door.

"Sounds good. If you're right, we're going to need some coffee," Stone headed for the front door.

As soon as he entered, Stone felt EAR's presence. A feeling of low voltage electric shock that started in his brain and surged through his body. It was almost a feeling of death as he walked through the house. Shoelaces, torn towels, an open bottle of Keri-Lotion, the large kitchen knife on the dresser in the master bedroom, and the herringbone tennis shoe impression in the mud just outside the kitchen window that matched the muddy print on the kitchen counter removed any doubt that EAR had struck once again.

Technicians were photographing the pieces of evidence, leaving them in place for further scrutiny, testing, and collection much later on in the investigation. They wouldn't be moved until the victim had an opportunity to walk Brockington and Stone through the attack.

"Coffee, black," Stone smiled at the young waitress taking the order.

"Make it two," Brockington added as he put his hands over his eyes and slowly shook his head in frustration, knowing the panic that would soon take over the previously quiet city.

"I hate to say it, Al, but you better add something strong to yours. This is the third hit in your town and you're going to be taking a lot of heat," Stone shook his head.

"No doubt in your mind it's EAR?" Brockington asked. "This is a college town and it could be a copycat."

"I don't think so. From what I saw and felt in the house, it's him. But why don't you run down what you know about this one," Stone replied.

Brockington opened his book.

"Patrol got the call around 4:30. Got there a couple of minutes later and met with the victim, Sheila Singleton, and her son at the next door neighbor's. She told them that her youngest son was still in the house and she didn't know if her attacker was still there or not. Of course, he was gone and the young fellow was still asleep.

"She said she had been on a date and returned home around 1:00 a.m. and went to bed. Next thing she knew, there was a light shining in her eyes. She said the man stated, 'Don't move or I'll blow your fuckin' head off. I'm going to blow your fuckin' head off, do you see this gun?' She said he told her several times that he would 'blow her fuckin' head off' and kill her kids. Told her to lie on her belly and he tied her hands behind her back and then tied her feet. Apparently he mentioned her two boys and said all he wanted was food and money for his van."

Stone felt the hair on the back of his head stand up when he heard 'food and money for the van.'

"He put his cock in her hands and asked her what it was and had her masturbate him. She said he kept telling her he would 'blow her fuckin' head off' if she made a noise," Brockington continued. "She said he stuttered at times and always acted angry. Apparently he performed every sex act, lubricated himself, blind folded her, everything you ran down to me the last time we got hit.

"Oh, yeah, apparently he was really sobbing at one point and said something like, 'I hate you, Bonny. I hate you, I hate you, I hate you'."

"Bonny or mommy?" Stone asked.

"The officer asked her if he could have said 'mommy,' and she told him she felt sure it was 'Bonny,' but, you know, she could be mistaken. She was pretty shook up," Brokington replied.

"She mention the size of his penis?" Stone asked.

"Yeah, said it was about three or four inches long, but never real stiff."

"Is she divorced or just separated?" Stone asked.

"Don't know for sure. Her husband or ex is a doctor and apparently hasn't lived with her for quite awhile," Brockington shrugged.

"Well, everything fits," Stone advised. "Open area, main thorough-fare within a few blocks, and State Highway 113 leads to Interstate 80. I think he's on the move and you're right in his path. The question is, will he hit you again or move on?" Stone raised his eyebrows.

"You think he's moving?" Brockington asked.

"He used to say he was moving to LA. And we thought it was a ploy on his part, but now I don't know. I do know he's getting more violent and angry. To be honest, I think he really does want to kill someone. It fits his profile that we got from D.O.J."

CHAPTER FIFTY-ONE

Sacramento Bee, 7-7-78

East Area Rapist Returns to Davis, Assaults Mother

DAVIS - A 33 year old mother of two young sons was raped early Thursday by a man believed to be the East Area Rapist, police reported...

7-7-78, Modesto

At 5:00 p.m. an officer was dispatched to a Palmilla Drive address, approximately one and a half miles from the Wilberta Montgomery rape. The revolver stolen during the rape was found near the canal behind Palmilla.

Sacramento Bee 7-10-78

Davis Council Session on Rapist Draws 400

DAVIS - Some 400 residents of this university community poured into a special city council meeting Tuesday night to hear tips on how to deal with the East Area Rapist, the sexual terrorist who recently added three Davis women to his list of 33 attacks.

"The level of paranoia is getting phenomenal," explained the mayor. "This is just raw fear."

The police chief said he has not seen Davis residents so upset "since the Vietnam War." He implied he did not blame them, saying the stymied police department has obtained a researcher to go through the police reports involving the ski-masked invader to see if there might be some common denominator in them the 40-member police force has overlooked.

Davis police are as stumped as Sacramento police, Sacramento county sheriff's deputies, Stockton police, and Modesto police in trying to identify or capture the East Area Rapist, who has terrorized 39 women and girls in those communities in the past two years.

"He [the rapist] has a pretty warped personality but he's also pretty shrewd," the chief said. "Every middle run murderer or rapist makes a mistake, but this guy hasn't made a mistake. We are convinced he does select his hits [victims] ahead of time. He

knows where he's going when he comes into town." The rapist also seems to know the best ways of escape.

The police chief of 16 years refused to answer some questions the audience raised in the two hour special meeting, saying "We could be raising a red flag in his face by telling everything he does." But he did try to dispel the rumors of mutilation that seem to have followed the rapist since he first emerged in Sacramento County June 18, 1976.

7-14-78, Davis

"Sergeant Brockington," the female began when Brockington answered the phone. "I am Lilliana Cervi, Sheila Singleton's neighbor. Sheila is in Europe on vacation and my ex-husband is looking after her house. Today he was cleaning her refrigerator and found a knife inside a Velveeta Cheese box. I know Sheila wouldn't put it there and I thought you should know."

"Thanks, Mrs. Cervi. I'll have an officer come over right away and pick it up. If it hasn't been handled, tell everyone to leave it just as it is," Brockington advised.

Epilogue

As I said, I wasn't there for the rapes at the beginning. I did read the reports and later had the opportunity to discuss the attacks at length with the lead investigator of the Sacramento Sheriff's Department's EAR Task Force.

The victims in the first thirty-seven rapes are real, their names have been changed to protect their privacy. The rapes were real. The beatings were real. The fear and the stark terror is real, more real than my words could possible describe. Black and white is insufficient. Only violent colors could remotely come close to describing what went through the minds of the victims, for they knew, each and every one of them that they were going to die a horrible and painful death at the hands of this masked maniac.

The investigations into possible suspects are real. Again, the names have been changed to protect the privacy of the innocent.

Jim Stone, Mike Burns, Greg Wayne, Peg Vickers, and all the other officers mentioned are not real. They are simply loosely based on the officers involved. They represent all police officers and deputy sheriffs who are deeply concerned with crime and the need to see that justice is meted out, even though they realize that all too often, it never is.

Any resemblance between the officers' personal lives as written, and those actually involved in the investigations, is purely coincidental and meant only to add a personal touch to the story.

If I brought back horrible memories that were dulled with time to any victim or their families, I sincerely apologize. This book is not written for that purpose.

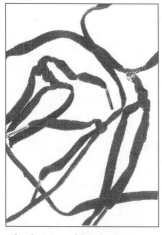

Shoelaces used by the rapist

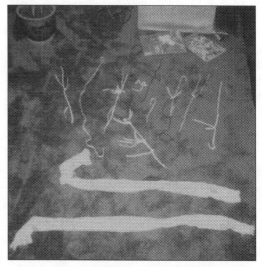

Typical knots and materials used by the rapist/murderer in his attacks

Knot used by the rapist

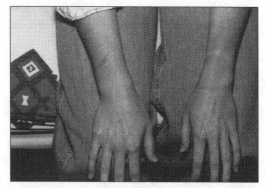

Marks on rape victim's wrists indicate how tght the bindings were to secure the victim during the attack

Chapter Fifty-two

The Contra Costa County
East Area Rapist Task Force

With Christmas, 1978 and New Years, 1979 over and forgotten, the EAR Task Force was in full swing. Although we were no closer to catching or even identifying our rapist, hopes were still high. Sergeant Bevins remained in constant contact, his need to reach closure as important as it was when the rapist was terrorizing his County.

While working on reports, Sergeant Rod Carpenter received a call from a deputy working the Danville area. Last March he had arrested a person for indecent exposure. A woman on Alviso Way had been in her living room around midnight and had looked out her sliding glass door and observed a man wearing a ski mask and no shirt. The man was masturbating. She and her husband had chased the man, however he got away. Later that morning the deputy had located the man. He had a lengthy record of indecent exposure, burglary and assault with contacts in Redding, San Diego and San Ramon.

Carpenter ran a criminal history on the subject. He had been in jail during the Contra Costa County rapes. Another dead end, another elimination.

On January 2nd, I received a call from an intern at the Crime Lab. She had responded to an illegal entry at a Thunderbird Place, San Ramon residence. Someone had broken into the house while the residents were out of town. Although nothing was missing, it was obvious that someone had been in the house.

At approximately 5:00 p.m., I contacted Richard Murphy by phone and set up a procedure between the Murphy's and Sheriff's Radio. At 1:30 and 3:00 a.m., Radio would call the Murphy residence. They would answer giving the code word "angel" if everything was all right.

The next day I met with Jamie Murphy, the thirty-year-old wife and mother of an eighteen-month-old baby. Mrs. Murphy, a five foot seven, one hundred and twenty pound redhead informed me that they had locked up when they left. In checking further, Mrs. Murphy noticed that her underwear drawer in her bedroom dresser was completely closed. This was unusual as the drawer malfunctioned, so she never closed it completely.

Mrs. Murphy had also received a phone call in early December in which the male caller had said in a slow, soft voice, "Would you like to talk to me while I masturbate?"

The Murphy residence was an upper middle class dwelling with the backyard bordering the golf course. The golf course was connected to Thunderbird Place by a wooden bridge just four houses from the Murphy's. They, in turn, were two houses from the Korbells, the couple who had found the rope secreted under the couch cushion. All indications were that EAR was active in the Danville/San Ramon area and that the probability of a hit was extremely high. Because of that, it was proposed that road blocks be set up in the area to check on those matching the physical profile of EAR. The Contra Costa County District Attorney's Office was contacted to rule on the legality of such a move.

On January 8th, the District Attorney responded: "The use of road-blocks to temporarily detain persons who match the physical profile of the East Area Rapist would not be permissible under California law. The fact that the person meets the description of the East Area Rapist is not reasonable suspicion to detain him. Both California and federal case law is clear that the proposal would be illegal."

Better that a thousand guilty go free than one innocent be inconvenienced. I wondered how the next victim would feel about Supreme Court decisions.

Also on January 8th, Voorhies and I met with Teresa McCrae for two reasons: one, to assure her that we were still actively pursuing the case and two, to go over her attack again in hopes of discovering something that was previously missing. McCrae was still emotionally terrorized and several times broke into tears and fits of uncontrollable shaking. As with most rape victims, she had not come to grips with the fact that she was not in any way to blame for becoming a victim. Over and over she repeated that she knew that she was going to die a horrible death that night.

In talking about the bedroom lamp that EAR had turned on and that I had retrieved the fingerprints from, McCrae assured me that to her knowledge, no one other than her boyfriend had been in her bedroom since she had unpacked the lamp.

On January 10th, Ford and I met with Sunny Walther, the San Ramon victim of October 28th. During her hypnosis she said that she had observed a beige Toyota drive by her residence the day of the rape. On November 16th, she had again seen the vehicle on San Ramon Boulevard and had copied down the license number. Ford had previously eliminated the driver of the vehicle as an EAR suspect after contacting him and learning that he had been looking at houses in hopes of purchasing one. The problem was that while under hypnosis, Walther stated that the image she related to investigators was of the driver of the beige Toyota. Now she was sure that it was the image she saw in her bedroom mirror. This raised doubt as to whether the composite done by investigators would be of any use.

During the interview of Sunny Walther I got the feeling that the rape incident really wasn't that frightening to her. It was almost like this was the ultimate turn-on. A fantasy that had been fulfilled. As we left I disclosed my feelings to Ford.

"It seemed like her eyes actually glazed over when she was describing the attack," I stated.

"I picked up on that also. Thought it was just me but I noticed her eyes when she was talking about being tied up and naked with EAR standing over her," Ford remarked.

"Well, she is definitely one of the prettiest he has hit, but I get a real strong feeling that this marriage is just about over," I replied.

"The part that threw me was when she said that when EAR told her to orally copulate him, she told him she needed a drink of water first. A woman being raped, would she really be worried that her mouth was dry?" Ford asked.

"It was almost like she was reliving it when she described EAR throwing water on her face and breasts but not reliving the terror like all the others describe. It was more like reliving an orgasm," I shook my head.

I didn't realize how accurate we were in our assessment until two years later when I was working as a patrol sergeant in Central County. I got a call from Dispatch to meet State and Federal narcotics officers. They were going to serve a search warrant on a methamphetamine lab in the unincorporated area of Concord and requested that I accompany them. They showed me two photographs, one of the "cooker," the person running the lab, and one of his girlfriend. I recognized the girlfriend as EAR victim, Sunny Walther.

During the search of the residence, although no one was home, I located several photographs of Walther and her biker boyfriend. Many of these were explicit photographs of Sunny Walther orally copulating her doper boyfriend while looking directly into the camera lens. Maybe the rape wasn't her ultimate fantasy, maybe this was. I felt sorry for her husband and her young son.

During the month each investigator was assigned a specific area to sift through: motels, pawn shops, other agency similars, suspect profile, victim profile, weapons, stolen autos, area profiles, sex registrants, evidence, fingerprints.

One of my subjects was fingerprints. Each case was gone over. How many fingerprints were collected? How many were eliminated? How many left? I contacted each agency and requested copies of the fingerprints that had not been eliminated. In turn these were turned over to our fingerprint examiner for comparison to see if any matched. None did.

On January 24th, I met with a fingerprint examiner of the California Department of Justice in Sacramento. I gave him a photocopy of the three fingerprints taken from the McCrae lamp to be run through their computer system.

"We can do that," the examiner replied, "unfortunately our system is not complete yet. We have hundreds of thousands of prints. Some of the prints we used are from arrestees who were probably dead, but the print was good.

"Someday we will catch up and all people arrested will be in the system, unfortunately, unless the person you are looking for was just recently arrested, the chances are the prints won't be in the system yet.

"We'll give it a try and if I come up with something, I'll give you a call. If not, I suggest you resubmit your request every two or three months. Just refer to the ISB case number and we'll do the rest. You might contact the FBI. Their system has been in place a lot longer than ours and is more up to date."

I thanked the analyst and left. Our luck remained consistent. No match was found. I contacted the FBI's Fingerprint Division to find out how I could submit a fingerprint. I couldn't. Their system wasn't set up to compare fingerprints. If I could give them the age, sex, height, weight, race, eye color, and any other characteristic we could determine, they could work on it. Their fingerprints were listed by suspect description. The narrower we could reduce the factors, the better the chance of finding a print. If I had that much information I wouldn't need them.

On January 25th, I met with Bevins and gave him copies of all the fingerprints from the Contra Costa cases. I also learned that the person who had burglarized the McCrae residence on October 30th had been eliminated as being the one leaving the prints on the lamp. Maybe we did have EAR's prints.

The burglar was also eliminated as an EAR suspect.

On January 26th, a memorandum was distributed throughout the Department of various sergeant openings. Gary Ford applied for a position in Crimes versus Persons and in Intelligence. Although he was probably one of the most qualified for either position, his request was denied due to the fact that he was number one on the new lieutenant's list and his promotion was a foregone conclusion. For the time being, he would stay with the Task Force.

A letter was sent on February 1st to ninety-four northern California Police Departments and twelve Sheriff's Departments requesting copies of any future burglaries involving a rape, and any past attacks where the victim was bound.

Carpenter compiled a twenty-five-page comprehensive crime study profile on the East Area Rapist from the four Contra Costa cases with comparisons to the other thirty-nine attacks. If EAR had a pattern, it certainly wasn't apparent. He had hit at least once in every month over the past thirty months and had hit every day of the week, although only once on Sunday with Friday and Saturday the most active. He had also hit on twenty different days of the month. His youngest victims were thirteen, his oldest, forty-one. Open side gates seemed to be the only visible evidence for patrolmen to look for.

I met with the owner of the Sun Shine Investment Corporation in San Jose. The owner, a nuclear physicist for General Electric, knew of no one by the name of Pippin and no one that fit Pippin's description. His employees, older and bigger than Pippin's description, were also physicists with no contact to the Sacramento area.

A deputy patrolling the Danville/San Ramon area while working the graveyard shift the morning of February 3rd noticed a gray primered 1968 Pontiac LeMans parked near the intersection of Sycamore Valley Road and Camino Tassajara, a non-residential area.

As vehicles don't normally park in the area, the deputy advised Radio at 5:30 a.m. that he was checking the vehicle. Upon approaching, he saw a white male who appeared to be sleeping in the back seat. The deputy woke the subject by tapping on the window and had him get out of the car. He noted that the subject resembled the description of EAR and asked for a driver's license. The subject, identified as John Walker, showed a Sacramento area address. When asked why he was parked in the area, Walker stated that he worked for the railroad in Milpitas and frequently stopped to sleep on the way home. He also stated that he was staying with a friend in West Pittsburg. In fear of jeopardizing any evidence found as a result of an illegal search, the deputy did not enter the vehicle nor check through a briefcase and several sales sample cases in plain sight.

The deputy ran a warrant check and found an outstanding traffic warrant. Walker was advised that he was under arrest and immediately became extremely upset stating he had just returned to work after being off ill for six weeks. His resistance was only verbal until the deputy started to take a Polaroid photograph of him. He then resisted physically until he was convinced that photographs would also be taken at the jail.

Walker's vehicle was locked and left at the scene. Enroute to the jail, Walker carried on a strange, one-sided conversation, mostly talking to himself. The comments were tape-recorded.

"If I call my old lady, it would give her a heart attack," Walker mumbled. "I'm going to give my mom a heart attack. If anyone fools with me, I'll poke his eyes out. I'll bite his tongue off."

The deputy watched his prisoner, slumped against the side window, through his rearview mirror.

"Would you shoot me if I tried to escape?" Walker mumbled.

"You don't want to escape, you'll be booked and released in a couple of hours."

"Nobody ever catches the real criminals, they always get away. Nixon ought to be shot. He lied to the American people. Look at Patty Hearst," Walker continued to ramble.

An "East Area Rapist Information" sheet was sent to the Task Force. Lieutenant Pitkin assigned the case to Harold Franklin, the D.A. investigator assigned to the Task Force.

"I've run up against a brick wall on Pippin," I remarked to Jack Harper. "I've got appointments with Mays and Hughs, the two real estate people, and if you're free, I'd appreciate your help."

"Glad to," Jack replied.

"I borrowed the IDENTA-KIT from Investigations. Want to give it a try?"

"Sure. I've used it several times. Maybe we'll get lucky."

On February 5th, Harper and I met with Mays and Hughs at separate times. Jack worked up composites from each. Thin faced with pockmarks and a turtleneck sweater was the major characteristics.

Stop and FI requests went out to neighboring agencies and our patrol force, requesting them to be on the lookout for an orange BMW driven by a subject possibly using the name Greg Pippin.

CHAPTER FIFTY-TWO

I contacted the sales manager at the Concord BMW dealership and learned that the BMW from 1967 through 1976 looked the same. In 1970 a buzzer was added that sounded when the door was opened with the key in the ignition. The manager said that the BMW in question was probably a 2002 or possibly a 1600.

I contacted the Sacramento office of the Department of Motor Vehicles and requested a printout of registered owners of 1967 through 1976 BMWs.

As everything was still coming up brick walls, I re-contacted Barbara Mays and asked her to undergo hypnosis in the hopes of learning something she may have forgotten. She was more than happy to help.

"Hey, Jim," I started when Bevins answered the phone. "I'm still working on this real estate deal. One of the women agreed to hypnosis."

"We tried that a few times. We had pretty good luck with it, but couldn't come up with what we needed. When are you going to do it?" Bevins asked.

"The sixteenth. A lieutenant at Concord P.D. does it for them and has agreed to work with us on this."

"Anything on the BMW?" Bevins asked.

"DMV is sending me a printout. Haven't got it yet and we put out a B.O.L.O. to all the agencies. If he's around, somebody should spot it. So far nothing has worked out with the real estate angle or the name Pippin. DMV came up with a few Pippins but none checked out," I replied.

"Well, nothing new up here. The boss says he's gone and good riddance. I think he'll be back. Just got the feeling that he's not through with us," Bevins stated.

"I talked to the search and rescue people with the bloodhounds. They all agree that if they took the dogs to Sun Valley Mall and EAR walked by, the dogs would go wild. Said the dogs got the scent and it was so weird they think the dogs will remember it. Said they think it has something to do with some kind of disability. Chemical imbalance or something," I continued.

"They probably have a better chance of catching him than we do, although I think I would pick up a scent if I passed him. When I go into a house after a rape, it's almost like I can feel him even before I talk to the victims," Bevins said.

"Well, you've got a lot more experience with him than I do, but I feel the same way. Thought it was just my imagination. Look, I'll give you a call after the hypnosis if we come up with anything," I added and we hung up.

"Hey, Russ," Carpenter walked into the office, "I just got off the phone with a Kay Rhea. She's a psychic that is well known. Been on the Johnny Carson Show and several other TV and radio shows. Says she has helped several law enforcement agencies solve crimes and wants to help us. Says she won't charge anything but she feels she can give us information so we can catch EAR.

"I've heard of her," Pitkin remarked.

"Says she has helped the FBI several times as well as LAPD and others," Carpenter continued.

"I don't know. I better run this by the Sheriff. We might look pretty silly contacting a crystal ball. The papers could have a field day," Pitkin shook his head.

"Well, she might be able to help us," Carpenter argued.

"I'll get back to you. Don't call her until I do," Pitkin dismissed him.

That afternoon we got our answer.

"The Assistant Sheriff said we will not, under any circumstances, meet with a psychic. He was adamant. If we meet with her, he will shut down the Task Force that day. Says if we have nothing to work on, we should be shut down anyway. Investigations are to be scientific, not psychic," Pitkin stated. "So I'm telling you no."

"What he doesn't know won't hurt him," Murdock commented. "I think we should look into it."

"And I'm telling you that Dillon will close us down. The answer is no," Pitkin left the office.

"I think we should talk to her," Murdock stated after Pitkin left.

"Count me out," I replied. "I feel the same as Dillon. I don't believe in psychic powers and I don't care what anyone says. I've never seen anything that would prove to me that any of these so-called psychics have ever helped anyone. After you catch them yourself the psychic can always say, 'See, I told you he would be near water when you found him,' and there he was, in the bathroom near the toilet. But they couldn't tell you what toilet, or what house, or even what town."

"I don't want to take the chance, either," Carpenter remarked.

"Me either," Ford chimed in.

"I've talked to enough nuts already," Voorhies added.

"Jack, you and Frank don't work for the Sheriff. How about going with me?" Murdock asked.

"I'll try anything," Harper replied. "We've done it before at Pleasant Hill. Didn't help us, but didn't hurt us either."

"Count me in," Fonda replied.

"Here's the phone number," Carpenter handed the paper to Murdock. "You're on your own."

A meeting with Kay Rhea was set for February 14th at 8:30 a.m. at her home office.

"Hey, boss," Harold Franklin sat down next to Lieutenant Pitkin's desk. "I think we've got EAR. That John Walker that patrol gave us the lead on looks real good. I ran a D.L. printout and he's had tickets in Sacramento in June of '76. Also Folsom, Fair Oaks, Elk Grove, and then in Walnut Creek in August of last year.

"He's living in Carmichael right now and commutes to Milpitas down near San Jose. He's also worked in Stockton and with the railroad he gets to travel through all the areas.

"I checked with his supervisor and he wasn't working any of the nights of the rapes in this county and he was off on sick leave from November twenty-first through January twenty-third.

"Carpenter did a drawing of Walker from his booking photo and another from the composite from the Sunny Walther rape and they're identical."

"Get hold of Voorhies and the two of you check this out. Also get his booking prints and have them checked against all the prints we have from our four cases, especially the ones from the McCrae lamp," Pitkin stated.

"You got it, boss," Franklin replied. "We'll hit his home in Carmichael and see if we can get him to chew on some gauze for us."

Franklin and Voorhies arrived at Walker's residence at 11:00 a.m. February 8th to be met by Walker's mother. The detectives did not tell her the reason for their visit and was told that John was in Fremont and would not be home for several days. She told the detectives that she would have him call when he returned.

Upon returning to the office, Franklin contacted the Chief of Security of the railroad and learned that Walker was at work in the Fremont yard. Franklin and Voorhies immediately left for Fremont only to learn that the crew had moved to Hayward.

They met with the Chief of Security and learned that Walker did not work on October 7th, 13th, and 23rd, November 4th, December 2nd, and 19th, the dates of the Bay Area rapes. He had worked on February

3rd, the night of his arrest; however, he had gotten off work at 3:45 a.m., as the crew had finished their work early.

Although Walker was permanently assigned to the Stockton Dispatch board, he had been working out of the San Jose Dispatch Board since September. He may have also worked on occasion at the Modesto yard.

Walker began working for the railroad in June of 1978. Prior to that he had done landscape work in Sacramento in May and June of 1978. No blood work had been done during the hiring process according to Walker's file.

Although his current address was Carmichael, he did live in West Pittsburg from August through October of 1978.

On February 13th, Franklin contacted Walker by phone and he agreed to an interview that morning. Franklin and Voorhies immediately left for Sacramento. They had not made it to the Benicia Bridge when they received a radio call to return to the office.

"Walker's mother called just after you left," Pitkin advised when they walked into the office. "She said if we wanted to talk to her son, we would have to go through her attorney. The phone number is on your desk."

"Attorney? If he's not guilty he wouldn't need an attorney. I knew we had him," Franklin grinned.

"Call the attorney before you get too excited," Pitkin warned. "Maybe it's just an overly protective mother."

"Bullshit. He's guilty and she knows it. She's protecting him or why else would she get an attorney that fast," Franklin ranted.

"Call the attorney," Pitkin remarked.

The next morning Franklin phoned Mrs. Walker and explained that all he wanted was for her son to chew on some gauze so he could be eliminated as the rapist.

"This has something to do with his arrest in San Ramon, doesn't it?" she remarked.

"No, not at all. He was arrested for an outstanding warrant and we have no interest in it," Franklin assured her.

"Well, I understand. I'll discuss it with our attorney and call you. I'm well aware of the East Area Rapist." She hung up.

Later, Mrs. Walker called back. Their attorney wanted some time to think it over. She would get back to Franklin.

Murdock, Harper, and Fonda met with Kathlyn 'Kay' Rhea, the psychic who had offered to help catch EAR. In preparation for the meeting, Murdock had prepared a series of forty-two matte boards with the victim's licenses, photographs and photographs of the victims' homes, both from the front and from an aerial view. Some of the boards also had photographs of bindings.

After introductions, Ms. Rhea told the detectives she did not have super natural powers and did not have a crystal ball.

"What I do, I can teach any of you to do. I am able to focus. Focus on the victim, focus on the attacker," she began.

Ms. Rhea, a para-psychologist, started by studying a few of the forty-two matte boards and began to develop information regarding EAR's appearance and his home. Later she went over each board and gave her thoughts on the victims. The meeting, tape recorded with her permission, lasted three hours.

Although the meeting was interesting. Very little was learned that could be used as investigative leads. The suspect, she felt, was in his late twenties with large hands and well developed leg muscles with brown leg hair. He preferred boxer shorts which might suggest a military background, she told the investigators. The military background was mentioned several times during the meeting.

She felt that EAR was laughing at the police for not catching him and he was thrilled for being able to outsmart people. An animal abuser as a child, he probably did not finish high school and if any remorse was shown, it would be false.

"He is not likely to kill," she stated, "as he prefers to frighten his victims. He must also work at the job of rape, as he has a real problem with erections."

The detectives played a tape recording of a call to a victim. Ms. Rhea felt the voice was not that of EAR as EAR was ten pounds lighter than the caller and EAR would not call and threaten to kill. She also felt that the poem written after the Modesto attack was not from EAR. She did feel that EAR would be caught and connected the arrest to two women in a house. It would occur in April and khaki uniforms would be present. She also stated that she felt we had a thumb print of him and fingerprints from a green kitchen.

A second meeting set for February 26th was scheduled in the hopes that Ms. Rhea would have additional job related information.

On February 15th, Harold Franklin called Bevins at Sacramento S.O.

"Jim, we're still trying to catch up with this John Walker person. His mother or attorney or somebody was supposed to call me back but haven't. Can you send somebody over to Walker's house and get a saliva sample and his shoe size?"

"No problem. I'll have a couple of our investigators head over now," Bevins replied.

A short time later Bevins called back. His two detectives had met with Walker's mother who stated that John was not home and they were not to talk to John. They were only to contact the attorney from now on. Bevins did contact the attorney, who stated: "In no way can you interview my client."

Franklin felt that all doubts had been dispelled. John Walker was EAR. Hot on the trail, he contacted Walker's roommate when he was living in West Pittsburg. The roommate was reluctant to talk and appeared to be very protective of Walker. Although he did not know the dates of the Contra Costa rapes, he was sure Walker had been home with him at the time. He further advised that Walker dated several girls; however, he refused to give names.

Franklin contacted his boss, the District Attorney, and had him call Walker's attorney in an attempt to obtain some cooperation. The attorney told the D.A. that he would have Walker sent to a private lab for blood typing; however, under no circumstance would he permit Walker to give a saliva sample as "it might be incriminating."

While Franklin was working the John Walker prospect, I continued to work the Greg Pippin incident. I had been in contact with Carol Gayley and had set up her hypnosis for 8:00 p.m. at Concord P.D. Pitkin and I arrived early to meet with the lieutenant to ensure everything was ready. When we walked into the Department, we were met by a lieutenant I had known back in my narcotics days when I worked with some of the Concord narcs.

"Hi, Larry," he greeted me and I introduced him to Pitkin. "How's the East Area Rapist thing going?"

"Slow. We're here for Straka to do a hypnosis for us on a possible witness," I replied.

"Well, he's sure got me nervous," the lieutenant began. "I built a box into the headboard of our bed and I sleep with my gun in it and then I sleep on my back with my hand over my head and in the box. If that bastard comes into my room, I'm ready."

"He's got a lot of us nervous," I replied as Pitkin looked at me with raised eyebrows.

"Well, I sure hope you get him. My wife is real nervous. You know he hit us here in Concord twice," he continued as though we might not know about the Concord rapes. "Good to see you again," He walked off.

"You know him?" Pitkin asked as if it was my fault.

"Know of him. Used to see him here when I was working with Jim Blackburn, one of Concord's narcs. I met his wife and believe me, EAR isn't going to go into their bedroom. For EAR to attack her, the good lieutenant would have to hold the gun to his head, and even then I doubt if he could get a hard on, even if it meant his life," I laughed.

Gayley and her husband arrived at the P.D. a little before 8:00 p.m. and after some small talk, Straka began his pre-hypnosis interview at 8:15 p.m. The husband, Pitkin, and I stayed in the room during the session which was videotaped and recorded.

Under hypnosis, Straka asked Gayley to put herself in a position where she was watching herself on television and tell us what was happening. During the session, she said that she had answered a knock on the door of an open house. A white male around thirty years old was standing on the steps. He looked nervous and was looking at the ground. He didn't say anything and she asked him in and gave him a cup of coffee. He told her that his name was Greg Pippin, walked to the backyard, and jumped up on the fence in the corner and looked at everything in the backyard.

Gayley felt real nervous watching him as he entered the house and went upstairs. When he came down he said he was hot and took off his red down jacket. That seemed strange to her as it wasn't warm in the house. He stood and drank his coffee. She didn't offer him more as she didn't want him to stay. She watched him go to the front window and pull and push on it. He said something about the house not being looked after and that he would have to put a lot of money in it.

She asked him again to repeat his name. He seemed irritated at her request; however repeated it for her and said he was a real estate agent for Sun Shine Investment in San Jose. She asked him how he had found the house and he said he had seen the sign. This was strange to her, as the house was not on a through street and the sign in the yard had fallen and she had not set it back up. She meant to earlier; however, she was too nervous while he was there to leave the house to stand it up.

She felt he was not looking at the right things for someone who wanted to buy a house. When he left she watched him get into an orange BMW. She could see the rear license plate: blue with orange lettering like a California plate. She could see the letter ZKH, but not numbers.

The hypnosis ended at 9:45 p.m.

"Every study I've ever seen or heard about says that parolees return to crime within the first three months of being paroled," I looked around the room at the Task Force members at our Monday morning meeting.

"We've all read the rape reports and Rod and Tom and Jack have gleaned all the information and what it shows us is that when EAR first hit on June 18, 1976, he had a plan. When he hit us on December 9th, he still used that plan. He's used it for forty-three rapes and he hasn't changed that plan. He's made it a little better and he's added a gun and he's added some statements, but he hasn't changed his pattern.

"I know some people think he's a cop because he knows how to get away. I don't. Hell, if he was a cop he'd be caught by now. Cops are the worst crooks in the world. If a cop raped a woman tonight, he couldn't keep it to himself. He'd have to tell everyone at line-up the next day. As cops we are not solitary animals. If EAR was a cop, he'd have to invite the shift to join him.

"I think the person has been in prison. No one wakes up one morning and says, 'Gee, I think I want to be a serial rapist and this is how I'm going to do it.' I think EAR started out as a peeping tom, a burglar, a lily-waver and graduated to rape and got caught. While he was in prison or jail, he had time to reflect on why he was caught and he had the chance to talk to others who were there under the same circumstances. I think EAR was paroled to the Sacramento area sometime within three to six months before their first rape and I think that if we got that list, he would be on it."

"Why don't you put something in writing to me," Pitkin said. "If your real estate person or Hal's railroad person doesn't pan out, maybe we can look at parolees. In the meantime, how has the fingerprint detail been going?"

"I've collected copies from all the agencies and turned them over to the Lab. Jim Cowger is comparing them to see if any match. We collected Davis, Stockton, and Modesto Friday and we already had the others," I replied.

"Yeah, Hal drove us to Davis, Sacramento, Stockton, and Modesto and had us back here before quitting time," Voorhies interjected. "He scared the hell out of us. He only has two speeds—a hundred or stopped.

"We were going down 80 and cars were moving out of his way like they knew Hal was driving. One person didn't, an Oriental, and Hal was screaming that Orientals shouldn't be allowed to get drivers licenses. A black man putting down Orientals. What next?" I smiled.

"Hey, they can't drive. Shouldn't be allowed on the road," Hal muttered.

"What about motels, Ron?" Pitkin asked.

"Larry and I checked the motels in Davis last week and the ones from Walnut Creek to San Ramon. We've got a couple of names to check out, but it doesn't look too promising," Voorhies replied.

"Hal, where do you stand with Walker?" Pitkin asked.

"I think he's EAR, boss. He was off every night a rape occurred," Franklin replied. "He won't talk to us, won't chew on gauze, and he's connected to every area. His lawyer and mother stop us at every stage."

"God damn it, Hal, he's not EAR," Voorhies broke in. "His crew said he was at work the night of the Concord rape and said there was no way he could have left early. Hal won't even believe his own elimination. His crew said they went to work at 11:00 p.m. and got off at 9:30 a.m. the night of the Concord rape."

"They get off when their job is done. They told us that they often get off early," Hal argued.

"But they said that they worked until 9:30 a.m. on October 13th and there was no way he got off," Voorhies replied.

"See if you can eliminate him some other way," Pitkin admonished.

Later that afternoon, Franklin and Tom Cassani met with Walker's supervisor at the Fremont rail yard. He brought Walker to the office to talk to the detectives.

"My attorney told me not to talk to you and besides, I don't trust police officers," Walker stated.

"Look, we don't want to talk to you, we just want to have you chew on a piece of gauze for us and we will be out of your hair. You don't have any right to refuse to chew on gauze," Franklin stated.

"Well, I'm not going to chew on any fuckin' gauze, so go ahead and arrest me. My attorney sent me to a private lab and had my blood tested. I think it's A negative," Walker glared at Franklin.

"What size shoe do you wear?" Cassani asked.

"Nine, ten. It depends," Walker replied. "And I'm not going to talk to you anymore. I'm going back to work."

On February 20th, I requested a movement list for the Department of Corrections Youth Authority inmates paroled between January 1, 1976 and June 18, 1976 to the Sacramento, Placer, and Yolo counties.

Although I felt that if EAR was a parolee, he was probably paroled to Sacramento County. Placer and Yolo were also within easy driving distance of the first twenty-two rapes.

When I talked to Bevins about the hypnosis session with Gayley, he mentioned that they had used Tom Macris, an officer from San Jose P.D., who was an excellent artist, to do sketches of suspects while witnesses were under hypnosis. I was willing to try anything.

I called Macris and he was willing to work with us and would be available to meet with Gayley to do a drawing of the person known as Greg Pippin. Macris needed a letter requesting his services sent to his Division Chief. He also wanted Gayley under hypnosis. Gayley agreed and the session was set for February 27th at 9:00 a.m., again with Lieutenant Straka.

On the 27th, Gayley and her mother met with Carpenter, Tom Macris, and me at Concord P.D. Straka began his session at 9:25 a.m.

"Carol, when do you see his face the clearest?" Straka asked after Gayley was placed under hypnosis.

"When he's at the table drinking coffee," she answered.

"Okay, I'm going to have you turn the television set off for a moment. Is it off?" Straka asked.

"Yes," Gayley answered.

"Okay. I'm going to have Sergeant Macris work with you. When I have you turn the set back on, I want you to watch Pippin drink his coffee. Sergeant Macris is going to talk to you and you're going to help him draw a picture. Can you do that?" Straka asked.

"Yes."

At 12:25 p.m., Straka brought Gayley out from under hypnosis. Macris showed her the colored picture of Greg Pippin he had drawn. It was so close to what she had remembered that she began to shake. The nervous feeling returned.

On February 28th at 2:30 p.m., Murdock, Cassani, and Harper met with Kay Rhea for their follow-up psychic meeting. Due to the availability of Tom Macris, it was decided that he would attempt a drawing of Ms. Rhea's vision of EAR. Rhea stated she felt EAR was due to hit again, soon, and if he hadn't hit three times in San Jose, he would.

She felt that EAR liked to wear turtleneck sweaters and felt he had been ill in January and had been thinking of visiting "back home" in Mississippi, Alabama, or Louisiana. He had been in the San Jose area a few times to pick up parts, drinks lots of coffee, misses work due to illness, possibly allergies, and had a fatalistic attitude that he was going to get caught.

"You may have him by June," she stated. "Road 70 or 97 ends near his residence."

She envisioned a dark haired female waiting for someone. "EAR enters from the bathroom area and punches the woman in the stomach. It's very windy outside. I believe it's the Sacramento area, eastern side. Music is playing around 10:00 p.m. There's snow in the mountains and it's beginning to thaw but it's still too cold to go swimming. I see a church. He feels very good after sex. Thoroughly enjoys it."

When asked about work, she envisioned a loading dock, newspapers, a truck with advertisements, a bell at his work place, and loud noises like machinery.

"He has lower back pain when he returns home from work and you've been close to him, real close," she told the investigators.

Pitkin released EAR cases number eighteen through number forty-three to the FBI for them to do a psychic profile.

On March 1st, Carpenter and I met with June Addison, the real estate agent who had shown the open house in Dublin where Pippin had shown up. Carpenter showed June the drawing done by Macris while Gayley was under hypnosis. Under June's direction, slight changes were made. The lips were thinner and paler, the complexion paler, side burns longer, and hair more combed back.

"That's him," Addison remarked after Carpenter had made the changes. "I've never been nervous at an open house before. I think I was suspicious because he didn't say anything when I answered the door. He just stood there. I just felt strange. He checked around the side of the house and the back fence even though he had to climb a small hill to get to it. He even checked the attic crawl space. The questions he asked just didn't relate to real estate."

On March 4th at 7:05 a.m., Deputy Phil Branum, returning to Martinez from the Danville area, saw a Sunkist orange BMW northbound on I80 near State Highway 24. Noting it matched the vehicle in my memo of February 3rd, Branum stopped the vehicle. The driver, a thirty-six year old male with mid-length sideburns, stated that he lived in Los Altos and frequently passed through the area. The driver, identified as Gregory Michale Ripon, was clear warrants, however had an arrest in this county in 1974 for sales and transportation of tear gas.

Branum filled out a field investigation form to be routed to me and released Ripon. A copy of Ripon's 1974 booking photo was similar to the artist's sketch done by Macris and altered by Carpenter.

I ran a history on Ripon and learned that he had a speeding ticket in Riverside County in 1963 and had applied for a real estate license in 1975 in addition to the one arrest that Branum had discovered.

A check with the State Real Estate Board showed that Ripon was licensed and did work for a San Jose development company. A copy of his fingerprints, taken at the time of his arrest, was taken to the lab for comparison to those taken at the rape scenes.

On March 6th, I contacted Ripon by phone at his residence and set up a meeting for 1:00 p.m. at his office.

After explaining the reason for our contact with him, Ripon stated he was looking at houses in the area for his brother who lived in Concord. He had gone to several open houses that he had seen advertised in the newspaper.

Ripon was five feet ten inches tall, one hundred and thirty-five pounds and wore a size ten shoe. He had worked in San Jose for the last four years. He had a brother in San Ramon as well as the one in Concord and had no contacts with Sacramento. He had been attending Foothill College in Los Altos since the spring of 1965, having registered for all four semesters in 1977 and both winter and spring in 1978.

Ripon agreed to chew on the gauze pad for the saliva sample. He did not know his blood type, however, agreed to call me if he could find it out.

As I was leaving he stated he had a blood condition and did have blood work done in 1960 in Wisconsin where he was born.

I took the saliva sample to the Lab for secretor status testing.

Although I had no link between Ripon and Sacramento, he was not eliminated.

CHAPTER FIFTY-THREE

ON MARCH 6, 1979 a memo was sent to Captain Rupf from Lieutenant Pitkin recommending that the EAR Task Force be reduced in size by April 1st to two sergeants.

Voorhies and I were to remain, working under the Crimes versus Persons Commander. Sergeant Gary Ford, presently on the lieutenant's list, would be transferred upon promotion. If not promoted by April 1st, he would remain as the third investigator until his promotion. Sergeant Mike Weymouth was to return to his old job in Inspection and Control, Carpenter and Peggy Bowen would transfer back to Investigations and Murdock would return to his job in the Crime Lab.

Fonda, Harper, Cassani, and Franklin would return to their departments. Secretary Caroline Clausen, who had returned from a leave of absence to handle the clerical duties, would resume her LOA status.

Lieutenant Pitkin would turn over his duties to Lieutenant John Gackowski on April 2nd, by formally briefing him on Task Force material.

When I returned from the lab after handing over the gauze that Ripon had chewed on, the investigators were all sitting around the room. I could tell they were pissed. Ford passed me a copy of Pitkin's memo. I was stunned. Each of us were actively working suspects, gathering physical evidence from past attacks, and had no inclination that Pitkin had decided on this move.

"What is this, Russ?" I asked.

"This is just a recommendation," Pitkin began. "EAR hasn't struck since December 9th so he has obviously left the area. I don't see any need to keep spending money. Ron and Larry can follow up on anything that's going on and can handle an attack if EAR does come back. I just don't think he will and we've done all we can."

"Russ, I've still got piles of lab work to do," Murdock stated.

"You should be able to finish it up in two weeks. Anything else you can do from the Lab," Pitkin replied. "The rest of you can make sure you pass your loose ends to Ron and Larry." Pitkin then got up and left the office.

"What brought this on?" I asked Ford after Pitkin had left.

"Oh, I know what it's all about. Russ wants the position on the Jail Transition Team. He's wanted it ever since it was mentioned and he knows that if he's here someone else will get it. If the Task Force is shut down, he gets the transfer," Ford shook his head.

"EAR hasn't quit. He's going to hit again, I can feel it, and he's going to hit us. I mean, I'm happy that he's recommending that I stay, but that doesn't mean that the Sheriff will agree and he may just shut us down completely. I'm still working Ripon and Hal is sure Walker is EAR. Doesn't it mean anything that this son of a bitch has raped our citizens and hasn't been caught. Christ, Russ must have some feeling for our job, or does that leave when you become an administrator?" I rambled.

"Well, maybe the Sheriff will see through Russ. He does live in a glass house and also don't discard his comment about spending money. I told you how he worked," Ford remarked.

On March 7th I received the parolee movement list for the Department of Corrections and the Youth Authority. Approximately six thousand parolees were listed as being paroled to Sacramento, Placer, and Yolo counties during the six month period.

On March 9th, Assistant Sheriff Dillon sent letters to Pleasant Hill, Walnut Creek, Concord, and the District Attorney's office of the intent to reduce the Task Force and thanking them for their cooperation and the use of their investigators.

"Larry, let's take another walk," Ford beckoned me as he headed for the door.

"What's up?" I asked.

"Let's go see Warren. Maybe he didn't get the truth about the Task Force," Gary replied.

When we arrived at the Investigations Division, Captain Rupf was standing in the bay talking to some of his detectives.

"Can we talk to you, Warren?" Ford asked.

"Sure," Rupf replied and headed for his office with us following.

"I know it's just a matter of time before I'm promoted, but this thing with the Task Force is wrong, Warren," Ford began.

"Why? Russ said you have completed all your investigations and there is nothing left for you to do," Rupf replied.

"Warren, the Task Force has so much left to do we can't even find our desks. Larry ordered his list of parolees from the Department of Corrections and just received about six thousand names. There's a darn good chance that EAR is on the list. The Ripon thing is still hanging, and Franklin is sure that John Walker is EAR and he is still working on him," Ford stated.

"Well, let me talk to the Assistant Sheriff. This is all news to me," Rupf stated.

"I figured it might be," Ford shrugged as we left.

"Think they'll change their mind?" I asked Ford.

"I think Russ will get his ass chewed but he'll probably get his transfer and that's all he cares about. I think the Sheriff will take another look at us, but we've done all we can do."

On March 12th, the results from Ripon's lab request was returned to me. Ripon was a non-secretor. Although his fingerprints did not match any of those from previous rape scenes, Gregory Michale Ripon was still a viable candidate for our serial rapist.

On March 13th, Hal Franklin contacted the Sacramento County District Attorney's office to obtain a copy of John Walker's probation report from a July 5, 1977 arrest for sales of marijuana. He had been arrested for setting up a sale with his roommate. Unfortunately for Walker, the buyer was an undercover agent for the Sacramento Sheriff's Office Narcotics Unit. Franklin and Voorhies met with Kerling, the person who sold the marijuana, at his Orangevale home.

Kerling stated that as part of their probation, he and Walker were not to have contact with each other. He did show the detectives a black ski cap that Walker had left at the house. This was taken by the detectives. Kerling stated that Walker often wore tennis shoes and drank beer. When asked about Walker's mother, Kerling described her as a "bitch" who wouldn't allow Walker to do anything and was always watching over him. Walker did not get along with his father.

"It's him, damn it," Franklin ranted as they left Kerling's house. "It's Walker and no one can tell me different. I can feel it and I know his train crew is protecting him."

"Hal, why would the train crew protect him? They've got no reason to protect a rapist. He was working and there is no way he got off early. You eliminated him and now you won't even believe your own work," Voorhies shook his head and threw his hands in the air in frustration.

"They're lying to protect themselves. They all got off early and put on their time cards that they worked until 9:30," Franklin stated.

"Bullshit, Hal. He's nuts, but he's not EAR," Voorhies ranted.

When they returned to Martinez, Franklin submitted the ski cap to the Lab for hair sample analysis. On March 16th, Assistant Sheriff Dillon received a letter from Gary Strankman, the Chief Assistant in the D.A.'s office. Due to Franklin working on an active suspect, the D.A.

would leave Hal with the Task Force. That would leave three investigators after the April 2nd transfers.

Three days later Franklin and Voorhies once again went to the Fremont railroad yard and met with Walker's supervisor to determine once and for all Walker's exact work schedule.

On June 22, 1978 Walker had reported to work in Sacramento at 11:55 p.m. At 1:30 a.m., June 23rd, EAR hit Modesto. Walker was off work the following night. EAR hit Davis at 3:15 a.m. on June 24th. Walker arrived at work at 7:55 a.m.

On June 28th Walker started work at the Stockton yard.

On October 12th, Walker arrived at work at the Fremont yard and worked until 9:30 a.m. on the 13th. EAR hit Concord at 4:30 a.m.

On November 3rd Walker arrived at work in Fremont at 11:30 p.m. and worked until 5:00 a.m. EAR hit Concord at 2:30 a.m. He arrived back at work that evening at 11:00 p.m. and worked until 5:00 a.m. San Jose was hit at 2:30 a.m.

Again Walker was eliminated as EAR due to his work schedule. Again Franklin refused to believe his own elimination.

"I know his work schedule reflects he was working on the dates of some of the rapes, but all the other rapes occurred while he was living in Carmichael. The rapes in our area and the rapes in San Jose didn't start until he moved to Pittsburg and started working down here," Franklin justified his views.

"Give it a fuckin' break, Hal. He's fuckin' eliminated. He was working. They proved it with his time cards, so give it up," Voorhies implored.

"His time cards are wrong. He's been in the area for every rape. When he lived in Carmichael, his home was right in the middle of all the Carmichael rapes, all eight of them, and he lived only two blocks from the second one. Not only that, he let it slip that he has blood type A positive and he wears a size nine shoe. He's EAR and I'm going to prove it," Franklin went on.

"Without me, Hal. I'm not driving down here again," Voorhies promised.

Tom Cassani received a call on March 20th from an anonymous citizen stating that a person who had been fired from the Contra Costa Sheriff's Department should be investigated as EAR.

"He was terminated for making blatant sexual advances to a juvenile female while on duty," the caller advised. "He's now a security guard."

Cassani checked with a female Walnut Creek officer who had worked security with the ex-deputy. She told him that the security guard was a "little strange" but had nothing specific to add. The information was given to Harper, who contacted the individual and had him chew on the gauze pad. He was eliminated as a secretor with type A negative blood.

At 10:30 a.m. that same day, I received a call from Bevins.

"Larry, I just came from an attempted rape over in Rancho Cordova. It looks like an EAR attack but the deputies didn't think to call me when they took the detail. Been almost a year since we've been hit and where there was no rape, they just handled it as an attempt rape and burglary. He beat her pretty bad so I only got to talk to her for a short time before she went to the hospital."

"What stopped the rape?" I asked.

"Don't know. She was asleep and felt someone on her holding her arms. When she woke she saw a nylon mask and started to scream. He beat her face pretty bad and told her to shut up and that all he wanted was money. Tied her, gagged her, and called her a bitch several times. She said he was wearing gloves and that's about as far as I got," Bevins explained.

"Well, Pitkin just had us shut down as of April 2nd. He'll probably blame one of us for staging this," I mused.

"Maybe this will change his mind. If it's EAR, he's going to start another summer session," Bevins remarked.

"We'll see. You going to check into this some more?" I asked.

"That's why I'm calling. I've got an appointment with the victim and her two kids at 6:00 this evening. I was hoping you could make it," Bevins advised.

"You bet. I'll meet you at your office around 5:00 and I'll bring Voo if he can make it." I hung up.

"Russ," I began, "Bevins just called and said they had an attempt rape last night that looks like EAR. He's got an interview with the victim at 6:00 and asked me to be there. You want Voo to go also?"

"No, he's working with Hal on the Walker extravaganza. Ask Rod if he can go. See if he thinks it's EAR," Pitkin replied.

"Bevins does. Nylon mask, tied, gagged, and called her 'bitch' several times. Apparently he beat her pretty bad when she screamed," I remarked.

"I think he's gone. I doubt if this is an EAR hit," Pitkin dismissed the conversation.

Maybe I was wrong. Maybe I was being selfish, but down deep, I really did want it to be EAR. He needed to be caught and if he left the area, he wouldn't be. I knew we could get him with a little more time.

Bevins, Carpenter, and I met with Marie Salinas and her twelve year old twins at a friend's house at 6:00 p.m. Her face was swollen and purple on the left side. Her lip was cut and swollen and her left eye was black and partially closed. She had trouble talking.

"After you left this morning, Sergeant," Salinas began, "I tried to turn my bedroom lamp on and it wouldn't work. I checked and it had been unplugged."

"You said you were awakened around 4:30 or 5:00," Bevins questioned. "Can you tell us how long this person was in your house before he left?"

"My alarm went off at ten to six," twelve year old Lynne remarked, "I let it ring for a long time before I turned it off. I noticed that my door was closed but I thought Mom closed it sometime during the night. I went back to sleep and my brother woke me at 6:15 and told me about what had happened to Mom."

"I didn't close it. Glen always sleeps with his door closed," Marie nodded toward her son, "but Lynne leaves hers open. When I heard him rummaging through the house I was afraid he would go into Lynne's room but I guess he just closed her door."

"What happened when you awoke?" Bevins asked.

"I started to scream and he hit me with his fist. He had something in his hand but I don't know what it was. I couldn't see it, but he hit me hard about four times and told me to shut up, he wasn't going to hurt me, he just wanted money.

"He told me to roll over and he tied my hands behind my back and tied a blindfold around my eyes. He was wearing some type of nylon mask but it was hanging loosely from his head. He was wearing tight fitting gloves that felt real soft.

"He threw the comforter over my head and I could hear him taking jewelry from my dresser and putting it in some sort of bag. He kept calling me 'bitch' and used the word 'fuck' all the time. It was like he was making gasping sounds when he was in the bedroom and then he would say 'bitch.' I heard him opening and shutting drawers in the kitchen."

"Did you hear him opening the refrigerator?" Carpenter asked.

"No, and it doesn't look like anything is missing," Marie answered.

"Did you have any beer in the refrigerator?" Carpenter asked.

"No," she replied.

"Did you hear him in any other room?" Bevins asked.

"It seemed like he was in every room except the children's. I was really afraid he would go in Lynne's room but he didn't. I don't know when he closed her door but I think it must have been before he woke me because Lynn didn't hear me scream."

"How long do you think he was rummaging before he came back into your bedroom?" Bevins asked.

"About forty-five minutes and then he came back into my room and lifted the comforter off my back and then he pulled my pajama bottoms down and then he just stood there and stared at me for about three minutes. And then he let go of the elastic and it snapped back and he said 'bitch' and then left the room and started rummaging again and then I didn't hear anything.

"After about ten minutes I was able to get up and wake Glen. When I did I saw that the front door was open.

"When he pulled my pajama bottoms down, he pressed something against my lower back. I think it was a knife, and then he told me it was my last chance to tell him where my money was. I begged him to believe me that I didn't have any. I knew he was going to rape me but he didn't."

"Do you have any idea why he didn't?" Carpenter asked.

"I've got a bad scar on my back and I think he was staring at it and I think it bothered him," Marie answered.

"Did he say anything about it?" Bevins asked.

"No, I just have that feeling."

"Did you hear Lynne's alarm clock go off?" I asked.

"No, but I had the comforter over my head," Marie replied.

"That must be about the time he left. He must have heard it and it scared him," Bevins remarked.

"I guess so," Marie whispered.

"All right. I think that's enough for now. I need you to try to remember anything else and if you feel you're up to it, I'd like to talk to you again tomorrow. We won't need to talk to the kids, but I would like to talk to you some more," Bevins remarked.

"I've got things I have to do in the morning. Is three o'clock okay?" she asked.

"At your house?" Bevins replied. "I'd like to take another look around."

"That's fine."

After leaving we stood near the cars and talked.

"He did a job on her, Jim," I remarked. "You sure she wasn't raped and just doesn't want the kids to know?" I asked.

"I don't think so, but that's one reason why I want to talk to her again without the kids around. Can you make it tomorrow?" Bevins asked.

"Oh, yeah," I replied.

"I can't," Rod said. "But I think I've got enough to convince me it was EAR."

"I do, also," Bevins stated. "The Department wants to stay quiet on this. They don't want the press to overreact. So far I haven't convinced my lieutenant that it's EAR."

"I didn't want to butt in, but what did he use to tie her with?" I asked.

"A nylon cord from the garage. He cut it from a tent that they have. The scarf that he gagged her with came from her dresser drawer so he was ready before he woke her. We don't know how he got in. Nothing seemed forced and she thinks she locked all the doors before she went to bed," Bevins answered.

"Sounds familiar," I remarked.

"Why don't you meet me tomorrow at noon. I'll buy you lunch and it will give us time to talk before we meet Marie," Bevins said.

"You're on. I'll meet you in your office around 11:30," I said and Rod and I left.

The next morning Rod and I met with Pitkin and other Task Force members.

"I'm convinced it was an EAR attack," Rod told the group after we explained what we had learned. "Sac wants to keep it from the press for now, but Bevins thinks it's EAR also. I've done a chart on Tuesday hits and each time he hit again within twenty-four days and each time he hit in a different city."

"If he didn't rape her, how can we even guess that it's EAR?" Pitkin asked.

"The other things all fit. The words, the tying, the gagging, rummaging. Said all he wanted was money, called her a bitch, wore a mask and gloves. I think he didn't rape her because the alarm went off and scared him, or at least frustrated him. In the past when he got frustrated he left without raping also," I remarked.

"Three other times he didn't complete a rape and all three times he hit again in another city within six to fifty-six days. I think it was EAR and I think we better plan on being hit," Rod explained.

"I think EAR left and won't be back. I think you're trying to convince yourselves it's EAR and so is Bevins. I don't think it was EAR," Pitkin remarked.

The following day I met Bevins in his office.

"The Sheriff still going to shut down the Task Force?" Bevins asked.

"Guess so. Except for Voorhies and me. We'll still work out of the same building we have now but we'll answer to Lieutenant Gackowski and Lieutenant Van Orden out of Investigations. Everybody else is being transferred back to their old jobs, except Hal Franklin. The D.A. wants him to stay and work on the railroad worker," I explained.

"I know he's weird and so is his mother, but I thought he had been eliminated because he had been working during a bunch of rapes," Bevins asked.

"Eliminated by everyone except Franklin. He refuses to admit he's eliminated and so far he won't chew on gauze. Hell, we've eliminated hundreds of suspects with a lot less than we have on Walker," I stated.

When Bevins and I arrived at Salinas's residence, I immediately had doubts as to it being an area that EAR would choose. Although it was a new residential area, all the homes were duplexes or tri-plexes. The victim's residence was a duplex. Backyards were surrounded by four-foot high fences with very small yards, and the buildings were close together.

During the taped conversation with Salinas, my doubts were quickly dismissed.

Glen, the twelve year old son, had heard someone outside the house around 12:30 the night of the attack, however did not tell his mother until the next day.

During the ordeal, her attacker returned to the bedroom several times to check her bindings. Each time he asked her where her money was and each time he called her a bitch. Marie said it seemed like it was a script he had pre-planned. She felt that her attacker was going to cut her and rape her. When he told her it was her last chance to tell him where her money was, she begged him to believe her. It was then that he snapped her pajama bottoms and again called her a bitch.

Also, Sunday evening around six, her son answered the phone. Although he could tell someone was on the line and kept saying hello, no one answered and he hung up.

"He seemed to talk through clenched teeth," Marie told us. "If it hadn't been for the scar on my back, I think he would have raped me. He just seemed to stare at it for three or four minutes."

"Well, what do you think?" Bevins asked me when we left.

"There's things missing, but there seems to be a reason for it. I think he didn't rape her because her daughter's alarm went off and upset his thought process and his control of the situation. He took about three thousand dollars worth of jewelry, but kept asking for money. Started out by telling her to shut up, just wanted money. The words 'fuckin' and 'bitch.' I think she's a very lucky lady she only got beat up. Personally, I think EAR was here.

"It's almost like he knows what's going on. Your Task Force is shut down except for you and ours will be in less than two weeks except for Voo and me, so maybe he just wants the publicity to start again," I stated.

"Well, we're shut down and even if the Sheriff agrees it's EAR, we won't be back in business. As far as I'm concerned, it's going to be you and me. If we get hit, I'll call you immediately. If you get hit, call me. We'll do these together and maybe we'll make it." Jim looked at me for agreement.

"Sounds right to me. One of us is going to get hit again. He didn't rape and he needs to. Maybe the next victim will blow his ass away," I answered.

"Well, we had one earlier on that should have taken him out. We didn't include it, but I know it was EAR. A woman in Rancho Cordova was afraid she would be attacked so she went out and bought a .357 and then went and took lessons on how to use it. Every night she sat on the kitchen floor with the gun in her hand. One night EAR did hit. He started to come through her kitchen window. She said she had him in her sights and was ready to pull the trigger and thought that if she killed him she would go to prison. Said she moved her aim over and shot the window frame. EAR slithered back out and disappeared. Must have shit his pants," Bevins said.

"Damn, she would have been a hero. Tickertape parade and the whole bit," I remarked.

"Yup. Didn't change things, though. He continued to hit." Bevins shook his head.

On March 22nd I was contacted by Gregory Ripon.

"I remembered after I talked to you. I had blood work done in 1961 at Columbia Hospital in Milwaukee, Wisconsin. I told you I had a blood disease and they were the ones who worked on me," he stated. "I lived on North 51st Street in Milwaukee at the time."

I called information and got the phone number of the hospital and called the medical records department. Gregory Ripon had a blood test and was determined to be O Negative. All other information agreed with the information I had on Ripon. After three months, two hypnosis sessions, composites, car stops, help from the L.A.P.D., North Hollywood P.D., and hundreds of phone calls, Gregory Michale Ripon was eliminated as an EAR suspect.

On March 23rd, Franklin sent a bulletin to Patrol requesting a stop and FI on any new suspicious pick-up trucks in the San Ramon/Danville area. If the driver happened to be Walker, Franklin requested a copy of the FI be sent to the Task Force. If nothing else, Franklin was determined.

The week before the Task Force was to close, Pitkin gave letters to each of the investigators, thanking them for their help. Although everyone knew it was the wrong move and definitely premature, the die had been cast. Was it Assistant Sheriff Dillon's promise to shut us down if anyone sought or accepted help from a psychic that drove the final nail in our coffin, or was it Lieutenant Pitkin's fear of losing a position he desired? Or had we really exhausted our usefulness? EAR had been out of the county for almost four months. He had never been gone for that length of time since his first attack. Were we failing to see the "big picture?" That was one of my failings: while others were looking through a wide angle lense, I was always looking through a macro. I saw the trees. Good administrators only looked for the forest.

We did have one thing to celebrate before Voo and I were to be left alone. Gary Ford was promoted to lieutenant the week of March 26th. On every department when someone is promoted, at least half of the officers grumble about the stupidity of the brass in making such a promotion. In this case, no one doubted the choice made by Sheriff Rainey. Gary was one of the last true gentlemen on the Department and had earned his promotion. His professionalism and dedication would only improve the Department.

On March 30th, Voorhies, Franklin, and I watched Gary Ford, Rod Carpenter, Mike Weymouth, John Murdock, Peggy Bowen, Jack

Harper, Tom Cassani, Frank Fonda, Caroline Clausen, and Russ Pitkin clean out their desks.

April 4, Fremont, California

Fremont is a city just north of San Jose on Interstate 680. Free of the high crime rate of other cities in the Bay Area, it is a bedroom community cherished by many who commute to other cities to work.

Darkness had settled over the quiet neighborhood when the dark figure silently moved through the shadows. Residents had grown accustomed to the traffic on Mission Boulevard just a block away. No other sounds interrupted the darkness. The silent figure strode directly to the Honda Way residence of Brad Erickson and his twenty-seven year old girlfriend, Jean Beaumont.

The figure walked across the lawn, stood on a planter box and peered through the window into the darkened house. No lights. No one home. The figure left the window and walked to the side gate and opened the latch. He pushed but the gate wouldn't move. A harder push and the gate moved a few inches. Bracing himself, the figure pushed harder and the gate moved. A loud scraping sound from inside the fence startled the figure as the stillness in the neighborhood was broken. Quickly the figure squeezed through the opening, stepping over the bricks piled against the gate. He moved down the side of the house toward the side window.

A door opened next door and the beam from a flashlight sliced through the darkness. The figure crouched in the darkness as the flashlight beam moved back and forth in the front yard. The light disappeared and once again the door opened and closed.

The figure remained crouched. No other sounds broke the silence as he rose and looked through the window into the empty bedroom. He began prying on the window frame near the lock. The window cracked, the sound amplified in the darkness. He looked toward the house next door: a light shined through the partially parted curtains. A face appeared, peering into the darkness, and then disappeared.

The dark figure moved to the back of the house and again pried, this time on the sliding glass door of the master bedroom. The lock broke free but the floor-mounted deadbolt held. Again the screwdriver flashed in the figure's hand as he pried the sliding glass door leading into the family room. The lock broke free and soon the floor-mounted deadbolt also broke loose. Silently he entered the house.

"What did you see out there?" Gloria Gobel asked her husband when he re-entered the house.

"I shined the light all around but didn't see anybody near our place," her husband Carl answered. "There was a scraping sound out there somewhere."

"Well, I heard glass break next door but when I looked out I couldn't see anyone in the dark," she remarked

"Something's going on," he answered.

"Well, the next door neighbors are on vacation, so they can't get hurt," she stated and walked back to the couch to resume watching television.

"Larry, Bevins here," Jim responded when I answered the Task Force telephone.

"Hi, Jim," I answered.

"I just got a call from a Detective Clark with Fremont P.D. They got hit early this morning and it looks like our man. I'm heading that way now. Able to join me?" Bevins asked.

"Want to pick me up here?" I responded.

"In an hour." Bevins hung up.

"Fremont got hit this morning," I told Voorhies and Franklin. "Bevins is going to pick me up on his way there."

"It's Walker. He's working down there now," Franklin pounded on the desk.

"Damn it, Hal, he's eliminated," Voorhies admonished.

"I'll call Gackowski and let him know about it," I remarked as I ignored Hal and Voo's banter and reached for the phone.

At approximately noon, Bevins and I met with Detective Steve Clark and his partner Bill Morse. Both detectives were extremely cooperative, asking for and offering any amount of help. A pleasant surprise as so far it seemed the only real cooperation between departments was between Bevins and our Task Force. Sacramento Sheriff's Department had readily given us copies of all their investigations. We, in turn, took them and made sure they knew all of our moves.

Clark and Morse showed us the exterior of the residence, the pry marks, broken window, and shoe impressions.

"The next door neighbors heard him push open the gate and heard the glass break, but didn't call because they knew no one was home. I guess burglary didn't enter their minds," Clark shook his head.

"That's the story of this bastard's life," Bevins stated. "You would think people would call, but they don't."

"Well apparently they didn't realize that sooner or later the people would return. I just don't understand some people," Morse added.

We met with the two victims inside the residence.

"We don't have too much furniture," Jean Beaumont remarked, "Brad's a contractor and we are only living here until we can sell. He builds them and sells them."

I looked at Erickson. I knew he was strong enough to pick the house up and take it with him if it didn't sell. EAR must have been real nervous until he was tied tight.

"I know you've gone over this too many times already," Clark looked at Beaumont and Erickson, "but I'd appreciate you doing it again. Sergeant Bevins works for Sacramento's East Area Rapist Task Force and Sergeant Crompton works for Contra Costa County's Task Force. They know more about these cases than anyone and they've offered to help us."

"Detective Morse told us that this was probably the East Area Rapist," Beaumont said.

"It sounds like it," Bevins stated. "Why don't you tell us what happened."

"Well, we left the house around 6:45 to go to dinner in San Jose and check on some of my rentals," Erickson began. "We got home around 9:00 and didn't notice anything wrong. The door to the bedroom with the broken window was closed. We always leave it open, but didn't think anything about it at the time."

"We went to bed and made love for about an hour and fell asleep. I'm on my period," Beaumont broke in, "and I didn't shower. I just cleaned up a bit and fell asleep nude."

"An hour or so later something woke me up and I saw this man standing in the doorway," Erickson continued. "He had a flashlight and a gun pointed at us. I could see a dark ski mask and some type of nylon jacket. He was about five eight; maybe six feet, one sixty-five or eighty, and maybe twenty-five to thirty years old by the way he talked.

"He shined the light on me and said, 'motherfucker, you're dead'. He told me to put my face down or he'd blow my fuckin' head off. He told Jean to tie my hands behind my back."

"He sounded uptight," Beaumont explained. "The voice sounded put-on, not his natural voice. He yelled at Brad several times, 'Don't you move or I'll blow you're fucking head off,' and one time he said he'd cut it off.

"He threw some shoelaces on Brad's back and told me to tie his hands. He kept saying, 'Don't look at me,' and "tighter, tighter.' Then he told me to lie down and he tied my hands and feet and Brad's feet."

"He tied my wrists again. Real tight. I've still got indentations." Brad showed us his wrists and the red indentations in the skin.

"The man kept threatening that he would blow our heads off. I could hear him in the hallway tearing towels. He kept repeating that he was hungry and wanted something to eat."

"Yeah, and he kept coming back into the bedroom and checking on us. One time he asked where my purse was," Beaumont stated. "I told him it was in the car in the garage. I heard him go into the garage and then he came back into the bedroom and told me to move farther away from Brad and then he told me to get on the floor and then he said he was taking me into another room so we wouldn't be together.

"When he helped me off the floor I could see his white legs and brown hair. He was wearing brown checkered socks with the elastic stretched and dirty white tennis shoes. I guess he didn't have any pants on or maybe he was wearing shorts.

"When we got into the front room he laid me down on the floor and threw a blanket over me and then he tied towels around my eyes. I heard glass clanging and then he went back into the bedroom."

"Yeah, he came back in and threatened to blow my head off again. Said he only wanted food for his van, whatever that meant. He gagged me and then tied the television cord around my ankles and stood some bottles, glasses, and jars on the bed next to me. At one point he ran the point of a knife down my back and then put a bunch of blankets over my head. He closed the bedroom door and I didn't hear anything else until Jean came in and we got loose," Erickson finished.

"When he came back to me he said something and I couldn't understand it. When I told him I couldn't hear him he got real mad and told me to whisper. He said something again and I told him I couldn't hear him. He got down real close to my ear and whispered, 'If you do what I want, I'll take the food and money and leave without hurting anybody.' I knew he was going to do something sexual to me.

"I was on my stomach with my hands tied behind my back and he took the blanket off me and sat on my buns with his penis in my hands. He didn't say to, but I knew he wanted me to stroke him, so I did. He began to change positions and I thought he was coming closer to my face, but he didn't. He sat on my buns again and I stroked him some more.

"He was erect, but not hard. More soft than hard. He untied my ankles and rolled me on my back and fondled my breasts and then entered my vagina for about a minute and then he put me on my side and entered me again.

"He squeezed my left breast real hard and then got up and threw the blankets over me and retied my ankles. Then he stuffed a towel in my mouth and then he tied my ankles to the bookcase with one of Brad's ties."

"Did he ever put his whole weight on you?" Bevins asked.

"No, never. Oh, one time he said, 'I'll just get these things together and put them in my van.' I never heard a car leave though. Before he had intercourse with me he turned on the television for light, but didn't turn on the sound. After intercourse, he turned the television off.

"After a while, I didn't hear him but before that I heard him go outside. I heard the front door squeak. He came back in and walked around and then I didn't hear anything. I got a knife and freed myself and then went and freed Brad. Then I called the police." Beaumont shrugged as if to say, "That's it."

"Did he bring the shoelaces with him?" I looked at Clark.

"Apparently so. Brad said he's missing one pair of laces, but that's all. The rest he must have had with him. He tied Brad with shoelaces, electric cord, neckties, and pieces of panty hose. Obviously he was afraid of Brad," Clark stated.

"You went to the hospital?" Bevins asked.

"Yeah, they did a rape examination," Morse answered

"Do you know if he ejaculated?" I asked.

"I don't know, but I don't think so. Like I said, we made love earlier and I'm on my period, so I was still pretty wet," Jean answered.

"Was he wearing gloves when he squeezed your breast?" Bevins asked.

"No. It felt like his bare hand."

"Oh, one thing I forgot to tell you earlier," Clark stated. "He took sixteen hundred dollars but that was only half of what was there. He just left the rest."

"Well, what do you think?" Clark asked when we were outside.

"Congratulations," Bevins commented. "There's not much doubt and he didn't leave too much out except calling her a bitch."

"Does he do that every time?" Morse asked.

"No, but he seems to be using it more and more and also 'fuck' or 'fuckin'," Bevins answered.

"They told me this morning that he used the word fuck in just about every sentence," Clark stated. "But they never mentioned 'bitch'."

"The size of Erickson's arms and wrists, I'm surprised that a shoelace went around him. EAR must have shit when he saw how big he was," Bevins remarked.

"As near as we can tell, he had four shoelaces tied around his wrists. He sure as hell didn't take any chances," Morse advised.

"How many times have you two been hit?" Clark asked.

"We've been hit twenty-eight times counting the one last month that he didn't complete. We think he got scared off when the daughter's alarm clock went off, but he beat the hell out of her face for screaming," Bevins answered. "Larry's been hit four times counting the two in Concord, and Sac P.D. had three, Stockton P.D. had two, Modesto two, Davis three, and we finally found out that San Jose had two."

"Don't feel bad. We didn't get any information from San Jose. I guess they don't need help from anyone," Clark stated.

"Seems to be a fact of life between police departments. Personally, I don't care who catches him as long as somebody does," Bevins said.

"That's the way I feel ," I remarked. "Look, we have copies of all the cases. Jim gave us everything he had and we picked up the San Jose rapes, so you're welcome to use our office to go over them. We're a lot closer to you than Sacramento and believe me, the more you know about EAR the better off you'll be."

"Thanks. We'll take you up on it and if we get hit again, if it's all right with the two of you, we'll call you right away," Morse stated.

"Call either one of us and we'll both show up," Bevins answered.

After the Fremont attack, Voorhies and I were reinstated on a stand-by schedule, each of us taking a week at a time. We both agreed that we would not receive any extra pay for the stand-by. The schedule would run from 5:00 p.m. Friday through 8:00 a.m. Monday and we would both carry pagers during the week. If an attack occurred, we would contact our lieutenant, John Gackowski.

On April 12th, John Walker was stopped for speeding on I-680 southbound near Crow Canyon Road at 1:00 p.m. by the California Highway Patrol. He was driving a 1979 maroon and white pick up. C.H.P. sent a copy of the citation to the Task Force.

In the meantime, I was working on the list of parolees I had received. Voorhies and I agreed to work on those paroled to Sacramento County first as we believed that EAR had lived in Sacramento during the first twenty-two rapes.

Other infamous rapists, including Berkeley's "Stinky," Sacramento's "Wooley Rapist," and San Jose's "Pillow Case Rapist," all started their rapes within four months of being released from prison. Most of these serial rapists had no prior rape arrests. We decided to stick with the six-month period I had requested from the Department of Justice files.

I narrowed the list of possible suspects to approximately seven hundred names and contacted the Department of Justice in Sacramento which in turn pulled the folders of the parolees released from the adult facilities.

During the next two weeks Voorhies, Franklin, and I traveled to Sacramento every day to go through the folders. By using elimination factors of black, in-custody during blocks of rapes, over six three, under five six, and over fifty years of age, the list was reduced further. To our amazement, several parolees had committed rapes using similar M.O.s as those used by EAR.

Forty-three parolees had been released from parole and their folders were kept in the archives at the California Medical Facility. These folders were pulled for us and again the process started. Twenty-two were eliminated, thirteen due to blood type.

Files on thirty-three inmates released from the California Youth Authority were pulled for us and eighteen were eliminated using the same elimination factors.

A copy of the remaining list of seventy-six names was sent to the Department of Justice to obtain fingerprints. The prints were given to the crime lab for comparison.

Placer, San Joaquin, and Yolo County parolees were researched using the same process. A beginning list of approximately four hundred was narrowed down to forty-one possible suspects.

Some parolees were eliminated after chewing on the gauze strips and showing as secretors. Physical disabilities eliminated others, and some had died or been killed.

By the end of May the list of parolees had been reduced from approximately eleven hundred to seventy-one: twenty-eight paroled to Sacramento County, ten to Yolo, twelve to Placer, and twenty-one to San Joaquin.

Forty-two were given a high priority listing. Nine of these would be eliminated over the next months in addition to eight from the lower priority list.

On the evening of May 16th, a thirty-eight year old San Ramon housewife was doing laundry in her garage. As she walked back into the residence she saw a twenty-five to thirty year old white male wearing a jogging suit and a black knit watch cap walking across her living room. Upon seeing the woman, the intruder ran out the patio door, through the open side gate, and north on Joaquin Drive toward Camino Ramon. Deputies Ron Britton and Buzz Walker searched the area with negative results.

CHAPTER FIFTY-FOUR

A **WALNUT CREEK** HOUSEWIFE, Sabrina Olivera, mother of a seventeen year old daughter, called Walnut Creek P.D. Someone had entered their San Carlos Drive home and stole a nightgown. An address book lying on the counter had also been taken.

June 2, 1979,
El Divisadero Drive, Walnut Creek. 11:34 p.m.

The pretty seventeen year old eleventh grader was sitting at the kitchen table doing her homework. "Saturday Night Live" had just started on television.

Although Pamela Olivera frequently babysat for the Beachwoods, it had been over a month since the last time. As she tried to ignore the sounds from the television in the next room and concentrate on the book in front of her, something drew her attention to the doorway leading from the kitchen to the hallway. She looked around and saw him.

He stood there, the white mask covering his face, the hunting knife still in the sheath in his right hand.

Her heart stopped, her breathing stopped, the world stopped as he ran toward her and pushed her head down onto the table with his gloved hand.

"Larry," the familiar voice began when I rolled over and picked up the ringing telephone beside my bed. "We just had a rape and I think you might be interested. Don't, under any circumstances, tell anyone I called or I'll get fired. No one knows I'm calling, but I think EAR hit. The victim's a seventeen year old babysitter. She's babysitting at a home on El Divisadero, just off Ygnacio Valley Road, down from the John Muir Hospital."

I looked at the clock: five minutes before midnight.

"I'll be right there. Thanks," I told my friend and hung up. I called Bevins at home. No answer, so I called Sacramento S.O. and left a message for him. Then I called Gackowski and gave him the news.

I arrived at the Walnut Creek residence around 1:00 a.m. and met with officers Ron O'Dell and Tom Cassani. Ron I knew from previous contacts. Tom I knew from his time with the EAR Task Force. O'Dell was photographing the exterior of the residence. Cassani walked me up the driveway.

"I just got here a while ago," Cassani began, "but I had a chance to talk to the victim before Steve Dorsey took her to John Muir. Masks, clenched teeth, threats, gloves, flashlight, knife, and she was bound real tight with her hands tied behind her back. Like to have you take a look inside and see what you think and then we can take a ride to the hospital and talk to the victim.

"She's a seventeen year old who was babysitting here. She was doing her homework at the kitchen table and looked up and there he was. Took her into the master bedroom and raped her. Two young kids slept through it and apparently he didn't disturb their rooms."

When we entered the house, the feeling was back: the presence of EAR was still there. Plastic bindings, similar to flex cuffs, had been used to secure the teenager's wrists and were lying on the floor where they had been dropped after being cut free. A knotted pantyhose, a knotted halter top, a cloth belt, and strips of torn towel, still knotted, were at the foot of the bed. All had been used to gag and blindfold the young girl.

"I called Gary Ford. He's the Patrol Watch Commander tonight. He said he would call your lieutenant and offer Search and Rescue bloodhounds and any other help you wanted," I advised.

"I heard he was transferred to Patrol after he was promoted and I'm glad for him. He'll make a good lieutenant. One of the dogs is already here, by the way. Judy somebody. Sergeant Dorsey is with her. She took the dog into the house and he immediately went to the master bedroom, jumped up and smelled the bathroom vanity, and took off out the door and down the street. I haven't heard anything so they must still be looking," Cassani explained.

"That would be Judy Robb. She's good and her dogs are excellent. I doubt if they'll go more than two blocks before they find where he left his car," I answered. "Did she have anybody else from Search and Rescue with her?"

"Yeah. I think he said his name was Milt."

"Milt Hall. He's one of the S.A.R. coordinators. Here's another dog handler now," I remarked as a station wagon pulled up in front of the residence and Lynn Hansen and her bloodhound, Betsy, got out. Cassani and I followed Lynn and her dog into the residence and Tom showed her the areas that the rapist had been known to have been. Her dog repeated the scenario that Tom had said Judy's dog had followed.

The dog became extremely excited when she entered the bathroom. Spittle flew from her mouth as she shook her head.

Tom and I followed as the dog exited through the bedroom sliding glass door, around the house to the side gate, through the open gate, down El Divisadero and San Carlos to San Jose Court where the dog lost the scent. Judy Robb, Pita, and Sergeant Dorsey were at the same location.

When we met with Dorsey, he told us that a juvenile on Los Banos Court near Ygnacio Valley Road had stopped an officer and told him a bicycle had been stolen from in front of his residence between 9:30 and 11:30 p.m. The bicycle had subsequently been located in front of a residence on El Divisadero. The chain was off the sprocket when it was found.

Had the rapist used the bicycle for transportation? EAR had on previous attacks.

Cassani and I met the victim Pamela Olivera, her mother, Chris, and Steve Dorsey at the hospital. Also present were two women from the Rape Crisis Center. Dorsey advised us that the rape examination had been completed and explained his observations when he first arrived on the scene.

After talking briefly with the victim and her mother, it was agreed that they would accompany Dorsey and me back to the scene so the victim could explain the sequence of events for processing. I further requested that Dorsey and I be allowed to accompany them to Pamela's residence for an in-depth interview as I felt she would feel more comfortable at her own home. I also recommended that the two Rape Crisis counselors be in attendance. Dorsey agreed with my request, as did the others.

Dorsey contacted Sergeant Sutton and advised him that we felt it was an EAR attack and that it might be appropriate to have the Crime Lab respond to help with the processing. Sutton advised that he would contact Ford to request the assistance. Dorsey and I returned to the scene and met with Pamela, who explained the scene for the techs. Cassani remained at the hospital to meet with criminalists John Patty and Dorothy Northey, who would be responding to collect the rape kit and help with the processing.

When I arrived at the scene, Sutton advised me that a Pleasant Hill officer had made a traffic stop on a subject who fit the description of Oliver's attacker. The subject had been arrested for drunk driving and subsequent to the arrest a hunting knife in a sheath and a pair of suede gloves had been found in the vehicle.

Officer O'Dell had responded to the traffic stop and with the subject's agreement had transported him to the Walnut Creek Police Department to wait for Dorsey and me to interview him.

A third S.A.R. dog handler, Bev Mestressat, and her bloodhound, Eli, had arrived prior to our return and Eli had followed the same trail as the first two dogs.

Later Dorsey and I met the Olivera family and the two Rape Crisis people at the Olivera residence. At my request, Pamela's parents left the room and allowed Dorsey and me to talk with Pamela. I felt she would be more open if the parents were not present at the time. Rape Crisis also remained during the taped conversation.

Pamela had been sitting at the kitchen table doing her homework when something had caught her attention. She looked toward the hallway and saw a male wearing a loose fitting white mask and holding a hunting knife still in the sheath in his right hand. He grabbed her and forced her head down onto the table, telling her to shut up and not look at him. He had threatened to slit her throat if she didn't do as he told her. He took her by the arm and walked her to the master bedroom and pushed her onto the bed telling her to shut up and put her hands behind her back. He then tied her wrists so tight she lost feeling in her hands. He had also tied her ankles.

She told us that he had rubbed the knife up and down her neck, telling her that if she wasn't quiet he would slit her throat. He continuously told her he wanted money; however, he never asked where it was. He also had used the word "fuck" during the whole ordeal. She had been blindfolded and gagged with a towel and pantyhose. Although she couldn't see she heard him rummaging throughout the bedroom and bathroom.

He rolled her onto her back and then untied her ankles and removed her shoes, socks, pants, and underpants. She heard him remove his pants and she could tell he was standing beside her. She said it sounded as though he were masturbating and then he was on top of her and telling her to spread her legs.

"Have you ever fucked before?" he had hissed. She couldn't tell him she was still a virgin because of the gag in her mouth. He pushed and pushed. He became frustrated when he couldn't enter her and got up off the bed. She felt herself being rolled onto her stomach and then felt his wet penis in her hands. He told her to play with it, feel it, move up and down.

Again he had rolled her onto her back and again he straddled her. She felt her sweater being lifted and felt him tearing at her bra, ripping it off. He bit her on the left nipple, once, twice, three times. Easy bites. Then he bit her hard, leaving teeth marks on her breast, bringing even more pain to the young girl. He pushed at her, this time succeeding. He got off her and rolled her onto her stomach.

"Don't move or I'll kill you," he hissed at her.

She could hear him getting dressed and then she felt the knife at her neck.

"I'm going to leave. Don't scream for help or anything or I'll cut your throat," he had threatened her, and then he was gone.

"When was the last time you babysat at this house?" I asked.

"Normally I babysit every Saturday night but I haven't for the last two months," Pamela replied.

"Have you received any phone calls lately where the caller hangs up or any obscene phone calls?" I asked.

"Yes. I got them at home and at places where I babysat. No one answered but I know they are there," Pamela answered.

"Do you babysit often? Other than where you were last night?"

"Yes, quite a bit."

"But you haven't been sitting for the Muirs for a couple of months?"

"No. At least two months."

When Dorsey and I left the Olivera residence we went directly to the Walnut Creek P.D. to talk to the person arrested by Pleasant Hill. He was willing to talk. He had been with friends all evening at a party and had left the party just minutes before he had been stopped. His alibi checked out. He was not Pamela Olivera's rapist. He was not EAR. He was booked for drunk driving and then released by O'Dell.

"The lieutenant wants to see you," Ron O'Dell advised me. "He's in his office."

I walked into the lieutenant's office and met with the Walnut Creek Watch Commander. "Lieutenant," I acknowledged him."

"Sergeant, understand something. We don't want your help, we don't need your help. We don't want you in our city. We don't want your Task Force in our city. We can do our own job. Understand?" the lieutenant glowered at me.

"Look, Lieutenant. I'm not here to interfere with your investigation or your Department. You were hit by the East Area Rapist tonight and up until two months ago you had an officer on the Task Force. He has access to our files and Sergeant Voorhies and I will be more than willing to help," I tried to explain.

"The East Area Rapist has not been in our town and will never be in our town. If you go to the press, we will deny it. We don't want you in our town," the lieutenant continued.

"You were hit by the East Area Rapist and this wasn't his intended victim. He's going to hit you again and it will be within the next month and in the same neighborhood. He wasn't after this one. He took her because she was there and he'll be back to get the one he had targeted," I replied.

"And I told you we would handle our city ourselves and I want you out of my town," he replied.

"You got it, Lieutenant. I'm gone."

On the way out I told Dorsey that the lieutenant didn't want any help and I was on my way home.

Tom Cassani, knowing that prior victims had received phone calls after the attacks, contacted Pacific Telephone Security and had phone traps placed on the Olivera and Muir lines. Tom called me at the Task Force and gave me an update. He had heard of the lieutenant's attitude toward the Task Force. He also advised that a canvass of the area had uncovered several people who had been receiving hang-up phone calls over the past month. He would also make sure we got copies of all the reports.

Three women living near the Walnut Creek Municipal Golf Course reported a prowler in their backyard. When the officer interviewed them, he learned that they had been receiving phone calls over the past two weeks. They were asked to check their photo albums for missing pictures. A picture of one of them in a bikini was missing as was one of her very well built daughter from the top of the dresser.

Cassani advised the women that the EAR Watch Units would be watching the house for the next couple of nights. He also advised them that several officers were working nights, riding bikes in the area. This would continue for a couple of weeks. Cassani also had a phone trap placed on the women's phone.

Contra Costa Times, 6-5-76

WALNUT CREEK - Authorities said Monday they still aren't sure if the East Area Rapist was responsible for the attack on a 17 year old babysitter over the weekend.

"There are as many dissimilarities in the case as similarities," said Lt. Robert Van Horst, head of investigations. "You run into the difficulty of a possible copycat."

Van Horst declined to elaborate further on the findings...

Van Horst said police investigators are conducting a "standard neighborhood search" of the area in hopes of producing new clues to the puzzling rape...

Contra Costa Times, 6-6-79

WALNUT CREEK - The East Area Rapist may have been responsible for an attack on a 17 year old babysitter late Saturday night in the Eikler - Rancho San Miguel subdivision.

Law enforcement officials have remained tightlipped about the investigation and refused to officially confirm or deny that the 10:00 p.m. attack in the quiet residential neighborhood near San Carlos Drive and Ygnacio Valley Road was committed by the East Area Rapist.

However, the Times has learned that at least two East Area Rapist task force investigators and members of the Contra Costa County crime lab were summoned late Saturday night to assist Walnut Creek police in the case.

"It's looking more and more like it was the East Area Rapist," a source said. "The attack was very violent, forceful, and aggressive..".

The El Capitan, Danville resident, a twenty year old, turned out the lights as he walked toward his bedroom. It was 11:45 p.m., June 10th, and he had to go to work in the morning. He hadn't yet fallen asleep when he heard footsteps crunching the lava rock path outside his bedroom window. Quietly he got out of bed and peered through the window curtains.

CHAPTER FIFTY-FOUR

A male wearing a dark t-shirt was standing just five feet away looking toward the neighbor's house. He watched as the male subject moved toward the front of the side yard and scrambled over the fence. For several minutes the twenty year old waited, watching out the window. Then he dressed and went outside. He walked east on El Capitan, and as he approached Allegheny Drive, he saw the subject get on a ten speed bicycle. When the subject saw him, he sped away, turning south on Mustang Drive.

The twenty year old returned home and called Sheriff's Dispatch.

On Delta Drive, a baby began to cry. The young mother checked on the infant, soothed her for a few minutes, and returned to bed.

At fifteen minutes past midnight, Deputy Keith Dale arrived and checked the area of El Capitan. He was unable to locate the subject on the bicycle.

At 2:30 a.m. an Allegheny Drive couple heard a noise outside their bedroom window. The husband looked out of the bedroom window. Nothing could be seen and the husband noted that the lights were off at Clay Cerro's house next door. He went back to bed. He did not notice his open side gate.

The dark figure waited in the shadows of the Cerro's backyard. He had checked the windows and doors and found one window that was unlocked. And still he waited.

The young couple sleeping inside, Clay and Ellen Cerro, were unaware of the unidentified stranger roaming their neighborhood. Soon they would be fully aware. Never again would they find peace in darkness.

The figure silently approached the unlocked window and slid it open. Effortlessly he slithered through and into the bedroom of the sleeping five year old child. He left the room, pieces of damp earth falling from his tennis shoes onto the soft carpet.

Ellen Cerro stirred from her sleep. Something had entered her subconscious. A noise? A voice? She looked toward the bedroom door and she saw him. A masked intruder holding a flashlight. She could see the reflection on the handgun he held in his right hand. She nudged her sleeping husband.

"Clay. Wake up," she whispered, her breath coming in short gasps.

"Neither one of you motherfuckers move or I'll blow your fucking heads off," the masked man hissed. "All I want is money."

He was quickly at Clay Cerro's side, the gun pressing against his temple.

"One move and I'll kill every motherfucker in the house," he threatened as he cocked the hammer back on the revolver, the sound echoing through Clay Cerro's brain. Clay started to swing his feet off the bed. The masked intruder grabbed his ankles, slinging his feet back onto the bed.

"Don't move again or I'll blow your fuckin' head off," he hissed through clenched teeth. "Get on your stomach and put your face in the pillow. Put your hands behind your back. Tie his hands," he demanded and threw shoelaces at Ellen.

She did as he ordered.

"Tighter, tighter," he ordered. "Get on your stomach," he hissed and grabbed her hands and tied her wrists. The white shoelaces cut into her skin as he pulled the laces tight. He retied Clay's wrists, cutting off the circulation to his hands. He tied their ankles, Clay's as tight as he had tied his wrists, Ellen's loose.

"Where's the money? All I want is the money, then I can get back to the city or I can kill every motherfucker here and leave," he hissed.

"In my purse under the bar," Ellen answered, her voice trembling.

"My wallet's in my pants pocket," Clay answered.

"Shut up and quit screaming," he hissed.

"All right. You asked me," Clay remarked.

"It's not here. Your wallet's not here. Don't lie to me. Where's your billfold?" he demanded.

"In my other pants in the den," Clay answered.

"Don't move or I'll kill you," the intruder hissed as he left the room. Minutes later he was back.

"You moved, didn't you? You tried to untie him, didn't you?" he challenged.

He checked Clay's wrists and then pulled Ellen from the bed and untied her ankles. He gagged Clay with a yellow hand towel and then gagged and blindfolded Ellen.

"Where's your purse? I can't find it," he hissed and pushed Ellen out the door and down the hall to the den.

"Shut up," he ordered as he lowered Ellen to the floor and retied her ankles. Then he was gone.

He was back in the bedroom, again checking Clay's ties. He pulled the bed sheet over him and lined several perfume bottles along his back.

"If I hear the bottles jingle, I'll blow your fuckin' head off," he threatened as he cocked the gun and pushed it against Clay's head. "You don't like it do you? There's nothing you can do about it," he taunted.

They could hear him rummaging, opening and closing cabinet doors and drawers.

"I'm hungry," he hissed as he stood over Ellen. "I need something to eat."

She could hear him in the refrigerator. She heard him open a can of beer, Olympia, the only canned drink in the house.

"I want to fuck you, Ellen," he was near her again. The use of her name startled her. Her purse. He had been in her purse.

She was on her stomach, her hands tied behind her. She felt his penis in her hands.

"Play with it. Stroke it," he demanded. He was not fully erect when he stood.

"I want you to suck me, Eileen," he hissed. He was mistaken. He didn't know her. He called her by the wrong name.

He forced her to do as he ordered. She could feel his bare hands run up and down her body from her neck to her thighs. He was beside her again, rolling her onto her back and again the laces were removed from her ankles. He bent her legs and he entered her.

He was away from her again, rummaging, and then he was back, touching her shoulder with something.

"I have to take these out to the van. Don't move or I'll blow your head off. I'll be back," he hissed.

He never did come back.

At 5:16 a.m. Deputy Keith Dale, 1Z14, received the call. "261 P.C., victims still tied." He arrived at the Allegheny address at 5:20 a.m. Two minutes later, 1Z13, Deputy Al Burt, arrived. Clay Cerro was standing in the driveway, his hands still tied behind his back. Ellen Cerro was still on her stomach on the den floor, tied, gagged, blindfolded, and naked.

Sergeant Tom Coggan, the patrol supervisor, arrived, took control of the scene, and called the Watch Commander, Lieutenant Gary Ford. It was an EAR attack.

Coggan had Burt transport Ellen Cerro to John Muir Hospital.

At 5:45 a.m., I received the call from Ford. I was to respond to John Muir to meet with the victim. Radio was calling Voorhies to respond to the scene. Search and Rescue, the Lab, and detectives would be called to help. As soon as I got off the phone with Ford, I called Bevins. He would meet me at the scene as soon as he could get there from Sacramento.

Judy Robb and her bloodhound had followed a trail from the scene to Delta Way, a few blocks away. As in previous attacks, the trail ended.

I met with Ellen Cerro at John Muir and after talking to her, agreed that it was an EAR attack. Karen Sheldon, the Criminalist, arrived to collect the rape kit and Cerro's clothing. Ellen told me that her attacker had touched her bare skin with his bare hands during the assault. Sheldon used a magna-brush on Cerro's chest, abdomen, and inner thigh areas in an attempt to develop fingerprints. None were located.

When I arrived at the scene I met with Voorhies and Peg Bowen and we went through the house with Clay Cerro.

At 9:00 a.m. Deputy Burt arrived back at the residence with Ellen Cerro. Voorhies, Bowen, and I interviewed her alone. During the interview, Bevins arrived and sat in on the taped conversation. Later we interviewed Clay. Although both victims were extremely upset, they handled the attack well. They would survive.

Shoe impressions were found in several yards in the area. All matches, and casts were made and photographed. Karen Sheldon took a photograph to a sporting goods store at the Sun Valley Mall and a clerk recognized the pattern as an Adidas "Tobacco" model, a non-sport casual shoe. After measuring it, it was determined that the shoe was a definite size nine and a half.

In talking to an Adidas representative, Karen learned that this particular shoe had been manufactured for eight years and approximately one and a half million pairs had been sold in the thirteen western states.

Voorhies, Bowen, Bevins, and I canvassed the neighborhood. At 3:00 p.m. Voorhies was contacted by a neighbor who had been on the way to work around 5:00 a.m. As he had turned onto Camino Ramon from El Capitan he saw a van, described as three to five years old, pulled close to the trees. The van was a dark blue-green, possibly a Chevrolet, with a double rear door with small windows and single rectangular taillights.

Before Bevins left, we talked.

"Thanks for coming, Jim." I remarked.

"Thanks for calling me. I guess he hasn't left the area, has he?" Bevins stated. "Anything else from the Walnut Creek hit?"

"Nope. They still refuse to cooperate. I don't think it's the investigators. They seem to be okay, so I guess it's just the Administration. Seems dumb, but egos have a way of making people dumb. Tom Cassani keeps us informed, but he has to walk on thin ice."

"Any chance of your Task Force being started up again?" Bevins asked.

"I don't know, but I wouldn't be surprised. Voo and I will talk to our lieutenant later today," I answered.

"Speaking of Voorhies, has he lost weight? He almost looks sick," Bevins stated.

"His wife left him awhile ago. Moved in with a long haired hippy dope smoker, I guess. Ron said he didn't suspect anything. I think they were married. Been together quite awhile. Anyway, Ron is into exercising, working out. I think he's doing okay now," I explained.

"Well, I'll head back home and let the Sheriff know that EAR's still alive and kicking in Contra Costa County. Let me know if I can give you a hand." Bevins left.

After briefing Gackowski, Lieutenant Van Orden, and Assistant Sheriff Dillon, Sheriff Rainey issued a press release.

News Release

Sheriff-Coroner Richard K. Rainey announced today that the department is investigating a reported rape in the Greenbrook area, Danville, believed to have been committed by the East Area Rapist.

The East Area Rapist is believed to be responsible for approximately 45 reported rapes in Sacramento, Davis, Stockton, Modesto, Concord, Danville, San Jose, Fremont, and Walnut Creek over a three year period of time.

The latest incident happened between 4:00 a.m. and 4:45 a.m. this date in a home in Danville. Entry was gained through an open bedroom window.

The suspect's description and activities inside the residence were similar to those as previously reported in other cases.

This incident is being jointly investigated by this agency, Walnut Creek P.D., Concord P.D., Sacramento S.O., and Pleasant Hill P.D.

Sheriff Rainey wishes to alert the residents of the county and request that windows and doors be kept secured and locked during the hours of darkness even when someone is awake; exterior lights should be left on; and any unusual or suspicious activity should be reported immediately to the police...

"The Sheriff is starting up the Task Force again," Lieutenant Van Orden told Voorhies and me. "Concord, Walnut Creek, and Pleasant Hill have agreed to send their people back on a limited time basis. I'm going to be in charge of the unit and Sergeant Carpenter will be acting lieutenant until further notice.

"The Sheriff is also starting up a Patrol Division Crisis Response Unit. They will work the Danville/San Ramon area with Sergeant Sizemore in charge of four deputies. They will work from 9:30 p.m. until 7:30 a.m. Three will have Monday, Tuesday, Wednesday off, and two will have Saturday, Sunday, Monday off so they'll cover every night. They've been instructed to coordinate with you two at all times.

"Larry, you and Voo will still take the stand-by and if there is a hit, radio has the call-out list. I've set up the five members of the Crime Prevention team to do the neighborhood canvass if you request them. This will all take effect as of now except for the Police Department members. They will be with us next Monday."

Contra Costa Times, 6-12-79

Danville Woman Latest Victim of East Area Rapist

DANVILLE - The East Area Rapist struck here around 5:00 a.m. Monday, assaulting a 35 year old Danville housewife only three blocks from an earlier victim's home.

Sheriff's officials said things that occurred inside the home Monday left little doubt that it was the East Area Rapist.

The victim was not beaten by her assailant, who crept in through a sleeping child's bedroom window which had been unlocked.

Valley Pioneer, 6-13-79

Special Meeting

A community meeting to discuss home security and rape prevention will be held tomorrow night in response to the latest attack by the East Area Rapist.

The meeting begins at 8:00 at Baldwin School, 741 Brook-side Drive, Danville, near where Monday morning's attack occurred.

Sheriff's officials and crime prevention members will discuss security measures.

On June 13th, Carpenter put a memo together for the Patrol Division. The memo was provided as a working guide for any beat patrol units responding as the first unit for an EAR attack. He also provided a comprehensive work sheet to be filled out by the first deputy on the scene.

The Patrol Crisis Response Team was actively working the Danville/San Ramon area. The night of June 15th, around midnight, as with the previous nights, members of the team had walked the railroad tracks, brushing clear any shoe impressions.

In the early morning light of the 16th, Deputy Bill Updegraff located shoe impressions in the dirt. The impressions were of a herringbone pattern and were located near Paraiso Drive. Similar impressions were located near El Capitan. The impressions were cast by Criminalist Steve Ojena.

Tri Valley Times, 6-17-79

East Area Rapist Unit asks for call if prowler spotted

DANVILLE - A crowd of worried women and men filled the Baldwin School library Thursday to find out how to protect themselves from the so-called East Area Rapist.

He is believed to have made his third strike in the San Ramon Valley early Monday when he entered a Danville Station home through an open window and bound the husband and raped the wife at gunpoint.

Five extra sheriff's patrol cars are on the streets of Danville these nights as a result of the attack, sheriff's officers told the tense crowd.

But residents themselves must take the responsibility to calling the law about anything unusual so those patrol officers can respond, speakers emphasized.

Sgt. Rod Carpenter, coordinator of the East Area Rapist Unit in Contra Costa County, said that after almost each of the approxi-

mately 45 attacks attributed to the rapist, neighbors have later said that they suspected prowlers nearby, but did not call police.

Even in the latest local incident, Carpenter said a woman around the corner from the victim's home heard a noise at 1:30 a.m. and saw a figure outside, but did not call.

In another case elsewhere, screams were heard but the neighbors just went back to sleep. In another instance, someone saw a masked man in dark clothes near a vacationing neighbor's home, but didn't call. Meantime, the neighbors returned and were attacked.

Callers should not ask the telephone company operator to help because of possible delays in answering. One rape victim counted 26 phone rings when she called the operator when she heard someone enter the house, according to Sgt. Larry Crompton, who also spoke.

Tensions between the audience and Carpenter put an edge on part of the meeting when the questioners' curiosity ran up against his reluctance to give away anything which would hamper investigation.

A woman who said she lived alone at the end of a cul de sac said, "I feel a hostility between us because of your reluctance to answer questions. I'm angry because you won't help me."

Another audience member said, "We are all serious but your answers are flip."

Crompton eased the crowd's dissatisfaction somewhat by briefly answering questions about the rapist's possible pattern. The man often returns to the same area for more attacks, Crompton said, but no pattern has been determined as to factors such as times, nearness to freeways, proximity to garage sales or houses for sale.

Carolyn Hendrickson of the San Ramon Crime Prevention Committee, who helped organize several community meetings after a San Ramon attack thought to be by the same intruder, reminded the group to put the local crime in perspective and "remember this person is not a superman." Statistics for 1978 show 217 rapes in Contra Costa, she said. Other speakers stressed the importance of keeping doors and windows locked and outside lights on.

CHAPTER FIFTY-FOUR

Neighborhood awareness was emphasized as a key to protection. People were urged to note strangers and unusual cars and to call the sheriff's office...

"Patrol is going to start making random car stops in the Strip," Carpenter advised the Task Force members. "Captain Al Moore made the decision to start stopping people after dark. Just uniformed deputies will be making the stops. They won't be running warrant checks, so hopefully there won't be too much flack."

"The ACLU will be up in arms if they hear about it. They seem to be against anything that helps citizens and hurts the bad guys," I remarked.

"Moore says we might get some information or at least we might chase him off before complaints stop us," Carpenter remarked. "By the way, it's good to see everybody back although it would be nice to have Gary Ford back as our lieutenant."

"Having him in patrol will help us. At least he'll keep things stirred up and moving forward," I said.

"Where do we stand on suspects? Larry, you eliminated the real estate guy, didn't you?" Carpenter asked.

"Yup. Wrong blood type. I hope we're right about EAR's blood type because Pippin is a non-secretor, although I don't think he's our rapist anyway. No real Sacramento contacts during the rapes."

"What about your railroad man, Hal?" Carpenter asked Franklin.

"He's still good. On the night of the Walnut Creek's hit he called in sick," Hal responded.

"What about the night of the Danville attack?" Carpenter continued.

"I've got an appointment to look at his time sheets this Wednesday. His supervisor says he worked the eleven p.m. to eleven a.m. shift, but I don't trust their scheduling," Franklin replied.

"God damn it, Hal, we've eliminated Walker. I eliminated him, you eliminated him, and you won't even believe your own work. He's weird, but he isn't EAR," Voorhies ranted.

"I've proven they can get off work at any time and I think he's EAR," Franklin responded.

"Larry, you want to go with Hal Wednesday?" Carpenter asked.

"Sure, as long as Hal doesn't drive. I'd like to live long enough to see EAR caught," I laughed.

"How about your list of parolees? Anything look good?" Carpenter asked.

"Hal and Voo really helped me on them. We went through about six thousand parolees altogether. I guess I still have less than a hundred to check on further. I've made personal contacts with several in Sacramento but there are quite a few I haven't been able to track down.

"More than one of them used the same M.O. as EAR, or least real similar. The first time we came across one we almost had a heart attack. Thought sure we had EAR, but the parolee was back in prison during most of the rapes. I'm still working them and I've got an appointment at the Vacaville Medical Facility with one of their psychologists who works with the sex offenders. She asked me to bring along some reports so she can look at them. I go to see her Friday," I advised.

"Anything more on the Danville rape?" Carpenter asked.

"Nothing. Sizemore has his people checking the tree farm in San Ramon, the golf courses and parks as well as looking for open side gates. He says they have chased a few prowlers and stopped a few hundred joggers, but so far nothing solid," Voorhies explained. "We did a hypnosis on the neighbor who saw the van the morning of the rape. Really does look like it was EAR's van, but we didn't get anything more from him than what we had. Patrol has the description, so maybe they'll turn it up."

"Well, they found Larry's real estate man for him, so maybe we'll get lucky," Carpenter commented.

"They stopped three orange BMWs. The last one was the jackpot. We've got some good deputies out there. If the van's there, they'll find it," I advised.

Franklin and I contacted the train master in Milpitas who checked Walker's schedule. He was scheduled to work the night of the Walnut Creek rape, however called in sick. He worked the night of the Danville rape from eleven p.m. on the 10th through eleven a.m. on the 11th.

It was explained that the train crews have a special series of duties. They have to have the Ford Motor yard set up by five a.m. Monday morning. Walker's crew was the crew that started "spotting the house," which means putting the cars in the Ford Motor plant.

"Are they allowed to leave when they finish?" Franklin asked.

"Yes, but that seldom happens," the train master answered.

"Did he work April 3rd and 4th?" Franklin asked.

"No, he called in sick."

The next day Voorhies and I found John Walker at his girlfriend's house in San Jose. He was uncooperative and reminded us that his attorney had ordered us to leave him alone.

"Look, I know you're not a rapist," I began, "All I want to do is eliminate you as a suspect so our boss will get off our case. All you have to do is chew on some gauze for me and that will be it. You'll never hear from us again."

"Fuck you. My attorney told me not to talk to you. I don't have to do anything you say," Walker stated.

"That's true, but if you're not guilty of anything, why not just chew on the gauze," I tried to explain.

"You might try to use it against me for something else, so I'm not going to do it," Walker remarked.

"We can't use it against you if you did do something. We didn't admonish you and your attorney told you not to talk to us, so no judge would ever let it into court. We just want to set you free," I continued.

"I don't trust cops. You're always hassling people. You hassle people who smoke marijuana and it doesn't hurt anyone. I know all about you," Walker started to leave.

"You smoke marijuana?" I asked.

"That's none of your business, but I know it doesn't hurt anybody. It isn't a dangerous drug and it should be legal," Walker ranted.

"Look, I don't care about your drug habit. I don't really care about you. Our boss tells us to do our job and our job is to eliminate you as a suspect. If I thought you were a rapist, we wouldn't be here. We would be watching every move you made. We don't want to be here any more than you want us here. All you need to do is chew on the gauze," I tried to explain.

"I'm going to call my mother and tell her you're still harassing me. Our attorney told you to stay away from me." Walker went into the house and closed the door.

"He's a stupid motherfucker, but he's still not EAR," Voorhies remarked.

"He's a good candidate for the loony bin, all right. Want to try talking to his boss again?" I asked.

"Might as well, but they're probably as sick of us as Walker is," Voorhies answered.

Once again Walker's supervisor went over the crew's schedule.

"You're sure that none of the crew can leave during their shift?" I asked.

"If they leave they have to turn in their time. If it shows they were working, they were working," the supervisor explained.

When we got back to the office, Carpenter was waiting.

"The sheriff got a call from Walker's attorney. He's going to court to get a restraining order. He just mentioned you, Larry, so apparently Ron didn't bother him," Carpenter informed us.

"He's not EAR. Ron and I went over his time sheets. He was working during some of the rapes. He refused to chew on the gauze for us, but if nothing else, he's too stupid to be EAR. He's a dope smoking, paranoid, brain dead momma's boy but he's not EAR. If Hal wants to make him a career case, that's his business, but as far as I'm concerned, he's eliminated," I ranted.

"Well, we've been told to stay away from him," Carpenter advised.

"Then this must be our lucky day," Voorhies remarked.

I met with the medical staff at the Vacaville Medical Center in Vacaville and left several rape synopses. The psychologist working with the prison sex offenders read the reports, talked to her sex offenders. She would give me her feedback the following week.

Many mentally deficient inmates are housed at the V.M.C., including Charles Manson and numerous repeat sex offenders.

5:00 a.m., June 25th

"Larry, Tom Cassani," Tom said when I picked up the phone. "You awake? We just got hit again."

"I've been awake since four wondering where EAR is and what we're missing. Who got hit? Walnut Creek?" I answered.

"Yeah, same area as last time only this time it was a thirteen year old. I'm going to start the call-out, but I wanted you to be here. I guess it's okay with my Department since the Task Force is back up," Tom remarked. "I'll call your watch commander."

"I'll meet you there," I told him after I had written down the address.

When I arrived, Sergeant Bruce Cockerham, the Walnut Creek supervisor, was standing outside the house. Doug Sizemore, the Sheriff's Patrol Response Team supervisor and Sergeant Tom Coggan, the Sheriff's patrol supervisor, were talking to him. Cockerham explained the scene and showed me the inside of the house.

The victim, thirteen year old Ashley Watkins, had been taken to John Muir Hospital. Criminalist Karen Sheldon and Ron Voorhies were to meet her there. Her sixteen year old sister, who had not been attacked, was with her as was her father.

When we entered the house, Cockerham stated that the only room that the rapist had been in was the victim's bedroom.

White bindings, still knotted, had been cut from the teenager's wrists and were lying on a cutting board in the kitchen. A bra that Cockerham explained had been used to gag the victim was lying on the father's bed.

On entering the girl's bedroom, my first observation was that the room had been trashed by the rapist. Clothes were strewn around the room, and dresser drawers were standing open, clothes hanging from them. Normal disarray, Cockerham explained to me. She had told him it was always like this.

More twine was on the floor at the foot of Ashley Watkins's bed as were the young girl's underpants.

Another piece of white twine was found on the ground outside the bedroom window. The father had stated that the twine did not come from his house. The rapist must have brought it with him.

We left the house just as Judy Robb and her bloodhound arrived. When Judy released the dog she immediately picked up the scent and tracked to the victim's house.

"No need to go inside," Judy explained. "She hasn't forgotten the scent from the last time."

Sizemore and I followed Judy and her dog into the backyard, where she gave the 'find' command. The dog went to two sliding glass doors in the back of the house, a window at the side of the house, and also a wooden door. From there the dog proceeded out the open side gate, west on San Pedro Court, right on San Carlos, and left on San Jose Court. Pita lost the scent at the same location as the dogs had tracked to after the first Walnut Creek rape, five minutes from the Watkins' house.

As we were following the trail, Cassani and Frank Fonda arrived. Deputy Bill Porter and Criminalist Steve Ojena arrived shortly after to process the scene.

Voorhies had met Criminalist Sheldon at John Muir Hospital and the two talked to the young victim. Sheldon collected the rape kit and photographed the indentations and bruising on Watkins's wrists.

Because the teenager preferred to have a female officer in attendance during the interview, it was agreed that Ashley, her sixteen year old sister, Bess, and her father would first return to the San Pedro Court residence to explain the scene to the detectives and then to go to the mother's apartment for the interview.

Voorhies arrived at the residence at 7:05 a.m. Carpenter arrived a short time later to coordinate the neighborhood canvass.

Ashley, an extremely beautiful young girl, and her family arrived at 7:35 a.m. and walked Cassani, Porter, and Ojena through the scene.

At 8:45 a.m. Detective Linda Hammes-Wells arrived to help with the interview of the young victim. Cassani briefed Hammes-Wells as to what had happened and also indoctrinated her in the use of the EAR victim interview format and what would be required during the interview.

Cassani and Hammes-Wells accompanied the Watkins to the mother's apartment in Concord and conducted the interview. Her sister and parents were requested to remain in another room.

Ashley had been sound asleep when her attacker had jumped on her back and placed a hand over her mouth.

"Don't say a word. I'm not going to kill you, all I'm looking for is money. All I want is money," were the first words she heard from her attacker.

She felt a knife against her neck and was told to put her hands behind her back. He told her that if she wasn't quiet he would stab her. She heard him rummaging in the bedroom after he had tied her wrists and ankles. When he returned to her bed he again admonished her to be quiet and again hissed, "I'm not going to kill you. All I'm looking for is money. All I want is money."

She heard him applying some kind of lotion to his hands or some part of his body. She heard the sloppy, slippery, sloshing sounds of lotion and then he was straddling her back. She felt his penis in her hand.

"You rub my cock and you better make it good or I'll kill you," he whispered. "I've got my long knife and if I cut you it will be instant death." He got off her and told her to roll onto her back. Her feet were untied and her underpants were taken down over her legs.

"Have you ever been fucked before?" he hissed. "I want you to spread your legs far apart." She felt him pushing into her young virgin body.

"Just do what I want and I won't hurt you. Gimme a good drop or I'll kill you," he threatened.

The investigators questioned her.

"Did he say, 'Give me a good drop?' Do you know what it means? Have you ever heard the expression before?"

Yes, he had, yet no one had ever heard the expression before.

He had pulled out of her and retied her feet.

"If I hear one word out of you, I'll kill you while I'm looking, looking, looky, for money, money, money," he whispered.

Her attacker had been wearing a loose fitting cheese cloth type mask and was described as about six feet tall and not heavy. When he was rummaging she could see he was wearing a type of jogging shorts.

She had been extremely frightened during the ordeal. She had even thought about being cool about it but remembered that a friend had told her that the East Area Rapist liked to be aggressive and the best thing to do when attacked is to act frightened so it wouldn't be so intense.

She recognized the lotion that her rapist had used as Johnson's Baby Lotion. EAR had brought it with him.

Contra Costa Times, 6-26-79

Walnut Creek Rape Under Investigation

WALNUT CREEK - Police are still undecided whether the pre-dawn rape of a 13 year old Walnut Creek girl Monday morning was the work of the notorious East Area Rapist.

"It might be and it might not be. There are similarities," said Lt. Gary R. Johnson of the Walnut Creek Police Department.

Police are sure the rapist who struck Monday was the same attacker who raped a 17 year old babysitter June 2 a short distance away from where the latest attack took place...

Johnson said the investigator who handled the June 2 rape case was positive Monday's rape was committed by the same man.

As a result of a profile study of the East Area Rapist and recent attacks in Contra Costa County during the month of June, Sheriff Rainey authorized a full scale assault on the San Ramon Valley over the upcoming weekend. The Sheriff's Department, California Highway Patrol, and the EAR Task Force, including Fonda, Harper, and Cassani, would provide maximum coverage.

The superintendent of the San Ramon Valley School District authorized the use of the California High School football field as a staging area and command post. Highway Patrol would supply their helicopter and pilot. The Sheriff would supply an observer who knew the area.

Personnel would be divided into two teams, one for the San Ramon area, one for the Danville area. Carpenter would be in charge of the Danville unit, Voorhies in charge of the San Ramon unit.

On Tuesday, June 26th, Carpenter addressed the Task Force members. "KPIX Channel 5 called Sheriff Rainey and asked for someone to be on their morning T.V. talk show this Thursday morning. They heard about EAR and are willing to let us use the show to get information out.

"Larry, the Sheriff wants you to volunteer since you've been involved the most and said to pick one other Task Force member. Anybody want to volunteer?"

"I'll go if no one else is interested," Franklin spoke up.

"It's yours. You and Larry can meet here and go over together," Carpenter advised.

"What kind of show is this and what time is it on?" I asked.

"It's a talk show called 'The Morning Show.' Comes on at six a.m. so they want you there by five. They want you to tell the viewers what to look for and how to protect themselves. Apparently they've had a few viewers call asking for the information. Think you two can handle it?" Carpenter answered.

"Sure, no problem. I drive. I still don't trust Hal behind the wheel. You got an address for the T.V. station?" I asked.

"It's on Van Ness Avenue in San Francisco. 2655 Van Ness. You know how the morning commute traffic is especially getting across the Bay Bridge, so be sure to give yourselves enough time. The show won't wait for you," Carpenter said.

"Dryden Watkins called and said they have had several hang-up phone calls," Cassani advised. "I'm going to call PT&T Security and get a trap set up. He also said that Ashley's hairbrush is missing from her bedroom dresser."

"I've been in the bedroom. How can they tell if anything is missing? Hell, EAR could still be there and we wouldn't be able to find him. My wife would go nuts if she walked in there. Our kids would be dead if they left their rooms like that," I commented.

"I thought the same thing but they're positive that the rapist took it," Cassani advised. "Another thing. We're going to start using bicycles again to try to catch our rapist."

"Your boss still saying it's not EAR?" Carpenter asked.

"Don't confuse me with facts. I've got my mind made up," Voorhies quipped

"That's what they told me," Cassani grinned at Voo's remark and continued, "Also a neighbor who lives directly behind the Watkins received a couple of suspicious phone calls, all hang-ups. He and his wife are in their late forties, so it may just be a coincidence."

Contra Costa Times, 6-27-79

WALNUT CREEK - The East Area Rapist was responsible for Monday's attack on a 13 year old girl in the Rancho San Miguel neighborhood in addition to a similar attack there two weeks ago, according to the county task force investigating the cases.

However, both Walnut Creek police and other investigators familiar with the two recent attacks are reluctant to confirm the task force findings.

Without citing specifics, Task Force Sergeant Rod Carpenter said Tuesday there were several key elements in the two Walnut Creek attacks which led him and fellow investigators to conclude they were committed by the East Area Rapist.

Carpenter noted that the East Area Rapist was responsible for attacking several teenagers, including one other 13 year old girl...

But some law enforcement officials Tuesday were not ready to attribute the two latest attacks to the East Area Rapist.

"My information has not confirmed that the latest incident was the East Area Rapist," Walnut Creek Police Captain Neil Stratton said...

Contra Costa Times, 6-27-79

A Profile of the East Area Rapist

MARTINEZ - A behavioral composite of the so-called East Area Rapist compiled from interviews with victims over the last three years was released Tuesday.

The man who began a string of more than 40 rapes in Sacramento's East Side three years ago dresses in dark clothing, frequently roams the neighborhood before his attack and has been armed in every reported case, said Sheriff Richard Rainey.

The rapist has selected victims between the ages of 13 and 42. He commits his assaults between the hours of 1 a.m. and 5 a.m. and a majority of his break-ins are made in homes with unsecured or poorly functioning locks.

He wears either a mask or a hood to conceal his facial features, but it has been determined that he is Caucasian between 25 and 35 years old, 5 feet 8 inches to 5 feet 11 inches tall, of medium build and very agile, said Rainey...

I met Franklin at the Task Force office at 4:00 a.m. on the 28th. Between 4 and 5 a.m. the trip to San Francisco took only forty-five minutes. After 5 a.m. the traffic backs up and the trip could be expected to take two hours, especially if there was an accident on the freeway.

We met Ross McGowan and Ann Fraser at the T.V. station. They were the co-anchors and went over the rules of the show, taught us how to act and where to look when we were talking.

McGowan introduced us to the real star of today's show, Kathleen Freeman, the Hollywood character actress. Ms. Freeman had a knack for making us forget the cameras and just talk to the audience. McGowan and Fraser professionally led us through the show. Before we knew it the show was over.

When we returned to the office we met with the usual comments, mostly negative, mostly in jest.

"Don't worry," we were told. "At that time of the morning the only ones watching was us. No one in their right mind would get up at that hour to watch T.V."

No one in their right mind? One hell of a prediction that I would come to realize.

At 10:30 a.m. the phone rang.

"Larry, it's for you," Carpenter advised me.

"Sergeant Crompton, can I help you?" I answered.

"Sergeant, this is Doctor Dell, Walter Dell. I'm a psychiatrist in San Francisco and saw you on T.V. this morning. I counsel homosexuals and people into bondage. After listening to you I got to thinking. If I could meet with you for an hour or so I can tell you whether your rapist is into bondage or whether he's tying the victims up just to secure them. It might help you in directing your investigation," the male voice said.

San Francisco. Sin City. Only in San Francisco. If San Francisco doesn't split off and sink into the Pacific Ocean, God owes Sodom and Gomorrah one hell of an apology.

"Really? To be honest, I don't think we ever thought of it in that light, but it might be important," I replied. I didn't mention that we think that EAR had homosexual tendencies or possibly was a homosexual. But then bondage wasn't just a homosexual game. Any nut could play.

"If you want, you can meet me in my office and I can show you what to look for to tell if he is into bondage. I teach a class for police officers at the university to help them investigate homosexual and bondage murders. I'd be glad to spend the time with you and I have all the equipment right here in my office," the doctor continued.

"We would really appreciate it, doctor. When would be a good time?" I asked.

"You name it, Sergeant. I'll make the time."

"Okay. Let me check and I'll call you back."

"I'll talk to you later, Sergeant." The doctor hung up.

After I explained the call to the Task Force, it was decided that Carpenter and Harper would meet with Doctor Dell. I was to call him back with a date and time. They could meet with the good psychiatrist. I would meet with the Vacaville Medical Center psychologist.

You win some. You lose some. This time I considered myself a winner.

Patrol sent us a list of deputies who would be working the EAR detail over the weekend. Eight volunteered for Friday and Saturday and thirteen for Sunday. Some of them volunteered for two nights. They would work from 9 p.m. until 7 a..m., working as two-man cars. Numerous Reserves, Search and Rescue personnel, and Sheriff's dispatchers also volunteered.

Carpenter also sent teletypes to Alameda S.O., Fremont P.D., Pleasanton P.D., and Livermore P.D. advising that we believed EAR would attempt an attack over the weekend and should our activity provoke an attack in their area, we would be available to respond.

Steve Ojena did a work-up on Ashley Watkins's sexual assault evidence and on a semen stain found on a quilt on her bed. Ashley was an ABO Group O secretor with a PGM type 1-1. The semen stain was from a non-secretor with a PGM 2-1, consistent with previous EAR evidence.

"Ron, if you get any thinner, you're going to have to run around in the shower just to get wet," Carpenter remarked.

"All muscle," Voorhies answered. "I work out every day. My body fat is down and I was supposed to take parachute lessons with my girlfriend this weekend. Guess that will have to wait until next weekend."

"Parachute? You got a death wish or you going through a second childhood?" someone asked.

"Live your life to the fullest," Voorhies laughed.

"Or end it," I remarked.

The next day I met with the Vacaville Medical Center psychologist, the most down-to-earth, realistic psychologist I had ever had the opportunity to talk with. Doctor Emily, as she was affectionately referred to, had worked many years with convicted sex offenders and fully understood the recidivism rate of parolees.

"I talked to my sex offender group," the Doctor began, "and they said that you had better catch this person because he wants to kill and he will kill. They say that he's giving them a bad name. Of course, they believe they're not doing anything seriously wrong."

I hadn't told her of the airman and his wife who had been killed in Sacramento during EAR's earlier attacks.

"Then why hasn't he killed yet?" I asked.

"Apparently he hasn't found the justification yet," she answered.

"If he finds the justification, will he then kill every time?" I asked.

"No, it's just that his justification would be less. I agree with my sex offender group, he really does want to kill each time he attacks, but something, maybe his upbringing, stops him. When he feels he's justified or in his mind, needs to kill, he will," she stated.

"Do you think he has ever been in one of your groups or at least in prison?" I asked.

"I don't know. I do know he's not your average garden variety rapist. He's violent and my sex offenders say he's dangerous. They feel that they really don't hurt their victims, your rapist will," she explained.

"That's a rather cavalier attitude, isn't it?" I remarked.

"We're not dealing with normal people here, but they are right about the East Area Rapist. I'm not afraid for myself. Nobody's going to rape this old lady, but I've got a beautiful daughter. My husband and I sleep with a gun and I've told him that if EAR breaks in and rapes our daughter and he doesn't do anything about it, I'll shoot his balls off. And he knows I mean it," the Doctor vented. "He's obviously getting more brazen and more violent."

"Does that mean he wants to get caught? As you read in the reports, he's been crying and sobbing after some of the attacks. Is it remorse?" I asked.

"He doesn't want to get caught and if he is cornered, he'll kill or kill himself if he gets the chance. Remorse? Maybe, but not enough to stop him. No one really wants to get caught, especially this one."

After about an hour of talking to the doctor and getting her insight as to the type of person we were dealing with, I thanked Doctor Emily and left. Her views of EAR were the same views that Bevins and I had agreed on.

Over the weekend the deputies were busy. Numerous traffic and pedestrian stops were made. A light, possibly a cigarette, maybe a small flashlight, was observed in a Christmas tree farm in San Ramon Saturday night. An extensive search of the area failed to locate the source of the light.

A prowler was heard at the bedroom window of a young housewife at 8:30 p.m., a half-hour before the patrol's EAR force began work. The patrol deputies responding failed to locate a suspect.

No attack occurred, much to the relief of Deputy Bill McGinnis, the deputy chosen to be the observer in the C.H.P. helicopter. No one knew at the time and he wasn't about to tell anyone, but he was scared to death of flying in the helicopter. Maybe his prayers saved an EAR victim that weekend.

Contra Costa Times, 7-3-79

Area Scoured for East Area Rapist

SAN RAMON - Aided by a helicopter and a Richmond police airplane, more than 30 lawmen from Contra Costa and Alameda counties participated in a weekend sweep aimed at catching or thwarting the East Area Rapist.

Operating from a field headquarters established in San Ramon, the lawmen cruised residential areas checking for unsecured and unlighted homes, a spokesman for the task force said.

When they found homes that were obviously occupied, the officers informed the residents of their search and asked them to close their windows and turn on their outside lights.

The task force's members have said that the rapist in almost every case has entered his victims' homes through an unlocked window after extensive prowling in the neighborhood. Locking windows and turning on outside lights is a security measure aimed at discouraging the rapist.

During the weekend sweep, the officers said they found several speeders, chased a stolen car that eluded them, and noted some suspicious persons.

The aircraft were available, lawmen said, to respond within minutes had the East Area Rapist struck anywhere between Concord and Fremont.

Future operations may be mounted, depending on manpower and other factors, but will not be announced in advance, officials said.

I had previously requested a list of parolees transferred from Contra Costa County to the Sacramento area prior to the first Concord rape. Monthly reports were received at the Task Force and names were checked against the original parolee list that Franklin, Voorhies, and I had worked on. No matches were made and parolees that fit the parameters of EAR were checked.

By July the Task Force had eliminated over four hundred suspects. Some were given to us by other police agencies, numerous were called in by concerned citizens who suspected a neighbor, a boyfriend, a husband, and many were sent to us on incident reports made out by patrol deputies.

Everyone was on edge, investigators wanted to catch him, deputies wanted to catch him, deputies wanted to make sure that he didn't hit during their watch, and citizens wanted assurance that they could be safe in their homes.

Hundreds of phone calls a day were coming in to the Task Force office. Many just needed someone to talk to, someone to comfort them. Some called to offer help and some to make lodge reservations for Yosemite National Park. Except for the area code, our number was the same as Yosemite's reservation office. Two of the calls came from Germany and Mexico. Carpenter had a rough time explaining that they were talking to the police, not a park ranger.

On July 2nd we had learned that Gary Ford would be returning to the Task Force on the 6th to take over as team leader allowing Carpenter to devote his time to analyzing all the rape reports in an attempt to relate EAR's activities to previous rapes in terms of time and place.

Anything that would give us a clue as to EAR's escape route and possible identity.

Carpenter scoured crime reports, citations, incident reports, and information called in to the office. Each call was recorded on an East Area Rapist information sheet and routed to an investigator for elimination.

Psychics began calling.

"You almost caught him over the weekend," one informed us.

"His thought is coming around to daytime attacks," from another.

"He's on the run," yet another.

"He was in Livermore three weeks ago, prowling," was the first time she had picked up on him, another advised. She was the power source of a group of psychics. They had information on EAR's looks, motel, travel, and work. "He moves like a cat. He's cautious," she added. And she would send in the information by mail. She didn't. She must have read Carpenter's mind.

Another one told Carpenter the name Johnson had come to him. An old Volkswagen, a mask, a leather jacket, Fort Alamo, Texas, a man tied up in a bathtub. He would also mail in further information. He didn't. He must have read Carpenter's mind.

CHAPTER FIFTY-FIVE

It was a three-quarter moon and the light shone brightly over the Sycamore Court condominiums as Brandon Garnett and his wife, Sylvia, prepared for bed. Their three-level condo was one of several surrounded by a greenbelt. Each building contained four residences, most owned by young married couples with no children.

Moonlight peeked through the drapes of their third-level bedroom as the young couple drifted off to sleep.

At 2:00 a.m. their next door neighbor heard someone on her porch. She did not investigate nor call the Sheriff's Office to report the prowler.

Brandon Garnett stirred. A rustling sound near the vanity drew his attention. The light from the moon played across the vanity mirror. The reflection in the mirror brought Garnett to a sitting position. A figure was pulling a dark mask over his head. The man's dark vinyl jacket was buttoned to his neck and his gloved hands were pulling the mask down, stretching it over his face. White shoelaces dangled from his hands.

Garnett sprang from the bed as the figure turned toward him, eyes staring unblinkingly, startled by the charging Garnett.

"Who the fuck do you think you are?" the six foot two, two hundred and twenty pound Garnett yelled. "What the fuck are you doing here?"

The masked man, astonished by the outburst, took a step backward, disorganized by the screaming Garnett.

"Who are you?" Garnett continued to yell as he blocked the masked intruder's exit, allowing Sylvia Garnett to run past the two of them and down the stairs. This was a path they had discussed many times since they had heard about the East Area Rapist.

"If you leave now, you can leave," Garnett continued to yell at the startled, motionless masked intruder. His wife safe, and not knowing if the man had a weapon, Garnett ran past him and down the stairs.

"Help. Help." Sylvia Garnett was yelling as he joined her in the yard.

A neighbor heard the yells and called Sheriff's Dispatch, then ran outside to help the Garnetts. The time was 3:57 a.m.

Deputies Steve Fuqua and Tim MacHugh arrived on the scene and took the initial report. A search of the area was negative. Neither of the Garnetts or their neighbor saw the masked man leave.

Sergeant Sizemore arrived and took charge of the scene. He had radio contact the on-call bloodhound handler, Gary Ford, Tom Cassani, the on-call Task Force investigator, Carpenter, and Deputy Bill Porter, the crime scene tech.

The intruder had searched dresser drawers and removed a pair of Brandon Garnett's shoes from the closet prior to Garnett awakening. It was unknown if he had a weapon or flashlight. Had he placed them aside while he pulled on his mask? Did he feel so secure in his attacks that he only donned his mask when he was ready to arouse his victims? Was it EAR?

At 5:00 a.m. Judy Robb and her dog arrived, as did Hal Drummond, the SAR team coordinator. Robb's dog picked up a slight scent in the living room. The scent became stronger in the backyard near the gate where Pita became excited. She followed the scent to the end of the court at Morninghome and Old Orchard, through the greenbelt area and to Sycamore Valley Road where the scent was lost. Judy felt that by the way Pita was acting, the scent pool was no more than a few minutes old.

During a canvass of the area, Carpenter talked to Garnetts' next door neighbor. She had heard the prowler on her porch at 2:00 a.m.

Later that day painters told her they had seen shoe prints on the porch, however had painted over them. The neighbor's porch and the Garnetts' are separated by a five foot high common wall.

Later Ford, Carpenter, and Brandon Garnett met with James Dean, a Vallejo police officer and credentialed hypnotist. Tom Macris, the San Jose artist, also sat in on the session and completed three drawings of the jacket the intruder had been wearing. The jacket was similar to the one described by Pamela Olivera, the seventeen year old Walnut Creek victim. It also had white lettering over the left breast area. Possibly "CORN" or something similar.

Contra Costa Times, 7-8-79

Husband Routs Ski-Masked Prowler from Danville Home

DANVILLE - A light-sleeping husband scared off a prowler—possibly the East Area Rapist— with a jet stream of obscenities and threats early Friday morning...

"It's good to have you back, Gary," I greeted Ford.

"It's good to be back. Graveyard really wasn't agreeing with me," Ford remarked. "Has Voo been sick? He's lost thirty pounds since I left."

"Since Anna left he's been on a health kick. Working out with weights, watching what he eats, and now he's into parachuting. He and his girlfriend have been taking lessons at the Antioch Airport. He says they're going to jump this weekend, but I think he's going to have to tie a rock to his ankles so he'll come down instead of up. He asked me to come out and watch him," I answered.

"You going?" Ford asked.

"We've been partners for quite awhile. Can't miss this one. At least I can tease him when his girlfriend jumps and he doesn't. By the way, you going with Rod to see the psychiatrist in San Francisco?" I answered.

"I'll have to talk to Rod. Sounds pretty sick," Ford answered.

Three of the Task Force investigators met with Dr. Walter Dell, the San Francisco psychiatrist who had called me after Franklin and I had been on T.V. As the good doctor explained, he counseled men and women who were into bondage and had trouble dealing with the lifestyle. As the investigators learned, he was also homosexual and a "trainer." He trained people to be submissive slaves. While a person was in bondage training, the doctor told them, he would live with his "training officer." At night he would sleep at the foot of the bed like a pet dog until this training had progressed far enough to where he could move onto the bed.

During the day he might be handcuffed or bound in a compromising position, a position that would allow his trainer to perform anal sex at any time. The bound and blindfolded "trainee" was at the trainer's mercy. Sometimes the training officer might have more than one slave at a time. This would be the time you might see several men with dog collars and a leash being walked down the streets of San Francisco.

Doctor Dell did have all the "equipment" in his office: hooks on the walls for bondage sessions; Crisco shortening, the only shortening living up to its reputation of no impurities; and his black bag of tricks.

"EAR," Doctor Dell emphatically explained after he was briefed on EAR's actions, "is not into tying his victims for bondage reasons. He is tying them for security reasons."

Whereas I couldn't make it to his meeting, the doctor extended me an invitation to attend his next four-hour class at a local university. Only police officers and reporters would be allowed to attend.

Hal Franklin received a call from a Davis, California resident who felt that her brother might be the East Area Rapist because of prior sexual acts their father had committed on them as children. The information was given to Voorhies and me to investigate.

We met the woman at her Davis home. She was married, however did not want her husband to know of our meeting as he was not familiar with their childhood. She told us that her mother and father wore stocking masks and carried a flashlight to scare them. The father molested both her and her sister and would place dishes on the other two children's backs while he had sex with one of the girls. The mother would blindfold the two girls and take them into the garage where her mother would have sex with her while her father had sex with her sister. They were both forced to have sex with a dog and at times they were forced to eat out of dishes on the floor like dogs.

Her sister would also be willing to talk to us, the woman advised.

She did. The sister confirmed, or at least echoed, the childhood charges, and expounded. The girls had been forced to stand in the shower while their father could see how close he could come to urinating in their mouths. At nineteen she was forced to go to her brother's bed. The father would send the brother out and then have sex with her. She had seen her brother recently and felt he was having sex with his dog and with his four year old daughter. She also felt that her brother tied his daughter with rope.

Her brother, who was living in Citrus Heights, was an avid baseball player, owned a blue VW van, and owned a blue vinyl jacket with the word "COORS" on it.

A van had been mentioned several times by EAR victims and Citrus Heights was the scene of earlier attacks. Brandon Garnett, under hypnosis, had described a blue vinyl jacket with white lettering, possibly "CORN" or something similar during the July 6th Danville attack.

Voorhies and I met with the brother who chewed on the gauze pad for us. He was a secretor and had no real contacts with Contra Cost County, Fremont, San Jose, Stockton, or Modesto. He was weird and we did pass on the information we had received from the sisters that he might be molesting his daughter to Child Protective Services in Sacramento.

The two sisters continued with their psychiatric counseling. It was true that the mother and father had been ordered to stay away from the two sisters while they were undergoing counseling.

And the beat goes on. The trouble was, we were finding out that EAR wasn't the only sick bastard out there. Hell, he wasn't even in the top ten.

During all the publicity in the news media, the extra patrols, the traffic and pedestrian stops, crime continued. And citizens still left their windows and doors unlocked.

Walnut Creek, the Department that refused to acknowledge that EAR had been in their city and who had spurned help from the Task Force, was hit three times in a two-week period by a person who entered women's bedrooms through unlocked doors or windows.

The man, wearing only underwear and a t-shirt, hit at least two times in the same general area as the two EAR attacks, the last one at 1:59 in the morning. Apparently he enjoyed making the women scream, as none were assaulted in any manner.

Carpenter received a call regarding a man who lived near the Garnett residence. The man previously lived in Sacramento and moved to Danville a year ago after he had raped his boss's wife.

Voorhies commenced an investigation into the forty year old camera salesman and found out he was a registered sex offender with contacts in Hayward, Oakland, Santa Barbara, San Bruno, Atascadero State Hospital, Sacramento, and Danville. No link could be made to the other areas.

On August 8th I was contacted by Captain Rupf. He had a letter from the District Attorney stating that D.A. Investigator Hal Franklin knew who the East Area Rapist was and we refused to believe it or do anything about it. His name was John Walker.

"Captain, Hal Franklin eliminated Walker and refused to believe his own elimination. Voo and Hal eliminated him and Voo and I eliminated him. He was working and couldn't have committed most of the rapes. He refused to chew on the gauze for us, but he's not EAR," I ranted in frustration.

"Well, I want him eliminated once and for all," Rupf explained.

"I've got a restraining order against me to stay away from him. His attorney went to court over the last time I talked to Walker. How do you want me to go any further?"

"I don't care. I want him eliminated. I don't like getting letters from other agencies telling me that we aren't doing our job." Rupf dismissed me.

That afternoon Voorhies and I went to San Jose to contact Walker one more time. When we arrived at his girlfriend's house, I knocked on the door. When Walker answered, I asked him to step outside.

"You're not supposed to harass me. You're supposed to stay away from me," Walker demanded.

"Look, you know why we're here. We know you're not a rapist, but I have to eliminate you. We're only here to help you, not hurt you," I explained.

"My attorney told me he could have you put in jail if you bothered me," Walker hollered.

"I know, but it's important to me to protect you. Some people think you're a rapist, and want you in jail. I know you're not. All I need is for you to chew on some gauze for me and I'll never bother you again," I argued.

"I won't chew on anything and I want you to leave. Now," Walker yelled.

"Ron, would you take a short walk. Just for a few minutes and let me talk to John," I asked Voorhies.

"Sure, I'll be in the car if you need me," Voorhies answered and walked off.

"Look, this is your girlfriend's house, right?" I asked Walker. "You live here with her, don't you?"

"Yeah. So what?" Walker answered.

"You really love her, don't you?" I continued.

"Yes, I do. We're going to get married," Walked answered.

"Well, I don't want to see either of you hurt, but if I call San Jose narcotics to come down here, they're going to take your marijuana plants and haul your girlfriend off to jail. Now, it's her house, so she's the one who will be convicted and go to prison just because you want to be a stupid asshole.

"I don't care about your dope. I'm here to eliminate you as a rapist. Now, if you want your girlfriend to go to prison, I can arrange it for you, but if you really love her, you'll cooperate and I'll be gone and you won't hear from me again. I promise you I won't call the narcs.

"Now, I'm only going to ask you one more time to chew on this piece of gauze." I looked at Walker.

"You mean before you order me to?" Walker asked, his eyes beginning to water.

"That's right." I handed him the gauze, he chewed on it, got it wet, and slipped it back into the package for me.

"Have a good day, John," I said as I walked off.

"You're not going to call the police about the plants are you?" Walked asked.

"You kept your end of the bargain. I'll keep mine." I waved.

When I returned to the car I smiled at Voorhies and showed him the package.

"How the fuck did you get that?" he asked.

I told him the story.

"How in hell did you see marijuana plants? I didn't see any. We weren't even in the house," Voo asked.

"I didn't. I know he's a dope smoker and I figured from what he told us before that he probably grew his own, so I pulled a bluff and it worked," I grinned.

"What if he didn't have any plants? What if the bluff didn't work?" Voo asked.

"The Captain said to eliminate him one way or the other. Guess I would have had to kill him," I replied. Voorhies just looked at me and shook his head.

Criminalist Ojena tested Walker's saliva. He was an A secretor. He was eliminated. At least in everybody's mind except Franklin's.

"I'm gonna jump Saturday," Voo stated.

"You said that last weekend," I replied.

"It's all set. The plane and pilot are all set up. You gonna watch?"

"What time?" I asked.

"Well, we train some more in the morning, around ten, so I guess we jump around noon," Voo explained.

"I'll be there," I answered.

EAR hadn't hit for a month and if the past was any indication, he probably wouldn't hit soon, but then he had been thwarted in his last attempt. Because of that we were still nervous.

I went home, ate dinner, fed the animals, and returned to work. Sizemore and his team were working the San Ramon area in plain clothes.

At 9:40 p.m. the call was received. A prowler seen in the backyard of a Pine Valley Road, San Ramon residence.

Sizemore and his team went directly to the private road between the residence and the tree farm. I went directly to the residence where I was met by a fifteen year old girl. The teenager told me that her dog barked at her rear sliding glass door just before 9:40 p.m. When she turned on the porch light she saw a man in his mid-thirties standing near the door with a long blade knife in his hand. The man turned and ran, climbing the back fence and disappearing into the Christmas tree farm behind her residence.

The California Highway Patrol helicopter and the Search and Rescue dog team were called. Although the time lapse was minimal, nobody was located.

Tennis shoe impressions were found near the fence, indicating a size nine to ten shoe. The prowler was described as a white male, five foot nine, medium build, with straight light brown hair. The teenager said he had been wearing a dark nylon jacket and faded jeans.

Saturday I stopped by the Antioch Airport and watched Voo and his girlfriend learn how to jump off a platform onto the ground without hurting themselves too much. I had flown in the Canadian Navy for four years off Canada's lone aircraft carrier. We were taught to go down with the plane, as it was safer than parachuting. Every time Voo jumped off the platform I was more convinced that the Canadian Navy was right.

After two hours, I left. Voo and his girlfriend were still jumping off the platform.

Sunday morning a man living on Plaza Circle in Danville got up to go to the bathroom at 4:20 a.m. He noticed a shadow in his backyard. When he looked closer, he saw a man wearing a mask and white t-shirt leave the backyard, go through the open side gate, and disappear.

Responding deputies failed to locate the prowler.

I responded from home and talked to the man. He described the prowler as a white male, maybe thirty-five, one sixty to one sixty-five, possibly with a silk stocking over his face and wearing a white t-shirt and light khaki pants.

The homes in the area were situated on three-quarter acre parcels and the prowler was last seen running along a cement wall, blending into the background. The victim, sixty-three years old, was not sure the prowler had seen him.

Monday morning we were all sitting around the Task Force office. All except Voorhies, who liked to be fashionably late.

"Did you watch Voo and his girlfriend parachute Saturday? Did he jump?" Ford asked.

"Well, it's a long story," I began. "Voo and his girlfriend went up and flew over the jump zone all right. His girlfriend jumped, but Voo hesitated too long so they had to go around again. The next time around the instructor told him to jump, but he waited too long again so they had to go around a third time. His girlfriend landed fine and was watching for Voo to jump, waving at the plane for encouragement.

"Voo told me later that the instructor whispered in his ear the third time around that he was gay and if he didn't jump he was going to shove a stiff one up his ass."

"Did he jump?" Carpenter asked as Voo sat down at his desk.

"Well, Voo said he did a little bit at first," I laughed.

"Fuck you," Voo growled as everyone laughed. "I jumped the first time around."

Activities continued in the Danville/San Ramon area. Fortunately citizens had become attuned to the terror of the East Area Rapist and were no longer hesitant in calling the Sheriff's Office. Neighborhood watch meetings and community meetings in which Task Force members spoke ensured that the level of alertness remained high. Those living near greenbelts and golf courses were cautioned by Sizemore and his team, their presence a daily reminder.

On August 17th a female resident on Plaza Circle, bordering the north of the Diablo Golf Course, saw a prowler with a flashlight around 2:00 a.m. Several neighbors also reported hearing noises. Responding deputies did not locate the prowler.

Two hours later a resident on the south side of the golf course heard noises and sent her sons out to investigate. Again no one was located.

All attempts to find a pattern were exhausted. Carpenter continued to extrapolate figures from all the attacks, still nothing seemed to help. Gut feelings by investigators appeared to be more accurate than any formula.

Detective Maloney, a Walnut Creek investigator, took data compiled by Carpenter to the Mathematics Department at Golden State University in San Francisco. Experts using computers were also unable to find a usable pattern.

Wednesday, August 29th, Carpenter and I attended Doctor Walter Dell's sexual assault investigation class presented through San Jose State University. The four-hour segment, made up a slide presentation, lecture, and visual display, was classic San Francisco.

"I am a social psychologist with a master's degree and a certified trainer." Doctor Dell began the class. "I have a slide presentation to show you and a bag of toys that we use. Part of my class is on S&M. Sadomasochism is a wide field now with over forty-five different areas we are into, from inflicting physical pain to mental pain.

"I am also a Master. Our organization has masters and slaves. I'm a true Master, which means I am into everything. A Mental Master deals with only one type of person that he controls.

"Currently I have about three hundred slaves and I am in the process of training a group of twenty-five. We will graduate six police officers, two military people, some doctors and nurses, and some ordinary citizens.

"These slaves are mine until they search out a master or a master seeks them out. We have auctions and masters can bid for the slaves through a point system we use. An accountant keeps track of our points. You get more points for training a police officer than say a teacher, and you can use those points for buying slaves. You also accumulate points by selling slaves.

"As for training, basic training is one month. During this time I am their teacher and I am good at what I do. I am gay, but not everyone into S&M is gay. Some are straight, they just enjoy bondage.

"During training the slaves may sleep at the foot of the bed on the floor. They must earn the right to sleep on the bed.

"Before anyone is allowed to be trained as a slave, they must fill out an application and go through an interview with me. They must sign a document that they are not being forced, coerced, or threatened into training. This is notarized at the time of signing and no one under the age of eighteen is allowed to enter.

"To be a good master, you must first be a good slave. I was a slave for two years.

"The largest S&M group is here in San Francisco; however Chicago and New York also have large groups. I have an S&M consulting company in San Francisco and I get calls and letters from all over the world. When people are getting into this field, we teach them. I love disciplining people. Every implement has been used on me and I won't use one on anybody that I have not first tested.

"We use handcuffs, alligator clips, clothes pins, ball stretchers, choke chain collars, whips, ropes, thongs, curtain hooks for lashing, paddles, cock rings, and cattle prods. You name it, we use it. Some even use batteries and wires to attach to the nipples. Choke chain collars are the most dangerous. They are used like you do for training dogs.

"Now as I said, not everyone is into pain. Some are just into water sports. Piss. Some are into feces, some into enemas. For those who are into pain, piercing, choke collars, ball stretchers, and cock rings with leather thongs are used. The person is totally secured and at your mercy.

They know that if they move they can either choke to death or castrate themselves. They must have total confidence in their master. Anything I need I can go into one of the toy shops in the city and pick up.

"There are ways of distinguishing masters from slaves when we are out. Hard core S&M's may not wear a signal. I do. A key ring hanging from one side means you are a master, the other side, a slave. A lock on the key chain means you're looking for a slave. We also have four main handkerchief colors. A white hanky means you're into standard S&M. A black hanky means you're looking for something heavy; yellow means you're into water sports; brown means you're into feces. Personally, I'm not into water sports or feces, but I have an associate who is.

"We also have a red hanky that means you're into fist fucking. This is where you insert your fingers into someone's anus. You start with your finger and keep going. We have fist fucking parties and because they can be dangerous, we have a doctor or nurse on hand. They don't participate while they are on duty. Sometimes someone will be carried away and pull someone's intestines out and that's why we have a medical staff on duty during the party. We do have many doctors and nurses who are into fist fucking. The association is called the FFA.

"It is because of the FFA that you can't buy a one pound can of Crisco shortening in San Francisco. They couldn't keep it on the shelves, so for San Francisco, Crisco started selling five-pound cans. Crisco has no impurities and is excellent for fist fucking. Here's a slide showing what I mean."

A picture on the screen showed a naked man bent over and a second man with his arm almost up to his elbow in the first person's ass. My ass puckered so tight that if I had broken wind only a dog would have heard it. I had to go to the back of the room and get a cup of coffee to try and relax. Houdini couldn't have done what I had just seen.

"For my birthday, my friends gave me twenty-five pounds of Crisco," Dell giggled. "We also have uniform clubs. A police uniform is the favorite, construction second."

After the slide show depicting all types of bondage, torture, two pound ball stretchers, whippings, cages, stocks, rack beds, etc., the doctor set his black bag of "toys" on the table and commenced to take them out one at a time and explain its use.

The Chinese string of balls, some bigger than a fist, huge dildos, alligator clips, and everything imaginable came from the bag. I was glad I was in my usual spot. In the back. The bag must have smelled like a two holer outhouse used by a family of fourteen. I know it was my imagination, but I swear I saw a blue haze rising from the bag.

"During the training, do the slaves stay with you all the time or do they go to work?" A female officer up front asked.

"It depends. Some work, some don't. It's between the slave and the trainer. I charge twenty dollars an hour for training," Dell answered, "and I don't allow my slaves to work."

"Is that Police Officer Standard and Training reimbursable?" Carpenter asked, and everyone laughed, except me. I knew he was joking, or at least I thought I knew he was joking. I did hug the door on the ride back to the office and I flinched every time he took his hand off the steering wheel.

By September, I had contacted several more parolees. All were eliminated as being EAR. From the approximately six thousand original names, over four thousand had been eliminated through information that had been included on the list, and eleven hundred were searched and eliminated by means of prison records at the California Medical Facility and California Youth Authority or personal contact. Seventy-one remained that I had not been able to locate, and forty-two of these remained on the high priority list.

EAR was due to hit again by early October. October was one of his most active months: four times in 1976, three times in 1977, and three times in 1978, each after a summer absence, except for the September 6, 1977, attack in Stockton.

The Murders

Does A Serial Rapist Become A Serial Murderer?

CHAPTER FIFTY-SIX

October 1, 1979, 2:00 a.m.
Queen Ann Lane, Goleta,
Santa Barbara County, California

"**WAKE UP! WAKE UP!**" The whispered voice broke the subconscious mind of Priscilla Duffy.

"Okay. Okay," she replied as the intruder kicked the bed. Priscilla and her boyfriend, Abel Playa, were wide awake as the flashlight beam moved across their eyes.

"Get on your stomachs," the intruder ordered. "Don't move, motherfucker, or I'll kill you. Don't move or turn your head," he hissed after they were on their stomachs. "I gotta have money. Tie his hands." He threw shoelaces onto the bed. "Tie it tight or I'll kill you."

She did as he ordered.

"Get on your stomach," he ordered the naked Duffy and she felt her wrists being tied, the circulation being cut off. Playa's wrists were retied by the masked intruder. Tight. Both victims' ankles were tied: his tight, hers loosely.

"Where's the money? Don't look at me, motherfucker," he hissed.

"In my purse in the kitchen," Duffy answered.

The intruder leaned close to the victims. "I'll kill you, you motherfuckers," he hissed. He left them. They heard him in other parts of the house and then he was back.

"I can't find your purse. One move, motherfucker," he threatened and again he was gone. They heard him ransacking, searching.

"Where's your purse? I can't find it," he hissed at Duffy.

"It's on the kitchen sink," she replied. She felt the ties on her ankles being removed.

"Show me," he whispered and pulled her from the bed and led her from the room. He had her lie on the living room floor and again her ankles were tied.

"Turn over." He ordered her to roll onto her back. She could feel the flashlight beam move over her naked body and she felt his eyes on her. She heard him rubbing himself. Masturbating?

He walked away from her and she rolled back onto her stomach. She heard him in the kitchen, walking down the hallway and then he was beside her again. He knelt at her shoulder and pulled a pair of shorts over her head, blindfolding her.

"Now, I'm going to kill you. Cut your throat," he hissed.

Fear she had never known surged through her body as he walked back into the kitchen.

"I'll kill 'em. I'll kill 'em. I'll kill 'em." She heard him muttering over and over and over.

She heard him walking down the hall and she rolled to her feet and started hopping toward the front door. She tripped, falling into the wall. She couldn't see. The blindfold. She got the door open and the bindings fell from her ankles. She ran outside, screaming for help. She ran into the side of the house in her blindness. She felt him grab her, pulling on her arm. She was thrown to the ground and felt his gloved thumb pulling on her mouth.

"I told you to be quiet," he hissed and she felt the knife pressed against her throat.

She was pulled to her feet and dragged back into the house. He pushed her to the floor and once again her ankles were tied.

Playa heard Duffy scream. He knew she was being killed. He swung his naked body from the bed and hopped to the sliding glass door. He opened it, and hopped into the backyard toward the fence. He hit the fence hard, trying to jar the boards free. They held and he fell to the ground behind the bushes. He saw the flashlight beam as the masked intruder searched the backyard. He rolled behind the orange tree and waited. His heart was beating so hard his body shook.

He saw the intruder re-enter the house and again he stood at the fence. His neighbor's lights were on. He began yelling.

"Help. I'm the neighbor. There's a burglar. Help!" He again fell to the ground hiding behind the tree.

Duffy again freed her feet. She heard a vehicle leave the area and she moved toward the bedroom. The blindfold had moved and she could see with one eye. Playa was not there. She tried to cover herself with her bathrobe and ran to the front door. As she left the house, her bathrobe fell to the ground. She saw car lights and she began screaming as they screeched to a halt in front of her.

At 2:00 a.m. deputies received a call of a woman screaming in the area of Queen Ann and Kellog. The person reporting was an off-duty FBI agent who was in pursuit of a male on a bicycle seen leaving the Queen Ann house.

Upon arrival the deputies located Priscilla Duffy on her front lawn, naked and screaming hysterically. Abel Playa was located, still hiding in the backyard.

The FBI agent had lost the masked intruder who had dropped the bicycle and ran between houses on San Patricio. The bicycle, a ten-speed, twenty-seven inch Nishiki, and a black-handled steak knife were recovered. The bicycle, registered to a U.S. Parole officer, had been taken from his North Patterson Avenue residence between 7:00 p.m. and midnight.

Sergeant Wells and Detective Chuck Kennedy located several shoe impressions in neighboring yards that matched impressions found in the victim's backyard as well as similar impressions in yards near where the bicycle had been stolen.

The suspect was described as a white male, five foot ten or eleven, wearing a Pendleton-type shirt and a ski mask. He also had some type of holster attached to his belt on his right side. He had pried open the rear sliding glass door to gain entry, apparently with a screwdriver-type tool.

In November, due to inactivity of the East Area Rapist in Contra Costa County, and our not knowing of the possible EAR activity in Southern California, the Task Force was once again reduced to three investigators: Carpenter, Voorhies, and me.

We continued to follow up on leads, parolees, and prowlers. We checked motel registers of motels near EAR attacks outside Sacramento and we stayed in constant contact with Bevins in Sacramento.

On December 29th, 1979, beginning sometime after 4:00 p.m., five burglaries occurred in Goleta. Sliding glass doors were pried open on four of the entries. Side gates were found open and at 11:15 p.m. a family returning home to their Windsor Court home saw a subject walk past their window inside their house. The suspect ran out the rear of the house and jumped over the rear fence. The family's small poodle had been beaten to death.

CHAPTER FIFTY-SIX

December 30, 1979
767 Avenida Pequena, Goleta,
Santa Barbara County

Approximately five hours after the unidentified subject fled from the Windsor Court home a male doctor, forty-four year old Robert Offerman and his female psychologist companion, thirty-five year old Alexandria Manning, were murdered in Offermans Avenida condominium.

Deputies responding to the scene found the doctors in the master bedroom. Alexandria Manning, naked and lying on the bed with a bullet wound to the back of her head, had her hands tied behind her back.

Offerman, also naked and with four bullet wounds to his upper torso, one to the upper chest and three to his back, was on the floor on his knees, his head on the floor and his buttocks in the air. He also had a white cord around his left wrist.

The thermostat was in the off position as were all the lights. No ransacking was noted. Pry marks were located on the sliding glass door and a plastic bag containing turkey bones and scraps of turkey was found on the back patio. Tennis shoe impressions determined to be the star shaped design of Adidas Runner were located on the soft earth in the back yard. They were the same shape, design and size of the shoe impressions found at the Duffy and Playa residence on October 1st and

Alexandria Manning

Robert Offerman

also matched shoe impressions in the neighbor's yard. Dog paw impressions were found along with the shoe impressions on the Offerman property. Neither Offerman nor his neighbor owned a dog.

During a neighborhood canvas, it was learned that several neighbors heard gunshots around 3:00 a.m. One neighbor, who was up at the time, reported one shot, a pause, three shots in succession, another pause and then a single shot. The same neighbor reported her son's bicycle had also been stolen during the night.

Other pieces of white twine were located in the rear yard of the residence where the bicycle had been stolen. The bicycle was located several blocks away.

Three sliding glass doors had pry marks. The one leading into the living room had been pried so hard the jamb had been pulled away from the wall.

Detectives determined that the killer had made several attempts to force entry. As with Duffy and Playa, Offerman and Manning were asleep and nude when they were attacked.

Jewelery belonging to Manning was found stuffed down between the mattress and the bed frame. Detectives speculated the killer confronted Offerman and Manning and told Manning to tie Offerman. Believing it was a robbery, Manning hid her jewelery. After being told to tie Offerman, Manning was tied by the killer. Offerman freed himself and confronted the killer who shot him to death. Manning was then executed.

The killer used a .38 caliber revolver loaded with Supervel brand, .38 caliber ammunition with 110 grain jacketed bullets. The weapon was probably a Smith and Wesson revolver. Manning had not been sexually assaulted however speculation was that Offerman had been. Apparently no evidence was collected from Offerman.

Although several neighbors heard the shots, no one called the Sheriff's Department.

During the canvas, detectives discovered that the condo next to the Offerman condo had also been entered. Pry marks were on the wooden frame of the front door and on the sliding glass doors.

A window screen had been removed and the same type shoe impressions were found below the window. The screen had been thrown on top of an eight-foot high hedge.

Inside the residence the same type of 1/16 inch three strand nylon twine used on Offerman, Manning, Duffy and Playa was located on the floor and under the sink of the master bathroom and on the floor of the master bedroom. The condo was vacant and for sale at the time of the murders.

Did the killer break into the vacant condo first or did he break in and hide after the murders? Detectives formed investigative theories in support of both positions.

———◦———

In February Jim Bevins heard of the Goleta homicide, the bindings, the stolen bicycle, the tennis shoe impressions in adjacent yards and the pry marks on the sliding glass doors. His calls to the Santa Barbara County Sheriff's Department proved futile. They had nothing similar, they said, to what he described.

Bevins and I discussed the rumors and I called Santa Barbara. Again, I too was stonewalled. They had not had any such attacks. Maybe the rumors were false.

In March our suspicions were confirmed. Two people were murdered in Santa Barbara County. Not only that, the deputy informed Bevins, who was attending a seminar, "the male had been sodomized after he had been killed."

Another Santa Barbara deputy told me of the attempted rape and escape of the couple in October. When I asked why we were unable to learn of these attacks and were in fact lied to when we made specific requests, I was given the answer.

"President Reagan has a ranch in Santa Barbara County. They don't want the news media to have a field day. They don't want the publicity," the deputy stated.

Bevins and I went over the two reports. The similarities were there. The initial contact with the flashlight and the threats to kill; the demand for money and the excuse to remove the female victim from the male's side to help the attacker find the purse; the tightly bound hands behind the back; ankles tied, the male tight, the female loosely; very little ransacking; ski mask, gloves; neighborhood prowling; tennis shoes; pry marks; stolen bicycles; the over-use of "motherfucker" in the first attack; eating in the second attack; masturbation; physical description; and yes, as the Vacaville Medical Center psychologist had predicted, "the homosexual tendency and the desire to kill."

Was it EAR? Bevins and I felt sure that it was. EAR attacks fifty and fifty-one.

CHAPTER FIFTY-SEVEN

March 13, 1980, late evening
573 High Point Drive, Ventura, California

A PROMINENT ATTORNEY, forty-three year old Lyman Smith and his thirty-three year old wife, Charlene, were murdered in their High Point Drive, Ventura home. Their bodies were not discovered until March 16th, when Lyman's twelve-year-old son, Charlene's stepson arrived from his mother's home to mow the lawn.

Ventura Police arrived at the scene at approximately 2:17 p.m.

Both victims had been bludgeoned to death with a fire log taken from the woodpile outside the home. The log, approximately twenty-one and a half inches long, was located on the floor near the end of the bed.

Charlene's ankles were tied together with a white drapery cord. Her wrists were bound together behind her back. She had been struck once or twice on the left side of her head.

Lyman and Charlene Smith

Lyman was naked and lying face down on the bed. His ankles were tied with a single length of drapery cord. His hands were bound behind his back with the same type of cord. Both victims' bindings had been secured with an uncommon decorative knot known as a "diamond knot."

Analysis of the blood splattering concluded that Lyman was struck before Charlene.

In the living room, officers noted that cushions on the main sofa had been disturbed. A piece of black cloth was found under one of the cushions. Cushions on the sofa in the family room were found standing upright against the back of the sofa.

Had the murderer entered the home earlier to secrete the bindings? Investigators never tested the theory.

Although there was no evidence of forced entry, the master bedroom window and the front door were unlocked.

A canvas of the area revealed prowler activity before and after the murders.

On Thursday, March 13th, at approximately 10:30 p.m., a resident on El Malabar saw a white mid- 1970's Pontiac sedan parked near the corner of High Point Road. It had been there since dusk. The neighbor had not seen the vehicle before. At around 2:00 a.m. he was awakened by screams. The screams came from near the Smith residence. He heard nothing else and went back to sleep. In the morning the Pontiac previously parked in the area was no longer there.

On Saturday, March 8th, a High Point resident heard someone prowling in her back yard. The prowler jiggled the bathroom window and moved it a couple of times. Nothing further occurred so she did not notify the police.

Friday, March 18th, another High Point resident heard a dog barking at approximately 4:00 a.m. The dog barked for 45 minutes, which was very unusual.

Another High Point resident advised that between midnight and 3:00 a.m. on the morning of Saturday, March 17th, or Sunday, March 18th, he was the victim of an attempted burglary. His infant son woke crying and the resident heard something in the infant's bedroom. His wife responded and settled the child down. At approximately 10:00 p.m., Tuesday, March 20th, he checked the perimeter of his house. He found that his son's bedroom window screen had been removed and was missing. A one and a half inch diameter hole was in the glass near the latch. He had the window replaced and notified Ventura Police approximately seven days later.

Detectives from Ventura P. D. and Santa Barbara County Sheriff's Department examined each other's homicides. Each agency rejected the theory that the Offerman/Manning and the Smith murders were related.

> August 19, 1980
> 33381 Cockleshell Drive, Laguna Miguel,
> Orange County, California

On Tuesday, August 19th, sometime after 11:05 p.m., twenty-four year old Keith and twenty-eight year old Patrice Harrington were murdered in bed in their Cockleshell Drive residence. Investigations indicated their killer was organized and had murdered before, murdering Lyman and Charlene Smith and possibly others.

The killer apparently entered through an unlocked door as no forced entry was noted.

Both victims were found lying face down on the bed. Both had multiple head injuries and a large amount of blood had saturated the underside of the comforter, which had been placed over the victim's heads before the bludgeoning.

Keith Harrington

Patty Harrington

Ligatures were found lying on top of Keith's lower body. Apparent ligature marks were noted on the wrists of both victims and on Patrice's ankles. A mark was also noted on Keith's ankle.

The killer had removed the bindings after killing the two and had disposed of them either on or close to the bed. The bindings were pieces of brown macramé type cord.

It appeared both victims had been on their bellies, hands tied behind their backs prior to the removal of the ligatures. The victims had been struck several times in the head with a blunt instrument while their heads were covered. A small brass fragment was recovered from Patrice's skull.

Semen was found on the vaginal swabs, on the back of Patrice's upper right leg and on the comforter.

In October 1996, DNA testing by the Orange County Sheriff's Forensic Science Division determined that the semen came from the killer.

Three days after the murders a left-handed blood stained leather motocross glove was found approximately ¾ of a mile from the Cockershell Drive scene.

February 6, 1981, 2:00 a.m.
35 Columbus, Irvine, California

The city of Irvine was not immune from violence. Twenty-eight year old Manuela Withuhn was murdered while lying on her bed.

Her cause of death was a skull fracture as a consequence of trauma to the head.

Manuela was found lying on her bed in a sleeping bag. It appeared she was attacked in her sleeping bag. The weapon was removed from the scene by the killer.

Ligature marks were noted on both wrists and on Manuela's right ankle. A ball of fibers was noted on her skin at the base of her spine.

A rear sliding glass door had pry marks and damage to the frame.

Several tennis type shoe impressions such as the "Tred 2" racquetball shoe were located in the back yard.

Wooden matches were found; two in front of the door leading into the garage and four in the flower bed alongside the garage. Similar matches had been collected at the Goleta murder scene.

During the neighborhood canvas a female neighbor directly behind the victim's residence said she returned home at approximately 11:00 p.m. and noted that her dead bolt was not locked. This was unusual,

Manuella Witthuhn

however she did not notice anything else as being disturbed and went to bed.

July 27, 1981, approximately 3:30 a.m.
449 Toltec Way, Goleta,
Santa Barbara County

Thirty-five year old Cheri Domingo and her friend, twenty-seven year old Gregory Sanchez were found murdered in Sanchez' Toltec Way residence.

Responding deputies found no evidence of forced entry although a small window in the master bath was open. The window screen had been removed and was found hidden a few feet away. The window was not large enough to gain entry, however detectives found they could reach in and unlock the door, which accessed the bathroom from outside.

Gregory Sanchez was found nude and lying face down on the floor, partially inside the bedroom closet. He had one gun shot wound to his cheek. The wound had not been fatal. Twenty-four blunt force wounds to his head were. The killer had removed clothing from the closet and placed them over Sanchez' head after his death. There was no evidence that Sanchez had been bound.

Cheri Domingo was found lying nude on the bed completely covered by the bedding. She was face down with both arms behind her back.

Ligature marks on her wrists and ankles indicated she had been bound with her ankles back over her buttocks and tied to her wrists. She had been killed with a single blow to the head with the same weapon used to kill Sanchez.

Investigators determined that Sanchez had been shot while in a kneeling position. He fell to the floor and was struck in the head. Sanchez later got up and was again struck by the killer. He stumbled to the closet and died.

During the neighborhood canvas a neighbor stated they had heard a gunshot between 3:20 and 3:35 a.m. on July 27, 1981. They then heard a scream and advised that dogs in the area barked for about a half hour. They did not call the Sheriff's Department.

Other neighbors also heard the gunshot, however no one reported it.

One neighbor stated he had seen a man standing behind a large tree at approximately 9:45 p.m. the night of the murder.

Another neighbor stated that he and his wife were walking in the neighborhood at approximately 10:00 p.m. when they saw a man following them. At one point he was approximately six to ten feet behind them. The subject was young, five foot eleven inches tall, slender, with blond neck length hair.

Cheri Domingo and Greg Sanchez

At 11:00 p.m., a mother and daughter were jogging in the area when they saw a white male standing on the sidewalk behind the Domingo residence. The man appeared to be in his twenties or early thirties, five foot ten inches tall, with neatly cut blond hair. The subject had a German Shepherd dog with him.

Detectives contacted two neighbors on Berkeley Road, approximately one block from the Sanchez home. They had likely seen the suspect approximately one week prior to the attack on Duffy and Playa on October 1st.

On Tuesday, September 25th, one of the neighbors was contacted by a subject stating that the previous evening he had been walking his dog without a leash and it had run into the residences' back yard. The dog returned and was bleeding badly.

The subject stated he had taken the dog to a veterinarian for emergency treatment.

Another neighbor was home the evening of September 24th when a subject came to her door asking to use the telephone to call a friend as his dog had been injured. The neighbor described the dog as a German Shepherd.

A man arrived in a car, picked up the subject and his dog and left.

The next morning the man returned and told the neighbor he had taken his dog to a veterinarian who told him the dog had been stabbed and required 70 stitches.

Later the neighbor received a single rose as a token of appreciation for allowing the subject to use the phone.

Ninety-seven days after the dog incident, Alexandria Manning and Robert Offerman were murdered. Paw prints from a large dog were located in the mud in the back yard.

Usually prowler calls happen once a month in these upper middle class neighborhoods. However, during these attacks and prior to the first attack on Queen Ann, neighbors reported several strange noises, open side gates, and shoe impressions in the back yards.

The activity indicated that the murderer was moving from one neighborhood to another, only to return a month later to prowl again.

CHAPTER FIFTY-EIGHT

ON AUGUST 20, 1981, detectives met with the police psychologist to discuss their three cases as well as the Ventura, Irvine, and Orange County cases that they knew about. The doctor felt that all the cases were connected to the same person. The bindings, tying the victims' hands behind their backs, the prowling, the pry marks, the tennis shoe impressions, the stealing of very few items, leaving money and expensive jewelry behind, eating and drinking after the attacks, stealing bicycles, and the progression of the killings all indicated to the doctor that the same person did commit all the attacks.

The screw-up in the Queen Ann case was a lesson the killer learned from. No longer would he lose control, the doctor said.

Had Doctor Emily at the Vacaville Medical Center been a prophet? Had EAR found his justification that he had been looking for? Was he now a serial killer?

The two doctors in Goleta? The male had attacked the intruder, the doctor explained to the detectives. He died for his efforts, but it was noisy. Bludgeoning was much quieter, but the first bludgeoning had left a lot of blood around the room and, obviously, on the killer. The next bludgeoning occurred after the person was covered with a blanket. Therefore less blood.

"In each of these cases," the doctor surmised, "the intruder entered with the full intent to murder."

He planned, he learned, and each time his motivation grew less, as Doctor Emily had predicted.

"This guy is not psychotic, and is not so far out of the way of all of us that he'd really be visible," the doctor said.

" A psychopath is something we use in the common language that really doesn't exist. A psychopath basically is an individual who had a high degree of really socially unacceptable kinds of behaviors, but he gives a pretty good appearance. They have superficial charm and very good intelligence.

"They do have delusional thinking, they are not irrational, very logical, not nervous, no neurotic manifestations, and you really can't scare them.

"This person would be perfectly capable of blowing you away and not even thinking about it. He lacks remorse and shame. A police officer might kill a person in the line of duty and learn from that to never kill anybody again and might even get out of that line of work. This guy will kill, he'll kill, and what he will learn is a more efficient way to do it."

"What about family? Would he deliberately kill a child?" the detective asked.

"He's done everything he can to avoid children to date. If a child walked in on him, I really don't know what he would do," the doctor answered. "If you have more than two crimes like this, you got kind of a compulsion. That's his life, that's his lifestyle, that's his life pattern, and you repeat these kinds of things. That's your best chance to catch him.

"He's going to get two people and he's going to get some guy who's going to trip him and knock him out. Somebody's going to have a gun under his pillow. This is scary, these kinds of guys. These are the only ones that scare me, they really do. If you get somebody like this, the minute you make a move to control it, it's over and done with."

CHAPTER FIFTY-NINE

DURING THE SANTA BARBARA and other southern California attacks, we continued to receive calls. There were leads to follow up on, however none were fruitful although the prowler calls diminished. Rapes, robberies, burglaries and murders still occurred, but that's life in these United States.

EAR seemed to have disappeared.

Carpenter received a call from a person claiming to be a psychic who had helped many police agencies solve crimes. The psychic stated that he had been working with Sacramento and he would like a call back. Rod gave me the call. The psychic wanted to be known by his code name "Fisherman."

I called. He was a professional, lots of degrees and a former intelligence agent, he told me. He also gave me the name of a person who was EAR. A person in jail for murder. I checked. The person in jail was not EAR.

Over the next few months I received several calls from the Fisherman. He wanted to help; he also wanted to be paid. Hell, if he confessed to being EAR, I would be happy to pay him; otherwise he had been, if nothing else, a pest. Still I talked to him. You never know.

He had contacted Channel 3, KCRA in Sacramento. They gave him money to help conduct an investigation with his "psychic" powers. He "visioned" a suspect who was a mechanic for the Sacramento Sheriff's Department. The mechanic was six foot three and was working in 1976 and 1977 in another area.

The Fisherman said he had been involved in locating the Red Brigade Terrorists in Italy. I gave the information to Bevins who checked out the psychic's activities. He had gone to Italy at the expense of the Italian government. The only thing he did, according to the Italian detectives, was to stay in expensive hotels and eat expensive meals. He did not help their investigation.

The next time he called me and said, "This is the Fisherman, is Sergeant Crompton in?"

I replied, "If you were really psychic, you would know." I hung up. He never called back. Maybe he was psychic. He knew I didn't like him.

Several agencies over the next few years told Carpenter and me that they had been contacted by the Fisherman offering to help them solve their crimes and that he had helped us in our investigations. We set them straight.

In 1985, the Fisherman reported that his house was being bombarded by FBI and police rays. Pacific Gas and Electric checked his residence. No rays were detected.

I continued to work on my parolee list until we were shut down completely. First Carpenter was transferred to Special Investigation's Intelligence Unit, then Voorhies was transferred to Homicide. My turn finally came and I was transferred to the Police Academy as the drill instructor and then to patrol as a shift supervisor.

Shortly after transferring to patrol, I received a phone call from Dispatch one night around 11:00 p.m.

Warren Rupf, who had recently been appointed Assistant Sheriff, had received a call from the Walnut Creek Police Department. They had arrested the East Area Rapist and needed someone to interview him. The Assistant Sheriff wanted me to respond.

"We arrested the East Area Rapist," the Walnut Creek Watch Commander advised me when I arrived, "and my detectives have interviewed him but they have gone as far as they can and we need your help. He hit us twice, but we need to have someone who knows about his other rapes to take it from here."

"He hit you twice? That's the first time you ever admitted that," I responded.

"Well we know it's him. We arrested him at his job in Pacheco," the lieutenant continued.

"Pacheco is in County area. Did you let our investigators know you were coming into our area to make an arrest?" I was out of line, but I was still upset that a thirteen-year-old child had been raped when it could possibly have been avoided if there had only been some cooperation. No, I wasn't upset, I was pissed.

"We didn't have time. We didn't want him to have a chance on leaving." He knew I was pissed.

"What makes you think he is EAR and how did you find out about him?" I asked.

"His grandmother turned him in. He moved down here from Oregon and is staying with her. He started telling her about EAR and she got scared and called us. He knew things that only the rapist would know, like using foreign objects, cutting the female's nipples off, and things like that," the lieutenant stated.

Now I was really pissed.

"EAR never cut off nipples or anything else," I stated.

"Oh yes, he has in several rapes," the lieutenant defended his statement.

"No, he hasn't. I know every rape inside and out. He's a violent bastard, but he hasn't done any of that," I remarked.

"Well we know it is him, so we need you to talk to him."

"Okay. Lead the way."

I met their prisoner in one of the interrogation rooms. He looked to be around thirty years old and a little on the stocky side. I introduced myself.

"Do you know why you are here?" I asked.

"I guess on a warrant for not paying spousal support. Nobody has told me." He shrugged his shoulders.

"You're divorced?" I asked.

"Yeah. My son and I moved down here so I could get a job. We're staying with my grandmother," he replied.

"Well, you may have a warrant, but they think you're a rapist. How's that feel?"

"A rapist? I never raped anyone in my life! A rapist? Are they fucking nuts? I swear to you, I've never raped anybody. For God's sake, I've got a son. I would never do anything that would hurt him." He ran his fingers through his hair, closed his eyes and shook his head in disbelief.

"Well, they told me that you know everything about the East Area Rapist," I remarked.

"The East Area Rapist? They think I'm the East Area Rapist? Look I don't know what's going on, but this is sick," he cried.

"How do you know about the rapist?" I asked.

"I read about him in the paper when I was in Oregon. I don't know anything about him," he blurted.

"You talked to your grandmother about him didn't you?" I asked.

"Well, yeah. I was curious because he raped those women here. Hell, I hate rapists," he stated.

"Well, I don't think you're a rapist either, but I've got to find something that can eliminate you. Have you ever been in jail before?" I asked.

"Once in Oregon," he stated.

"What for?" I continued.

"For not paying spousal support. I didn't have a job and couldn't pay so they put me in jail for a couple of months," he stated.

"Do you know when it was?" I asked.

"No, not really. A few years ago. I know it was summer. Look I swear to you, I never raped anybody. I'm really getting scared here. I've got a son to take care of," he stated and I could see his eyes starting to tear.

"Sit here a minute. Let me do some checking and I'll be right back. I know you're not EAR, so just stay calm," I assured him.

I met the lieutenant in his office. "Did you run a criminal history on him to see if he ever spent time in jail?" I asked.

"I don't think so," the lieutenant replied.

"Can you have someone do it for me?" I asked.

"Sure."

A few minutes later a sergeant informed us that the man they held had been in jail in Oregon from the middle of May 1979 through the first week of July.

"Do these dates ring a bell?" I asked the lieutenant.

"What do you mean?" he asked.

"He was in jail during both of your rapes. In Oregon," I remarked.

"Damn. We were sure he was the rapist. Now what do we do?" the lieutenant put his head in his hands.

"I don't know about you, lieutenant, but I'm going to go back in and tell that fellow that he is not a rapist and then I'm going home to get some sleep. If I were you, I'd take him out and buy him the biggest steak dinner you can afford and hope he accepts an apology," I stated.

To myself, I said "And kick me out of your town one more time, please."

When I got home I called the Assistant Sheriff and told him EAR was still free and Walnut Creek had finally admitted that EAR had been in their town.

On October 21st, 1982, Jim Bevins called me at home. Margarita Lopez, EAR's twenty-fourth victim, had received a phone call the previous night. She said it was the rapist's voice, which said: "Hi, it's me again. Remember me? I'm going to come over and fuck you again. You're going to suck my cock again."

Bevins placed a trap on Lopez's phone and put extra patrol on her residence.

CHAPTER SIXTY

IT WAS DEVASTATING to all of us when the EAR Task Force was shut down.

"EAR has left our area. He's no longer our worry," was the final word. Reality.

My problem, as with many police officers, is that we don't see the "big picture." We tend to look at the world through a macro lens, while administrators look through a wide-angle lens. That's probably why many officers go out with high blood pressure or heart attacks. Administrators rarely do. The trick is to promote until you can see the "big picture."

It's a bitter pill to swallow when a case is not closed by an arrest. Most of us take it personal. What did I miss? What did I do wrong? What didn't I do that I should have? We all have the same thoughts.

There may never be an answer to our questions. There may never be an ending to our mission. Did EAR move south and proceed to the next level? Is he the murderer who started raping in Sacramento on June 18, 1976? Bevins and I thought so but we were the minority.

I still wake up in the middle of the night and wonder, where is he? Who is he? And I wonder how many victims still wake up in the middle of the night and shiver with fear.

At times I still blame myself for not being good enough to catch him. I know the others feel the same way. I pray that some day we will find the clue that we missed.

At times I blame the system. Agencies that won't cooperate; investigators who won't cooperate; officers who do less than the job they are paid to do.

A criminal moves to another area and the slate is wiped clean. He's someone else's problem.

If fire departments worked this way, fires would have to burn themselves out. Fortunately, they don't. Firemen clamor to help each other. Jealousies never enter. Cooperation abounds.

But we are cops. We don't need help. We can be the heroes. And the criminals can remain free. And we can all lose.

This isn't a story about cops. It's life. Real, ugly, violent life and the victims who were a part of it. Victims who will never know why they were picked to endure the terror inflicted by one man, a sick, sadistic, serial rapist; a sick, sadistic serial murderer. The one they called the East Area Rapist.

———⇒❖⇐———

Government statistics state that nearly 18 percent of women in the United States have been raped or are the victims of attempted rape at some point during their lives. That amounts to 17.7 million American women. More than half were under seventeen when first raped.

CHAPTER SIXTY-ONE

CONTRA COSTA TIMES, Sunday, October 1, 1982

Where is the East Area Rapist Now?

By John Van Landingham

Lesher News Service

MARTINEZ- It has been more than three years since the East Area Rapist last struck in Contra Costa County and police admit they are no nearer to catching him than they were after his first attack in October, 1978.

Already the statute of limitations has run out on four of the seven attacks credited to the shadowy terrorist whose name was derived from a wave of sexual assaults in Sacramento's east area in 1976 and 1977.

Had the legislature not extended the statute of limitations on sexual assaults from three to six years, the East Area Rapist could have returned to Contra Costa last June and identified himself without fear of criminal prosecution.

He attacked at night, often through unlocked doors or windows, inflicting terror that his victims never forgot, all the while confounding lawmen in five counties.

Cases from Miami, Fla. To Texas and Louisiana were followed with great interest by a seven-member Contra Costa task force assembled in 1979. While they never caught their quarry, they did help solve some of those crimes, according to Sgt. Rod Carpenter, a member of the now-defunct task force.

Airplanes equipped with powerful searchlights were sent aloft to search neighborhoods the elusive rapist seemed to favor. The sheriff's office and affected police departments issued "Lock, Light, and Look" warnings to fearful residents.

Seminars on rape prevention and the East Area Rapist's methods of operation-those that investigators dared disclose-and self defense for women sprung up throughout the county.

At the height of the East Area Rapist scare in Contra Costa, the task force trying to catch him reported as many as 30 reports a day related or possibly related to him.

Rape is not an unusual crime in Contra Costa, so what was it about the East Area Rapist that produced the massive media and police response?

"The fear that he put into people," remarked Sheriff's Sergeant Larry Crompton, a member of the task force.

"He just emanated fear. It was knowledge that he wanted to kill somebody and his victims realized it; that's why nobody fought him," Crompton added.

Victims told of such terror that several of them were unable to go back to their homes...

CHAPTER SIXTY-TWO

Sunday, May 4, 1986
13 Encina, Irvine, California

FOUR YEARS, NINE MONTHS AND EIGHT DAYS after the last known murder of Cheri Domingo and Gregory Sanchez, Janelle Lisa Cruz, born July 11th, 1967 became the murderers youngest known victim.

A male co-worker of Janelle visited her the evening of May 4th. There had been no sexual contact between the two friends, however they were sitting in Janelle's bedroom when they heard noises outside the bedroom window. Janelle looked outside but saw nothing. Later they heard noises again. It sounded like a door shutting in the garage or a gate closing in the side yard. Again they saw nothing.

At approximately 10:45 p.m. Janelle's friend left.

At 11:15 p.m. a neighbor heard Janelle's Chevette drive up to her home. One car door slammed. He knew it was Janelle's car because of the defective muffler.

A real estate agent previewing the home discovered Janelle's body at approximately 5:00 p.m., Monday, May 5th, 1986.

Officers responding to the scene found Janelle's body lying diagonally across her bed. Her bloodied head, face and neck were covered with a blanket. She had been battered about the face with the most serious injury to her forehead. Blades of grass were located at the head of the bed and near her feet and knees. Her bra had been pulled down to her waist.

Medium blue colored lint was found on and near her body. The Orange County Crime Lab determined them to be pieces of fabric from material that had been ripped. This would be consistent with EAR's earlier northern California rape scenes where he tore towels to use as blindfolds and gags.

Although there were no ligature marks, fresh abrasions and scrapes were present on Janelle's wrists.

Blood was noted on the kitchen floor, kitchen cabinets, on the wood flooring inside of the front door and on the wooden shutters and at the head of Janelle's bed.

No weapons were found at the scene, however a pipe wrench that had been in the back yard was missing. Tennis shoe impressions were located on the east side of the residence.

There was no forced entry and all the doors except a rear sliding glass door were locked. Friends stated Janelle often left doors unlocked.

Janelle Cruz

CHAPTER SIXTY-THREE

ON JANUARY 1ST, 1997, the Countywide Law Enforcement Unsolved Element, (CLUE) was formed by the Orange County Sheriff's Department. The unit was charged with investigating unsolved homicides and assumed responsibility for the Harrington investigation.

On June 23rd, 1997, CLUE investigators Brian Heaney and Dave Wilson began a review of the Harrington case. On August 15th, 1997, Research Analyst Janet Wilder examined the Harrington, Witthuhn and Cruz murders. Wilder developed victimologies and a link analysis diagram of the murders. CLUE investigators met with Irvine Police Detective Larry Montgomery who was the case agent for the Witthuhn and Cruz murders in September 1997.

Additional homicides within the southern California counties appeared to be linked. They were: March 13, 1980, Ventura murder of Lyman and Charlene Smith, the December 30, 1979 Goleta murder of Robert Offerman and Alexandria Manning and the July 27, 1981 Goleta murder of Gregory Sanchez and Cheri Domingo.

Significant evidence also linked the October 1, 1979 Priscilla Duffy and Abel Playa attempt, rape/murder to the Offerman/Manning and Domingo/Sanchez murders.

CLUE investigators contacted the Santa Barbara Sheriff's Department to discuss the Goleta cases. The lieutenant contacted was hesitant to discuss the cases as he felt it would only be a duplication of the work he had already put into it and it would take a lot of time and effort to retrieve the case files.

The development of DNA profiling and other advances in forensic science provided new opportunities in crime scene investigations.

DNA profiling did not exist when the Orange County Harrington murder occurred in 1980. Now it did. Orange County Sheriff's Forensic Scientist Elizabeth Thompson examined biological evidence collected during the initial investigation of the Harrington case. Forensic examination determined that semen deposited in and on Patrice Harrington was from the murderer.

In the Los Angeles Times, Sunday, August 2nd, 1981 edition, staff writer John Hurst wrote an article entitled *"Night Stalker," Theory Connecting Eight Southland Slayings Disputed.* He opened the story asking,

Is a psychopathic "Night Stalker" murdering southern California couples in their beds?"

With DNA profiling and the killer's method of operation, fifteen years later his question was about to be answered.

———⟫●⟪———

In March 1998, CLUE Research Analyst Janet Wilder resigned and was replaced by Michael Hynes in January 1999. On April 3, 1998 Investigator Larry Pool replaced Dave Wilson. On Monday, April 27, 1998 Pool assumed the lead investigator responsibility.

On January 23, 1999, Forensic Scientist Mary Hong matched DNA evidence from Ventura Police Department's Lyman and Charlene Smith murders to the suspect's DNA from Harrington, Witthuhn and Cruz homicides.

Twelve years after the Janelle Cruz murder, DNA evidence had proven what CLUE investigators had believed; the murders were committed by the same person.

The suspect's M.O. and the type of crimes appeared similar to the Domingo/Sanchez and Offerman/Manning homicides and the Duffy/Playa attempt, all in Santa Barbara County. Santa Barbara Sheriff's Department, however, concluded that their homicides were not related to the serial murderer and refused to participate in a coordinated investigation.

After becoming the lead investigator, Pool examined previously convicted violent sex offenders within Ventura, Santa Barbara and Orange counties. Pool utilized the Megan's Law CD Rom program provided by the California Department of Justice. He also met with Sergeant John Yarbrough of the Los Angeles County Sheriff's Homicide Unit. Yarbrough, a graduate of the FBI's National Center for the Analysis of Violent Crime, (NCAVC), was trained and qualified to conduct offender behavioral analyses. With preliminary information Yarbrough felt that the Harrington serial killer would be between eighteen and thirty-five years of age in 1980 and probably had a history of burglary, prowling and rape.

Pool also queried the Violent Crime Information Network, (VCIN). He entered blood serology information from the Harrington killer and conducted an ADHOC search. Harrington's murderer was a non-secretor with the following blood serology information: PGM=2-1; PGM SUB=2+1-; PEP-A=1-1 or 1, and a LEWIS of A=B- or A-B-.

Although a number of offenders were identified within the VCIN system, none were the serial killer Pool was looking for.

Killers condemned to California's Death Row were examined. Blood samples were requested from those who were possible suspects. This request was refused, as it would be a violation of the prisoner's rights. The Sacramento County Superior Court issued an injunction January 1997 prohibiting the drawing of blood. Although the injunction had been appealed by the State three times, it still stands. The crux of the death row inmates' argument is: incarceration prohibits death row inmates from further victimizing the world outside the confines of prison. They therefore should not be required to relinquish DNA samples because their incarceration thwarts their ability to commit additional offenses within society. They must have put a lot of thought into that decision. Somewhere there might even be some logic in it.

California State prisoners discharged from prison between January 1, 1986 and June 30, 1986 were identified while state prisoners admitted to the California prison system after May 5, 1986 for rape and murder, between thirty-eight and forty-nine years of age were also identified. Males who died between May 1, 1986 and May 7, 1987 who were Orange County Coroner's cases were also identified.

Nationwide teletypes were sent to law enforcement, parole and probation departments. Teletypes were also sent to INTERPOL for worldwide law enforcement dissemination.

Monday, October 12, 1987, 2215 hrs
Oakdale, California

On Monday, October 12th, 1987, a thirty-one year old Oakdale woman was attacked by an unknown assailant.

The woman was sleeping when a subject entered the rear yard of the residence, retrieved an oak log from a woodpile and entered the house through a laundry room window. The intruder struck her in the head several times with the log fracturing her skull multiple times.

The woman woke up screaming, thinking she had a nightmare. Noting blood, she thought she had cut herself while sleeping. Approximately one hour later she called the police.

Her ten-year-old daughter sleeping in a separate room was unharmed.

Investigator Pool was contacted by a Stanislaus County probation officer on Friday, February 19th, 1999 after receiving a request for assistance teletype sent by Pool to California's four parole regions.

Pool responded to Oakdale, however after talking to investigators he could not establish that the attack was related to the southern California murders.

Chapter Sixty-four

AFTER SEVERAL KNEE OPERATIONS culminating in a total knee replacement I retired in October 1998 and moved out of state.

In April 2000 I received a call from Contra Costa County Sheriff's Criminalist Paul Holes. He had heard I had been an investigator on the EAR Task Force and as a DNA expert he wanted to link EAR cases through DNA. I gave him the names of the rape victims in Contra Costa County.

On July 8th, 2000, Holes called back. He had linked Sunny Walther and Teresa McCrae as definitely raped by the same man. On July 15th Ellen Cerro was added to the link. The statute of limitations had run out on the rapes, but at least we finally learned that above all else, we were right. Bevins was right, we were right. EAR did exist.

"Paul," I told Holes, "I know EAR hit down south. Santa Barbara Sheriff's Department wouldn't cooperate with us but if you can get with a criminalist down there to cooperate, I know they have evidence. If you can get it I know you can match EAR to their homicides. I think they had at least five attacks. All I can say is good luck. I know it's EAR."

Tuesday October 3rd, 2000, the *L.A. Times* did an article on the southern California homicides and the DNA link:

DNA Tests Reveal a Serial Killer

Crimes: O.C. Sheriff's cold-case unit believes the man may have committed 10 murders in Orange, Santa Barbara and Ventura counties between 1979 and 1986.

The mystery began to take shape four years ago when scientists at the Orange County Sheriff's Department's DNA lab started applying new technology to old murder cases and found three with striking similarities.

The next year, the departments new "cold case" unit found evidence that a previously undetected serial killer may have left at least 10 victims in three Southern California counties from 1979 to 1986.

On Monday, investigators revealed that they have been silently tracking a man who carefully picked his victims from upscale communities in Orange, Santa Barbara and Ventura counties and who now could be dead, in prison or still on the loose.

DNA tests of semen and hair found at four crime scenes and a common method have led investigators to believe that a single man was involved in six attacks.

The idea that the killer may still be alive has spurred Orange County Sheriff's Detective Larry Pool to conduct a desperate search to match a face to the trail of DNA.

But after years of reviewing hundreds of sexual assault cases and a trip to San Quentin's death row, Pool said Monday that the killer's identity remains a mystery.

"This is the kind of case that wakes me up at 3 in the morning because a person with this kind of desire, this kind of murder driven by fantasy, these people can't stop," Pool said. "The only thing that will stop them is something beyond their control, like death."

Pool explained the stakes of his investigation. "He could be in prison and for all we know get out tomorrow," he said. "And then he'll do it again."

The killer has left some broad clues. He is believed to be white. Sometimes he brought a German Shepherd with him. Officials guess he was living in the Goleta area of Santa Barbara County when he surfaced.

Authorities say the series of crimes began in the fall of 1979...

In March 2001 Holes called me back. "Guess what?" Holes began, "They didn't have five attacks down south, they had ten homicides and we linked six of them to our rapist. EAR did move down south."

"I knew it," I replied, "I knew it had to be him

"Well Orange County Sheriff's Office has put a Task Force together to work on the unsolved homicides. They would like you to call them. The investigator is Larry Pool. I didn't give him your phone number but he really wants to talk to you."

I called Larry Pool at the Sheriff's Department CLUE unit. I went over some of the cases, the description we had, the way EAR attacked, the words he used.

"We linked our homicides by DNA but Santa Barbara says they have no evidence and they know it's not the same person because he shot their victims and the rapist never used a gun," Pool said.

"Never used a gun? He always had a gun, especially when a male was present," I told him.

Pool knew nothing about EAR and needed information. Their unit was formed to investigate unsolved homicides and they had the full backing of the Sheriff. Any help was welcome.

"Well, I'll do anything I can to help you but you need to understand, I'm writing a book on EAR. I'll give you everything I have but I would like to have copies of the initial homicides," I told Pool. "My only concern is catching this person and that's why I started writing this book. I'll tell you something else, you won't get much cooperation from some of the northern California agencies."

"Anything you can give us will be appreciated," Pool advised.

"Well, I have copies of all the reports. My department was throwing everything out because they had no room to store it. I caught it before the janitor had hauled everything off and have had them ever since. A lot of stuff did get thrown away, especially names and investigations of suspects. I do have a copy of a fingerprint from a lamp in a Danville rape. Our department is supposed to be running it through the system periodically. I'll call Paul Holes and have him send you a copy. Look, I'm going to be out of the state for the next couple of weeks. I'll call you when I get back and we can talk."

We would appreciate it," Pool stated and we hung up.

When I returned home in April I had a phone message. The Crime Lab had somehow thrown out the fingerprint from the McCrae lamp. I had the only copy. Why I had kept it all these years I did not know. For some reason I had a copy made and kept it in my desk drawer. Was it EAR's? We never did eliminate the print.

In April 2001, the *Contra Costa Times* had printed an article linking the East Area Rapist to the southern California murderer.

DNA Links '70s Rapist to Deaths

Although unknown, the East Area attacker has been connected to several killings by criminalists using new methods on old evidence.

Decades after he struck fear in thousands of East Bay women, the man known as the East Area Rapist is also a serial killer believed to have slain at least six southern California residents, according to discoveries by criminalists.

The nameless, faceless rapist and killer is known to authorities only by his DNA. While criminalists have connected the crimes through DNA, investigators are still trying to match the DNA profile – considered better identification than even a fingerprint – to a person.

Authorities think the East Area Rapist attacked as many as 40 women between Sacramento and San Ramon during a two-year period in the 1970's. After a few similar rapes in the San Jose area, he reportedly disappeared. It was rumored he had moved to southern California.

Biological evidence from three of the rapes was saved over the years. As technology improved, the crime lab began routinely analyzing its cold cases, looking for ways to solve the crimes based on new fingerprinting technology and DNA profiling, said Karen Sheldon, director of the Contra Costa County Crime Lab.

Early last year, when the crime lab began analyzing evidence from the East Area Rapist cases, someone recalled that there had been some rape homicides in southern California that appeared similar, Sheldon said. A few phone calls were made and the two crime labs kept in touch.

In October, the Orange County Sheriff's Department's cold-case unit linked six unsolved killings to one person through DNA evidence. Those slayings occurred in Ventura, Laguna Niguel and Irvine between 1980 and 1986. Based on the method of the crime, investigators also believe the unknown killer is linked to four other slayings in southern California. In each case, the killer broke into a house at night and raped the female victims first.

The DNA profiles proved the East Area Rapist cases in Contra Costa County were linked to the southern California cases...

I called Larry Pool and told him about the fingerprint having been thrown out.

"Can you fax us a copy of the print you have?" Pool asked.

"I'll try and I'll try to get a photo copy made for you," I said.

"One other thing, the Sheriff would like to have you come down and talk to us. We will pay your way down and pay all expenses. We really would like to spend a few days with you," Pool advised.

"Look I appreciate your offer but I think it would be better if you come here. We've got plenty of room to put you up and you can read through all the reports. There is no way you will get copies from all the agencies involved and I do have copies," I replied.

"Let me talk to the Sheriff and I'll get back to you," Pool responded.

Pool called back a few days later and said if I would the Sheriff would rather I come to Orange County. I agreed and on April 25th I arrived at John Wayne Airport with copies of all the rape reports and notes I had made while writing the book. I also gave them a copy of the fingerprint from the McCrae rape.

I was excited to finally see an agency that was actively trying to solve cases. Excited but apprehensive. Too many times I had found that politics and administrative decisions had squelched proper investigations.

After talking to Pool and Michael Hynes, a civilian member of the CLUE unit I knew the investigation would be thorough. My meetings with the Assistant Sheriff Tim Simon, Captain Steve Carroll, Lieutenant Larry Jones, Sergeant Bob Blackburn and Deputy Yvonne Shull showed that the dedication and total backing was there. If the cases were ever solved, this unit would be an integral part of the investigation.

It was apparent during my stay in Orange County that with very few exceptions, cooperation from other agencies was lacking. Welcome to our world, the world of law enforcement.

Upon learning of the connection between the northern California rapes and the southern California homicides a meeting was set up in Sacramento by the Sacramento D.A.'s office to discuss the investigative procedures. Orange County was not invited! Although I requested to be invited, I was turned down. It was decided that only commanders would attend. Unfortunately none had been involved in any of the rapes and no northern California agency had a crime that the statute of limitations had not run out on. I was later told by one of the attendees that the Santa Barbara Sheriff's Department representative had complained about Orange County's CLUE unit and had proposed that no retired investigator be involved in the investigation. One more time a road block to help the criminal. Cooperation.....you will find it in the dictionary somewhere between constipation and copulation.

Investigator Pool and his unit actively pursued the investigation. Over 120 three ring binders, all cross referenced sit on shelves in Pool's office. Mike Hynes input all into the CLUE unit computerized system.

Agencies throughout the United States were sent teletypes asking for help in identifying the serial rapist/murderer.

NATION – WIDE FIRST TIME BROADCAST

ATTENTION ALL INVESTIGATIVE UNITS: the Orange County Sheriff's Department, California, is seeking to identify a serial rapist/killer – living or deceased.

In March 2001, DNA linked a southern California rapist/serial killer (Responsible for no less than six murders between March 1980 and May 1986) to a series of Sacramento area rapes perpetrated by a suspect known as the East Area Rapist (EAR). The EAR terrorized Sacramento/Contra Costa Counties between June 1976 and July 1979, then migrated south along the California coast. The suspect is described as:

Probably White (Fair to light olive complexion), 47 to 51 (Today),

5'9" to 5'11"; 150 to 170 pounds, dark hair and dark eyes.

Possibly has a tattoo of a bull on his left or right forearm.

The suspect was a nighttime prowler who prowled/burglarized the victim's neighborhood days/weeks in advance of his attack. He often burglarized the victim's home and victim's neighborhood in advance and telephoned the victim and their neighbors prior to his attack (The calls were usually 'hang-ups' however, the suspect occasionally spoke and threatened to return to the victims days/weeks/years after attacking them).

The suspect wore a ski mask and gloves and generally wore dark clothing and long sleeves. He usually wore tennis shoes or military style boots. He generally brought a knife and gun (.45 or

.357) and controlled the victims utilizing the firearm. He generally selected single-story detached dwellings and forced entry if necessary utilizing sliding-glass doors with a screwdriver. The suspect attacked during the hours of darkness but most often attacked between midnight and 4:00 a.m. He would attack even though children or dogs were present within the victim's home. He initially attacked single females but evolved into attacking male/female couples after they fell asleep. (Though primarily preying on couples, the suspect has still struck lone females) When confronting the victims the suspect:

- Habitually talked/whispered to the victims through clenched teeth.

- Generally confronted the victims while they were sleeping.

- Woke the victim(s) by shining the flashlight beam on them or by speaking to them. He usually told the victims to "Wake up."

- Initially told the victims all he wanted was "money and food."

- Often pressed his gun or knife against the victim's skin when threatening.

- Brought ligatures with him. He generally used shoestrings, twine or cord.

- Threw ligatures to the female and made her tie the male victim's wrists behind his back. The suspect then bound the female's wrists behind her back, and her ankles together. The suspect subsequently tied the male's ankles together and retied the male's wrist ligatures. The suspect tied the ligatures extremely tight.

- Covered the victim's heads with an object or blindfolded them with a towel.

- Separated the female from the male, moving her into another room of the house where he raped and sometimes sodomized her — sometimes made the victim orally copulate him (the suspect sometimes copulated the victim). The suspect often placed dishes, or similar objects on the male victim's back prior to moving the female — He told the male that if the dishes, Etc. moved and made a sound, he would kill everyone. Often sexually assaulted the female victim multiple times.

- Repeatedly threatened to kill the victims and often said, "Muthafucka." And "Bitch."

- *Initially told the victims all he wanted was food and money. Repeatedly asked where money was located (Seldom actually took much of value). Took some money, jewelry, food items from refrigerator before leaving.*
- *Lubricated himself with lotions he brought with him or obtained within the victim's home.*
- *Masturbated and had difficulty obtaining and maintaining an erection.*
- *Straddled the female victims as they lay face down – had them rub his penis with their hands which were tied tightly behind their backs.*
- *Spent a significant amount of time in the victim's kitchen – drinking and eating. Spent between five minutes to four hours with the victims.*
- *Left all ligatures tied tightly on the victims.*

The suspect evolved into a killer. He generally bludgeoned his victims to death – striking them in the head multiple times with a blunt object. Victims whom he evidently lost control of were shot. He appeared to become more evidence conscious as he evolved and began removing ligatures from the victim's bodies before he departed the crime scene.

We suspect the East Area Rapist/Killer is either dead or in prison. Please contact our agency with similar cases or any information which might assist us in identifying the suspect – Dead or Alive.

Chapter Sixty-five

On June 1st, 2001 I learned that the Contra Costa County Sheriff was putting a letter together to be sent to the Orange County Sheriff's Department. The letter was to state that he had learned that the retired investigator Larry Crompton had taken a truck load of evidence regarding the East Area Rapist to Orange County. It would further state that Crompton had no right to have this evidence and that he demanded all originals be returned to the Contra Costa County Sheriff's Department.

Two things bothered me about this. Ninety-nine percent of what I had were not originals. They were copies that were being thrown out by the Contra Costa County Sheriff's Department in the early 1980's by the order of the Sheriff. Members of the Department knew I had them. Secondly, no one from Contra Costa County ever called me to ask about the evidence. To this day I have not been contacted.

I did talk to Investigator Pool. His Sheriff had received a letter from Sheriff Rupf, however the contents were not divulged to Pool other than all originals were to be returned. I told Pool which single piece of paper was original. All the rest were copies I had made and collected from the trash.

Once again cooperation had reared its' ugly head.

In May, 2001, Sheriff Michael Corona authorized additional personnel to the CLUE unit.

In June, 2001, Larry Pool called me. They had a hit on the fingerprint I had given him from the McCrae lamp, (rape #43).

The FBI had matched the fingerprint to a person who had been in the witness protection program. Unfortunately he was now dead from natural causes and buried back east.

A record for extortion, bank robbery, carrying a concealed firearm, burglary, several AKA's, and in California during the rapes; he looked good. Born in 1934, 5'7" and 190 pounds; he didn't look good. On top of that, he was a name that we had looked at, not as a suspect, but as an elimination factor as having at one time, access to the McCrae residence.

Why hadn't our fingerprint examiners matched the prints? Pool explained that the prints on file for the subject were so poor that comparison was not possible.

"How do you feel?" Pool asked me.

McCrae had told me that this person had not been in the house after the lamp had been unpacked. McCrae had no reason to lie to me. Was he the rapist? My gut said no. The rest of me said, 'Please God, let it be.'

"McCrae had no reason to lie to me," I told Pool.

"Well, the Sheriff is prepared to let me fly back east to exhume the body to collect DNA," Pool told me.

"I'll keep my fingers crossed and do a lot of praying," I told Pool.

In July Pool traveled east. The body was exhumed. Teeth, hair, bone were extracted for DNA testing.

Fingerprints were also taken from the left hand utilizing a latex-type casting method known as microsil to ensure that the right body had been exhumed.

The evidence was returned to the Orange County Sheriff's Crime Lab by a forensic scientist accompanying Pool during the exhumation.

On Friday July 19th, it was settled. My gut had been right. We still did not have EAR. No DNA match.

During Investigator Pool's research into the northern California attacks, he noted that although Walter Hamilton, (a suspect in the third EAR attack, 8-29-1976, on victim Rose Scott,) had been eliminated as EAR, the elimination was, at best, questionable.

Pool located Hamilton in Illinois.

On September 27, 2001, Pool and his partner, investigator Yvonne Shull traveled to Illinois and met with the State Attorney.

A search warrant was subsequently authorized by the Ninth Circuit Court Judge for the DNA, finger and palm prints of Walter Hamilton.

Pool and Shull met with and interviewed Hamilton. He was photographed and DNA, finger and palm prints were collected.

DNA typing was completed on November 29, 2001. Hamilton was eliminated as the East Area Rapist/Serial Killer as a result.

One more dead end in a twenty-five year span of dead ends.

Chapter Sixty-six

I CONTINUED TO STAY IN CONTACT with Larry Pool. The dedication and professionalism of the Orange County Sheriff's Department and the CLUE unit personnel was obvious. During this time Pool kept me informed of cases the unit closed while working on the EAR/Night Stalker case. The frustration in his voice was evident in that although cases were closed, the one case that was uppermost on his mind remained a mystery.

I'm sure Pool and his team wanted closure in this serial rapist/ murderer case as much as I did.

In 2003, I was contacted by Pool. A Chicago based Production Company was interested in doing an episode on the rapist/murderer cases to be shown on their A&E Cold Case File program. They wanted to interview several investigators and others who had been a part of the investigation, and would I be willing to talk to them? After twenty-seven years of frustrations, a chance to open the case to a national audience. I readily agreed and met with the Production Company in Sacramento to tape the interview.

In September, 2003, the A&E Network aired the production, "The Original Night Stalker". It aired several times over the years and each time calls came into the CLUE unit. Again, over and over, they ended up a dead end.

In May, 2004, after an episode of "The Original Night Stalker" had aired, Michael Schott, a private investigator and a retired sergeant from the Contra Costa County Sheriff's Department called me. Mike and I had worked together for years and his dedication to his job as a burglary detective had obviously not left him. He was excited about the renewal of the EAR cases and had some ideas that might help.

Mike knew of a professor of criminology at Texas State University and had contacted him to see if he would help in identifying the areas where EAR may have lived during his crimes. Professor Kim Rossmo had developed a geographic profiling technique using zip codes of at-

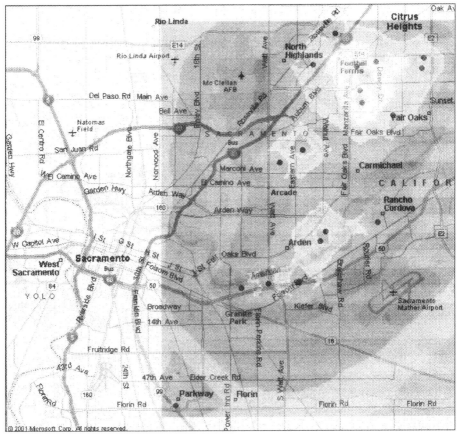

In his geographic profile study Professor Rossomo used the addresses of the East Area Rapist attacks to determine the highest priority zip codes of Sacramento County, California, where the attacker would have lived. His profiling determined that the 95608 zip code, Carmichael, would have been the most likely, followed in order of priority by 95621, Citrus Heights area, and 95610, Citrus Heights area.

tacks. His study was based on numerous cases of serial criminals, their initial attacks and their relationship to their place of residence.

I gave Mike the addresses of attacks by EAR with the understanding that he would contact Professor Rossmo and ask him to use the addresses in his study. Professor Rossmo agreed to look at the data however would prefer to have a request from a law enforcement agency. I contacted Larry

 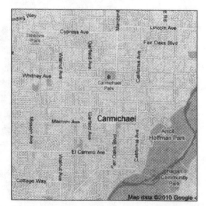

Professor Kim Rossomo's geographic profile study shows that the rapist could possibly have lived in the area of zip code 95608 (Carmichael), 95621 or 95610 (Citrus Heights).

Pool who agreed to send the request to Rossmo along with psychological profiles on the EAR rapes and on the southern California murders to help him in his study.

The Professor did his part and worked out the areas where he believed the rapist/murderer lived during the attacks.

Once again Mike Schott came through, this time with a contact who worked for a computer company that kept names and addresses of California residents. Through Mike and Larry Pool a request was made to give Orange County Sheriff's Department a list of names of those living in the zip code areas that Professor Rossmo had provided. Although the chance of the rapist/murderer's name being on the list was a high probability, the computer company, due to law suites and investigations into releasing such information was apprehensive and backed out of the request.

Not to be stymied Schott contacted another company he had worked with during some of his investigative work and again the process commenced. This time, after extensive communication between Schott, Pool and the company a list of names was provided. Unfortunately the list comprised of names and locations, however the dates that coincided with the attacks were not used and the addresses were not listed in chronological order, again due to the fear of law suites. The list comprised of four to five thousand names, a number that made it impossible to work with. Is the name amongst this list? A good possibility. Once again, better that a million guilty go free than one innocent be inconvenienced. I do not blame the computer company for being paranoid over possible repercussions. Past experience proves the point.

In May, 2008 I was contacted by Todd Lindsey of E! Networks, a Los Angeles movie company. They were interested in doing a program on the rapist/murderer with a emphasis on the rapes as more information was available from the initial attacks prior to EAR turning into a serial murderer.

I met with Todd Lindsey and his Producer Randy Ferrell and camera crew in Concord, California. They professionally took me through the video taped interview and then we visited some of the rape scenes in the area. Todd said that they had previously interviewed several investigators from the Sacramento Sheriff's Office and would be interviewing several southern California investigators. E! Networks planned on having their program "True Hollywood Story Investigates the Original Nitestalker" in early 2009.

Due to production times and the in-depth study by Todd Lindsey and the E! Network crew the program time for airing was delayed.

A rape victim was interviewed on tape for the show explaining the terror she went through at the hands of EAR.

John Formichella, E! Entertainment Producer and his camera crew contacted me at my residence for an interview to explain areas of concern and the show "True Hollywood Investigates: The Original Night Stalker" was aired for the first time May 5th, 2009. It has been aired several times since as has the A&E show "The Original Night Stalker".

Would this help bring a close to one of California's most infamous serial rapist/murderer investigations? Would someone watching the program know a brother, a relative, a friend, a fellow worker who lived in Sacramento in 1976, moved to the Contra Costa County area of Concord around 1978 and to the Santa Barbara area of southern California in late 1979? Would that person come forward?

Who would have the ability to move through those areas, have the time to prowl the neighborhoods and who would have access to the several vehicles seen at and near the crimes?

In the meantime Investigator Larry Pool will continue to work the cases as his current position allows. Private investigator Mike Schott will continue in his quest to eliminate names provided by the computer company to a usable number. Mike's dedication to this investigation is the same dedication he showed during his years as an investigator with the Contra Costa County Sheriff's Office. Working with the Haynes

Directory he has narrowed the list to a few hundred names. Much better than the few thousand he started with yet still too much for law enforcement to work.

Over the years I would wake in the middle of the night wondering where I went wrong. What did I miss? I wanted this monster to get caught so I could sleep through the night. Then I realized. It wasn't about me. It was about the victims of this rapist/murderer. It was about those who were raped and their families. It was about young girls who never had the chance to grow up before being attacked, their virginity taken from them by the worst type of human being. It was about the families of those murdered and those who were not murdered yet in their minds knew that they were going to die at the hands of a mad man.

No, it is not about me. Closure can only come to those who suffered at the hands of this monster when he is caught and punished. There are dedicated men and women still in the hunt. My prayers are with them.

CHAPTER SIXTY-SIX

Typical residential area neighborhood attacked by EAR

Method of entry often used by EAR

DEDICATION

THIS BOOK IS DEDICATED to the victims, their families and the communities terrorized by the East Area Rapist (EAR) / The Original Night Stalker, the most violent serial rapist/murderer in California history.

My prayers are that this book will help in the identification of this monster and bring closure to the minds of those terrorized and to the officers and citizens involved in the hunt.

EAST AREA RAPIST/
ORIGINAL NIGHT STALKER ATTACKS

Date	Time	Location	Zip Code
06-18-76	0400	Rancho Cordova	95670
07-17-76	0200	Carmichael	95608
08-29-76	0320	Rancho Cordova	95670
09-4/5-76	2330	Carmichael	95608
10-05-76	0645	Citrus Heights	95610
10-09-76	0430	Rancho Cordova	95670
10-18-76	0230	Carmichael	95608
10-18-76	2300	Rancho Cordova	95670
11-10-76	1930	Citrus Heights	95610
12-18-76	1920	Fair Oaks	95628
01-18/19-77	2330	Sacramento	95826
01-24-77	0100	Citrus Heights	95610
02-07-77	0650	Carmichael	95608
03-08-77	0400	Sacramento	95826
03-18-77	2245	Rancho Cordova	95670
04-02-77	0320	Orangevale	95662
04-15-77	0230	Carmichael	95608
05-03-77	0300	Sacramento	95826
05-05-77	0015	Orangevale	95662
05-14-77	0345	Citrus Heights	95610
05-17-77	0130	Carmichael	95608
05-28-77	0220	Sacramento	95823
09-06-77	0130	Stockton	95207
10-01-77	0100	Rancho Cordova	95670
10-21-77	0300	Sacramento	95842
10-29-77	0145	Sacramento	95821
11-10-77	0330	Sacramento	95826
12-2/3-77	2330	Sacramento	95842
01-28-78	2230	Carmichael	95608
03-18-78	0105	Stockton	95207
04-14-78	2150	Sacramento	95822
06-05-78	0300	Modesto	95356

ATTACKS

06-07-78	0355	Davis	95616
06-23-78	0130	Modesto	95356
06-24-78	0315	Davis	95616
07-06-78	0250	Davis	95616
10-07-78	0230	Concord	94518
10-13-78	0430	Concord	94518
10-28-78	0230	San Ramon	94583
11-04-78	0345	San Jose	95132
12-02-78	0200	San Jose	95132
12-09-78	0200	Danville	94526
03-20-79	0515	Rancho Cordova	95670
04-04-79	0020	Fremont	94539
06-02-79	2230	Walnut Creek	94598
06-11-79	0400	Danville	94526
06-25-79	0415	Walnut Creek	94598
07-10-79	0357	Danville	94526
10-01-79	0200	Goleta	93111

MURDERS BEGIN

12-30-79	0400?	Goleta	93111
03-13-80	?	Ventura	93003
08-19-80	?	Orange County	92677
02-16-81	0200	Irvine	92620
07-27-81	0330	Goleta	93111
05-04-86	?	Irvine	92620

OTHER POSSIBLES

10-21-75	0400	Rancho Cordova	95670
01-16-76	0445	Carmichael	95608
10-26-76	2330	Rancho Cordova	95670
02-16-77	?	Sacramento	95826
		16 year old boy shot chasing suspect	
02-02-78	?	Rancho Cordova	95670
		Double homicide	
06-27-78	0230	Sacramento	95825
12-18-78	daytime	San Ramon	94583
		Secreted rope found in house	
12-29-79	1600	Goleta Five burglaries	
03-13-80		Ventura, Prowlers and burglaries	